ADVANCE PRAISE FOR

The Competent Public Speaker

"There is a useful Latin saying, 'Res ipsa loquitur,' which translates to 'The thing speaks for itself.' This is an apt description of *The Competent Public Speaker* by Sherwyn P. Morreale. Professor Morreale is herself the model of a competent speaker, and has both the academic background and professional qualifications to write a practical and readable textbook for the beginning but aspiring public speaker."
—*Frank E.X. Dance, John Evans Professor Emeritus, University of Denver*

"*The Competent Public Speaker* is comprehensive, has new material not found in other public speaking texts, and is written to encourage and support developing public speaking excellence. Although a research-based text, students will find the text readable, supportive, and truly outstanding."
—*Pamela Shockley-Zalabak, Chancellor, University of Colorado, Colorado Springs*

"*The Competent Public Speaker* is much more than a competent textbook. Based on the National Communication Association's conceptual model for teaching and evaluating undergraduate public speeches, this new public speaking textbook successfully combines traditional approaches to public speaking with current theory and research. The book's unique blending of eight core competencies with globalization, technology, ethics, culture, and diversity provides both students and faculty with highly applicable knowledge and skills. A strength of the book is its highly accessible and easy-to-use approach to this important skill. The content is well supported by examples of student speaking experiences, useful assessment tools, applicable competence building activities, and sample speeches. The combination of the core competencies, traditional and current theory, along with very useful pedagogical tools makes this textbook a winner for any public speaking class."
—*Phil Backlund, Professor, Central Washington University,*
and NCA Educational Policies Board member

"Sherwyn P. Morreale's *The Competent Public Speaker* is an excellent text for the beginning public speaking course. Based upon the most frequently used assessment rubric in the field, the text is very readable and personal. Morreale grasps the student perspective and builds upon it. The learning aids—including definitions, knowledge checks, and class and individual activities—are creative and will assist students in identifying and applying the concepts presented. This is also a good text for a course that is often first for many communication majors. It introduces theories and frameworks that students will consider in later course work. *The Competent Public Speaker* provides the thorough foundation students need to become strong public speakers and begin their study in the discipline."
—*Ellen Hay, Professor of Communication Studies, Augustana College*

The Competent Public Speaker

This book is part of the Peter Lang Media and Communication list.
Every volume is peer reviewed and meets
the highest quality standards for content and production.

PETER LANG
New York • Washington, D.C./Baltimore • Bern
Frankfurt • Berlin • Brussels • Vienna • Oxford

Sherwyn P. Morreale

The Competent Public Speaker

PETER LANG
New York • Washington, D.C./Baltimore • Bern
Frankfurt • Berlin • Brussels • Vienna • Oxford

Library of Congress Cataloging-in-Publication Data

Morreale, Sherwyn P.
The competent public speaker / Sherwyn P. Morreale.
p. cm.
Includes bibliographical references and index.
1. Public speaking. I. Title.
PN4121.M647   808.5'1—dc22   2010029955
ISBN 978-1-4331-0857-0 (hardcover)
ISBN 978-1-4331-0856-3 (paperback)

Bibliographic information published by **Die Deutsche Nationalbibliothek**.
Die Deutsche Nationalbibliothek lists this publication in the "Deutsche
Nationalbibliografie"; detailed bibliographic data are available
on the Internet at http://dnb.d-nb.de/.

CONTENTS IN BRIEF

DETAILED CONTENTS

PART TWO: PREPARING A SPEECH

PART THREE: PRESENTING A SPEECH

PART FOUR: SPEAKING IN DIFFERENT SITUATIONS

PREFACE

A past president of the National Communication Association, Dan O'Hair, once said something profound in its simplicity: "The promise of communication is understanding." I agree with Dan and believe improved communication—including the ability to give a good speech—enhances relationships, bridges differences, and encourages dialogue. Regardless of your own personal or professional goals, everything you do in the future will be influenced by how well you communicate. My own research supports this claim. Our analysis of 93 journal and newspaper articles, reports, and national surveys provides evidence of the importance of effective and appropriate communication to: your personal development, psychologically and socially; succeeding in school; becoming a responsible citizen and participant in the world; and succeeding in your career, in business, and in organizational life.

What you learn from this book and the communication course you are now enrolled in will help you grow as a competent communicator and public speaker. Your learning in this book begins with a general introduction to studying communication and public speaking. Then you focus on preparing and presenting speeches, and applying those public speaking skills to different types of speeches and speaking situations.

UNIQUE FEATURES OF *THE COMPETENT PUBLIC SPEAKER*

Based on the National Communication Association's conceptual model for teaching and evaluating undergraduate public speeches (as developed by this author and others), this new textbook offers a highly accessible, easy-to-teach, easy-to-learn approach to public speaking. The competence approach embedded in the book includes eight public speaking competencies—four focused on speech preparation and four on speech delivery. The eight competencies are enhanced by discussing their relationship to globalization, technology, ethics, credibility, culture, and diversity.

Because it is based on a nationally recognized model for teaching and learning about public speaking, *The Competent Public Speaker* offers a distinctive but practical approach for exploring speaking in public.

- Part One covers foundational topics in communication. Chapter 1 introduces the key communication concepts that help put public speaking into a larger context. Chapter 2 introduces public speaking fundamentals, including the history of public speaking in rhetoric, why public speaking is important, and some common myths about public speaking many of us may think are true. Chapter 3 introduces the eight competencies for preparing and presenting a first speech and provides guidelines for unlearning public speaking anxiety. Chapter 4 provides essential coverage of the critical first steps to speaking well in public—audience analysis and listening, a key responsibility of audience members.

- Part Two outlines the first four competencies of the *Competent Speaker Model* and focuses on speech preparation. Chapter 4 addresses choosing and narrowing a speech topic. Chapters that follow address developing a speech purpose and thesis/central claim (Chapter 5), researching and gathering support materials for the speech (Chapter 6), and organizing the materials into a useful and coherent outline (Chapter 7).

- Part Three describes the last four competencies of the *Competent Speaker Model* and covers speech presentation and delivery. Chapters in this part address verbal communication using words and language (Chapter 8), using the voice and vocal variety (Chapter 9), effective and appropriate pronunciation, articulation, and grammar (Chapter 10), and nonverbal communication (Chapter 11).

- Part Four considers public speaking based on different purposes or objectives, and in different situations. Preparing and speaking with presentational aids, with an emphasis on technology in public speaking, is covered in Chapter 12. The next two chapters cover different types of speeches and ways of organizing based on the speech objective, speaking to inform (Chapter 13) and speaking to persuade (Chapter 14). Both of these two chapters conclude with a discussion of ethics and credibility and challenges to informative speaking and persuasive speaking. A final chapter in Part Four provides an overview of public speaking at work and on special occasions (Chapter 15).

SPECIAL FEATURES IN EVERY CHAPTER

All 15 chapters in *The Competent Public Speaker* include unique features designed to enhance teaching and learning.

- Each chapter begins with a *story of a student* experiencing the content of that chapter. The student's experience is discussed and used as an example throughout the chapter. Different students are introduced in various chapters, and the reader follows their real stories as they learn more and more about public speaking.

- Each chapter also contains *tables and boxes* related to an important topic in that chapter. The boxes are derived from the writings of communication experts and from websites and blog discussions available on the Internet.

- *Building Competence Activities* also are included at the end of each chapter. Individual and group activities provide opportunities to apply chapter concepts and practice public speaking strategies in the classroom or as take home assignments.

- *Competency Checkpoints and Self-Assessment Tool* appear at the end of each chapter and are available electronically on the book's website. These assessments outline what a student needs to know and be able to do regarding the chapter content. Knowledge, skills, ethics, and credibility checks are included in each self-assessment tool.

APPLICATION OF COMMUNICATION THEORY AND RESEARCH

Highly accessible descriptions of some of the best thinking of communication theorists and researchers are included in every chapter. Here are a few examples:

- The introduction to communication extends the discussion to include recent writings about mediated communication and social media, as those contexts relate to communication in general and to public speaking.
- The introduction to public speaking explores the historical roots of contemporary public speaking in classical Western rhetoric. The reader is provided recommendations for applying the ideas of Greek and Roman orators and writers to public speaking today.
- The description of rhetoric also includes an account of non-Western rhetoric including Asian, African, and Islamic rhetorical traditions. The contributions and relevance of these non-Western traditions to contemporary public speaking are explored.
- In the recommendations for conducting audience analysis, the work of Milton Bennett on developing intercultural sensitivity is explored. Bennett provides a useful tool for judging how well each of us, as public speakers, analyze and understand the diverse perspectives of multicultural audiences.
- The discussion of nonverbal communication and public speaking is based on the work of communication researcher Judee Burgoon and her thinking about how nonverbal cues are used to build interpersonal relationships. Burgoon's ideas about relating to others nonverbally are applied to public speaking.
- The advice on using presentation aids is based on recent research on technology-assisted communication and public speaking. Frank Dance's concept for achieving a transparent delivery helps to clarify a discussion about the pros and cons of computerized presentations.
- Speaking at work and in 21st century organizations is informed by advice on using web-based presentation and communication technology—web cast presentations, web conferencing, and webinars.
- Presenting in face-to-face and geo-dispersed teams is derived from the work of Pamela Shockley on team-based organizations. We explore how technology is being used to communicate across time and space, using meeting technologies like teleconferencing and computer conferencing.

TEACHING AND LEARNING RESOURCES

Instructors and students reading this textbook are pointed to the following resources in the book itself, on the companion website, and in the instructors' manual.

- Four extraordinary speeches are analyzed and annotated in the appendix to the book. The exemplary informative and persuasive speeches are prizewinning speeches presented by students at the National Interstate Oratorical Society Contest in 2008 and 2009. A moving special occasion speech recently delivered at a convocation on a college campus and a fictitious speech developed by Kumar in the textbook also are annotated.

- An electronic version of a fill-in-the blank standard format for a speech outline is included in the book's appendix and on the website. A format for a motivated sequence speech outline also is in the appendix and on the website.
- An instructors' manual and companion website contain sample syllabi and PowerPoint presentations, extra in-class activities, and a test bank of questions for each chapter.
- Resources in the instructors' manual for gathering data for assessment and accountability include instructions for inter-rater reliability training and behavior expectation matrices for the eight competencies and sub-competencies outlined in the textbook and the Competent Speaker Speech Evaluation Form.

If the promise of communication is understanding, then the purpose of these resources, to say nothing of this textbook, is to help deliver on that promise. The author stands ready to communicate with public speaking instructors and their students, to help in any way to achieve this promise.

Cordially,

Sherry Morreale

ACKNOWLEDGMENTS

I first express my gratitude to the countless students and communication colleagues, faculty, administrators, and leaders in the discipline who, over the years, have expressed their belief in my knowledge and skills in the areas of instructional communication, communication education, and communication assessment.

With regard to this particular textbook, it only exists because of the seminal efforts of those colleagues who developed, tested, and revised the *Competent Speaker Speech Evaluation Program*: Michael Moore, Donna Surges-Tatum, and Linda Webster.

Committed graduate research assistants contributed immeasurably over several years to the book's development: Britney DeLaughter, Rose Fortune, Marcelle Hureau, Rayven Irons, Corlea Keeney, Jenny Mayo, and Katie Puryear. Their research efforts and continuous reading and re-reading of all 15 chapters helped to ensure an error-free manuscript—we hope!

Special thanks go to Mary Savigar and Bernadette Shade at Peter Lang, who guided this book skillfully through conceptualization and production to completion. In addition, Mary had the foresight to involve a reviewer whose knowledge of communication theory and public speaking contributed immeasurably to enhancing the depth and breadth of several key chapters. I also appreciate the photographs provided by Terry Fortune and Zachary Miller that effectively open and conclude each chapter.

On the home front, my family and friends continued to understand, as I spent countless hours, writing, revising, and staring at my computer: Samantha and Steve, Jesse, Bella and Sissy, Sam and Cyndy, Don and Nancy, and of course, Zak and Vanny, and my colleague, Pam Shockley.

PART 1:

APPROACHING

PUBLIC SPEAKING

A Personal Note from the Author to the Reader of this Textbook!

Before you start Chapter 1, I would like to talk with you as a friend and as a public speaking coach. You may read this book as you read many textbooks...looking just for what you'll be tested on. I would like to suggest another approach based on what's in it for you! If you read this textbook thoughtfully and participate actively in your public speaking class, you definitely will become more confident and better at communicating in public. But, there is another surprise benefit. I promise you, as you improve your public speaking skills, you will become better at communicating in many other life situations.

To help accomplish these goals, you will meet Angelique in Chapter 1, a real public speaking student like yourself. We'll use Angelique's experiences to illustrate key concepts and practical ideas for learning more about communication. You'll meet other students at the start of each chapter who will share their stories about public speaking with you. You also can contact me personally and ask me any questions through our shared website.

Your learning in this book begins with a general introduction to studying communication and public speaking in Part One. Part Two is about preparing speeches and Part Three focuses on presenting speeches. Part Four concludes with how you give speeches in different types of situations. Follow this logical organization and apply the recommendations in each chapter to your daily communication interactions, in the public speaking class, and outside it. At the end of each chapter, assess whether or not you are ready to go on to the next chapter. I promise you will grow as a communicator and that could be a real life-enhancing experience. Let me know how it goes for you and have a great time of it.

Dr. Sherry Morreale

1

UNDERSTANDING COMMUNICATION

"We live in a world in which we are able to communicate very quickly in many different ways, and yet we find communicating more difficult than ever. In fact, we need communication more urgently than ever."
Tom Cruise, American actor, b. 1962

• •
• •

Shaking off summer and rolling out of bed for an 8 a.m. class was a disappointing way for Angelique to start her fall semester. As she ran across campus, still tired, she realized she forgot her book. "Ugh, this is going to be a rough morning and now I'm late for class!" she thought. After running back, book now in hand, she couldn't believe she was taking a communication class. She heard from other students that the professor actually made you give formal public speeches—that made her nervous. But, the class filled her elective requirement. Still . . . 8 a.m.

As Angelique hustled across campus, all the while she thought "I already know how to talk. I talk a lot. Plus, I constantly e-mail and text my friends. Why do I need to learn about communication and how to be a public speaker? I'm not going to be a politician. I don't even know what my major is—I may never have to give a speech." Angelique's anxiety calmed a little knowing her good friends were in the same class. They would get through this one together.

• •
• •

Angelique is right about one thing. As adults, we already know how to talk. But as you may have noticed in your own life, we don't always succeed in communicating what we think and feel. This chapter sets the stage for learning about public speaking by first understanding what communication is and how it works. To do that, we'll touch on these key areas of vital importance to becoming a competent public speaker:

• The processes of communication and communication competence
• The importance of communication in your day-to-day life
• A description of communication in different contexts and situations
• The impact of culture and diversity on communication and public speaking
• The role of ethics and credibility when you communicate

WHAT IS COMMUNICATION?

Communication is such an integral part of our daily lives that we tend to take it for granted until we say or do something that is misunderstood. Then we wonder why the other person does not understand. Conversely, we may not understand what the other person is trying to communicate. At best, poor communication results in a minor disagreement or lack of appreciation of the other person's point of view. At worst, it results in major arguments and deteriorating relationships. Failure to communicate is not limited to interpersonal relationships, however. Communication mishaps also occur in group situations, at school, at work, and even when people speak in public. A good starting point for probing these kinds of problems is to consider what communication is and how it works.

Many terms, such as message transmission, speech, or spoken language,[1] have been used to describe human communication. Webster's dictionary says that communication is "a process by which information is exchanged between individuals through a common system of symbols, signs, or behavior."[2] Communication scholars think that a broad conceptual definition is most useful to describe communication in any situation, such as this: **Communication** is the process of managing messages and media for the purpose of creating meaning and promoting understanding.[3]

Think about that definition. It is saying you should be able to use any communicative message, from speaking, to listening, to instant messaging, in such a way that others fully understand what you mean. As important, you should be able to understand the meaning of messages others send to you. The true promise of communication is that it is a tool any of us can use to create meaning and promote understanding whether we're communicating with a stranger, our best friend, or a group of different and diverse people in a public situation.[4]

1.1 COMMUNICATION is the process of managing messages and media for the purpose of creating meaning and promoting understanding.

COMMUNICATION'S KEY CONCEPTS

Take a closer look at the definition and the promise of communication. Four key concepts are mentioned that are critical to learning about successful and competent communication:[5]

- Messages
- Media
- Meaning
- Understanding

Messages are the words, sounds, actions, and gestures that people use to communicate with one another. We use two types of symbols—verbal and nonverbal—to create communication messages. A **symbol** represents or stands for something else, but it is not that something else. The American flag, for example, stands for and represents the principles on which the country was founded. Verbal symbols are the words we use when we communicate using language, spoken or written. For instance, the word *chair* is not the thing that you actually sit on. Rather, *chair* is the symbol that stands for and represents our understanding of the piece of furniture on which we sit. Nonverbal symbols include various aspects of our physical appearance and

1.2 MESSAGES are the words, sounds, actions, and gestures that people use to communicate with one another.

1.3 SYMBOLS represent or stand for something else, but it is not that something else.

Table 1.1: Four Key Concepts of Communication

KEY CONCEPT	DEFINITION OF THE CONCEPT
Messages	The words, sounds, actions, and gestures that people use to communicate with one another.
Media	Any means or channels people use to transmit and exchange messages with one another.
Meaning	The interpretation and understanding of a message that is sent or received using various media.
Understanding	What occurs when we use messages and media in such a way that we fully grasp the meaning of the other person or persons' message.

body language, facial expression, and eye contact. For example, when we wave to another person, we are using a nonverbal symbol to send a message of greeting or get a person's attention. When we avert our gaze and avoid eye contact, we are saying nonverbally that we prefer not to communicate or feel shy in the particular situation.

The most important thing to remember about symbols is that *people* assign meaning to them—their meaning is not absolute and fixed. The meaning of any symbol may vary based on the culture and situation where communication is occurring and based on each person's individual and personal interpretation of that symbol. Therefore, the messages we send and receive, using verbal and nonverbal symbols, may be easily misread or misunderstood by others. Think back to a time when the message you intended to send was misunderstood because the other person misread your verbal or nonverbal use of symbols. In the opening story for this chapter, Angelique arrived five minutes after class started and apologized for being *late*. But the instructor's sense of *late* may be different than Angelique's and she may wonder why Angelique is apologizing. In any communication situation, including public speaking, we all need to be aware of how the verbal and nonverbal symbols we use may be interpreted by the other person or persons in the audience.

Media are any means or channels people use to transmit and exchange messages with one another. When humankind first started to communicate eons ago, their media choices and channels were quite simple and limited. Humans mainly communicated using natural media such as the voice or human behaviors. The first humans may have grunted and pointed to their mouths to indicate hunger or to a spear to say, "Let's go hunting." As well, the first organized societies were primarily oral and were restricted to using spoken language to communicate. Over time, communication became far more complex as people learned to read and write, use technology such as the printing press, and then transmit messages using more sophisticated mass media.

1.4 MEDIA are any means or channels people use to transmit and exchange messages with one another.

Today, added to natural media are various types of technological media such as electronic personal digital assistants, video phones, cell phones with cameras, and the list goes on. We have many media alternatives, from phones and faxes, to e-mail and instant messaging, to putting your life story up on YouTube for a large audience to see.

Every day, without thinking, people make unconscious choices about the medium or channel for sending communicative messages to one another. When we need to send an important message, we tend to use the medium that is most comfortable for us, even though it may not always be the most appropriate. For example, some people prefer to avoid face-to-face communication as a medium of choice, if they need to communicate very bad news to somebody else. One study even found that people prefer using e-mail, rather than voicemail, to deliver evaluative feedback to another person.[6] In fact, several national corporations were roundly criticized for giving some employees their termination notices by e-mail. The employees were told that they were fired and that, by the end of the day, they should depart the building. While this is an extreme example, it illustrates the importance of choosing the right medium for communicating messages. Angelique has a choice of media for communicating with her professor. If the professor appears busy and distracted on the first day of class, it might be more considerate to send a quick e-mail message after class explaining her lateness.

Meaning is the interpretation and understanding of a message that is sent or received using various media. As social beings, we have agreed to the meaning of most words and nonverbal symbols. When you communicate with a person or group of people who share the same meaning of most words and symbols as you, communication flows more readily. But when you communicate with people different from yourself—based on culture, age, personal history and background, or political or religious beliefs—they may interpret and understand your message differently than you intend. When that is the case, you need to make an extra effort to communicate and construct a sense of shared meaning and understanding. Constructing shared meaning is a process that first involves assigning meaning to a speaker's message and then clarifying your understanding of it to ensure you are both "on the same page." Angelique could construct a sense of shared meaning with her professor by asking what her expectations will be regarding punctuality and the start of class.

> **1.5 MEANING is the interpretation and understanding of a message that is sent or received using various media.**

Understanding occurs when we use messages and media in such a way that we fully grasp the meaning of the other person or persons' message. The goal of mutual understanding is achieved by learning how to use verbal and nonverbal messages to get your point across effectively. This does not mean that you want everybody else to agree with you, but it does mean the other person or persons need to understand what you think and feel, whether they agree with you or not.

> **1.6 UNDERSTANDING occurs when we use messages and media in such a way that we fully grasp the meaning of the other person or persons' message.**

For all of us as communicators, the most frustrating situation is feeling that others just don't understand what we are trying to say. Two doctors outside the communication discipline summarized this situation quite well: "Talking, listening, reading, writing…it all seems so simple. Yet we know how easily 'wires can get crossed,' when we don't listen to what somebody is saying (How many times has that caused arguments between you and your significant other?), or when we misread a letter or e-mail, or when we don't talk to or phone someone at a crucial time."[7]

To address misunderstandings such as these, we need to pay more attention to how we manage the entire process of sending and receiving verbal and nonverbal messages. We need to be aware of differences in how others interpret our verbal and nonverbal messages, and we need to choose the appropriate media to transmit our messages. The goal is not just that the other person or persons hear you. The goal is that they understand you and you understand them.

MODELS OF COMMUNICATION

To better appreciate the process of creating meaning and promoting understanding through communication, one picture will be worth a thousand words. Over the years, communication scholars have chosen to draw pictorial models of the communication process. Just as you would better understand the inner workings of an automobile engine by seeing a diagram of it, communication as a process is best presented visually.

....
1.7 A SOURCE is the sender of a message.

....
1.8 A CHANNEL is the medium through which the message is sent.

....
1.9 A RECEIVER is the recipient of the message.

Figure 1.1 is what most communication scholars consider a basic model of communication. It includes the essential components of any communication interaction: a **source** or sender of a **message**; the medium or **channel** through which the message is sent (voice, e-mail, phone, newspaper, etc.); and the **receiver** of the message. This model also sometimes identifies the possibility of "noise" entering into the communication process, which would affect the transmission of the message. Noise could be actual physical distractions in the environment such as loud music in the room or psychological distractions such as the listeners not caring about the topic you are discussing. In this traditional model, you will notice that the senders and the receivers of messages are one and the same. When people send messages (talking to another person), at the same time, they are receiving messages (perhaps the nonverbal cues the other person is sending while listening).

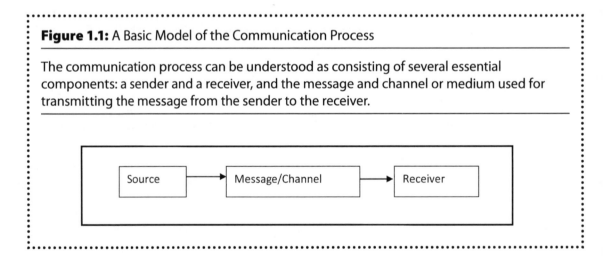

Figure 1.1: A Basic Model of the Communication Process

The communication process can be understood as consisting of several essential components: a sender and a receiver, and the message and channel or medium used for transmitting the message from the sender to the receiver.

Figure 1.2 is a somewhat more sophisticated model and depicts communication as the process of creating meaning and promoting understanding. This model would hold true of any communication interaction or situation, from an interpersonal conversation to giving a public speech. It includes the four key concepts or components: messages, media, meaning, and understanding.

Now think back to the story at the start of this chapter. Angelique did not know it on the first day of her public speaking class, but she and her friends were on the verge of learning about the promise of communication—how to competently use messages in various media to create meaning and promote understanding.

Figure 1.2: A Model of the Communication Process: Creating Meaning and Promoting Understanding

One way to sort out messages, media, meanings, and understanding is this model depicting how senders and receivers create shared meaning through the communication process.

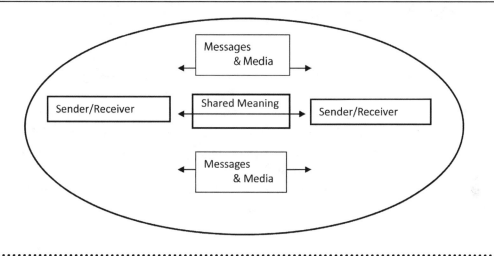

WHAT IS COMPETENT COMMUNICATION?

By now we should be in agreement that the goal in most communication situations, including public speaking, is to create shared meaning and promote understanding. When you accomplish that goal, you are engaging in what some communication professionals refer to as competent communication.[8] You may be asking yourself—what constitutes competent communication? Competent communication is critical to your personal, career, and educational success. **Competent communication** is both *effective* and *appropriate* for the particular situation.

Effective communication means you are able to achieve the goal or purpose for which you are communicating. You need to possess the necessary communication skills and be able and willing to use them, whether you are at home with family and friends, or at work in any employment situation. If it is an interpersonal conversation, you need to know how to self-disclose, share information about yourself, and listen actively to the other person. If it is a small group or team meeting, you need to engage in collaborative problem solving and discuss difficulties in an open and fair manner. If you're using technology, whether text messaging on a cell phone or using e-mail, you need to know how to use the equipment effectively. And if it is a public speaking situation, you need to know how to analyze an audience and prepare and present a speech effectively. That may mean knowing how to give an electronic presentation effectively using a presentation program like Microsoft's PowerPoint.

Appropriate communication means you are aware and respectful of the norms and expectations for communication behavior in the particular situation. You communicate in a manner that is

1.10 COMPETENT COMMUNICATION is both *effective* **and** *appropriate* **for the particular situation.**

1.11 EFFECTIVE COMMUNICATION means you are able to achieve the goal or purpose for which you are communicating.

1.12 APPROPRIATE COMMUNICATION means you are aware and respectful of the norms and expectations for communication behavior in the particular situation.

sensitive and respectful of everyone involved. In a new interpersonal relationship or with a group of strangers, you avoid inappropriate or early self-disclosure. At work, in a group or team meeting, you respect different opinions and encourage others to share ideas. If you're using technology, you are aware and respectful of the etiquette and right way to communicate—no terse messages that may offend the recipient. In a public speaking situation, you communicate respect for the beliefs, attitudes, and values of a diverse audience. You appropriately acknowledge the sources of the content of your speech and thus avoid any appearance of plagiarizing the work of others. In sum, you don't just know what to say, you know *how* to say it.

As Angelique approaches her first communication class, she needs to *effectively* tell the professor why she is late; it was not disinterest but the result of forgetting her book. She also should communicate this message to her professor *appropriately*. Rather than blurting it out when entering class on the first day, she could tell her professor in a one-on-one situation during a break or after class. That said, we know that Angelique questioned whether taking a public speaking class is a good idea at all, even as an elective. Let's answer that question now, for Angelique and for you.

IS COMMUNICATION IMPORTANT?

Being able to communicate competently *is* critical to your personal and professional success, right now as a student, and as you advance in your chosen career or profession in the future. Our economy is changing and we are becoming more service and knowledge-based, with most jobs relying heavily on a worker's ability to communicate, sometimes using technology and sometimes not. Communication skills and communication competence have never been more important.

A careful analysis of 93 journal and newspaper articles, reports, and national surveys, all published from 1998 to 2006, provides evidence of the importance of effective and appropriate communication to: your personal development, psychologically and socially; succeeding in school; becoming a responsible citizen and participant in the world; and succeeding in a career, in business, and in organizational life.[9] In addition, good communication is considered necessary to our ability to address emerging social concerns in the 21st century including health communication issues, crisis communication situations, and crime and policing problems.

Several of the 93 articles specifically highlight the importance of business communication and public speaking skills. For instance, one article discusses changes in communication across generations as people grow and mature.[10] According to the author, "this [current] generation may be technologically savvier than their bosses, but will they be able to have a professional discussion?" Barker points to a 2005 report for Achieve, a non-profit organization that helps states raise academic standards. The report found that employers were very dissatisfied with the oral communication skills of graduates; and, 45 percent of college students and 46 percent of high school graduates said they struggled particularly with their public speaking abilities. Another of the articles says employers are looking for strong communication skills when evaluating college graduates as potential new hires ("Job market still soft for the class of 2003"). This article states that "Employers have placed communication skills at the top of their wish lists" and that "new graduates come up short on many of these [communication] skills." The employers believe that new graduates are not proficient at speaking or writing and students should work on skills to improve verbal and written communication by enrolling in public speaking and writing courses. Good advice for Angelique and her friends and for you and your classmates.

Think about it. Every human endeavor and every relationship in which you engage could be more successful and rewarding if you communicate competently. Furthermore, if you master what most people think is the most difficult communication skill—the ability to communicate in public speaking situations—research suggests you will become a better communicator in a variety of life's situations and communication contexts. For example, if you are able to use your communication skills, particularly public speaking, to speak out publicly on behalf of important issues in our society, you will be able to contribute significantly to the greater social good. Some might argue that effective and appropriate communication and speech are at the core of a free and democratic society.

COMMUNICATION CONTEXTS

We all know there are different situations in life when communication is of the utmost importance. Communication experts refer to these "life situations" as communication contexts. Put simply, **communication contexts** are the life situations in which you communicate. Context provides the boundaries and rules for what and how communication should occur in a given situation. The most traditional way to think about communication contexts is what we call a levels approach.

1.13 COMMUNICATION CONTEXTS are the life situations in which you communicate.

LEVELS OF CONTEXT

Context level refers to the number of people involved in the communication event and the distance between or among the communicators. The levels differ according to whether you are communicating on a one-to-one basis, one-to-several, or one-to-many, and whether some type of technological media is involved, which may result in more physical distance among the communicators. For example, face-to-face interpersonal communication is characterized by less distance between two communicators than interpersonal communication that takes place by phone or e-mail.

1.14 CONTEXT LEVEL refers to the number of people involved in the communication event and the distance between or among the communicators.

Figure 1.3 illustrates the various levels of communication starting with the least complex (fewer communicators and no media) to more complex (more communicators and media or technology are involved). In this model, computer-mediated communication is placed after mass media, because some experts say it brings the communication process full circle. People are communicating interpersonally when they communicate by computer, even though the computer is mediating their one-on-one communication.

Intrapersonal communication is one way communication with yourself—only one person is involved. Interpersonal communication involves two people communicating, whether face-to-face, by phone, e-mail, or even text messaging. Small group communication is an interaction among a number of people—typically three to twelve—that sometimes involves a team-oriented activity or

Figure 1.3: A Diagram of the Levels of Communication

The situations or levels of communication are distinguished by how many people are involved, the direction of communication in the situation, and the use of technological media.

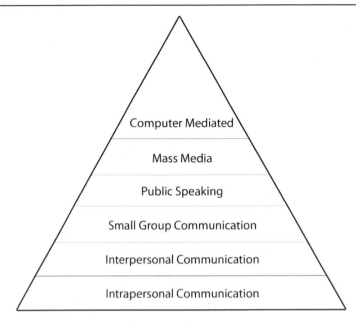

Computer Mediated

Mass Media

Public Speaking

Small Group Communication

Interpersonal Communication

Intrapersonal Communication

project. The public speaking context involves one person or a small group of people speaking to a larger number of people, an audience that typically has little or no "speaking" role. Mass communication takes place using some type of mass media as the channel for sending and receiving messages such as television, radio, advertising, public relationships, newspapers, books, and magazines.

Some assumptions about competent communication hold true across all the context levels. For example, in all contexts, you should communicate effectively and appropriately, but how those two goals are achieved may change from one context level to the next. As the number of people increases, the possibility of varying interpretations of the meaning of your message also increases. So when speaking in public, you need to be aware that your message may be varyingly interpreted by different audience members. As the distance among communicators increases because of the use of communication technology (phones, e-mail, etc.), the potential for misinterpretation of your message may increase. When talking on the phone or exchanging e-mail messages, you need to realize that there is a lack of nonverbal cues such as facial expression and eye contact. Your message is conveyed with only your words and how you say or write them.

MEDIATED COMMUNICATION AND SOCIAL MEDIA

The context level taking on greater importance in the 21st century is mediated communication that may be one-to-one or one-to-many. This context involves any mediated communication interaction using cell phones, e-mail, or any use of the Internet and World Wide Web. Today, communication researchers are very interested in **computer-mediated communication** (CMC), which is defined as any human symbolic interaction through digitally-based technologies. These researchers are looking at the more traditional ways people communicate, but they examine the traditional contexts through the lens of CMC.

....

1.15 COMPUTER-MEDIATED COMMUNICATION (CMC) is any human symbolic interaction through digitally based technologies.

Interpersonal communication researchers are studying how people use technology to initiate interpersonal relationships,[11] to develop on-line relationships,[12] and to manage on-line romantic relationships.[13] Other researchers are probing loneliness and the use of computer-mediated communication. They have found that socially anxious adolescents tend to prefer communicating on the Internet rather than face-to-face;[14] and, CMC users who are more lonely, tend to communicate in CMC situations more and differently than their less lonely counterparts.[15] Gender styles and differences in e-mail and computer-mediated communication also are under investigation. For example, females tend to use more exclamation points than males in their e-mail messages as markers or indicators of friendly interaction.[16]

Small group communication researchers also are studying the use of CMC. They are examining how groups make decisions and solve problems[17] and whether and how group participants conform to group norms in computer-mediated communication environments.[18] One researcher examined the impact of anonymity on participants' collaboration in computer-mediated group discussions.[19] The ability to remain anonymous in these discussions tends to minimize differences in status and frees group participants to make comments without fear of any payback.

CMC also is making its mark in intercultural communication situations. One researcher examined whether contributors to Wikipedia from different cultures (French, German, Japanese, and Dutch) would demonstrate any cultural differences in the style of their contributions to the on-line encyclopedia.[20] Indeed, communication was impacted significantly by the cultural background of the contributors to the encyclopedia.

Finally, a context you probably are very familiar with and perhaps use every day is referred to as social media. **Social media** involve any sort of communication created by people using highly accessible publishing technologies. Over the past decade, social media such as blogs, wikis, social networking

....

1.16 SOCIAL MEDIA involves any sort of communication created by people using highly accessible publishing technologies.

sites (SNS) like *MySpace* and *Facebook*, and the micro-blog/SNS hybrid *Twitter* have become an important part of communication all over the world. For example, in a populist uprising in the streets of Iran after that country's 2009 presidential election, ordinary citizens posted graphic images and videos of the unrest to SNS websites using their cell phones. Without any use of traditional media, they alerted the rest of the world thousands of miles away to what they were experiencing.

In a very basic way, social media are a shift in how people discover, read, and share news and information about the world and about one another. As a communication context, social media have become extremely popular, allowing people to connect in the online world to form relationships for personal and business reasons. If you want to find out what an old friend is up to, you check out their *Facebook* page; if you want to find a new job, social networking sites often are used more than the classified pages of the local newspaper. As Shel Holtz, of *Holtz Communication + Technology*, and others simply explain: "Social media is the mechanism for having a conversation and telling your story."[21]

A competent communicator is aware and respectful of all dimensions and characteristics of the context level and communication situation. The number of people involved in the communication event is critical. Is it one other person, a small group, or a cast of thousands? Equally important is the physical and psychological environment. Will an interpersonal conversation be better served if it takes place in a quiet environment rather than a noisy bar? Is a big lecture hall conducive to audience members identifying with you personally as a public speaker and reacting favorably to your speech?

All of us communicate in these various contexts on a fairly regular basis. Interpersonally, we communicate with friends and family, teachers, and medical providers. Small groups and teams are a common practice in schools, businesses, and most organizations. Mediated communication and the use of cell phones and e-mail are permanent fixtures in our daily lives, and we interact regularly with mass media with hardly a second thought. And remember, communication in all these situations and contexts is affected by the cultural background of the people participating in the communication event.

CULTURE AND DIVERSITY

As Angelique plans for her public speaking class, she is assuming the other students in the class will be somewhat like her and her friends. That may not be the case. They may differ from Angelique and from one another based on cultural characteristics that may not be readily apparent. Some cultural differences, race for example, are observable, but a person's ethnicity, religious, or political preferences are not as obvious but may equally impact the communication process.

THE IMPACT OF CULTURE ON COMMUNICATION

Culture consists of the enduring patterns of thought, values, and behaviors that define a group of people.[22] Cultural factors of importance include but are not limited to the communicators' ethnicity, race, nationality, gender, and, their belief systems and ways of thinking and behaving. Any of these cultural characteristics may affect how others react to you and your communication message, whether you are meeting someone for the first time or presenting a speech. In fact, some researchers discovered that people tend to perceive others who are more like themselves as more competent and more socially attractive.[23] Another study compared Hispanic cultures and Anglo-Americans and found that cultural background significantly affects whether you are perceived to be a competent communicator.[24]

> 1.17 CULTURE consists of the enduring patterns of thought, values, and behaviors that define a group of people.

Other intercultural communication researchers have learned that cultural background and cultural differences may affect building successful business relationships,[25] the performance of multicultural teams,[26] and communication among students on college campuses.[27] Even the researchers themselves are impacted by cultural differences. A study of professional communication in the former Soviet republics indicates that scholars writing in these regions, where democracy is new and even alien to the culture, bring their own set of biased assumptions and practices to their work.[28]

As you begin to understand communication and communicating competently across cultures, you want to ask yourselves some questions. Have you considered the other person or the audience's cultural preferences and orientations as you prepare to communicate? If it is a public speaking situation, did you choose a topic that the majority of the audience will find interesting? Will the cultural background and the *diversity* of the audience play a role in how your speech is received?

Box 1.1: Thinking Outside the Box: Business Blunders in Other Countries

An American businessperson learned some lessons about communicating in other cultures when he refused an offer of a cup of coffee from a Saudi businessman. That rejection of hospitality is considered very rude in Saudi Arabia, and negotiations between the two businesspeople and their companies stalled. International business blunders such as this are more frequent than you might think and could derail the very best of international and intercultural relationships. According to respected cultural anthropologist, E.T. Hall, "The single greatest barrier to business success is the one erected by culture." In the era of globalization, culture is now recognized as having a major impact on sales, marketing, recruitment, management and mergers. In short, culture is behind everything we should say or do. So what lesson can we learn from intercultural business blunders of others like these?

1. Managers at one American company were startled when they discovered that the brand name of the cooking oil they were marketing in a Latin American country translated into Spanish as "Jackass Oil."

2. American Motors tried to market its new car, the Matador, based on the bullfighter's image of courage and strength. However, in Puerto Rico the name Matador means "killer" and was not popular on the hazardous roads in the country.

3. A sales manager in Hong Kong tried to promote employees' promptness at work. He insisted they come to work on time instead of 15 minutes late. They complied, but then left exactly on time instead of working into the evening as they had in the past. Much work was left unfinished until the manager relented and the employees returned to their usual time schedule.

4. A U.S. telephone company tried to market its products and services to Latinos by showing a commercial in which a Latino wife tells her husband to call a friend to say they would be late for dinner. The commercial bombed since Latino women do not order their husbands around and being a little late would not require a call about lateness.

5. A cologne for men pictured a pastoral scene with a man and his dog. It failed in Islamic countries where dogs are considered unclean.

6. Proctor & Gamble used a television commercial in Japan that was popular in Europe. The ad showed a woman bathing and her husband entering the bathroom and then touching her. The Japanese considered this ad an invasion of privacy, inappropriate behavior, and in very poor taste.

7. A Japanese manager in an American company was told to give critical feedback to a subordinate during a performance evaluation. Japanese are very uncomfortable giving direct feedback. It took the manager five tries before he could be direct enough to discuss the poor performance so that the American understood.

8. One company printed the "OK" finger sign on each page of its catalogue. In many parts of Latin America that is considered an obscene gesture. Six months of work were lost because they had to reprint all the catalogues.

9. Leona Helmsley should have done her homework before she approved a promotion or marketing campaign that compared her Helmsley Palace Hotel in New York to the Taj Mahal—a mausoleum in India.

10. A golf ball manufacturing company packaged golf balls in packs of four for convenient purchase in Japan. Unfortunately, pronunciation of the word "four" in Japanese sounds like the word "death" and items packaged in fours are unpopular.

Continued on next page

Continued from previous page

11. FEDEX (Federal Express) wisely chose to expand overseas when it discovered the domestic market was saturated. However, the centralized or "hub and spoke" delivery system so successful domestically was inappropriate for overseas distribution. In addition, they failed to consider cultural differences: In Spain, the workers preferred very late office hours, and in Russia the workers took truck cleaning soap home due to consumer shortages. FEDEX finally shut down over 100 European operations after $1.2 billion in losses.

12. Mountain Bell Company tried to promote its telephone services in Saudi Arabia. Its ad portrayed an executive talking on the phone with his feet propped up on the desk, showing the soles of his shoes—something an Arab would never do!

The big lesson learned: Be sure you are aware of the cultural norms and expected behaviors when communicating with someone from a culture different than your own. Unlike these business blunders, your communication with people from other cultures could be successful but only if you are aware of cultural differences. Sometimes we don't know what we don't know. It is your job to find out about the cultural expectations of other people, other countries, and other cultures. Visit the *Kwintessential Cross Cultural Solutions* website to learn more about proper etiquette in different countries and to take a personal cultural awareness quiz.

THE IMPACT OF DIVERSITY ON COMMUNICATION

Diversity merely means how much alike or unlike the members of any group of people may be in terms of their cultural background. This concept is extremely important in contemporary society because our population today represents a far richer mix of cultures than in the past. In fact, statisticians say that the United States is becoming increasingly multicultural and multiracial.[29] By the year 2050, the racial and ethnic demographics of the United States will shift significantly with White Americans being about equal in number to the total number of those people now considered minority populations (Hispanic, Black, American Indian, and Asian).

1.18 DIVERSITY means how much alike or unlike the members of any group of people may be in terms of their cultural background.

Given the globalization of the world economy in the 21st century, some communication scholars are calling for a new form of intercultural dialogue to deal with these cultural differences and manage conflicts.[30] A glance at the chaos in the Middle East and other troubled spots around the world supports this call for improving intercultural communication.

The result of increased diversity is that we cannot expect others, including audiences for public speeches and presentations, to be highly similar to ourselves in cultural background and beliefs, attitudes, and values. A competent communicator and speaker is aware of the need to communicate in an inclusive manner that respects and honors multiple and various ways of looking at the world. Inclusive communication calls for using communication strategies that adapt to the culturally and ethnically diverse ways that people communicate. The chapter on audience analysis (Chapter 4) in this textbook discusses this topic in much more detail.

Becoming aware of the reality of cultural diversity is a critical first step toward communication competence. It will help you create and transmit messages effectively and appropriately, but there are other benefits. A speaker who shows respect for other cultures is communicating ethically and, as a result, establishes a high level of credibility.[31] Ethical communication and speaker credibility are inextricably related to one another, so let's now examine these concepts and their relationship.

ETHICS, COMMUNICATION, AND CREDIBILITY

Ethics is a branch of philosophy that explores what constitutes good and bad or right and wrong. Ethicists are concerned about how people decide whether a particular decision or activity is good or bad.[32] Each of us has our own internal sense of right and wrong that we regularly apply to how we interact and communicate with others. There are times when most people think it is alright to tell a lie. "Yes, your new haircut is very flattering." "No, you do not look fat in that pair of pants." There are

1.19 ETHICS is a branch of philosophy that explores what constitutes good (or right) and bad (or wrong); and, how people decide whether a particular decision or activity is good or bad.

Box 1.2: A Credo for Ethical Communication

The leading scholarly communication organization gives these guidelines for communicating ethically.

Credo for Ethical Communication of the National Communication Association (approved by the NCA Legislative Council in 1999)

Questions of right and wrong arise whenever people communicate. Ethical communication is fundamental to responsible thinking, decision making, and the development of relationships and communities within and across contexts, cultures, channels, and media. Moreover, ethical communication enhances human worth and dignity by fostering truthfulness, fairness, responsibility, personal integrity, and respect for self and others. We believe that unethical communication threatens the quality of all communication and consequently the well-being of individuals and the society in which we live. Therefore we, the members of the National Communication Association, endorse and are committed to practicing the following principles of ethical communication:

- We advocate truthfulness, accuracy, honesty, and reason as essential to the integrity of communication.
- We endorse freedom of expression, diversity of perspective, and tolerance of dissent to achieve the informed and responsible decision making fundamental to a civil society.
- We strive to understand and respect other communicators before evaluating and responding to their messages.
- We promote access to communication resources and opportunities as necessary to fulfill human potential and contribute to the well-being of families, communities, and society.
- We promote communication climates of caring and mutual understanding that respect the unique needs and characteristics of individual communicators.
- We condemn communication that degrades individuals and humanity through distortion, intimidation, coercion, and violence, and through the expression of intolerance and hatred.
- We are committed to the courageous expression of personal convictions in pursuit of fairness and justice.
- We advocate sharing information, opinions, and feelings when facing significant choices while also respecting privacy and confidentiality.
- We accept responsibility for the short- and long-term consequences for our own communication and expect the same of others.

Source: National Communication Association. Retrieved from www/natcom.org

other times when we as a culture or society think it is unethical to lie. We don't lie under oath, for example, in the U.S. justice system. What each of us thinks is ethical does vary, based on our cultural background. We will talk a little more about cultural variations in a later chapter. Let's now consider some descriptive models of ethics and communication.

MODELS OF ETHICAL COMMUNICATION

What is ethical communication and how does it relate to public speaking—the topic of this book? Communication ethics has been debated by scholars for centuries, since the time of the ancient Greeks and Romans. Plato said communication should always be used to serve truth and the civic good; otherwise it could be used to exploit and manipulate other people. Plato's student, Aristotle, argued against that idea. He claimed the best defense against being exploited is to understand how communication can be used or misused.

That debate aside, it is not surprising today that we see many calls for guidelines to help us decide how to make ethical judgments and communicate more ethically.[33] For instance, the National Communication Association, a major organization of communication scholars and teachers, spent lots of time and energy developing and approving a national model for ethical communication.[34] After much discussion about whether their model should be general in nature or focus on specific communication practices, the group decided to craft a credo that would apply to all forms and settings of people's communication interactions in our democratic society. The credo suggests that communicating ethically with other people benefits society collectively and ourselves as individuals. Accordingly, ethical communication fosters truthfulness, fairness, responsibility, personal integrity, and perhaps most important, respect for self and others. The credo, presented in Box 1.2, gives you a good idea of what experts on this topic specifically think is the right thing to do when communicating in any situation.

While we're at it, here's another way to think about ethical communication you may find useful. The concept of competent communication as effectiveness and appropriateness can help us make ethical communication judgments. Effectiveness could be viewed as primarily serving our self interest and accomplishing our own communication goals. By contrast, appropriateness could be viewed as primarily an interest in the other person or persons with whom we are communicating. Logic would say that if we fairly balance our own interests and those of the other people with whom we are communicating, we would be close to an ethical course of action.

Put more plainly, **ethical communication** means sharing sufficient and appropriate information with others, such that they can make fully informed decisions about matters of importance to

....

1.20 ETHICAL COMMUNICATION means sharing sufficient and appropriate information with others such that they can make fully informed decisions about matters of importance to themselves.

themselves. To return to the earlier example, you would have an ethical responsibility to tell your friend the truth if: (a) the haircut looks ridiculous and he is on the way to an important job interview; or (b) the pants are much too tight and she is on the way to meet her future in-laws for the first time. These events might be considered matters of importance for your friends and telling them the truth would be the ethical thing to do. In the same way, as you are researching and developing a speech, you have an ethical responsibility to make note of your sources of information. When you present your speech, you have an ethical responsibility to tell the audience about those sources and where you got your information. That challenge is most important when you research your speech on the Internet. You have an ethical responsibility to question the credibility of the Internet source and share that information candidly with your audience.

ETHICAL COMMUNICATION AND CREDIBILITY

Closely linked to ethical communication is your credibility as a speaker. A communicator who tries to communicate ethically is typically perceived by most people as reasonably credible. Like ethics, the early philosophers debated what it means to be credible. In the 4th century, B.C., Aristotle referred to credibility as the *ethos* of a speaker and said that it was as important as a speaker's ability to use logic or emotion to persuade. Four centuries later, a Roman writer and orator, Quintilian, said that to possess ethos or credibility a speaker needs to be "a good person speaking well." He was suggesting that to be perceived as credible, a communicator must be thought of as a good person and as competent and trustworthy. The definition of credibility has not changed much over the years. Today, **credibility** for a communicator means being perceived by others as both well-intended and qualified and able to speak informedly on the given topic.

1.21 CREDIBILITY means being perceived by others as both well-intended and qualified and able to speak informedly on the given topic.

As you and Angelique approach your first public speaking class, your reputation and character are not yet established. You are a blank slate in many ways, but Quintilian's advice still holds true. It is important in any communication interaction, including the public speaking context, to be a "good person" and consider the impact of your remarks on others as well as yourself. It is also important to know your topic well.

The recommendations for communication introduced in this chapter are applicable to all communication contexts, perhaps especially public speaking, the topic of this textbook. More than you might expect and throughout your life, you will need to be able to speak out publicly, with confidence and competence—at community events, public gatherings of all kinds, and on the job. From a wedding toast to a professional training or briefing, effective and appropriate communication skills and public speaking skills will serve you and Angelique, the star of our opening story, quite well. Chapter 2 shows what happens to Angelique and her friends in their first public speaking class.

CHAPTER SUMMARY

Communication may be defined as the process of managing messages and media in order to create meaning and promote understanding. The messages people use to communicate with one another make use of verbal and nonverbal symbols. Various media or channels are used to transmit and exchange these messages. As messages are sent or received using various media, meaning is assigned to the messages by the communicators. When we grasp the meaning of the message, understanding occurs. To better appreciate this process, communication scholars use pictorial models that contain components such as the source or sender, medium or channel, the message, the receiver,

and noise. When this process works well, we are engaging in competent communication, which is both effective—achieves the goal for communicating—and appropriate —is respectful of the norms and expectations for communication in the situation. Many studies and surveys call attention to the importance of communication to success in a variety of life situations or contexts. Cultural factors and the diversity of the communicators may have a positive or negative impact on the communication process. Regardless of such factors, communicators have a responsibility to communicate ethically, which means sharing sufficient and appropriate information with others so they can make fully informed decisions about any matters of importance to themselves. Ethical communicators typically are perceived as credible, that is, well-intended, qualified, and able to speak well on the given topic.

KEY TERMS

The key terms below are defined in this chapter and presented alphabetically with definitions in the Glossary at the end of the book.

- communication
- messages
- symbol
- media
- meaning
- understanding
- source
- channel
- receiver
- competent communication
- effective communication
- appropriate communication
- communication contexts
- levels of communication
- computer-mediated communication
- social media
- culture
- diversity
- ethics
- ethical communication
- credibility

BUILDING COMPETENCE ACTIVITIES

INDIVIDUAL ACTIVITIES

1. Think of a recent communication experience or event that you think was not competent. On a piece of paper, describe the event and what happened. Think about the key concepts of communication (message, media, meaning, and understanding) and write each one down on the piece of paper. Analyze why the communication event was not competent based on each of the four concepts.
2. Reflect on the previous week in your life and all the communication interactions you had with other people. Identify which interactions were most affected by communication and why communication was important in those interactions.
3. Think of a time when you were faced with an ethical choice about what to do as a communicator that may have represented an ethical *tight spot*. Use the definitions and models of ethical communication in this chapter to analyze what you decided to do in that situation.

GROUP ACTIVITIES

1. Form groups of four to five students. Use a big piece of blank paper and magic markers and draw a model of communication that captures your collective opinion of what communication "looks like." Present your models to the class and discuss the strengths and weaknesses of each model.

2. With a partner, leave the class and go to a computer on campus and access the website of the National Communication Association at www.natcom.org. Look over the website and then, with your partner, summarize what you learned about the communication discipline that you did not know before. Present what you learned to the class.

3. Form groups of four to five students. Share examples of significant competent or incompetent communication situations that you have experienced. Develop a list of guidelines for competent communication based on the discussion. Present your list of guidelines to the class.

4. Form groups of four to five students. Share examples of significant ethical or unethical communication situations that you have experienced. Develop a list of guidelines for ethical communication based on the discussion. Present your list of guidelines to the class.

5. Form groups of four to five students. Share examples of times when you were particularly credible as a communicator. Develop a list of guidelines for credible communication based on the discussion. Present your list of guidelines to the class.

COMPETENCY CHECKPOINTS AND SELF-ASSESSMENT TOOL

Here is what you need to know and be able to do regarding the communication process. Determine your level of competency and whether you are ready to proceed to the next chapter. Give yourself one point for each checkpoint you answer satisfactorily.

COMPETENCY CHECKPOINTS	NUMBER OF POINTS
KNOWLEDGE 1. Define communication. 2. Describe each of the four key communication concepts: messages, media, meaning, and understanding. 3. Define competent communication, including what it means to communicate effectively and appropriately.	
SKILLS 1. Draw a pictorial model of the communication process. 2. Give an example of the importance of communication based on your own life experience. 3. Give an example of communication in your life in each of the different communication contexts or levels, including computer-mediated communication. 4. Give an example of how cultural differences or diversity impacted you as a communicator in the recent past.	

ETHICS AND CREDIBILITY
1. Provide an example of ethical communication.
2. Provide an example of unethical communication.
3. Identify what you need to do to be perceived by others as a credible communicator.

TOTAL CHECKPOINTS (OUT OF A POSSIBLE TEN POINTS)

ENDNOTES

1. Littlejohn, S., & Foss, S. (2005). *Theories of human communication* (8th ed.). Belmont, CA: Wadsworth.

2. Foltz, J., & Wilson, C. (2007). Communicating in the feed and grain business: Are you getting what I'm saying? *Manager's Notebook, 4*(2), 40.

3. Frey, L. R., Botan, C. H., & Kreps, G. L. (2000). *Investigating communication: An introduction to research methods* (2nd ed.). Needham Heights, MA: Allyn & Bacon.

4. O'Hair, H. (2007, February). The promise of communication: A presidential address. (Cover story). *Spectra, 43*(2), 1–10. Retrieved from NCA Collection database.

5. Morreale, S. P., Spitzberg, B. H., & Barge, J. K. (2006). *Human communication: Motivation, knowledge, and skills* (2nd ed.). Belmont, CA: Wadsworth.

6. Watts, S.A. (2007). Evaluative feedback: Perspectives on media effects. *Journal of Computer-Mediated Communication, 12*(2), 50–77.

7. Foltz, J., & Wilson, C. (2007). Communicating in the feed and grain business: Are you getting what I'm saying? *Manager's Notebook, 4*(2), 40.

8. Morreale, S. P., Spitzberg, B. H., & Barge, J. K. (2006). *Human communication: Motivation, knowledge, and skills* (2nd ed.). Belmont, CA: Wadsworth.

9. Morreale, S.P., & Pearson, J.C. (2008). Why communication education is important: The centrality of the discipline in the 21st century. *Communication Education, 57*(2). 224-240.

10. Barker, O. (2006). *Technology leaves teens speechless.* Retrieved from http://www.usatoday.com/tech/news/techinnovations/2006-05-29-teen-texting_x.htm; Job market still soft for the class of 2003. (2002). Retrieved from http://www.collegejournal.com/resourcecenter/nace/20021127-nace.html

11. McQuillen, J.S. (2003). The influence of technology on the initiation of interpersonal relationships. *Education, 123*(3), 616–624.

12. Lee, B., Sim, L., Tan, T., & Detenber, B. (2003, May). *Getting to know you: Exploring the development of relational intimacy in computer-mediated communication.* Paper presented at the meeting of the International Communication Association, San Diego, CA.

13. Anderson, T. & Emmers-Sommer, T. (2006). Predictors of relationship satisfaction in online romantic relationships. *Communication Studies, 57*(2), 153–172.

14. Peter, J. & Valkenburg, P. (2006). Individual differences in perceptions of Internet communication. *European Journal of Communication, 21*(2), 213–226.

15. Chung, D. (2003, May). *I am not a lonely person any more: Interpersonal relationship in computer-mediated-communication.* Paper presented at the meeting of the International Communication Association, San Diego, CA.

16. Waseleski, C. (2006). Gender and the use of exclamation points in computer-mediated communication: An analysis of exclamations posted to two electronic discussion lists. *Journal of Computer-Mediated Communication, 11*, 1012–1024.

17. Turman, P.D. (2005). Norm development, decision making, and structuration in CMC group interaction. *Communication Teachers, 19*(4), 121–125.

18. Lee, E. (2006). When and how does depersonalization increase conformity to group norms in computer-mediated communication? *Communication Research, 23*(6), 423–447.

19. Rains, S.A. (2007). The impact of anonymity on perceptions of source credibility and influence in computer-mediated group communication. *Communication Research, 34*(1), 100–125.

20. Pfeil, U., Zaphiris, P., & Chee, S. (2006). Cultural differences in collaborative authoring of Wikipedia. *Journal of Computer-Mediated Communication, 12*(1), 88–113.

21. Holtz, S. (2009, March 11). Social Media Boot Camp. Presentation at the Social Media for Communicators Conference, Las Vegas, NV; Bernoff, J. & Li, C. (2008). *Groundswell: Winning a world transformed by social technologies.* Boston, MA: Harvard Business School Press.

22. Samovar, L.A., & Porter, R.E. (1995). *Communication between cultures* (2nd ed.). Belmont, CA: Wadsworth.

23. Feldstein, S., Dohm, F.A., & Crown, C. (2001). Gender and speech rate in the perception of competence and social attractiveness. *Journal of Social Psychology, 141*(6), 785–806.

24. Johnson, P., Lindsey, A., & Zakahi, W. (2001). Anglo American, Hispanic American, Chilean, Mexican and Spanish perceptions of competent communication. *Communication Research Reports, 18*(1), 36–43.

25. Zhu, Y., Nel, P., Bhat, R. (2006). A cross cultural study of communication strategies for building business relationships. *International Journal of Cross Cultural Management, 6*(3), 319–341

26. Matveev A.V., & Nelson, P.E. (2004). Cross cultural communication competence and multicultural team performance: Perceptions of American and Russian managers. *International Journal of Cross Cultural Management, 4*(2), 253–270.

27. Halualani, R., Chitgopekar, A., Morrison, J., & Dodge, P. (2004). Diverse in name only? Intercultural interaction at a multicultural university. *Journal of Communication, 54*(2), 270–286.

28. Harootunian, G. (2007). Dancing the *Kochari*: Challenging the U.S. Perspective on Communication in Newly Democratic Cultures. *Journal of Business and Technical Communication, 21*(1), 91–105

29. U.S. Census Bureau. (2003). America's families and living arrangements. Retrieved from http://www.census.gov/population/www/socdemo/hh-fam.html

30. Baraldi, C. (2006). New forms of intercultural communication in a globalized world. *International Communication Gazette, 68*(1), 53–69.

31. Makau, J.M., & Arnett, R.C. (Eds.). (1997). *Communication ethics in an age of diversity.* Chicago: University of Illinois Press.

32. Morreale, S.P., & Bovee, C.L. (1998). *Excellence in public speaking.* Ft. Worth, TX: Harcourt Brace.

33. Walker, G.S. (2005, September-October). Survey: Communicators seek ethics guidance. *Communication World,* 19.

34. Andersen, K E. (2000). Developments in communication ethics: The Ethics Commission, Code of Professional Responsibilities, Credo for Ethical Communication. *Journal of the Association for Communication Administration, 29,* 131–144.

2

UNDERSTANDING PUBLIC SPEAKING

- **What is Public Speaking?**
  The History of Public Speaking and Rhetoric
  Types of Speeches
  Types of Delivery
- **Is Public Speaking Important?**
  Benefits for Society
  Personal and Professional Benefits
- **Myths about Public Speaking**

"You can speak well if your tongue can deliver the message of your heart."
John Ford, American film director of Irish heritage, 1894–1973

• •
• • •

On the first day of class, Angelique was glad to see her friend, Zak, who chose the same section of public speaking. She and Zak have a lot in common. He is a cool guy and will give her support in the class. Angelique's relief at seeing familiar faces turned to dismay at the sight of a well-dressed Chinese woman at the front of the room with the teacher. Angelique thought, "Oh god, we're starting off on the first day with everybody giving speeches." The instructor introduced Lin Wang who shared her personal story about taking a public speaking class: "I am here today to tell you I avoided public speaking until my last semester as an undergraduate because my English is not perfect and I was very nervous. I was surprised I did well in the class and actually got an 'A' in the course. I was yet more surprised when I went on an interview for my first job. I was asked to present a few remarks about my qualifications and why I wanted the position. Later that week, I got a call saying I got the job. When I met with the personnel manager, she said I was chosen from a large pool of equally qualified applicants because of my ability to clearly present my best thinking! Nobody was more surprised than me."

• •
• • •

Angelique and Zak arrived in class with one thing in common—their lack of enthusiasm about learning to give a good speech. But they both were surprised and motivated by Lin Wang's personal story. At that point, they decided it was time to learn more about public speaking and some basic public speaking skills. This chapter introduces you and these somewhat unenthusiastic students to the fundamentals of public speaking by addressing these topics:

- What public speaking is, including its history in rhetoric in different cultures
- The various types of speeches you will be giving and different ways to deliver a speech
- The importance of knowing how to give a speech
- Some myths or false beliefs about public speaking that could hinder your development of public speaking competence

WHAT IS PUBLIC SPEAKING?

Public speaking is most easily understood by revisiting our discussion of communication contexts in Chapter 1. If you recall, context level refers to the number of people involved in a communication event and the distance among the communicators. As a communication context, **public speaking** involves one person or a small group of people speaking to a larger number of people, an audience that typically has little or no "speaking" role except for questions and answers at the end of the presentation. This definition provides some subtle insight into public speaking anxiety to be discussed later in Chapter 3. When you give a public speech or presentation, a number of people may be evaluating and judging you and your message. Who wouldn't be at least a little bit nervous?

2.1 PUBLIC SPEAKING involves one person or a small group of people speaking to a larger number of people, an audience that typically has little or no "speaking" role except for questions and answers at the end of the presentation.

Let's now begin to understand public speaking by learning about its history in the study and practice of rhetoric in Western and non-Western cultures.

THE HISTORY OF PUBLIC SPEAKING AND RHETORIC

As you begin to plan and present your public speeches, you are participating in the tradition of rhetoric that is over 2,000 years old. **Rhetoric** is defined by some as the art of discovering the available means of persuasion in the situation and influencing an audience through words.[1] That is exactly what you will be doing in your public speaking class.

However you define it, rhetoric does date back many centuries to the Greek and Roman periods of Western history. Since those early beginnings, rhetoric has been studied and practiced in various forms throughout the world and in many cultures. We will focus on rhetoric in Western culture, that is the Greek and Roman traditions, and in some non-Western cultures includ-

2.2 RHETORIC is the art of discovering the available means of persuasion in the situation and influencing an audience through words.

ing Asian, African, and Islamic rhetoric. The growing importance of these areas of the world tells us we need to think about public speaking more expansively and comparatively, just like we study comparative religions and comparative literature. With globalization and the increasing diversity in the United States, an awareness of the rich history of rhetoric and public speaking internationally will prove valuable to you as a well-informed communicator.[2]

The Greek Period. The art of rhetoric in Western culture is said to have originated in the 5th century, BCE, with a Greek teacher, Corax, and his student, Tisias, on the island of Sicily. The island's government had been overthrown, a democracy was established, and the Greek courts were flooded with conflicting property claims. Corax recognized the need for organized public speaking instruction and taught ordinary citizens how to speak persuasively in the Greek courts of law. He is said to have proposed the first system for organizing speeches, declaring an effective speech needs three major components: an introduction, an argument or proof, and a conclusion. Does that system of organization sound familiar to you?

The work of Corax and Tisias led to the expansion of rhetoric to the mainland of ancient Greece. A group of Greek philosophers and teachers called **Sophists** began teaching Corax's methods of speaking persuasively throughout Greece (c. 481 BCE). The Greek word "sophos" means knowledge or wisdom, so essentially a Sophist was a teacher of wisdom.

The Sophists, however, were not entirely accepted in Greece. Many were foreigners and distrusted, while others were criticized for charging too much for their services. Despite this, the Sophist movement did make many contributions to the evolution of rhetoric and public speaking.

One Sophist named Protagoras (480–411 BCE) is still known today as the *father of debate*. He required his students to first speak in favor of an issue and then argue against it, to develop an understanding of the thinking and reasoning on both sides. Gorgias (480–375 BCE) is perhaps the most famous Sophist. He established a school of rhetoric and became known for his emphasis on the poetic use of language. He is also called the *father of impromptu speaking*, a skill you will learn more about later in this chapter.

2.3 SOPHISTS were a group of Greek philosophers and teachers who began teaching Corax's methods of thinking and speaking persuasively throughout Greece in about 481 BCE.

One of the most famous Greek philosophers, Plato (427–347 BCE), was considered an opponent of the rhetorical movement. Plato was a wealthy Athenian who rejected the practical nature of rhetoric and political involvement as advocated by the Sophists. He favored a focus on philosophy and stressed participation in **dialectic**, a question and answer process used to examine all sides of an issue in search of the truth. His writings often took the form of dialogues or conversations between characters who debated important issues like the nature of knowledge and the immortality of the soul.

2.4 DIALECTIC is a question and answer process and logical discussion used to examine all sides of an issue in search of the truth that was advocated by the Greek philosopher Plato.

Another famous Greek philosopher and writer, Aristotle (384–322 BCE), was a student of Plato and responsible for the first fully developed and unified body of rhetorical thought. His book, *Rhetoric*, is considered the foundation of the communication discipline, and he is referred to by some as the *father of modern communication*. He was the first to systematically describe a system of persuasion for Western culture based on the logic of the argument (logos), the emotion of the argument (pathos), and the speaker's character and credibility (ethos). That system is still used today to help students understand how to speak effectively and persuasively.

The Roman Period. After their ascent to power in the Mediterranean region, the Romans continued the tradition of public speaking begun by the Greeks, though some scholars consider the Roman contributions less impressive. One famous statesman, Cicero (106–43 BCE), represented the epitome of Roman rhetoric. In addition to writing about rhetoric, he also was an accomplished orator and considered the world's greatest speaker during that time period. Cicero's major contribution to the study of rhetoric was his attempt to restore the union of rhetoric and philosophy (like Plato) by arguing that rhetoric should be taught as an art form useful for dealing with all practical and public affairs. When preparing a speech, he recommended first thinking about the audience's interests and then using humor, questions, and other techniques to reach the listeners. Today, public speakers still adhere to Cicero's recommendations to analyze your audience, which we will discuss in Chapter 3.

In the first century AD, a Roman lawyer and educator, Quintilian (35–95 AD) extended the Roman tradition of public speaking. He is credited with a concern for being an ethical speaker as well as an effective one. In his writings, he described the ideal speaker as *a good man speaking well*. By that, Quintilian meant that a *good* speaker is ethical and of high character, and *speaking well* meant being well informed and presenting the speech effectively. Quintilian's phrase is still used by many communication instructors today to describe an ideal for public speaking competence.

The foundational ideas of the Greeks and Romans about rhetoric have endured through the centuries and into modern times. In the first quarter of the twentieth century, the academic study of rhetoric began to be taught at colleges and universities throughout the United States. Some scholars now use rhetoric as a research tool, engaging in rhetorical analysis of spoken and written works. Other researchers are challenging the fundamental assumptions about rhetoric embedded in Western culture. They criticize Western rhetoric based on the grounds that it has been dominated for 2500 years by elite male viewpoints and experiences.[3] The communication skills that you can take away from the Greek and Roman traditions emphasize organization of a speech and audience analysis.

Other scholars are turning their attention from the traditional study of Western rhetoric to non-Western cultures, including Asian, African, and Islamic rhetoric. A closer look at rhetoric in these non-Western cultures may add valuable insights into how we think about rhetoric and public speaking.

Non-Western Rhetoric. Asian rhetoric, as a formal discipline, is young, tracing back only to the 1960s.[4] But a glance at the basic concepts of the rhetorical history of the East reveals interesting contrasts to Western rhetoric. Western rhetoric highly values direct verbal expression, clear organization, cause and effect (logical) reasoning, and open debate of opposing views so the truth emerges from the debate. Our U.S. court system exemplifies this process with two lawyers arguing both sides to get to the truth. By comparison, Eastern rhetoric honors non-expression and silence, or at a minimum, indirectness and politeness are valued; a clash of opinions is avoided in order to preserve harmony. With our high value of forthrightness and individualism in the West, we may sometimes fail to appreciate the Eastern values of group harmony above the individual and relationships based on respect for authority, age, and wisdom. When you think about the geographical scope and long history of the countries of Asia—including China, Japan, Korea, Vietnam, Cambodia, and many more—it's obvious a conversation about the rhetoric of this vast area could enrich our understanding of public speaking.

As with Asia, focusing only on contemporary African culture limits our appreciation of the long history of rhetoric in Africa.[5] The early Nubian and Ethiopian cultures were highly civilized though no writings on rhetoric have been preserved comparable to those of the Greeks and Romans. One explanation is that communication and historical preservation in early African societies was achieved with a complex and widespread message system using drums. So while no great rhetorical essays were preserved, African society and culture were probably as verbally expressive as the West. Also like Asia, African society essentially honors harmony, the compatibility of people, and the smooth and peaceful running of the community. Since speech and public speaking are logically linked to the values of any society, African rhetoric in the past and present focuses on achieving social harmony and supporting the stability of society. The smooth operation of a village or tribe is important and, in instances of conflict among members of society, public speech functions to restore stability. Even today, when speaking publicly, the African speaker may try to restore harmony using a more subdued tone, volume, and rhythm. Public speaking is directed toward maintaining community harmony. Kofi Annan, a Ghanaian diplomat who served as the seventh Secretary-General of the United Nations from 1997–2007, is a good example of this unique African rhetorical style. When talking with world leaders, even about the most contentious events, Annan's rhetoric was restrained and quietly respectful of everyone involved. As a result, he and the United Nations were the corecipients of the 2001 Nobel Peace Prize.

The communication skills that you can take away from both the Asian and African traditions are to respect the audience and use public speaking to help create harmony in any community in which you find yourself. While presenting your own opinions, you will want to voice respect for any dissenting viewpoints of listeners.

Closely related to the African tradition is Islamic rhetoric.[6] Islam represents one of the world's major cultural and rhetorical traditions with more than a half a billion members from northern Africa to Indonesia. The Islamic or Muslim tradition and its writings originated in 622 AD, with the life and teachings of Mohammed. His work gave birth to a new form of rhetoric that became the basis for all future Islamic preaching. The goal of the Muslim faith was to use oral discourse and persuasion to promote the "ultimate truth" of Allah's word as presented in the *Koran*. This understanding of the power of persuasion closely parallels similar ideas in the Greek and Roman traditions and in Arab culture. The Arab discipline of rhetoric defines eloquence as the attainment of verbal effectiveness. A milestone in the systematic study of Arab rhetoric was an encyclopedic work entitled *Miftah al-ulum (Key to Success)*, written in the 12th century by al-Sakkaki of Khwarizmi. This writing divided rhetoric into three main parts, a division which remains in Arab thought until today. The three parts focus on the effective use of grammatical forms and sentences, achieving lucid style and clarity of expression, and embellishing speech using schemes and tropes. The communication skill you can take away from the Islamic tradition is the effective use of a clear style during a speech. Chapter 8 in this book goes into more detail about how to use language clearly and vividly.

Scholars and speakers over the centuries have made good use of the recommendations of the early rhetoricians. For example, the classical organization for a speech espoused long ago by Cicero—a good speech has an introduction, body, and conclusion—is still taught in college classrooms and textbooks. Contemporary political and business leaders around the world use the age-old public speaking techniques of the Greeks, Romans, and non-Western traditions to motivate audiences and to speak publicly in all kinds of rhetorical situations, in their communities and at work.

Now that you have some idea of the rich historical foundation for public speaking in various cultures, let's turn our attention to the speeches you will present in your class. Speeches today are grouped according to the type of speech and how the speech is delivered. Let's first consider the most popular types of speeches.

TYPES OF SPEECHES

Speech types are categorized based on the speaker's purpose for speaking. You may give a speech with the intention to entertain and amuse an audience. David Letterman's opening remarks on his late night show are a good example. On a special occasion, you may be invited to give a speech to commemorate a particular event such as the toast at a wedding or a keynote address at a meeting or convention. While these two types of speeches are important, they don't occur very often in most people's lives. More common are the two types of speeches covered in most beginning public speaking classes—speeches to inform or to persuade.

An **informative speech** has the purpose of communicating something new or a new perspective to an audience and moving listeners to greater understanding or insight. Speakers at training seminars and college professors both have the purpose of sharing new information with the audience and achieving greater understanding. A **persuasive speech** has the purpose of influencing an audience's attitudes, beliefs, values, or behaviors. Motivational speakers, religious leaders, and even sales people have the purpose of persuading their listeners to change in some way. Many political speeches fall into this category because politicians try to persuade you that their positions on public issues represent

2.5 AN INFORMATIVE SPEECH has the purpose of communicating something new or a new perspective to an audience and moving listeners to greater understanding or insight.

what you should think or do. President Franklin Roosevelt was famous for his persuasive speaking in what he called "fireside chats" broadcast by radio to the entire country.[7]

Some years ago, a well-respected communication scholar expanded this discussion of the types of speeches college students should learn.[8] His advice was true then and is still true today. Yeager contended that students need to learn to prepare the types of talks that an average business or professional person is called on to present most often. To make public speaking training more useful and to meet modern needs, we must teach practical types of talks and train students to handle the ordinary, everyday speech problems that confront them. Yeager was quick to point out that the speech types based on general purposes, such as to inform or to persuade, are quite useful. But he suggests that these general ends or purposes should be examined more closely to determine what sub-types or specific purposes, under each general purpose, are most useful for students speaking in the business world and contemporary organizations. While Yeager's observations were provided some time ago, his recommendations continue to be relevant for public speaking students, like you, Angelique, and your classmates.

Table 2.1 provides Yeager's list of speech sub-types based on the specific purpose they serve. Review the list and try to identify which sub-types you would consider speeches to inform and which you would consider speeches to persuade. We allow space on the table for you to make your best

> **2.6 A PERSUASIVE SPEECH** has the purpose of influencing an audience's attitudes, beliefs, values, or behaviors.

Table 2.1: Types of Speeches Important in Business and Organizations

Guess whether each type of speech presented in businesses is informative or persuasive.

MORE IMPORTANT TYPES	INFORMATIVE OR PERSUASIVE
Instructions	
Explanations	
Oral reports	
Sales talks	
Promotional talks	
Good-will talks	
Discussions of policy	
Inspirational talks	
LESS IMPORTANT TYPES—COURTESY TALKS	
Introduction	
Presentation	
Acceptance	
Welcome	
Farewell	
After-dinner (or lunch) talks	

Source: Yeager, W. H. (1929). Teaching business speaking—a modern trend. *Quarterly Journal of Speech, 25*(4), 485–495.

guess. Then we need to consider the different ways you can present and deliver any of these speeches. Some communication scholars, in fact, say how a speech is delivered is central to its ultimate success.[9]

TYPES OF DELIVERY

An informative or persuasive speech may be presented using any one of four different types of delivery: impromptu, extemporaneous, manuscript, or memorized. A fifth type of delivery that bears consideration is a technology-aided speech, which means that some kind of technology is used to enhance the presentation of your remarks. The delivery types mainly differ based on how much time is available to prepare the speech and the degree of formality when they are presented. For instance, many public speaking classes start out on the first day of class with students presenting an impromptu speech of self-introduction. You have very little time to prepare and the style of presentation may be somewhat informal. Later on in the class, you probably will use an extemporaneous style, which allows you more time to prepare the speech before class, but it is delivered somewhat more formally. Table 2.2 provides a quick sketch of the various types of delivery.

Interestingly, the type of delivery seems to influence some students' levels of public speaking anxiety.[10] The lowest level of anxiety is experienced for manuscript reading (less chance of making a mistake). Anxiety is higher for an extemporaneous speech (more chance of making a mistake). The highest level of anxiety is experienced with an impromptu speech (less time to prepare and even more chance of making a mistake). Witt and Behnke did not study anxiety related to memorized or technology-aided speeches. However, most instructors observe some anxiety with memorized speeches (you may forget your lines) and not as much with technology-aided speeches (you rely on the projected slides to help deliver the speech).

Let's now consider these types of delivery in a little more detail starting with the type that requires the least amount of preparation.

Table 2.2: Types of Speech Delivery

You can deliver a speech in several different ways based on how much time you have to prepare and how formally the speech may be presented.

TYPE OF DELIVERY	DESCRIPTION OF DELIVERY
Impromptu	Minimal preparation, little or no time to plan and develop the speech Most anxiety-producing
Extemporaneous	Carefully planned and prepared ahead of time, presented with note cards or outline More anxiety-producing
Manuscript	Written out ahead of time and read word for word to audience Lowest level of anxiety
Memorized	Written out and memorized ahead of time and spoken to audience Somewhat anxiety-producing
Technology-aided	Developed using computer software and presented using projector Not as anxiety-producing

An **impromptu speech** is delivered with minimal preparation, usually with little or no time to plan and develop your talk. At a social event like a wedding or a surprise party, guests are often invited to provide impromptu remarks about the bride, the groom, or the guest of honor. At a staff meeting at work, you may be called on to present an impromptu description of a project or a plan for solving a company problem you are responsible for. If you find yourself in any one of these impromptu speaking situations, here are some simple hints that will help you speak most effectively in the moment:

2.7 AN IMPROMPTU SPEECH is delivered with minimal preparation, usually little or no time to plan and develop your talk.

- Most important, stay calm and try to relax. Nobody expects the Gettysburg Address from an impromptu speaker.
- Quickly write down some brief notes to help focus and organize your remarks.
- Mentally identify your single most important point and an example or story to illustrate it. This will keep your remarks focused and your listeners interested in what you are saying.
- Organize your remarks around a simple introduction, middle, and conclusion. Remember that Cicero recommended this strategy and it still works today.
- When you reach the conclusion, just say it and stop talking. Often impromptu speakers try to compensate for the brevity of their remarks by rambling on and on. Know when to stop but do not say, "That is all I have, I guess I'm done." Instead, end on a quick summary of what you said and revisit your main point.
- Above all, be yourself. This is your impromptu speech, own it and be authentic.

An **extemporaneous speech** is carefully planned and prepared ahead of time and delivered using a conversational tone of voice. You may have spent a great deal of time researching, organizing, and practicing, but you do not create a manuscript of the speech. Rather you create presentational note cards or an outline that you use to guide your presentation and ensure that you cover your main ideas in the right order. As a result, the delivery of your speech is natural, as if you're presenting the information for the very first time. Since your note cards or outline contain only key words to remind you of what to say, the wording of the speech varies each time it is presented.

2.8 AN EXTEMPORANEOUS SPEECH is carefully planned and prepared ahead of time and is delivered using a conversational tone of voice.

While extemporaneous speaking is one of the most popular types of delivery today in classrooms, businesses, and organizations, it does present some challenges. For some extemporaneous speakers, it can be difficult to stay within the allotted time and still cover all of their material. Most speakers tend to include too much information and then they are surprised when they run out of time. Here are two very simple suggestions to help you avoid this problem:

- When you are preparing, include less information in the speech and on your note cards. Thus you will keep your speech simpler and far more manageable.
- Practice the speech ahead of time. If it seems like you have too much information, take something out. Speech instructors agree that students who practice give better, more focused speeches and have much less speech anxiety, which we will talk about in more detail in Chapter 3.[11]

By comparison to impromptu and extemporaneous speaking, a **manuscript speech** is written out ahead of time and read word for word to the audience. This type of delivery is used when accuracy is

necessary, like a keynote address at an important conference or
if you are the spokesperson to the media for a prominent organization. The President's State of the Union address is always
presented using a manuscript, because each word needs to be
carefully chosen and presented without error.

One problem with this type of delivery is losing the sense
of spontaneity and audience contact that characterizes extemporaneous and impromptu speaking.
That is because manuscript speakers tend to make fewer eye contact with the audience and use less
nonverbal cues, such as gestures. If you find yourself in a situation where you need to use a manuscript, here are a few hints to help you deliver that speech well:

- When preparing the manuscript, use more adverbs and adjectives to liven up the speech
  for the listeners.
- Use shorter paragraphs, which are easier to come back to after making eye contact with the
  audience.
- Type the manuscript in all capital letters and a big typeface, so you can read it easily when
  presenting.
- Practice with the manuscript several times, so you memorize some parts of it and can say them
  instead of just reading them. The better you know the speech, the more relaxed you will be
  when reading it to the audience.

A **memorized speech** requires the most time to prepare because it is fully written out and memorized ahead of time, then spoken to the audience word for word. This type of delivery, like a manuscript speech, is used when it is important to be highly accurate. That said, this type of delivery
may not be very effective unless you are a very good actor. The main problem is that you may appear
rehearsed and lacking in sincerity. Worse yet, if the speech is interrupted for any reason, you may

lose your place in the memorized text. The best recommendation for avoiding these problems is to practice the speech so
much that you can appear spontaneous and relaxed when you
present it. Even consider practicing in front of a few friends, a
live audience, ahead of time.

A **technology-aided speech** is developed using a computer software program such as PowerPoint, and it is presented
using some form of projection equipment. This type of delivery is gaining, if not dominating, the public speaking circuit
in schools, businesses, and organizations. Nearly 25 percent of
speakers claim to use projection equipment for most of their
presentations, more than 40 percent use multimedia on occasion, and 94 percent of professional speakers say they depend
on PowerPoint.[12] Since you will be using PowerPoint exten-
sively, now and in the future, here are a few hints for using it
most effectively:

- Keep your slides simple and focused on one topic per slide.
- Use a slide layout, design, and color scheme that enhances rather than distracts from the
  information you are presenting.

- Maintain a sense of audience contact and use the slides to support, not replace, your remarks. Don't let the PowerPoint presentation take the place of you as the presenter.

You will learn more about various presentation technologies in Chapter 12. For now, let's talk about why you should be enthusiastic about learning to deliver an effective speech. In Chapter 1, we discussed how important general communication skills are. Here we argue particularly for public speaking being as an important communication skill for you to master.

IS PUBLIC SPEAKING IMPORTANT?

When you think about learning to be a better public speaker, it may seem a bit intimidating, but there are some good reasons for addressing this challenge. As mentioned in Chapter 1, the ability to speak well in public yields civic benefits for everyone in our society as well as benefits for you in your personal and professional life.

BENEFITS FOR SOCIETY

Just as in the days of Plato and Aristotle, public speaking continues to have a role in achieving the ideals of democracy in modern society. Public speaking skills significantly contribute to the common good by serving as a powerful tool for effecting change in communities and society. People who can communicate ideas publicly—whether arguing for policy change or championing human rights—are in a better position to contribute in a positive way to the well-being of everyone. By speaking out, they help those who can't be heard to coordinate their efforts to create better communities. Being able to speak your mind publicly on behalf of a cause enables you to mobilize the power and energy of diverse individuals and groups to achieve common goals. In this way, public speaking serves as the primary basis for facilitating the exchange of ideas in the public sphere of democratic society. We can look to contemporary public figures as examples of this: Oprah Winfrey, Michael J. Fox, and Lance Armstrong, to name but a few.

On a more local level, suppose a tuition hike is planned for your campus, one that most students cannot afford. The students keep meeting informally to talk about the problem, but they don't seem able to unite with a common voice and do anything about it. By speaking up and offering to be a spokesperson at one of the meetings, you could help the students get their story straight and bring it clearly to the attention of the campus' administrators. By presenting their collective ideas effectively, you could see to it that their argument would be heard and their concerns and rights respected.

PERSONAL AND PROFESSIONAL BENEFITS

Putting civic motives aside, you will benefit as an individual by improving your public speaking competence. If you become a better public speaker, you will feel more confident about yourself and possess an invaluable set of communication skills. You'll use your public speaking skills in your personal life giving toasts and eulogies and speaking out and presenting your ideas in class, on campus, and at work.

2.12 CRITICAL THINKING is the process of evaluating evidence, assumptions, and ideas based on sound reasoning and logic.

Another personal reason for improving your public speaking skills is that it will help you to become a more critical thinker. **Critical thinking** is the process of evaluating evidence, assumptions, and ideas based on sound reasoning and logic. When you prepare a speech, you collect, evaluate, and organize evidence and ideas logically. These activities involve critical thinking; so while preparing your speech and improving your public speaking skills, you also hone your ability to think critically.[13] Professionally, the ability to think critically, organize your thinking, and communicate your ideas clearly to others may have surprising benefits. You may get a job you want because of your improved communication abilities. Plus, you will use public speaking skills in your work life presenting reports, briefings, and trainings.

The story about Lin Wang at the start of this chapter clearly illustrates how important it is for you to be able to speak well in public. If you do so with confidence and competence, your ideas will be respected and you will be perceived as a credible individual whose professional presentations are worth paying attention to. Let's reinforce this argument by dispelling a few false beliefs you may have about public speaking.

MYTHS ABOUT PUBLIC SPEAKING

Given the importance of developing your public speaking abilities, it will be helpful to start with a reality check of some common myths that may hinder your skills development. Every person who has ever sought guidance in preparing for a speech has probably heard at least one of these myths.

One of the most popular myths: "Imagine the crowd naked" is intended to help speakers get over their nervousness. Really, if you saw a room full of naked people, would you be relaxed? "Look over the heads of the crowd," suggests that even if you do not like public speaking, you can do it by not looking at or connecting with anyone in the audience. Absolute myth! It is always good to make eye contact with an audience to let them know they are included and respected and to find out if they understand what is being discussed. Yet another myth: "Start with a joke." Here the hope is that if the speaker can get the audience laughing, they will be relaxed and that will allow the rest of the speech to go smoothly. The problem with this myth is that it only works if the speaker is a good joke teller and the audience gets the joke. If the joke does not come off well, that makes for a very long speech. The best way to incorporate humor into a speech is to make it part of a story with which you are very familiar. This way the audience will see you as a real person, more human and more likeable.

A few more myths: "You are born to be a public speaker." This suggests you cannot learn to become a speaker, you either are born with the talent or not. Without a doubt some individuals are more comfortable presenting before an audience than others, but people can be trained to become good, even great public speakers. Recall the story about Lin Wang from the beginning of this chapter. Her experience in her job interview was a perfect example of how an inexperienced presenter can gain confidence by taking a public speaking class. If you are willing to commit to work hard to learn how to present a speech, you can become a professional and competent presenter; however, it does take time, commitment, experience, and lots of practice. OK, one more myth: "I can wing it so I do not need to practice!" The thought here is if a speaker knows the subject well, they do not need to plan or practice the presentation. The opposite actually is true. Impressive presenters and experienced speakers spend a great deal of time developing and rehearsing their presentations. That is why these speakers make their presentations look so smooth, almost without effort.

The next chapter clearly spells out eight competencies you need to know and do in order to speak in public like a real pro. Before going on, take a last look at the summary of public speaking myths and the facts that dispel them in Box 2.1.

Box 2.1 : Thinking Outside the Box: Public Speaking Myths and Facts

Check and see which myths you may think are true and what the facts really are.

MYTHS	FACTS
You are an experienced speaker so you don't need to practice.	Experienced speakers spend a large amount of time practicing and developing their presentations prior to delivery. Practice is extremely important.
An experienced speaker uses the lectern.	An experienced speaker uses the lectern to hold notes or an outline of the speech. If the microphone is attached to the lectern, the speaker should not move about. However, if the microphone is free standing or a clip-on, the presenter should get out in front of the audience and interact with them. The lectern can act as a barrier to making contact with the audience.
Memorize your speech.	It is good to memorize the opening and closing sections of a speech. However, most presenters should not memorize their speech verbatim. Things happen during a presentation, questions or interruptions and you may forget where you were.
Don't talk with your hands.	Using gestures is a natural part of talking! Watch someone talking on the phone, they are always gesturing and they can't even be seen. Using natural gestures is appropriate and effective.
You are born to be a public speaker.	People learn and develop their skills as public speakers and presenters. Through persistence, preparation, and practice most people can become good, even great at public speaking.
Structure isn't important in a speech.	Structure is essential to preparing and delivering a speech. Keeping the flow of the speech moving in the right direction is important. A lack of structure results in the audience not following what is being said.
Start with a joke.	Only if you are good at joke-telling! Know your strengths. Know your audience.
Timing is not very important.	Everyone cares about timing! The meeting planner and your audience care! Going overtime will annoy everyone present at your speech.

CHAPTER SUMMARY

Public speaking involves one person or a small group of people speaking to a larger number of people, an audience that typically has little or no "speaking" role except for questions and answers at the end of the presentation. The history of public speaking is in rhetoric, defined by some as the art of discovering the available means of persuasion in the situation and influencing an audience through words. With globalization and as the United States becomes more diverse, we are interested in the traditional study of Western rhetoric, the Greeks and Romans, but also non-Western cultures, including Asian, African, and Islamic rhetoric. From Western rhetoric, we learn about classical organization for  a speech and how to lead and motivate audiences. Asian and African traditions teach us to respect the audience and use public speaking to help create harmony. The Islamic tradition encourages the effective use of clear style during a speech. In addition to understanding rhetoric, it also is important to be aware of how speeches are categorized based on the type of speech and how it is delivered. An informative speech communicates something new or a new perspective to an audience and moves listeners to greater understanding or insight. A persuasive speech influences an audience's attitudes, beliefs, values, or behaviors. The four main types of delivery are: impromptu, extemporaneous, manuscript, or memorized. A fifth type of delivery is a technology-aided speech. Finally, understanding the myths of public speaking is important as well. The ability to separate myths from facts can make a difference in how you prepare, practice, and deliver any given presentation.

KEY TERMS

The key terms below are defined in this chapter and presented alphabetically with definitions in the Glossary at the end of the book.

- public speaking
- rhetoric
- Sophists
- dialectic
- informative speech
- persuasive speech

- impromptu speech
- extemporaneous speech
- manuscript speech
- memorized speech
- technology-aided speech
- critical thinking

BUILDING COMPETENCE ACTIVITIES

INDIVIDUAL ACTIVITIES

1. Attend a live lecture or speech. Analyze the speech based on the following questions.
   - Identify the purpose of the speech (informative or persuasive) and decide how effectively the speaker achieved the purpose.
   - What type of delivery was used and was it used effectively?

- Was the speech delivered effectively and appropriately?

Write up a one-page summary of your analysis of the speech.

2. Go the website of the Public Address Division of the National Communication Association (http://www.ncapublicaddress.org/publicaddressarchives.htm) that links to many other sites that contain speeches such as the Top 100 Speeches of the 20th Century. Choose one speech, view it, and analyze it based on the questions presented above in Activity 1.

GROUP ACTIVITIES

1. Form groups of four to five students. Attend a live lecture or speech. Analyze the speech based on your impression of how well the speaker used the eight public speaking competencies summarized in this chapter. Present your analysis to the class and discuss the strengths and weaknesses of the speech that you attended.

2. With a partner, go to a computer and access the White House website (http://www.whitehouse.gov) and find the web page that provides manuscripts of the president's recent major speeches. Select a speech that interests both of you and prepare and present an analysis of it in class.

3. Form groups of four to five students. Share examples of significant competent or incompetent public speeches you have attended. These could be in-class lectures. Develop a list of characteristics and behaviors of competent public speakers based on the group discussion. Present your list of characteristics and behaviors to the class.

4. Form groups of four to five students. Share examples of significant ethical or unethical public speakers or speeches (could be lectures) you have observed. Develop a list of characteristics and behaviors of ethical speakers and of unethical speakers based on the group discussion. Present your two lists to the class.

5. Form groups of four to five students. Share examples of times when you were perceived as a credible public speaker (could be a presentation you did in another class). Develop a list of characteristics and behaviors for credible public speaking based on the group discussion. Present your list to the class.

6. Form two groups with two to three students in each group. Choose a topic for the next speech in your class. Have one group put together a short outline and practice the speech for ten minutes. The second group 'wings' it with no outline or practice. Have each group present the speech and then discuss the strengths and weaknesses of each speech.

COMPETENCY CHECKPOINTS AND SELF-ASSESSMENT TOOL

Here is what you need to know and be able to do regarding the public speaking process. Determine your level of competency and whether you are ready to proceed to the next chapter. Give yourself one point for each checkpoint you answer satisfactorily.

COMPETENCY CHECKPOINTS	NUMBER OF POINTS
KNOWLEDGE 1. Define public speaking. 2. Explain why the study of rhetoric is relevant to you as a public speaker. 3. Describe Western and non-Western rhetoric and what we can learn about public speaking from each. 4. Identify two myths about public speaking you may have believed in the past and say what the facts are about those two myths. 5. Of the benefits of improving public speaking (society/civic, personal, or professional), which is most important to you and why?	
SKILLS 1. Give an example of a time when you presented an informative speech and what you did to present it competently. 2. Give an example of a time when you presented a persuasive speech and what you did to present it competently. 3. Of the main types of speech delivery (impromptu, extemporaneous, manuscript, memorized, technology-aided), which are you better at and why? What should you do to improve your skills?	
ETHICS AND CREDIBILITY 1. Provide an example of ethical or unethical public speaker you have observed in the past. Say why the speech was ethical or unethical and the impact it had on the listeners. 2. Identify what you need to do to be perceived by other students in the class as a credible public speaker when you present your first speech.	
TOTAL CHECKPOINTS (OUT OF A POSSIBLE TEN POINTS)	

ENDNOTES

1. Charland, M. (2003). *The constitution of rhetoric's tradition*. Retrieved from: http://search.ebscohost.com/login.asp z?Direct=true&db=ufh&AN=10323875&site=ehost-live">The Constitution of Rhetoric's Tradition.

2. Asante, M. K. (2006). The rhetoric of globalisation: The Europeanisation of human ideas. *Journal of Multicultural Discourses, 1*(2), 152–158.

3. Royster, J.J. (2003). Disciplinary landscaping, or contemporary challenges in the history of rhetoric. *Philosophy & Rhetoric, 36*(2), 148–167.

4. Wang, B. (2004). A survey of research in Asian rhetoric. *Rhetoric Review, 23*(2), 171–181.

5. Campbell, K.F. (2006). Rhetoric from the ruins of African antiquity. *Rhetorica, 24*(3), 255–274.

6. Merriam, A.H. (1974). Rhetoric and the Islamic tradition. *Today's Speech, 22*(1), 43–49.

7. Keiko, A. (2006). A study of Franklin Delano Roosevelt's persuasive communication within the fireside chat: An analysis of language and style. *Human Communication, 9*(1), 71–81.

8. Yeager, W. H. (1929). Teaching business speaking—a modern trend. *Quarterly Journal of Speech, 25*(4), 485–495.

9. Johnstone, C.L. (2001). Communicating in classical contexts: The centrality of delivery. *Quarterly Journal of Speech, 87*(2), 121–144.

10. Witt, P.L., & Behnke, R.R. (2006). Anticipatory speech anxiety as a function of public speaking assignment type. *Communication Education, 55*(2), 167–177.

11. Feldman, P., Cohen, S., Hamrick, N., & Lepore, S. (2004). Psychological stress, appraisal, emotional and cardiovascular response in a public speaking task. *Psychology and Health, 19*(3), 353–368.

12. Cyphert, D. (2007). Presentation technology in the age of electronic eloquence: From visual aid to visual rhetoric. *Communication Education, 56*(2), 168–192.

13. Allen, M., Berkowitz, S., Hunt, S., & Louden, A. (1999). A meta-analysis of the impact of forensics and communication education on critical thinking. *Communication Education,48,* 18–30.

3

BUILDING PUBLIC SPEAKING COMPETENCE

"According to most studies, people's number one fear is public speaking. Number two is death. This means to the average person, if you go to a funeral, you're better off in the casket than doing the eulogy." Jerry Seinfeld, actor and comedian, b. 1954

• •
• •

Richard sighed as he reviewed his public speaking syllabus. After ten years on the police force, there were no more opportunities for a promotion without a college degree. A major in communication seemed like a logical choice, but now he had to face public speaking. His stomach twisted at the thought of getting up in front of the class and giving a speech, while all those faces stared intently right at him. He began to feel very alone in his anxiety. But Richard was not alone in his lack of enthusiasm for giving speeches. During a conversation in the hallway, he learned that most of the other students in the class were also a bit afraid of public speaking.

"I totally break out in hives," Mario admitted. "That's nothing," LaTisha retorted. "Every time I give a speech in class, I can hear my voice shaking, so it makes me even more nervous. My hands start twitching, my notes become shaky and hard to read; I end up forgetting what I am talking about." "I can beat that," Angelique added. "The last time I gave a speech, I got so nervous that I had to stop right in the middle. Not a pretty sight." With that, Richard thought to himself, "This is going to be an interesting semester!"

• •
• •

Richard, Mario, LaTisha, and Angelique may be from different backgrounds, but they have one thing in common—their nervousness about learning to give a good speech. What they don't know yet is understanding more about public speaking and learning some basic public speaking skills will transform their negativity and anxiety into a valuable set of communication skills. This chapter prepares you to give your first in-class speech. But if your next speech is coming up quickly and you need help getting organized, a format for a speech outline is presented in Figure 3.1 and electronically on the website for this book. Specifically, this chapter introduces you to the fundamentals of public speaking competence by addressing these topics:

- What it means to give a speech competently and ethically, including how to prepare and present your first speech.
- Why public speaking anxiety happens and how to overcome it.

WHAT IS PUBLIC SPEAKING COMPETENCE?

The basic ideas about competent public speaking introduced centuries ago by the Greeks and Romans are still with us today, though contemporary communication scholars and teachers may phrase the ideas a bit differently. If you recall from Chapter 1, we said that competent communication is both *effective* and *appropriate* for the particular situation. Effective communication means you achieve your communicative goal or purpose, and appropriate communication means you are aware and respectful of the norms and expectations for communicating in the particular situation. Applying this definition to public speaking, **competent public speaking** is both effective and appropriate for the particular rhetorical situation. This simply means you accomplish the purpose of your speech in a way that is respectful of the situation you are speaking in and the other people involved. Your choice of topic, the material you include, and your way of delivering the speech are all informed by what is going on in the particular situation.

3.1 COMPETENT PUBLIC SPEAKING is both effective and appropriate for the particular rhetorical situation.

Interestingly, psychologists tell us some people tend to think they are more competent than they really are, even in public speaking. They are not competent, but they are unaware of their own incompetence.[1] They tend to overestimate their abilities, and this overestimation is sometimes a bigger problem than knowing their limitations and being willing to learn. You have probably attended a speech or a lecture when the speaker fell into this category. Closely related to true public speaking competence is the matter of interacting ethically with the audience.

ETHICS AND PUBLIC SPEAKING

To be perceived as competent, it is critical that you communicate ethically with your audience. In Chapter 1, ethical communication was described as sharing sufficient and appropriate information with others so they can make good decisions about matters important to themselves. Let's apply that general definition to public speaking. Your ethical responsibility as a public speaker is to engage in research that fully explores your topic, as you develop your speech. You have an ethical responsibility to fully disclose what you learn and what you know about the topic in your speech in a forthcoming and open manner and without personal bias. The benefit to this ethical approach is that it will enhance your ethos or credibility with the audience and you will be perceived as a more competent speaker.

Now let's pull these ideas together in a set of tangible skills to summarize what you do to prepare and present a speech competently.

EIGHT PUBLIC SPEAKING COMPETENCIES AND YOUR FIRST SPEECH

The Competent Speaker is a model for public speaking developed in 1990 and revised in 2006 by a committee of the National Communication Association and representatives of 12 colleges and universities.[2] The model contains eight competencies for public speaking presented in Table 3.1. The first four competencies focus on preparation and the second four on delivery. Each of these eight

Table 3.1: Eight Public Speaking Competencies of the National Communication Association's Competent Speaker Model

These public speaking competencies, developed nationally by public speaking experts may be applied to any type of speech, from informative to persuasive and from impromptu to fully scripted.

Competency One	Chooses and narrows a topic appropriately for the audience and occasion.
Competency Two	Communicates the thesis/specific purpose in a manner appropriate for the audience and occasion.
Competency Three	Provides supporting material (including electronic and non-electronic presentational aids) appropriate for the audience and occasion.
Competency Four	Uses an organizational pattern appropriate to the topic, audience, occasion, and purpose.
Competency Five	Uses language appropriate to the audience and occasion.
Competency Six	Uses vocal variety in rate, pitch, and intensity (volume) to heighten and maintain interest appropriate to the audience and occasion.
Competency Seven	Uses pronunciation, grammar, and articulation effectively and appropriate to the audience and occasion.
Competency Eight	Uses physical behaviors that support the verbal message.

competencies will be explored in depth in a later chapters, but, for now, here is how you can apply them to preparing and presenting your first speech.

PREPARING YOUR SPEECH

No matter what type of speech your instructor assigns; how you prepare and deliver it competently is the same. You begin with *Competency One* by choosing and narrowing a topic for your speech based on thoughtful analysis of the audience and their needs and interests. This information about your listeners will guide and shape every aspect of what you include in your speech. Then you think about factors like the occasion for the speech, the length requirements, and your personal knowledge of the topic you are considering. Are there aspects of the speaking occasion that should influence what you say and how you say it? Can you cover the topic you are considering in the time allotted; and, are you fairly knowledgeable about the topic? These factors are important, even when a topic is assigned by your instructor. Any topic needs to be narrowed and focused so it appeals to the particular audience and works within the time constraints. Suppose, for example, your first speech is assigned as a speech of self-introduction to be presented in four to five minutes. You cannot tell the class everything about yourself in that length of time. But you could acquaint them with who you are or what you care about by discussing your work, a hobby or favorite activity, a significant personal experience, or your professional or academic goals. If you have only five minutes, developing one of these as a specific topic is better than trying to cover all of them.

After choosing a specific topic, *Competency Two* says you should determine a thesis/specific purpose for your speech that you will communicate to the audience when you present. The general purpose of a speech is based on the type of speech that is assigned—a speech to inform, to persuade, or perhaps to motivate or entertain. The specific purpose is narrower than the general purpose, and it tells the audience exactly where the speech is headed.

For example, in a self-introduction speech, your specific purpose might be "to acquaint the audience with the health and recreational benefits you have experienced through the use of a regular exercise and workout program."

Competency Three encourages you to gather and provide supporting material that will help to accomplish the specific purpose of your speech. These materials should include a variety of types of information. In order to enhance your credibility, they should come from your own personal experiences but also other outside sources. Through research in the library, electronic sources, and from interviews with experts, you can find material such as statistics, facts and figures, and stories or examples that will help to make your speech appealing and memorable. Be sure to balance the amount of hard information and data with the amount of personal stories and examples. Too much hard information in one speech is overwhelming to listeners and not nearly as interesting. For the speech about the benefits of a regular exercise and workout program, you could get hard information from the National Institutes of Health. You could interview the director of wellness for a YMCA. A personal story about your own enhanced health regimen could help to introduce you to the other students. As you gather these materials, keep good records, perhaps putting each piece of information on a separate note card. That extra effort will help you with the last preparation step, which is organizing your speech.

Competency Four focuses on arranging your information in an organizational pattern that is appropriate to the topic, audience, occasion, and purpose of your speech. First, return to the specific purpose of the speech, examine the support materials and research notes you gathered, and identify two or three main points for your speech. Keep the time limit in mind as you decide on main points and err on the side of fewer main points rather than more. Arrange the main points in a logical order and break each main point down into several subpoints. Then choose the best supporting materials for each main point and set of subpoints. Try to be creative in the use of the materials and include at least one meaningful example or impressive statistic for each main point. Now you are ready to give your speech some shape.

Remember Cicero's advice and divide your speech into three main sections: the introduction, body, and conclusion. The introduction is the first section of the speech in which you capture the listeners' attention and engage them in the topic of your speech. You could use a startling quotation or a moving story as an opening device followed by a clear statement of your specific purpose and a preview of the content of the speech. The body of the speech consists of your main points but be sure there is a clear and logical progression among the main points. The conclusion ends the speech on a resounding and summative note. It lets the audience know the speech is over, summarizes and reinforces what you have presented, and if appropriate, it motivates the audience to some kind of action. The conclusion should leave some kind of lasting impression and bring your speech to a memorable ending.

To help you develop an effective outline for your first speech, Figure 3.1 contains a standard outline format that you could use as a model. Plus, each of these preparation steps is developed in more detail in later chapters. For now, let's think about presenting your first speech.

Figure 3.1: Outline Format for a First Speech

All speeches can be organized using a standard outline format such as this one that contains all of the components essential to an effective speech.

Speech Title: (Indicate the speech topic, pique curiosity, be concise)

General Purpose: (to inform, persuade, or entertain)

Specific Purpose: (infinitive statement indicating the goal of the speech)

INTRODUCTION (written out in full sentences)
  I. Attention-getting or lead-in device
  II. Thesis statement (declarative sentence stating the central idea or claim of the speech and its significance to the audience)
  III. Preview of main points

BODY (support material that accomplishes the speech purpose organized into 3–4 main points with subpoints for each main point)
  I. First main point (can be written out as a complete sentence)
    A. First subpoint
      1. Support material
        a. Support material
        b. Support material
      2. Support material
        a. Support material
        b. Support material
    B. Second subpoint
      1. Support material
        a. Support material
        b. Support material
      2. Support material
        a. Support material
        b. Support material
        * Transition to next main point
  II. Second main point (can be written out as a complete sentence)
    A. subpoint
    B. subpoint
    * Transition to next main point or to conclusion

CONCLUSION (written out in full sentences)
  I. Review of main points
  II. Restatement of the thesis statement
  III. Closing device

PRESENTING YOUR SPEECH

Once you have prepared your speech competently, you need to think about how to present it most effectively and most appropriately. *Competency Five* says you should use appropriate language for the audience and occasion. When you are up in front of an audience and have very little time, your choice of words is critical to the effectiveness of your speech. You should use language that is exceptionally *clear* to ensure audience understanding, *vivid* to ensure their enthusiasm for your speech, and *appropriate* for the particular occasion. Choose words that clarify your meaning, develop understanding, and paint mental images for your listeners. For instance, if you want to describe the intensity of your fitness training program, don't say you had to lie down for awhile right after the first class. Rather tell the audience how you "collapsed at the end of the first hour, unable to move even your little finger." Be excited about the topic and use exciting language, but choose words that are natural to you and not pretentious or condescending. Be respectful of all of your listeners and avoid words that might offend or embarrass anyone in the audience.

According to *Competency Six*, you should enliven your delivery by varying how you say what you say. Vary the rate or pace at which you talk, sometimes faster and sometimes slower. Vary your pitch, the highness or lowness of your voice, and vary your intensity or volume. Use a conversational style of speaking, but at the same time, be sure that you talk loudly enough to be easily heard by all audience members. If you have ever sat through a lecture with an instructor using only a monotone voice, that should tell you how *not* to speak. Instead, use your voice as a tool to heighten and maintain interest in your speech and its content.

Competency Seven also focuses on how you speak but with an emphasis on effective and appropriate pronunciation, grammar, and articulation. If you mispronounce a word or you don't articulate speech sounds correctly, your listeners may not understand what you say. If your speech is full of grammatical errors, listeners will pay attention to those mistakes and not to what your speech is about. Any such errors will have a negative effect on your credibility as a speaker, no matter how well you have planned and developed the content of your speech.

Competency Eight is about understanding and using physical behaviors, nonverbal cues, to support and enhance your verbal/spoken message. Like your use of language, your use of nonverbal communication has a significant impact on the audience's reaction to you and to your speech. The nonverbal cues that most impact how you are perceived as a public speaker are: your appearance, posture and body movement, gestures, facial expressions, and eye contact. You should modify your appearance—clothing, jewelry, hair style—to make a favorable first impression on the audience. By making an effort to appear professional and competent, you also tell the listeners that you respect and appreciate their attention. In addition to dressing professionally, you should sit, stand, and walk with confidence, your head up and shoulders erect. Whether standing or moving, keep your hands and arms free and relaxed, so you can use gestures to reinforce and emphasize what you are saying. The important thing is to gesture naturally, not in a stilted or stylized way. Your facial expressions can be used to communicate to the listener how you feel about the topic of your speech. Be sure that your expression matches and reflects what you are saying. You can use eye contact to promote a sense of audience contact and let the audience know that you are involved with them. If you avoid eye contact with your listeners, they will think you are either nervous or not interested in their reactions to your speech.

As you begin to contemplate the challenge of your first speech, one final suggestion will help you and your classmates immeasurably…prepare, prepare, prepare and practice, practice, practice! According to one recent study, overall preparation time correlated significantly with higher speech grades and students who spent more time practicing their speeches also earned higher grades.[3] In another study, students who practiced their speeches before an audience received higher evaluation scores than did students who practiced without an audience, and students who practiced their speech before larger audiences received higher scores than students who practiced before smaller audiences.[4] To reinforce this recommendation, an article in a management journal states that rehearsal before a presentation helps a speaker connect with the audience intellectually, emotionally, and kinesthetically.[5]

Let's return for a moment to Richard, Mario, LaTisha, and Angelique's main concern about giving speeches. If you recall in our opening story, these students break out in hives and become very nervous at the thought of giving a speech. Communication instructors find these reactions to be relatively normal and refer to this challenge as public speaking anxiety. If you have not dealt with and learned to manage your public speaking anxiety, all the preparation in the world will not ensure that you present your speeches competently. What's worse, if you delay and put off preparing your speech, some researchers tell us that your anxiety will be much worse.[6] To address this challenge to public speaking competence, let's first think about what public speaking anxiety is and how it works in most people.

WHAT IS PUBLIC SPEAKING ANXIETY?

Public speaking anxiety refers to a person's level of fear or anxiety associated with a real or anticipated public speaking event. Anyone who has experienced nervous anticipation prior to presenting a speech understands this definition without any further explanation. Even Cicero, the greatest of all Roman orators, suffered from public speaking anxiety. He confessed, "I turn pale at the outset of a speech, and quake in every limb and in all my soul."[7] Because he was able to become a great orator, Cicero proved that if you harness and overcome your inner feelings of nervousness, you'll become a better speaker for it.

3.2 PUBLIC SPEAKING ANXIETY refers to a person's level of fear or anxiety associated with a real or anticipated public speaking event.

Furthermore, Cicero also is evidence that having some anxiety, at least a little, may be positive. A manageable amount of anxiety indicates that you understand and take seriously your responsibilities as a public speaker. Indeed, speech instructors tell us that overly confident students often underperform, by comparison to students whose appropriate level of anxiety encourages them to work hard to develop their public speaking skills.

So how does public speaking anxiety show itself—physically and emotionally? Students, and most people for that matter, experience *physiological* or physical anxiety right at the beginning of a speech. Suddenly, our hands shake, legs quiver, voices quake, and stomachs churn. We are frequently surprised by these physiological reactions, particularly if we aren't aware of feeling very anxious before the speech. While these symptoms typically lessen or disappear for students identified as low-anxiety speakers, students identified as high-anxiety speakers often report a significant increase in these same stress symptoms immediately after the speech has ended.[8] Researchers think that these high-anxiety students experience anxious remorse and regret about how well they did and they are afraid of a negative evaluation of their performance. We all have also heard about actors getting the emotional jitters right before they go on stage. Research seems to support this notion. Most public speakers experience their highest level of *psychological* or emotional anxiety immediately prior to

Box 3.1: Thinking Outside the Blog: They're All Just Staring at Me!

This blogger's story about public speaking anxiety may help you manage yours.

Tim Tiah, learned some lessons about public speaking anxiety and giving an effective speech, and then shared them on the Internet on his blog, *The Journal of Nuffnang*. "My Speech at Bloggers Buff" outlines Tim's experience in his own words as he planned and delivered a speech about blogging as an income generator in Malaysia. Tim is cofounder of Nuffnang, a company that promotes blog advertising in Malaysia. He was invited to present a speech on Sunday morning to a crowd of 60 blogging enthusiasts. Guess when he got started on the speech…you guessed it… Saturday night!

"That night, I sat in front of my Mac with Word open, trying to figure out at least what I was about to say. I was a little nervous. Dear God…whatever it is, please don't let me make a fool of myself tomorrow. I promise I'll spend more time preparing my next speech."

LESSON ONE: Don't wait until the last minute to prepare your speech!

"The next morning, I got into the car and just drove straight to the event. I saw a few familiar faces and shook hands. I was supposed to be in the VIP room but I told them I felt much more comfortable mixing with everyone."

LESSON TWO: Mix and mingle with the audience before your speech!

"When my name was called, I sat still for a split second with thoughts racing in my head. An easy way out would be to read from my script. But I hate speeches like that and was determined not to give one like that."

LESSON THREE: Prepare some good notes and talk to the audience; don't read your speech.

"My heart whispered to me….You are here to talk about something you believe in…just talk naturally. If people don't like your speech, at least they'll appreciate your sincerity."

LESSON FOUR: Talk about something you love and know a lot about.

"I don't remember how I started, but I remember asking the audience to interrupt me at any time with questions. They did that and it made a difference. The speech was if anything…fun"

LESSON FIVE: Involve the audience during your speech.

"Then came the Q&A, the part where everyone sits still and doesn't say anything because we're all shy here. But Danny Foo asked one question and it opened a floodgate of questions all around the room."

LESSON SIX: Encourage at least one good friend to ask the first question.

Tim's blog concludes: "I was supposed to speak for 15 minutes but it lasted over 45. Everyone in the room seemed happy and I didn't catch anyone sleeping through the speech. The event turned out to be quite a success."

Like Tim, your speeches can be successful and you can feel confident and in control. Plan ahead, choose a topic you like, develop a good outline rather than a manuscript, and get involved with the audience before, during, and at the end of your speech. Visit Tim's blog and read some of the comments of those who actually attended his speech.

Source: Tiah, T. (2007). My speech at bloggers buff. Retrieved from http://timothytiah.blogspot.com/2007/07/my-speech-at-bloggers-buff.html

speaking rather than during or after a speech.[9] Following that initial anxiety, most people become progressively more psychologically comfortable while presenting their speeches.[10,11]

Think about these patterns of anxiety and what you experience when giving a speech. By knowing when anxiety might occur and what is considered "normal" for most people, you can be better prepared to handle your anxiety and to make use of some anxiety-reducing techniques discussed later in this chapter. But first, let's think about why we are anxious about public speaking in the first place.

Table 3.2: Public Speaking Anxiety: Causes, Reactions, and Solutions

Examine these causes of anxiety and how people react to them. Which causes are most true for you? Then look at the possible solution you could use to handle your negative reactions.

CAUSE OF ANXIETY AND REACTION	POSSIBLE SOLUTIONS
CAUSE: Previous negative experiences with public speaking. REACTION: Avoid public speaking so you won't look foolish and stupid.	Forget the past and don't allow it to shape the present.
CAUSE: Identification with the wrong role models. REACTION: Avoid public speaking because you'll make mistakes and embarrass yourself.	Make a conscious effort to identify with speakers who appear confident and in control. Watch those people and think about yourself being a public speaker just like them.
CAUSE: Unrealistic expectations about public speaking and premonition of disaster or catastrophic failure.	Become aware of which unrealistic expectations affect you as a public speaker.
REACTION: Avoid public speaking because you can't possibly do well.	Realize that it is unlikely that anything catastrophic will occur. And if something does go wrong, it isn't the end of the world.
Desire for total acceptance.	Realize it's impossible to please everyone all the time, just as it's impossible for everyone to please you all the time. Be yourself and do the best job you can.
Desire for absolute perfection.	Don't expect perfection. Realize that no speech is perfect, then accept your imperfections and learn from mistakes. Don't dwell on what goes wrong.
Desire for total confidence.	Expect anxiety. Realize that fear is natural and everyone has it. Accept your insecurities, knowing the audience can't see your fears and they are probably supportive of you.

CAUSES OF ANXIETY

One cause of anxiety is remembering negative experiences that happened to you in the past when you spoke in public. It may have been something trivial, like answering a question incorrectly in an elementary school class and others laughed or made fun of you. Or it may have been more significant, like presenting a speech and having the audience strongly disagree and challenge your remarks in public. In any case, the lesson was learned: When I speak in public, I feel foolish or stupid.

A second cause of anxiety is identifying with ineffective public speakers as your role models rather than effective speakers. You watch someone speak on television or at a meeting who makes mistakes or who is poorly organized. You identify with that person, perhaps another student, rather than with someone who speaks effectively and impressively. You say to yourself, now that's the kind of speaker I am. The lesson is learned: When I speak in public, I am uncomfortable and make embarrassing mistakes.

A third cause of public speaking anxiety is holding negative and unrealistic expectations about public speaking in general and about yourself as a public speaker. For example, you may have the expectation that your speech is going to be a big disaster, a catastrophic failure. You expect something awful to happen, like forgetting everything you plan to say. Or, you may have an unrealistic desire to be totally accepted and liked by all the listeners in the audience. Your speech needs to be

Table 3.3: Number 1 Fear: Public Speaking

Public speaking is the top fear of 45% of North American adults, followed by financial problems, heights, deep water, and then death.

FEARED EVENT	TOTAL	WOMEN	MEN
Speaking before a group	45%	54%	34%
Financial problems	40%	42%	38%
Heights	40%	50%	29%
Deep water	33%	45%	19%
Death	31%	34%	28%
Sickness	28%	34%	21%
Insects and bugs	24%	34%	13%
Loneliness	23%	27%	18%
Flying	22%	30%	15%
Driving/riding in a car	10%	13%	7%
Dogs	10%	11%	8%
Darkness	9%	14%	4%
Elevators	8%	13%	4%
Escalators	8%	13%	4%

Source: Bruskin/Goldring Research Report (Feb. 1993). *America's number 1 fear: Public speaking.* Bruskin/Goldring Research, Inc., p. 4.

perceived by the audience as absolutely perfect and flawless in every way, no mistakes. Or you may expect that you should feel completely confident, calm, and in control. All of these expectations are unrealistic and again, a negative lesson is learned: I cannot possibly be a good public speaker and present my speech effectively.

Table 3.2 summarizes these causes of public speaking anxiety, how we react to each cause, and some solutions for each of the negative reactions. See which cause you relate to the most and make note of the suggestions for handling that cause and its reaction.

Richard and his friends probably can point to similar causes of their public speaking anxiety. In fact, most researchers agree that public speaking anxiety is one of the greatest fears of most North Americans. In a survey of 1000 randomly selected people, respondents were asked to identify their greatest fears. You guessed it—public speaking was number one, feared more than financial problems, heights, deep water, or even dying.[12] Speaking before a group of other people is the top fear of 45 percent of adults. Table 3.3 presents the survey results. If that is how widespread fear of public speaking is, how can we go about controlling it?

UNLEARNING ANXIETY

Now that you know some of the causes of public speaking anxiety, we can consider how to manage it. Rest assured that practically all speakers have some degree of nervousness about speaking in public. The key is to control that anxiety so it doesn't take over and distract you from doing a good job of your speech. You need to learn how to use the nervousness to your advantage and as a way to energize your presentation.

Over the years, communication teachers have discovered some clever ways to address anxiety; for example, anxiety may be reduced for some students by participating in small group discussions in which they first communicate in a semipublic setting. Viewing videos on the topic of anxiety reduction has proven helpful to some students. Also, those who view videos of themselves giving speeches often report a decrease in apprehension and anxiety and an increase in perceptions of their own communication competence, particularly in the classroom setting.

....
3.3 SYSTEMATIC DESENSITIZATION is a process that changes how you feel about public speaking by using relaxation and positive visualization when you think about a public speaking event.

In addition to these teacher-tested ideas, there are three other approaches to reducing public speaking anxiety based on the ways most people have learned to be anxious. Public speaking anxiety is a result of fear of communicating (emotions and feelings), unrealistic beliefs about public speaking (knowledge), and/or a lack of skills (behaviors). Therefore, reducing anxiety involves changing how you feel (your feelings and emotions), what you think (your beliefs and thoughts), or what you do (your skills and behaviors).

Changing how you feel is approached through systematic desensitization; changing what you think can be achieved through cognitive modification; and a lack of skills can be remedied through goal setting. Read on and see which of these three methods might work best for you.

Systematic desensitization is a process that changes how you feel about public speaking by using relaxation and positive visualization when you think about a public speaking event. This method is based on the idea that negative feelings are the source of the anxiety. By changing how you feel and your emotions, the anxiety is reduced. This is accomplished by engaging in deep relaxation, mentally constructing a hierarchy of steps that lead up to the feared communication event, and practicing relaxation while visualizing each step.

Here's how systematic desensitization works: First, you think about a series of situations that logically lead up to the feared public speaking event. You start with a comfortable, non-threatening situation that represents the first step toward the anxious situation. That could be the day you enrolled in the public speaking course. You then visualize increasingly more threatening and anxiety-producing situations: perhaps the first day of the course, then the self-introductions in front of the class, and then choosing the topic for your first speech. With each situation, you engage in relaxation techniques. Eventually, you should be able to think about the situation of presenting a speech without feeling an uncontrollable amount of anxiety.

Remember that earlier we said that public speaking anxiety is highest right before you give your speech, when you anticipate getting up and talking in front of the audience. Systematic desensitization is an approach that is good for addressing this anticipatory anxiety. It works because a human being cannot be relaxed and fearful at the same time. By visualizing the feared communication event, but relaxing at the same time, you gain control of the fear.

3.4 COGNITIVE MODIFICATION is a process that changes or modifies your unrealistic expectations and beliefs about public speaking.

Cognitive modification is a process that changes or modifies your unrealistic expectations and beliefs about public speaking. This method is based on the idea that negative thinking is the source of anxiety. By changing your beliefs and thoughts, the anxiety is reduced. This is accomplished by identifying and challenging any negative thought patterns you have about speaking in public. This method enables you to confront your beliefs and question their soundness and worth.

Here's how cognitive modification works: You begin by identifying any unrealistic and negative thoughts you hold about yourself as a public speaker. Then you substitute more realistic, positive beliefs that produce less anxiety than the unrealistic ones. You actually write down the negative thoughts that come to mind about an upcoming public speaking event. Then you rewrite each thought in a more reasonable and positive way. You frequently read over and review the revised belief statements during the time period prior to the speech.

An example of an unrealistic or negative belief is: "I feel so nervous about giving a speech that there's nothing I can do about it." You could rewrite this negative thought more realistically and more positively this way: "It's counter productive to feel nervous about giving a speech, so I will apply myself to becoming a little more relaxed." Note that the unrealistic statements are extreme, misleading, and produce high anxiety. The revised statements should be less extreme, more realistic, and result in a more moderate emotional reaction.

Cognitive modification works because it provides you with a different way of looking at yourself as a public speaker. Your negative thinking is derailed and replaced with positive statements about an upcoming public speaking event. Basically, you talk yourself out of negative thought patterns into positive ways of thinking.

3.5 GOAL SETTING is a process for alleviating anxiety that provides a structured plan for changing your communication and public speaking behaviors.

Goal setting is a process for alleviating anxiety that provides a structured plan for changing your communication and public speaking behaviors. This method is based on the idea that a lack of skills' development is the main cause of anxiety, rather than negative feelings or thoughts. By changing your communication behaviors over time, you ultimately reduce your public speaking anxiety. This is accomplished by creating a set of personal goal statements about desirable behaviors and following the necessary steps to accomplish those goals.

Here's how goal setting works: You begin by identifying a general goal for improvement, such as reducing your overall public speaking anxiety. Then for that general goal, you formulate specific goal statements in behavioral terms. The specific goal statements could be that you will: (1) contribute more frequently and confidently to class discussions; (2) contribute more frequently and confidently to small group discussions; and (3) discuss your ideas (for speeches) more comfortably with your professor. Next, you write out specific behavioral criteria for each goal statement to create benchmarks for its accomplishment. The criteria would be to make a minimum of two contributions per day in each class, two suggestions in each group discussion in which you participate, and discuss your ideas for presentations with your professor once a week.

Goal setting works because it gives you an organized structure for accomplishing behavioral change. By accomplishing each specific goal, you move steadily toward the accomplishment of the general goal. As you communicate with greater confidence, your overall anxiety is reduced.

As you consider the use of systematic desensitization (changing how you feel), cognitive modification (changing what you think), or goal setting (changing your communication skills), it may

---

Box 3.2:: Six Surprising Ways to Overcome Your Fear of Public Speaking

Instructions: Get together a group of students who particularly fear public speaking and try some of these techniques. Use an available classroom to try them out. Each student comes forward and takes a turn using one of these techniques. The others in the audience should applaud and whistle wildly as each person comes up, during and at the end of each performance.

1. Bashing a bar or other stool: Use a rolled-up newspaper or hard foam water noodle and bash the platform or podium while yelling motivational slogans like: "My name is ____ and I am a great public speaker….I am a fearless presenter!"

2. Tabletop poetry: Each student brings a short poem, no more than 15 lines, and stands on a very low table and delivers the poem—enthusiastically and with lots of drama.

3. Happy/sad nursery rhymes: Each student chooses a different nursery rhyme and presents it first with exaggerated humor and then with exaggerated sorrow.

4. Three-way sayings: Repeat the same short sentence—e.g. "What can I do for you?" "When do the speeches start?" "Tell me how you feel"—first in an angry tone, then a puzzled tone, and then with exaggerated politeness.

5. Simultaneous debates: Two students pair off and select a debate topic. The two stand up and start debating the topic and try to drown each other out. After 30 seconds, they reverse and take the opposite position on the topic.

6. Singing Happy Birthday: Take turns singing happy birthday to one another with wild enthusiasm. If you get over your fear of singing publicly, public speaking will be a piece of cake!

Source: Grenby, M. (2003, March). Six ways to overcome your fear of public speaking. *Harvard Management Communication Letter*, 3–4.

be helpful to know that you are already busy with an activity that will reduce your anxiety. Several communication scholars recently found that a very good way to reduce public speaking anxiety is simply to take a standard public speaking class.[13] Apparently, you, Richard, and the other students in his class are already on the right track. But if none of these suggestions appeals to you, take a look at the six funny techniques presented in Box 3.2 for students at the Harvard Business School.[14] Some of the techniques may seem a little strange, but they could help you face down your fear and step up to the podium with greater confidence.

Box 3.3: Thinking Outside the Box: Public Speaking Etiquette for Speakers and Listeners

You may not realize there is such a thing as "Public Speaking Etiquette." Both the speaker and the listener have ethical responsibilities that come into play at any public speaking event.

Speakers' Responsibilities

1. Always come prepared to address your audience. Don't offend your listeners by trying to "wing it" during a presentation. They will know if you are not prepared.

2. Be considerate of time. Your listeners have taken time out of their day to be your audience. The planners have allotted you a specific window of time, do not go overtime.

3. Dress professionally. Show respect for your listeners by dressing appropriately. Men should wear a collared shirt and slacks. Women should wear a dress, or pants or a skirt, with a professional blouse. No jeans, no tee-shirts, no tennis shoes or flip flops for either sex. You may distract the listeners from your message with too casual an appearance.

4. Look at your audience and speak with a strong, public voice. It's your job to ensure all listeners can see and hear you throughout your speech.

5. Finally, be prepared for anything that may go wrong; technology isn't perfect. The flash drive might fail or the computer could shut down. Plan for the unexpected.

Listeners' Responsibilities

1. Be respectful and arrive on time. Find a seat and be in it before the speaker begins talking.

2. Turn off your cell phone, pager, beeper or Blackberry. If absolutely necessary, turn the device to vibrate so calls won't interrupt the presentation.

3. Do not get up and leave or enter the room during a presentation.

4. Wait until there is a pause in the presentation before opening up your briefcase or backpack or purse. These activities make noise and can distract from the speech.

5. Do not eat or drink or send or receive text messages, while the speaker is presenting.

6. Give speakers the respect of listening by facing and looking at them directly during their presentation.

7. Focus your full attention on the speaker's message and prepare to participate in a Q&A after the speech. If you expect others to listen to you, then be prepared to do the same.

Source: Marcelle Hureau and Corlea Keeney, University of Colorado at Colorado Springs (2009).

PREPARING AND PRESENTING YOUR FIRST SPEECH COMPETENTLY

You now know what it means to be a really awesome public speaker—what some communication instructors refer to as a highly competent communicator. If you apply the eight public speaking competencies to your next speech, you may be surprised you do so with more confidence and less anxiety. No matter what the next speech assignment is, prepare for it carefully: choose the right topic, focus your purpose and thesis statement, engage in thorough research for support materials, and develop a solid outline containing an introduction, main points, and conclusion. Then practice the speech ahead of time, preferably before a live audience even if that is only one person. Pay attention to any feedback about how you use words and language, your voice, and all sorts of nonverbal cues. If you don't have access to a willing listener, consider taping or recording your speech, and becoming your own best critic.

Each of the eight competencies is explored in detail in a later chapter of this book. We conclude this chapter with some practical suggestions from two graduate teaching assistants for speaking and listening etiquette, listed in Box 3.3. Good luck with your next speech! Richard and some other students will see you in Chapter 4 to talk more about the importance of audience analysis and listening.

CHAPTER SUMMARY

Competent public speaking is both effective and appropriate for the particular rhetorical situation, which means you accomplish the purpose of your speech in a way that is respectful of the situation and people involved. These eight public speaking competencies will help you become a competent public speaker:

- Chooses and narrows a topic appropriately for the audience and occasion.
- Communicates the thesis/specific purpose in a manner appropriate for the audience and occasion.
- Provides supporting material (including electronic and non-electronic presentational aids) appropriate for the audience and occasion.
- Uses an organizational pattern appropriate to the topic, audience, occasion, and purpose.
- Uses language appropriate to the audience and occasion.
- Uses vocal variety in rate, pitch, and intensity (volume) to heighten and maintain interest appropriate to the audience and occasion.
- Uses pronunciation, grammar, and articulation effectively and appropriate to the audience and occasion.
- Uses physical behaviors that support the verbal message.

In accomplishing these competencies, many speakers experience public speaking anxiety, which refers to a person's level of fear or anxiety associated with a real or anticipated public speaking event. This anxiety may be caused by remembering negative public speaking experiences, identifying with ineffective speakers, or holding negative and unrealistic expectations about public speaking and yourself as a speaker. You can reduce your public speaking anxiety by changing how you feel (your emotions and feelings) through systematic desensitization, what you think (your beliefs and thoughts) through cognitive modification, or what you do (your skills and behaviors) through goal setting.

KEY TERMS

The key terms below are defined in this chapter and presented alphabetically with definitions in the Glossary at the end of the book.

- competent public speaking
- public speaking anxiety
- systematic desensitization

- cognitive modification
- goal setting

BUILDING COMPETENCE ACTIVITIES

INDIVIDUAL ACTIVITIES

1. Attend a live lecture or speech. Analyze the speech based on the following questions:
   - What was the purpose of the speech (informative or persuasive) and how effectively the did speaker achieve the purpose?
   - What type of delivery was used and was it used effectively?
   - Was the speech delivered effectively and appropriately?

   Write a one-page summary of your analysis of the speech.

2. Go the website of the Public Address Division of the National Communication Association (http://www.ncapublicaddress.org/publicaddressarchives.htm) that links to many other sites that contain speeches such as the Top 100 Speeches of the 20th century. Choose one speech, view it, and analyze it based on the questions presented in Individual Activity 1.

3. Try at home to use any one of the three approaches to managing public speaking anxiety (systematic desensitization, cognitive modification, or goal setting). Write a one-page summary of how well it worked or did not work for you.

GROUP ACTIVITIES

1. Form groups of four to five students. Attend a live lecture or speech. Analyze the speech based on your impression of how well the speaker used the eight public speaking competencies summarized in this chapter. Present your analysis to the class and discuss the strengths and weaknesses of the speech that you attended.

2. With a partner, go to a computer and access the White House website (http://www.whitehouse.gov) and find the web page that provides manuscripts of the president's recent major speeches. Select a speech that interests both of you. Prepare and present an analysis of it in class.

3. Form groups of four to five students. Share examples of significant competent or incompetent public speeches that you have attended. These could be in-class lectures. Develop a list of characteristics and behaviors of competent public speakers based on the group discussion. Present your list of characteristics and behaviors to the class.

4. Form groups of four to five students. Share examples of significant ethical or unethical public speakers or speeches (could be lectures) you have observed. Develop a list of characteristics and behaviors of ethical speakers and of unethical speakers based on the group discussion. Present your two lists to the class.

5. Form groups of four to five students. Share examples of times when you were perceived as a credible public speaker (could be a presentation you did in another class). Develop a list of characteristics and behaviors for credible public speaking based on the group discussion. Present your list to the class.

COMPETENCY CHECKPOINTS AND SELF-ASSESSMENT TOOL

Here is what you need to know and be able to do regarding the public speaking process. Determine your level of competency and whether you are ready to proceed to the next chapter. Give yourself one point for each checkpoint you answer satisfactorily.

COMPETENCY CHECKPOINTS	NUMBER OF POINTS
KNOWLEDGE 1. Define public speaking competence. 2. Explain why the study of rhetoric is relevant to you as a public speaker. 3. Outline the four competencies for preparing a speech. 4. Outline the four competencies for presenting a speech.	
SKILLS 1. Give an example of a time when you presented a speech and what you did to present it competently. 2. Give an example of a time when you presented a speech and what you did to present it incompetently. 3. Of the eight competencies, which should you do to improve your skills? 4. Of the approaches to managing public speaking anxiety presented in this chapter, which would work best for you and why?	
ETHICS AND CREDIBILITY 1. Provide an example of an ethical or unethical public speaker you have observed in the past. Say why the speech was ethical or unethical and the impact it had on the listeners. 2. Identify what you need to do to be perceived by other students in the class as a credible public speaker when you present your first speech.	
TOTAL CHECKPOINTS (OUT OF A POSSIBLE TEN POINTS)	

ENDNOTES

1. Kruger, J. & Dunning, D. (1999). Unskilled and unaware of it: How difficulties in recognizing one's own incompetence leads to inflated self-assessments. *Journal of Personality and Social Psychology, 77*(6), 1121–1134.

2. Morreale, S., Moore, M., Surges-Tatum, D., & Webster, L. (2006). *The competent speaker speech evaluation program,* 2nd ed. Washington, DC: National Communication Association Non-Serial Publications Program.

3. Pearson, J.C., Child, J.T., & Kahl, D.H. Jr. (2006). Preparation meeting opportunity: How do college students prepare for public speeches? *Communication Quarterly, 54*(3), 351–366.

4. Smith, T.E. & Frymier, A.B. (2006). Get 'real': Does practicing speeches before an audience improve performance? *Communication Quarterly, 54*(1), 111–125.

5. Morgan, N. (2004). Preparing to be real. *Harvard Management Communication Letter, 1*(1), 3–5.

6. Behnke, R. R., & Sawyer, C.R. (1999). Public speaking procrastination as a correlate of public speaking communication apprehension and self-perceived public speaking competence. *Communication Research Reports, 16*(1), 40–47.

7. Dickens, M. (1954). *Speech: Dynamic communication*. New York: Harcourt Brace, p. 41

8. Witt, P.L., Brown, K.C., Roberts, J.B., Weisel, J., Sawyer, C.R., & Behnke, R.R. (2006). Somatic anxiety patterns before, during, and after giving a public speech. *Southern Communication Journal, 71*(1), 87–100

9. Finn, A.M., Sawyer, C.R., & Behnke, R.R. (2003). Audience-perceived anxiety patterns of public speakers. *Communication Quarterly, 51*(4), 470–481.

10. McCullough, S.C., Russell, S.G., Behnke, R.R., Sawyer, C.R., & Witt, P.L. (2006). Anticipatory public speaking state anxiety as a function of body sensations and state of mind. *Communication Quarterly, 54*(1), 101–109.

11. Clay, E., Fisher, R.L., Xie, S., Sawyer, C.R., & Behnke, R.R. (2005). Affect intensity and sensitivity to punishment as predictors of sensitization (arousal) during public speaking. *Communication Reports, 18*(2), 95–103.

12. Bruskin/Goldring Research Report (Feb. 1993). *America's number 1 fear: Public speaking.* Bruskin/Goldring Research, Inc., p. 4.

13. Duff, D. C., Levine, T. R., Beatty, M. J., Woolbright, J., & Sun Park, H. (2007). Testing public anxiety treatments against a credible placebo control. *Communication Education, 56*(1), 72–88

14. Grenby, M. (2003, March). Six ways to overcome your fear of public speaking. *Harvard Management Communication Letter,* 3–4.

4

LISTENING AND ANALYZING YOUR AUDIENCE

"To listen well is as powerful a means of communication and influence as to talk well." John Marshall, influential Chief Justice of the Supreme Court of the United States, 1755–1835

• • •

At the start of Richard's speech, Kumar could see why the police officer might be pretty confident in his public speaking abilities. Richard had a commanding presence—his voice was steady, his opening question captivating, and he hardly used his outline or notes. But after the first 60 seconds of Richard's speech, Kumar found his attention wandering and he decided to catch up on some text messages with friends. He was sitting in the back of the classroom so he could easily respond to a few messages. Kumar figured there was nothing wrong with sending messages and listening to Richard at the same time.

As he looked around the room, Kumar noticed other classmates also seemed disinterested in Richard's speech. At one point, he looked over at Angelique who shrugged her shoulders in either confusion or disinterest and picked up her phone to check messages. Mario looked as if he might be listening to music but his hair concealed the wireless earpiece quite well. At that point Kumar thought to himself, "Maybe Richard isn't quite the public speaker he thinks he is. Or maybe we aren't quite the listeners we thought we were."

• • •

Although Richard had a mature and commanding presence in the classroom and an impressive PowerPoint presentation, he had not analyzed how the rest of the class would react to the topic of his speech—violent crime statistics in their community. As a result, his audience had a difficult time paying attention and listening to his speech. This chapter will help you avoid some of the mistakes Richard made by addressing the following topics related to listening and analyzing the audience for your next speech:

- The importance of listening compared to just hearing.
- Barriers affecting how well you listen *and* whether the audience will listen to your speech.
- How to listen as a good audience member (and that means **no** text messaging!).
- How to analyze your audience, including their culture and diversity.

IS LISTENING IMPORTANT?

Being a good listener is probably one of the most crucial (but neglected) human communication skills anyone can have.[1] More arguments could be avoided, more marriages saved, more jobs and careers enriched, if all of us took the time to listen better. According to one author, there is "nearly universal agreement that effective listening skills are critical in people's public, private, and work lives."[2]

The importance of listening is intensified today as a result of globalization, the all-pervading use of technology to communicate, and diversity in today's world. In a writing on learning to listen across cultural divides, Bill Eadie is quoted as saying: "...we need to make a special effort to hear the voices of those who are not like us, to listen for their truth, and to celebrate both how we are similar and how we are different."[3] Eadie's observation about listening across cultural divides and differences is an important lesson to learn.[4] It may be particularly important for college students. A study of 554 university students found the scope of their listening skills is rather limited, even among experienced listeners. Yet, these same students dedicate roughly 50 percent of their time to listening every day.[5]

It also will motivate you to know that listening skills are highly valued in a variety of work settings. The Harvard Business School provides readers of its newsletter with pointers on how to listen to business speeches—a skill emphasized later in this chapter.[6] Leaders in organizations are advised to turn listening from a passive, compliant activity into an active, influential one that contributes to more dynamic, trusting, and collaborative relationships.[7] Some trainers in the business world are encouraging what they call **precision listening,** a type of listening that is a basic tool for gathering and assessing information needed for timely and effective decision making.[8] Managers are being trained to assess their own listening effectiveness.[9] Even bankers and pharmaceutical representatives are provided with recommendations for becoming better listeners.[10,11]

4.1 PRECISION LISTENING is a type of listening that is a basic tool for gathering and assessing information needed for timely and effective decision making.

In support of these recommendations from the world of business, Box 4.1, Thinking Outside the Box: the Ethics of Listening argues for listening as an ethical communication activity. Look at it this way. If we expect others to listen to us (and our speeches), as ethical communicators, we should listen to them. The box also calls your attention to how listening compares to hearing.

LISTENING COMPARED TO HEARING

Some people confuse hearing a message with actively listening to it. Often we hear sounds, even someone speaking, but we fail to listen and grasp the meaning of the person's message. The old expression, "It went in one ear and out the other," calls attention to this failure to listen. By contrast, experts from the International Listening Association define **listening** as the process of receiving, constructing meaning from, and responding to spoken and/or nonverbal messages.[12]

4.2 LISTENING is the process of receiving, constructing meaning from, and responding to spoken and/or nonverbal messages.

4.3 RECEIVING means tuning in to a speaker's entire message, including both its verbal and nonverbal aspects, and consciously paying attention to it.

Three key steps in the listening process are clearly identified in this definition: *receiving, constructing meaning, and responding.* **Receiving** means tuning in to a speaker's entire

---

Box 4.1: Thinking Outside the Box: The Ethics of Listening

Hearing and listening are different from each other. Hearing is mostly a physiological process by which sound waves pass through the ears and are decoded by our brains. Listening, on the other hand, involves interacting with our environment and deciding what elements of that environment deserve our attention. Some elements literally demand to be attended to, usually sounds that are much louder than others, such as a police or ambulance siren. Some sounds we learn are important, and we react to those sounds without really having to think about doing so. We not only look both ways before we cross the street, but we also listen for vehicles that might be approaching. If someone calls our name, we immediately pay attention.

But, quite a bit of our listening behavior involves making decisions, and any time we make decisions we encounter the potential for ethics to come into play. So, what sorts of ethical standards might we use so that we can listen responsibly? I addressed that question a number of years ago in a speech I gave to honors graduates at the university where I was a faculty member.

To listen responsibly, I told the students and their families, requires responsiveness. Listening passively may or may not be irresponsible, but it doesn't allow us to make conscious ethical decisions. Being responsive, for example, means that we are aware of the nature of our relationship with another person. Even if our grandfather has told a story many times over, he is still entitled to believe that we hear the story as if he's never told it before.

Some other duties we have as a responsible listener are to take particular care to understand positions that are different from our own; to appreciate the perspectives of individuals who are different from us; to realize the therapeutic role we can play merely by listening to someone, rather than trying to "fix" them or their problem; and to support others in gentle and humorous way to understand the blind spots that all of us experience.

Source: Eadie, W.F. (July 15, 1989). Hearing what we ought to hear, *Vital Speeches of the Day, 55*(19), 587–588.

---

message, including both its verbal and nonverbal aspects, and consciously paying attention to it. This means you make choices about what you pay attention to and what you ignore. **Constructing meaning** involves assigning meaning to the speaker's message and mentally clarifying your understanding of it. This step is more difficult than you might expect. Often the meaning a listener assigns to a message is different from the speaker's meaning. **Responding** completes the listening process and is the step in which the listener lets the speaker know the message, its verbal and nonverbal content, has been received and understood. This last step is often overlooked and leads to misunderstandings between speakers and listeners.

4.4 CONSTRUCTING MEANING involves assigning meaning to the speaker's message and mentally clarifying your understanding of it.

4.5 RESPONDING completes the listening process and is the step in which the listener lets the speaker know the message, its verbal and nonverbal content, has been received and understood.

Let's simplify this listening process by relating it to Richard's speech and the other students' reactions to it. Richard apparently chose a topic of limited interest to his classmates, and perhaps presented some boring statistics and numbers about violent crimes on his PowerPoint slides. Therefore, most of the students failed to *receive* and pay attention to most of his speech. In fact, Kumar tuned Richard out completely and started texting his friends. Since most of Richard's message was not received by the listeners, little information was available to them for *constructing meaning* about it. In the third step, *responding*, Richard should have noticed the audience's lack of response and disinterest. None of the students were making eye contact with him or shaking their heads to express concern about increases in violent crimes. Had Richard noticed their lack of response, he could have returned to the type of interactive questioning he used to open his speech. In so doing, he would have encouraged more active listening.

In sum, what we are saying may be surprising; listening is a very critical part of the public speaking process. In the past, you may have thought about giving a speech only as *speaking* effectively, not listening. Again, think back to Richard's speech and the reactions of Kumar and other students to it. Why didn't the students listen and pay attention? An array of barriers to listening may have worked against their desire to listen. Let's think about these barriers, and what we all can do to become better listeners and better audience members.

BARRIERS TO THE AUDIENCE LISTENING

Most listening researchers call our attention to three basic challenges to listening, any of which affect whether an audience pays attention to a speech. Physical, psychological, and interaction barriers are elements present in any and all communication situations, from interpersonal to public speaking. They affect all three steps in the listening process—receiving, constructing meaning, and responding to the message. We also need to consider two other challenges unique to communication in today's society—the impact of culture and of technology.

PHYSICAL, PSYCHOLOGICAL, AND INTERACTION BARRIERS

Physical barriers include interferences from the physical environment and distracting characteristics or behaviors of the speaker or other listeners. Phones ringing, other people talking, an uncomfortable chair or hot room, even being very hungry will distract you from actively listening. Unique mannerisms of the speaker such as stuttering, pacing, or nervous gestures will distract even a well-intended listener. In the case of Richard's speech, Kumar was distracted by the communication behaviors of other listeners in the class who appeared disinterested in the speech. Becoming aware of any potential physical barriers to listening is a first step to avoiding them. For instance, if you need to have an important conversation with a friend or coworker, don't choose a noisy restaurant or the company cafeteria at lunchtime for that chat. Once you are aware of any physical distractions, concentrate your energy and focus your attention on the speaker and the message, not the distraction.

4.6 PHYSICAL BARRIERS include interferences from the physical environment and distracting characteristics or behaviors of the speaker or other listeners.

Psychological barriers include mental and emotional distractions to listening, for instance, daydreaming, being emotionally preoccupied with something else, thinking listening takes too much time, or strong personal reactions to the speaker or the topic. When we are not interested in the message or if it is vague, confusing, or difficult to understand, we tend to tune out or jump to conclusions about what the speaker is saying.[13] If we strongly disagree with the speaker, we fail to listen and

4.7 PSYCHOLOGICAL BARRIERS include mental and emotional distractions to listening, for instance, daydreaming, being emotionally preoccupied with something else, thinking listening takes too much time, or strong personal reactions to the speaker or the topic.

instead spend time developing a counter argument or rehearsing a response to what the speaker is saying. Even when we agree with the speaker, what is said may cause us to "detour" or think of something else. Finally, if we are self-absorbed and focused on protecting our own ideas, we may not listen to the ideas of others.[14]

Many of these psychological barriers take place because of a difference in speaking versus listening rates. In today's world, people now speak at approximately 200 words per minute but listen at about 500 to 600 words per minute. This vast difference leaves a lot of mental and psychological down time, so your mind and attention tend to wander from what the speaker is saying. Again, awareness of this barrier and the tendency for your attention to wander is a first step to better listening. Every time your mind wanders, instead try to focus on thinking critically about the message. Yoga and meditation instructors often give this same advice, when they say to focus on being in the present moment.

Interaction barriers to listening result from characteristics or elements of the particular communication situation and the people involved. For instance, when a communication interaction spirals into a strong disagreement and verbal battle, very little listening takes place.[15] Verbal aggressiveness or using language such as inappropriate slang dissuades even the best listener from focusing on the message. At a less volatile level, if you have difficulty interpreting the nonverbal behaviors of the speaker, you may focus on those cues rather than on the speaker's message. You can manage interaction barriers by consciously controlling your own use of aggressive or inflammatory language. If the speaker is com-

> **4.8 INTERACTION BARRIERS to listening result from characteristics or elements of the particular communication situation and the people involved.**

municating in an aggressive manner, consider suggesting that the conversation be postponed to a calmer time. If you are listening to an antagonistic public speaker, try to focus on the essence of the message and not its intensity.

CULTURE, TECHNOLOGY, AND 21ST CENTURY BARRIERS

Closely linked to the three basic barriers to listening is a set of barriers that are increasingly important to communication in the world as we know it today. This set of barriers arise from two factors—communicating with people from other cultures and cultural backgrounds and communicating using technology, which often results in message overload and complexity.

Cultural barriers, which encompass characteristics of listeners like race, ethnicity, gender, and age, may affect listening in significant but not obvious ways. As globalization becomes a reality and the world and our workplaces become more diverse, two key ideas about listening across cultural barriers are important.

First, people from other regions, ethnic groups, and other countries may speak or send messages differently than you and that may affect how well you listen to them. Recall in Chapter 2, you learned about different approaches to public speaking in Western and non-Western cultures. So if you are listening to

> **4.9 CULTURAL BARRIERS encompass characteristics of listeners like race, ethnicity, gender, and age.**

a speech or a speaker from a different culture, be aware and respectful of any differences in speaking or presentation style and focus your attention on the message, not the dialect or distractions.[16]

Second, if *you* are the speaker and members of your audience are culturally different from you in any way, don't expect them to use the listening styles of your culture. In the United States and other Western cultures, listeners use nonverbal cues like making eye contact and head nodding to indicate

Table 4.1: Barriers to Listening and Overcoming Them

Five different types of barriers affect our ability to listen but they can be easily managed through awareness of these specific strategies.

FIVE BARRIERS TO LISTENING	OVERCOMING EACH BARRIER
Physical barriers: Environment, distracting characteristics and behaviors of speaker or other listeners	Become aware of physical distractions and then concentrate your energy and focus your attention on the message.
Psychological barriers: Mental and emotional distractions	Become aware of the tendency for your mind to wander and then focus on critically evaluating the message instead.
Interaction barriers: Characteristics or elements of the situation and people involved	Avoid using aggressive or inflammatory language and focus on the essence of a message, not its intensity.
Cultural barriers like race, ethnicity, gender, and age.	Be aware and respectful of cultural differences in the speaking or presentation style of the speaker. Pay attention to cultural differences in listening styles of your audience when you are speaking.
Technology barriers such as use of cell phones, the Internet, etc.	Avoid multitasking when you should be listening. Turn off the technology so you can listen to the speaker.

they're paying attention. In some Eastern and Middle Eastern cultures, it's considered disrespectful for listeners to look directly at a speaker and periods of silence in conversations are quite acceptable.

You can deal with these cultural differences and barriers and move toward effective intercultural listening by suspending judgment and not making assumptions about a message or speech until you have patiently listened with an open and alert mind and heart. Try to listen beyond the differences and use intercultural listening to build what culture researchers refer to as "mutuality."[17] What they mean is that the listener and the speaker use listening to *mutually* shape and reshape their common understanding and satisfaction with the communication situation. In the story at the start of this chapter, Richard may have been from a different professional group than most of his audience members, which could be considered a different cultural group. His job as a police officer resulted in his interest in violent crime statistics. Clearly, most of the other students didn't share that interest, so they failed to listen attentively to his speech.

Technology barriers, and related message overload and complexity, also are affecting listening in 21st century U.S. society. **Message overload** refers to the quantity of messages you process every day and **message complexity** is about how detailed and complicated those messages are. To get a sense of these listening barriers, think about the sheer volume of information and messages you sort through everyday, using cell phones, land lines, the Internet, e-mail, text messages, blogs, and social media websites, to say nothing of listening to teach-

4.10 TECHNOLOGY BARRIERS result from the use of cell phones, land lines, the Internet, e-mail, text messages, blogs and social media websites, and television, radio, and music on iPods.

4.11 MESSAGE OVERLOAD refers to the quantity of messages you process and **MESSAGE COMPLEXITY** is about how detailed and complicated those messages are.

ers and bosses and coworkers, and television, radio, and music on iPods. Several recent studies call attention to how prevalent message overload is in today's society. For instance, one study of how people use information and communications technology (ICT) found over 50 percent of American adults are what they call elite tech or middle of the road tech users, which means they make extensive use of technology to communicate every day.[18] Other researchers asked college students how much time they spend in different types of communication activities, and the students reported spending less time reading, writing, speaking, and listening, and more time on e-mail than in the past.[19] Yet another study looked at phone usage in the United States and found that over eight in ten (81%) say they have a landline phone, and over three quarters (77%) say they also have a wireless or cell phone.[20] If people are using all this technology to send all these messages, then somebody also is on the listening end of it, even if it's an e-mail message or a message left on a cell phone. The result is that most of us do experience some degree of message overload. In addition, sometimes the messages we receive are too complex or complicated to understand, and then we tend to tune them out.

Richard's speech may have been a problem for Kumar and others because of its level of complexity and the message overload resulting from sending text messages and listening to Richard's speech at the same time. Even the best listeners in the class may have become distracted by too many statistics, and then they failed to listen to valuable information for safeguarding themselves against violence. The best approach to handling technological barriers to listening may be the "golden rule" that says: *do for others what you want them to do for you.* Although it is tempting to multi-task when you are listening, instead turn off your cell phone or iPod, when you should be listening to someone else.

Table 4.1 will help you remember the barriers to listening and how to overcome them. But by now, you may think listening is a very difficult challenge. Let's consider a few good ideas for improving your listening skills.

LISTENING BETTER AS AN AUDIENCE MEMBER

An easy way to think about listening better is to return to the three steps in the listening process—receiving messages, constructing meaning, and responding—and consider the communication skills critical to each step. First, what are the receiving skills to help you become a better listener?

- Prepare yourself to listen and don't take the process for granted. Be mentally, physically, and emotionally ready to listen whether you're at work, in class, or having dinner with a friend.
- Think about your purpose for listening in the situation. If you're clear about your purpose, you're more likely to achieve it at the end of the speech, lecture, or conversation.
- Be aware of any physical barriers in the listening situation and, to the best of your ability, eliminate the barriers or focus on ways to minimize them.
- Concentrate your full attention on the speaker and the message and rein your mind back in whenever it tends to wander.

Second, if you have listened and received the message, what constructing meaning skills do you need as an effective listener?

- Avoid judging the speaker or the message until the speech or conversation is over—this may be one of the most difficult things to do when listening.
- Leave behind any personal biases or prejudices that may color your perception of the speaker's message. Realize you would want the same courtesy, when you speak.

- Analyze the message objectively by listening for the speaker's main points and supporting evidence. Weigh the evidence and argument and avoid listening for where the speaker is wrong. Try listening for where others may be right.

Third, what skills will help you respond to other speakers most effectively after listening?

- Don't respond emotionally to what the speaker says. Rather, listen to the entire message and then decide how you feel about it. You may be surprised to find you feel differently.
- While the other person is speaking, provide verbal and nonverbal feedback to demonstrate you are interested and listening. Be sensitive to cultural differences about what is appropriate feedback.
- Develop a mental summary of the meaning of the speech or message in your own mind.
- Provide that summary to the speaker without sounding like you are evaluating it. Ask the speaker to comment on your feedback and clarify any possible misunderstandings.

Now, to ensure the audience does all of these things and is motivated to listen to *your* speech, let's talk about engaging in audience analysis.

WHAT IS AUDIENCE ANALYSIS?

If you want to give a speech your audience listens to attentively, you need to think about who they are and what they are like ahead of time. Professionals whose work involves communicating with the public regularly, including legislators, healthcare providers, and corporate trainers, all recognize and call attention to this need to know more about one's listeners by engaging in audience analysis.[21, 22, 23]

Audience analysis is the process speakers use to determine facts and information about the listeners and the speaking situation and occasion that will influence reactions to the speech and how the speech is prepared and delivered. While you don't need to know everything about the audience, you do need to know anything that will affect how they react to your speech.

> **4.12 AUDIENCE ANALYSIS is the process speakers use to determine facts and information about the listeners and the speaking situation and occasion that will influence reactions to the speech and how the speech is prepared and delivered.**

ANALYZING THE LISTENERS

Everything about your speech, from choosing a topic, to developing it, to delivering it should be guided by what you learn ahead of time about your listeners. Three types of characteristics of the listeners are most important: personal demographics, cultural characteristics, and psychological characteristics.[24] If your audience is very similar on these characteristics (audience members are much alike), choosing an appealing topic will be easier. If the audience is diverse in personal, cultural, or psychological characteristics, the speech development process is more challenging. That was precisely the problem Richard experienced in our opening story; he was not aware of how diverse the listeners were in his class.

If you're already in a speech class or if you have a presentation coming up at work, think about the audience for that speech or presentation. Use the following audience characteristics to help you choose a topic or develop a focus on an assigned topic that is appealing to the audience.

Personal or demographic characteristics most relevant include the listeners' ages, the types of households they live in, their occupations, income, and education levels. *Age* is one of the first indicators of the possible interests of an audience. Listeners in their 50s or 60s are more likely concerned about changes in social security benefits than listeners in their 20s or 30s, who might be more interested in new job opportunities due to globalization. *Household type* describes who currently lives in the households of the listeners. Households in the United States are now very diverse, including single parent families, step-families, households with two working parents, and gay/lesbian families, to name just a few. If your speech in any way references house or home, be sure you are respectful of all these possibilities. What your listeners do for a living and how much they earn also may influence the topics they find appealing. Their *occupations* could help you figure out what they like or dislike and their *income* could tell you what they are able to do or not do in life. If most of your listeners are working in restaurants and have little extra income, a speech about cruises to the Caribbean Islands will probably fall flat. Finally, *education level* may suggest topics of interest, but it is not a litmus test for any topic. Many people who have not attained advanced degrees are vitally interested in all kinds of topics. They may be quite intelligent and have inquiring minds but don't hold advanced degrees. If your topic requires information only available through education, provide those facts so the entire audience appreciates your speech.

> **4.13 PERSONAL OR DEMOGRAPHIC CHARACTERISTICS include the listeners' ages, the types of households they live in, their occupations, income, and education levels.**

Cultural characteristics of importance can be divided into two groups your listeners belong to—groups they were born into and groups they grew up in. The "born into" groups include things like their biological sex, race, ethnicity, or the region of the United States or the country they come from. The "grew up in" groups include their religion, political affiliations, and clubs or organizations they either grew up around or chose to join. We now know the United States is becoming increasingly diverse in culture, race, and ethnicity. As a public speaker, if you learn about the cultural backgrounds of your listeners, you can choose or develop a topic for your speech that will appeal to and respect any cultural differences. But to clarify, this is not to suggest that you should misrepresent a topic; rather, you should analyze the diversity of your audience and adapt your speech so it is appropriate and appealing to the listeners. Also, don't rule out the possibility your career will require you to speak publicly in countries and cultures outside the United States To prepare for that very real possibility, check out the practical suggestions in Box 4.2, Thinking Outside the Blog: Public Speaking in Diverse Cultures.

> **4.14 CULTURAL CHARACTERISTICS can be divided into two groups your listeners belong to—groups they were born into and groups they grew up in.**

> **4.15 PSYCHOLOGICAL CHARACTERISTICS include the listeners' needs and motivations and their beliefs, attitudes, and values.**

Psychological characteristics to be analyzed include the listeners' *needs* and *motivations* and their *beliefs*, *attitudes*, and *values*. If you are thinking these psychological characteristics are closely related to the cultural backgrounds of the listeners, you are quite right. The tough part is that psychological characteristics are not easily identified because they relate to internal states of the listeners that cannot be observed. Without directly asking, it may be difficult to know what the audience needs or finds important, and knowing their needs is critical to developing a meaningful speech.[25] Most of us are more highly motivated to pay attention to a topic that addresses what we perceive as our own real needs or interests. If I need to file for social security in the foreseeable future, I want to

Box 4.2: Thinking Outside the Blog: Public Speaking in Diverse Cultures.

The Internet and various websites and blogs provide a wealth of information on presenting speeches to different cultural groups. The following suggestions will prove helpful whether you are talking to listeners in the United States who are natives of another country or if you are speaking to an audience in a foreign country. But, while it is good to be aware of cultural differences in public speaking, the world is in a state of flux as we all cope with globalization. What may have been stereotypical approaches to public speaking may have been replaced by new norms borrowed from other, more influential cultures.

General Hints for Public Speaking Across Cultures

"Public speaking is an art of communication that needs to be guided by a special sense of integrity, even more so today in our world of cultural globalization."[1]
These general hints can guide how you approach public speaking across cultures:

1. Linguistic (verbal) and non-linguistic (nonverbal) politeness are essential to any public speaker, but more so in some cultures than others.

2. The appropriate use in a speech of gestures, eye contact, silence, use of space and time, and touching may vary based on the culture. Be aware of any cultural differences and expectations.

3. Formality and informality also are specific to cultures. For example, the degree of expected formality in the introduction of a speech is higher in Singapore and Finland than in American speeches.

4. Contrary to some other cultures, American speakers often personalize their own experiences with regard to the topic of a presentation. American speakers also interact with the audience through the use of rhetorical questions. Be sure you are aware of whether these public speaking strategies are considered appropriate for a non-American audience.

Hints for Using Humor Cross Culturally

"Every culture enjoys some form of humor. But, humor has difficulty crossing cultural boundaries because what is humorous in one country is often not humorous in another."[2] According to Cultural Savvy, some basic rules regarding humor should guide any public speaker[3]:

1. Humor is very difficult to export—or import!

2. Each culture has its own style of humor, so be aware of the types of humor appreciated by a specific cultural audience.

3. Americans often begin speeches with a joke. Be cautious when taking this style to other cultures where humor at the start of a speech may be considered disrespectful.

4. Humor requires extensive knowledge and understanding of a language, otherwise your great joke may fall quite flat in a different culture or country.

5. When in doubt, avoid humor. Erring on the side of the cautious use of humor is a good idea for any public speaker.

Sources: [1] Vartia-Paukku, N. (ND). *Culture and politeness in public speaking. Observations on American, Finnish and Singaporean Chinese speeches.* Retrieved from http://www.nord.helsinki.fi/clpg/CLPG/Niini%20Vartia-Paukku.pdf

[2] Axtell, R. (1999). *Do's and taboos of humor around the world*, (pp. 77–78). New York. John Wiley & Sons, Inc. Intercultural Press.

[3] Cultural Savvy, (2009). *Humor.* Retrieved from http://www.culturalsavvy.com/humor.htm Editorial assistance from Marcelle Hureau (2009). University of Colorado at Colorado Springs.

4.16 ATTITUDES are the listeners' psychological reactions, positive or negative, to another person, object, or concept. They represent what people like or dislike.

4.17 BELIEFS are your listeners' convictions about reality, based on their cultural background, knowledge, and experiences in life. They represent what people think is true or untrue.

4.18 VALUES are an extension of your listeners' attitudes and beliefs and reflect what they consider to be important and unimportant.

know of any changes in the program. If I need a new job fairly soon, opportunities in a global economy will hold my interest.

Closely related to your listeners' needs are their attitudes, beliefs, and values, which are part of their psychological makeup and need to be analyzed. **Attitudes** are the listeners' psychological reactions, positive or negative, to another person, object, or concept. They represent what we like or dislike. **Beliefs** are your listeners' convictions about reality, based on their cultural background, knowledge, and experiences in life. They represent what we think is true or untrue. **Values** are an extension of your listeners' attitudes and beliefs and reflect what they consider to be important and unimportant. They represent what we hold as worthy or unworthy and they help us make big decisions in life.[26] Attitudes, beliefs, and values are intertwined. As an example, if you highly value freedom of expression, you probably will believe in the rights of private citizens to engage in public protests, and you will have a negative attitude toward police officers who appear to obstruct public demonstrations. For your speech to be effective, you need to carefully analyze the attitudes, beliefs, and values of your audience. They will listen more attentively to information that supports or at least shows respect for their position on the topic of your speech.

Table 4.2 provides a summary of the characteristics of listeners (and the situation and occasion) that you should consider when analyzing your audience. The need to analyze all of these characteristics of listeners is obvious, if you think back to Richard's ill-fated speech about violent crime. Did Richard fail to consider his audience's personal, cultural, or psychological characteristics? The story doesn't give us a lot of details, but we do know the audience was culturally diverse and Richard had a different type of job than the other students and may have been a bit older. The topic he chose was well suited to his own background but did not necessarily appeal to the needs or personal and psychological characteristics of the audience.

Table 4.2: Audience Analysis: Analyzing Listeners' Characteristics, the Occasion, and Situation

The first step in planning and developing any speech is to engage in careful analysis of the audience, occasion, and situation.

Analyzing the listeners	Personal or demographic characteristics: Ages, type of households, occupations, income, education level. Cultural characteristics: Groups listeners were born into and groups they grew up in. Psychological characteristics: Needs, motivations, beliefs, attitudes, and values.
Analyzing the occasion and situation	Timing: When speech is presented, time of day, how much time for the speech. Place: Physical environment and surroundings including technology. Occasion and situation: Nature of the event and your role as a speaker in the event.

ANALYZING THE SPEAKING SITUATION

In addition to thinking about who your listeners are, you also need to engage in situation analysis. A well-known 20th century communication scholar was famous for introducing us to this notion of analyzing the *rhetorical situation* in which a speech occurs.[27] **Situation analysis** includes careful consideration of the time, place, and occasion for the speech.

Timing involves when the speech is presented, the time of day, and how much time you are given to speak. If your speech (or the class you find yourself in) is in the morning, your listeners will be more alert than in the afternoon. For an afternoon speech, avoid an overly complex presentation and liven it up with a story or examples. In either time slot, pay attention to how much time you are given to talk and don't run over or under. Inexperienced speakers often try to cover too much and end up rushing through their remarks at the end. Practice your speech ahead of time, with an eye on the clock, to avoid this problem and cut it down if you have to. The other aspect of timing that is important is the sequence of speakers. Whether you are first, last, or in the middle, sticking to the time limit is considerate of other speakers.

Place considers where the speech is presented, the physical environment and surroundings. This includes everything from the furnishings in the room to audio visual equipment and lighting. Good public speakers visit the place ahead of time and check out where they will stand, the location of the podium or lectern, how the listeners will be seated, and most important, the equipment and how it works in the room. Even the best of speakers has, on occasion, used PowerPoint slides that were too dark for listeners to read given the lighting in the room. You can avoid these problems by checking out the physical environment and even doing a practice run of your speech in the room and space.

Occasion refers to any unique aspects of the speaking situation that will impact the presentation, for example, if you are the keynote speaker at a luncheon or dinner. If you are presenting a training at work while listeners are eating lunch, that is a very different occasion than a room of listeners in a public speaking class. Even in a public speaking class, occasions occur that could and should be noted in your speech. If your speech falls on the anniversary of September 11, 2001, some acknowledgement of the terrorists' attacks might be appropriate at some point in the speech.

In sum, analyzing your audience and listeners is important, perhaps most important. But some attention to details in the speaking situation—the time, place, and occasion—will help you avoid any problems and maximize the effectiveness of your speech in the particular environment.

> 4.19 SITUATION ANALYSIS includes careful consideration of the time, place, and occasion for the speech.
>
> 4.20 TIMING involves when the speech is presented, the time of day, and how much time you are given to speak.
>
> 4.21 PLACE considers where the speech is presented, the physical environment and surroundings.
>
> 4.22 OCCASION refers to any unique aspects of the speaking situation that will impact the presentation.

UNDERSTANDING YOUR AUDIENCE

All the recommendations about audience analysis may be more useful with a few last suggestions from some experts and communication theorists, past and present. One or more of these ideas may spark your interest and motivate you to take the audience analysis process a little more seriously. The effort will pay off immeasurably how the audience reacts to your next speech, we promise!

LISTENING TO THE EXPERTS

In a landmark article actually entitled "Audience Analysis," Charles Redding describes the use by students of opinion polls in their public speaking classes, much like the public opinion polling conducted by Gallup and other organizations.[28] Redding says this technique will help stimulate your creative thinking about possible topics for your speeches, and it will help you build more objective attitudes toward those topics.

More recently, Eunkyong Yook tells us how to conduct such classroom polls using different types of questions to survey your audience's attitudes, knowledge, and interest in your speech topic.[29] Yook says surveying the audience is a method of audience analysis that focuses on the following question types. *Open ended questions* require the interviewees to answer in detail. "Tell me of any experiences you have or know about related to violent crimes in our community." *Closed questions* are answerable in a few words, usually with a fixed set of responses. "Do you think an increase in violent crimes is taking place in our community?" *Leading questions* are the questions in which the interviewer suggests the desired answer. "Is a significant increase in violent crimes worth worrying about?" *Neutral questions* are the ones that give the interviewees a chance to respond without any influence from the interviewer. "Why are violent crimes on the increase in our community?" In the opening story, if Richard had asked his classmates these types of questions, he could have adapted his speech more effectively based on what he learned.

Two other nationally recognized scholars, Frank Dance and Carol Zak-Dance, promote the concept of **decentering** in order to move away from your own center, a self-centered view of your topic and the world, and pay more attention to the diverse views of the audience members.[30] Through decentering, you learn about the personal experiences and thoughts of the audience in order to understand how they may react to your speech. While our own views are important, by decentering, we consider the alternative views of often diverse and multicultural audiences. Richard probably did not decenter and did not consider the diverse views of others in the class, including perhaps the instructor.

4.23 DECENTERING involves moving away from your own center, a self-centered view of your topic and the world, and paying more attention to the diverse views of the audience members.

4.24 INTERCULTURAL SENSITIVITY involves the various stages of sensitivity to cultural differences people go through in order to arrive at a point where they relate most productively and nonjudgmentally to others.

DEVELOPING INTERCULTURAL SENSITIVITY

Finally, Milton Bennett provides a useful tool we can use to judge how well we analyze and understand the diverse perspectives of multicultural audiences.[31] Bennett's *Developmental Model of Intercultural Sensitivity* describes the stages of sensitivity to cultural differences people go through in order to arrive at a point where they relate most productively to others unlike themselves. The six stages in the model, and some typical statements people make if they are at that stage, are presented in Table 4.3. Examine the stages and statements and think honestly about which stage you may be

Table 4.3: The Developmental Model of Intercultural Sensitivity

Look at the statements people typically make indicating their stage of intercultural sensitivity. See which statements most closely sound like what you might think or say about other cultures.

SIX STAGES TO INTERCULTURAL SENSITIVITY	AT THIS STAGE, LEARNERS SAY:
DENIAL OF DIFFERENCE The inability to construe or understand cultural differences.	Live and let live, that's what I say. As long as we all speak the same language, there's no problem. With my experience, I can be successful in any culture without any special effort. I never experience culture shock.
DEFENSE AGAINST DIFFERENCE Recognition of cultural difference coupled with negative evaluation of most variations from one's native culture.	I wish these people would just talk the way we do. Even though I'm speaking their language, they're still rude to me. When you go to other cultures, you realize how much better the United States is. Boy, could we teach these people a lot of stuff.
MINIMIZATION OF DIFFERENCE Recognition and acceptance of superficial cultural differences like eating customs, while holding all people are essentially the same.	The key to getting along in any culture is to just be yourself, authentic and honest. Customs differ, of course, but when you get to know them, they're pretty much like us. I have this intuitive sense of other people, no matter what their culture. While the context may be different, the basic need to communicate remains the same around the world.
ACCEPTANCE OF DIFFERENCE Recognition and appreciation of cultural differences in behavior and values.	The more difference the better; more difference equals more creative ideas. You certainly wouldn't want to have the same kind of people around; the ideas get stale and besides it's boring. I always try to study about a new culture before I go there. Where I can I learn more about Mexican culture to be effective in my communication while there.
ADAPTATION TO DIFFERENCE The development of communication skills that enable intercultural communication, such as use of empathy or frame of reference shifting (decentering).	To solve this dispute, I'm going to have to change my approach. They're really trying hard to adapt to my style, so it's fair I try to meet them halfway. I can maintain my values and also behave in culturally appropriate ways. The more I understand this culture, the better I get at the language.
INTEGRATION OF DIFFERENCE The internalization of bicultural or multicultural frames of reference.	Everywhere is home, if you know enough about how things work there. Whatever the situation, I can usually look at it from a variety of cultural points of view. In an intercultural world, everyone needs to have a trans-cultural mindset. My decision-making skills are enhanced by having multiple frames of reference.

Source: Bennett, M. J. (1994). A developmental model of intercultural sensitivity. *Perry Network Newsletter, 16*(1), 6–7.

at right now. By knowing yourself and how you presently relate to other cultures, you can develop a higher level of intercultural sensitivity. That personal awareness will help you determine how best to develop a speech for a multicultural audience. If you seem to be at *Denial of Difference, Defense Against Difference,* or *Minimization of Difference* that might impede your ability to engage in good audience analysis. If you are at *Acceptance, Adaptation,* or *Integration of Difference* you may be better able to adjust your presentation style to different cultural groups.

We have focused our attention in this chapter on how you, as a public speaker, should develop your speech to maximize its appeal to your audience and motivate them to pay attention —more than they did to Richard's crime statistics speech. But communication is a two way street. In addition to developing an appealing speech, when we are the listeners in the audience, we have an ethical responsibility to listen. Richard's story is a good example of audience members not listening and a speaker not analyzing his audience. In the chapters that follow, audience analysis will be interwoven in our discussion of how to develop and then present your speeches most effectively and appropriately.

CHAPTER SUMMARY

Listening may be defined as the process of receiving, constructing meaning from, and responding to spoken and/or nonverbal messages. Three steps in the listening process are receiving, constructing meaning, and responding. Receiving means tuning in to a speaker's entire message, including both its verbal and nonverbal aspects, and consciously paying attention to it. Constructing meaning involves assigning meaning to the speaker's message and mentally clarifying your understanding of it. Responding completes the listening process and is the step in which the listener lets the speaker know the message, its verbal and nonverbal content, has been received and  understood. Three basic barriers to listening need to be considered. Physical barriers include interferences from the physical environment and distracting characteristics or behaviors of the speaker or other listeners. Psychological barriers include mental and emotional distractions to listening. Interaction barriers result from characteristics or elements of the particular communication situation and the people involved. In the 21st century, we are also concerned about cultural barriers, which encompass characteristics of the listeners like race, ethnicity, gender, and age. Technological barriers, including message overload and message complexity, also affect listening in today's society. To become a better listener, you need to consider the communication skills critical to each of the three steps in the listening process and use what you know about listening to become a better listener as an audience member.

Listening is important to public speaking because you want to give a speech your audience listens to attentively, which means you engage in audience analysis. Audience analysis is the process speakers use to determine facts and information about the listeners and the speaking situation and occasion that will influence reactions to the speech and how the speech is prepared and delivered. You analyze listeners by considering their personal or demographic, cultural, and psychological characteristics. Psychological characteristics include the listeners' attitudes, beliefs, and values. Situation analysis includes careful consideration of the time, place, and occasion for the speech. Communication theorists advise us to employ opinion polls in public speaking classes using different types of questions to survey the audience's attitudes, knowledge, and interest in a speech topic.

They also advise us to decenter and move away from an egocentric view and consider the views or perspectives of audience members. To analyze the diversity of a multi-cultural audience, we need to be aware of the stage of intercultural sensitivity at which we find ourselves.

KEY TERMS

The key terms below are defined in this chapter and presented alphabetically with definitions in the Glossary at the end of the book.

- precision listening
- listening
- receiving
- constructing meaning
- responding
- physical barriers
- psychological barriers
- interaction barriers
- cultural barriers
- technology barriers
- message overload and complexity
- audience analysis

- personal or demographic characteristics
- cultural characteristics
- psychological characteristics
- attitudes
- beliefs
- values
- situation analysis
- timing
- place
- occasion
- decentering
- intercultural sensitivity

BUILDING COMPETENCE ACTIVITIES

INDIVIDUAL ACTIVITIES

1. Identify a personal communication interaction or situation in which it is important to listen and develop a list of skills you can use to improve how you listen in that situation.
2. Identify a public speaking situation in which you observe barriers to listening for yourself. Develop a list of the barriers and some effective listening behaviors you could use in that public situation.
3. Choose a possible topic for your next speech and use the audience analysis techniques presented in this chapter to develop a list of the possible reactions to the topic of the listeners in your class. Identify how you could adapt and accommodate that topic to the interests and needs of the audience.
4. Examine the stages described in the intercultural sensitivity model in Table 4.3. Consider how you could move to the next stage using your experiences in this public speaking class.

GROUP ACTIVITIES

1. In groups of four or five students, have each student first identify a person who is a good listener. Develop a composite list of behaviors of the good listeners. Then have each student identify a person who is a bad listener and develop a list of behaviors of bad listeners. Share your two lists with the class.
2. With a partner, identify what each of you think are barriers to listening in your public speaking class. Develop a set of recommendations and creative ideas for overcoming those barriers. Share the ideas with the class and make a commitment to implementing the recommendations.

3. Form groups of four to five students and develop a general description of the class as an audience, including the listeners' personal/demographic, cultural, and psychological characteristics. Present your descriptions to the class.
4. Choose a topic for your next speech and then interview several other students in the class and get their reaction to the topic. Adapt and modify the topic based on what you learn.
5. In dyads, two students, share your opinion of the stage you are at on the intercultural sensitivity model (in Table 4.3). Discuss ways that each of you could move to the next stage and what benefits you would get from doing so.

COMPETENCY CHECKPOINTS AND SELF-ASSESSMENT TOOL

Here is what you need to know and be able to do regarding the listening process and audience analysis. Determine your level of competency and whether you are ready to proceed to the next chapter. Give yourself one point for each checkpoint you answer satisfactorily.

COMPETENCY CHECKPOINTS	NUMBER OF POINTS
KNOWLEDGE 1. Define listening and describe the three steps in the listening process: receiving, constructing meaning, and responding. 2. Explain the relationship of listening skills and audience analysis. 3. Describe the most important tasks involved in effective audience analysis for a speech.	
SKILLS 1. Give an example of a time when you used good listening skills to overcome one of the three basic barriers to listening: physical, psychological, and interaction, and one of the 21st century barriers to listening. 2. Anyone can become a better listener than they are now, so what could you do to improve your skills? 3. Think about your ability to "decenter" and take the audience or other person's perspective. Identify ways that you could improve your decentering skills. 4. Identify the stage you are at on the intercultural sensitivity model and state what you could do to move to the next stage. 5. What can you do in your next speech to demonstrate a high level of intercultural sensitivity?	
ETHICS AND CREDIBILITY 1. Provide an example of ethical or unethical listening you have observed in the past. Say why the listening event was ethical or unethical and the impact it had on the listeners. 2. Would audience members perceive you as more credible and believable if you have engaged in audience analysis? Why?	
TOTAL CHECKPOINTS (OUT OF A POSSIBLE TEN POINTS)	

ENDNOTES

1. Wolvin, A.D. &, Coakley, C.G. (2000). Listening education in the 21st century. *International Journal of Listening, 14,* 143–153.

2. McCracken, S. (2006). Listening and new approaches to the creation of communication centers. *International Journal of Listening, 20,* 60–61.

3. Eadie, W. F. (July 15, 1989). Hearing what we ought to hear. *Vital Speeches of the Day, 55*(19), 587–588.

4. Harris, J.A. (2003). Learning to listen across cultural divides. *Listening Professional, 2*(1), 4–21. Retrieved from Communication and Mass Media Complete database.

5. Imhof, M. (1998). What makes a good listener? Listening behavior in instructional settings. *International Journal of Listening, 12,* 81–105.

6. Bierck, R. (2001, January). How to listen. *Harvard Management Communication Letter, 4*(1), 45.

7. Harris, R.M. (2006). *The listening leader: Powerful new strategies for becoming an influential communicator.* Westport, CT: Praeger Publishers/Greenwood Publishing.

8. Glaser, J.E. (2004, August). Precision listening. *Executive Excellence, 2l* (8), 9–10. Retrieved August 25, 2008, from Business Source Premier database.

9. Pearce, C.G., Johnson, I.W., & Barker, R.T. (2003, January). Assessment of the Listening Styles Inventory. *Journal of Business and Technical Communication, 17*(1), 84–113.

10. Become a better listener. (2007, April). *Community Banker.* Retrieved from Business Source Premier database.

11. Brody, M. (2005, March). Learn to listen. *Pharmaceutical Representative, 35*(3), 31.

12. International Listening Association (2008). www.listen.org.

13. deLisser, P. (2004, Summer) Listening training: A professional communication coach reveals his formula for designing a workshop on listening to difficult messages. *Listening Professional, 3*(1), 8–10.

14. McDaniel, T. (2007, April). The power of listening. *Academic Leader, 23*(4), 8.

15. Worthington, D.L. (2005). Exploring the relationship between listening style preference and verbal aggressiveness. *International Journal of Listening, 19,* 3–11.

16. Major, R., Fitzmaurice, S., Bunta, F., & Balasubramanian, C. (2005). Testing the effects of regional, ethnic, and international dialects of English on listening comprehension. *Language Learning, 55*(1), 37–69.

17. Starosta, W. & Chen, G. (2005, January). Intercultural listening: Collected reflections, collated refractions. *International & Intercultural Communication Annual, 28,* 274–285.

18. Horrigan, J.B. (2007, May 7). *A typology of information and communication technology users.* Washington, DC: Pew Internet & American Life Project.

19. Janusik, L. &, Wolvin, A. (2006) *24 hours in a day: A listening update to the time studies.* Paper presented at the meeting of the International Listening Association, Salem, OR.

20. Harris Poll #51 (2007, June 7). *Cell phones widely used by those under 30.* Retrieved from http://www.harrisinteractive.com/harris_poll/index.asp?PID=767.

21. Detz, J. (2007, July/August), Tips for a more powerful presentation. *State Legislatures, 33*(7), 72–73.

22. Lauer, C.S. (2002). Be prepared. *Modern Healthcare, 32*(6), 26.

23. Petrini, C. (1990, September). A survival guide to public speaking. *Training & Development Journal, 44* (9), 15–24. Retrieved from Business Source Premier database.

24. Morreale, S.P., Spitzberg, B.H., & Barge, J.K. (2007). *Human communication: Motivation, knowledge, and skills* (2nd ed.). Belmont, CA: Thomson Wadsworth.

25. Monroe, M. & Nelson, K. (2004). The value of assessing public perceptions: Wildland fire and defensible space. *Applied Environmental Education and Communication: An International Journal, 3*(2), 109–117.

26. Johannessen, R.L. (2001). *Ethics in human communication* (5th ed.). Prospect Heights, IL: Waveland.

27. Bitzer, L.F. (1968, Winter). The rhetorical situation. *Philosophy & Rhetoric, 1*(1), 1–14.

28. Redding, C.W. (1947, October). Audience analysis. *Western speech, 11*(3), 19–20.

29. Yook, E.L. (2004). Any questions? Knowing the audience through question types. *Communication Teacher, 18*(3), 91–93.

30. Dance, F. & Zak-Dance, C. (2007). *Voice, speech, and thought.* Dallas, Texas: Fountainhead Press, pp. 38–44.

31. Bennett, M. J. (1994). A developmental model of intercultural sensitivity. *Perry Network Newsletter, 16*(1), 6–7. See also www.idrinstitute.org.

PART TWO:
PREPARING A SPEECH

In Part One, you learned about communication in general and public speaking competence in particular. We also discussed the importance of listening and audience analysis to public speaking. Part Two now builds on the discussion about analyzing your listeners by focusing on four critical competencies for preparing speeches.

Effective preparation has a direct and significant impact on how well your speech is received by the audience. One early research study, involving 119 public speaking students just like you, investigated the relationship between preparation and public speaking performance.[1] The actual quality of students' speech performances was related directly to students' total preparation time, including: time spent preparing a visual aid, the number of times the speech was rehearsed before an audience, the amount of time spent rehearsing silently and out loud, and the amount of research conducted. Students who spent more time on all of these preparation activities got better grades on their speeches than students who spent less time. A more recent study came up with the same findings; overall preparation and practice time correlate significantly with higher speech grades.[2] The lesson is clear: Preparation is an important part of public speaking competence. Four steps, vital in the preparation process, are explored in Part Two:

- Chapter 5: Choosing and Narrowing a Speech Topic: Competency One
- Chapter 6: Developing a Purpose and Thesis Statement: Competency Two
- Chapter 7: Researching and Supporting Your Speech: Competency Three
- Chapter 8: Organizing and Outlining Your Speech: Competency Four

5

CHOOSING AND NARROWING
A SPEECH TOPIC: COMPETENCY ONE

- **Finding a Good Topic**
    Subject Area versus Topic
    Personal Resources
    Internet and Databases
- **Adapting Topic to Audience and Occasion**
    Adapting to the Listeners
    Adapting to the Occasion and Narrowing
    to Time Constraints

"Let thy speech be better than silence, or be silent." Dionysius of Halicarnassus, Greek historian and teacher of rhetoric, c. 60 BC–after 7 BC

• • •

In the third week of the public speaking class, most students faced a common problem— choosing a good topic for their next speech assignment. They had already presented impromptu speeches on some pretty funny topics and then there was the speech of self-introduction. It was fairly easy to stand up and talk about yourself. But for the next speech, their first challenge was to figure out a topic other students would find interesting. Hana was concerned that the first topics she came up with would not impress her classmates. Given her Asian background, her first thought was to talk about the immigration process her family recently experienced. She wondered if the other students she was getting to know in the class—Angelique, Zak, Richard, Kumar, Mario, and LaTisha—would appreciate a speech about immigration. Richard, the police officer, drew on his personal experiences when he talked about crime statistics; but the other students seemed bored by that topic. Maybe she could go with immigration but figure out how to focus the topic by analyzing the audience's possible interest in it. Hana thought to herself: "When all else fails, read the textbook! Chapter 5 might help me find a different topic or figure out how to adapt immigration in an effective way for my new friends."

• • •

Hana is on the right track. Choosing and narrowing a topic is the first public speaking competency for a good reason. If you choose, narrow, and adapt a topic effectively for the particular audience, your speech is far more likely to be well received. This is not some brand new idea in the 21st century. In Chapter 2, we talked about classical rhetoric as the centuries-old foundation of competent public speaking. The great Roman orator, Cicero, outlined **five principles or canons for public speaking**: invention, arrangement, style, memory, and delivery. Invention and arrangement are the classical equivalent of the speech preparation steps. Likewise, style, memory, and delivery are the classical equivalent of speech presentation. The key point here is that **invention** comes first and calls for discovering or inventing what you will say creatively—the content of your speech.[3] Moreover, the first step in inventing what you will say is finding a good

....
5.1 THE FIVE PRINCIPLES OR CANONS FOR PUBLIC SPEAKING are invention, arrangement, style, memory, and delivery.

....
5.2 INVENTION calls for discovering or inventing what you will say creatively—the content of your speech.

topic. **Arrangement** then focuses on how you arrange or organize what you say in your speech. But we're getting ahead of ourselves. For now, let's think about Hana's concern about just finding a good topic for her speech. Based on what you and

....
5.3 ARRANGEMENT focuses on how you arrange or organize what you say in a speech.

Hana learn in this chapter, you will be able to: *choose and narrow a topic appropriately for the audience and occasion/situation.* This is Competency One and it includes the ability to:

- Choose and focus a topic that is clearly consistent with the purpose of the speech.
- Adapt the topic based on insightful analysis of the audience.
- Narrow the topic based on time constraints for the speech.
- Adapt the topic and speech to the speaking occasion.

FINDING A GOOD TOPIC

Let's start with some solid advice from an American legend in public speaking. Dale Carnegie was a writer, lecturer, and developer of famous courses in self-improvement, salesmanship, and public speaking. Born in poverty on a farm in Missouri, Carnegie was the author of *How to Win Friends and Influence People*, first published in 1936.[4] The book became an international bestseller and by the time of Carnegie's death, it had sold five million copies in 31 languages, and 450,000 people had graduated from the Dale Carnegie Institute. It has been said that Carnegie critiqued over 150,000 speeches during his days in the adult education movement.

According to Carnegie, *the key to a successful public speech is speaking on the right topic.* He goes further and provides us with an effective formula for identifying the right topic.[5] Carnegie's three easy pieces of advice are as follows:

- Know the topic well.
- Care about the topic.
- Have a strong desire to tell the audience about it.

The way Carnegie puts it, you have to earn the right to talk about your topic, you have to be passionate about the topic, and you must have a burning desire to talk about it. If you are not convinced Carnegie is right, consider the advice of another notable author from the communication discipline. John Brilhart noted a correlation between the subject of a speech, the speaker's personal involvement with the topic, and the effectiveness of the speech.[6] He said the main factor to consider in choosing a topic to talk about is to be vitally interested in it.

Think back to a speech that really impressed you; it could be a political talk, a class lecture, or maybe a religious sermon. You can bet the speaker knew the topic well and was highly motivated to talk about it to the audience. Here are some advantages of this approach. If you know a lot about the topic, you will be confident about what you know and therefore not easily distracted from delivering the speech. If you care a lot about it, you will be less aware of yourself and more concerned about getting your message across to the listeners. As a result, your anxiety level will be lower. You will be more enthusiastic and that enthusiasm will be contagious and motivate the audience to get involved and pay attention. But how do you know if you know enough about a topic? At a minimum, you need to know more about it than most of the audience members.

What about Hana and the immigration topic? Yes, she probably knows more about immigration than her classmates, but does it sound to you like she has a burning desire to tell the audience about it? As you consider Dale Carnegie's good advice, here are some suggestions to help you find a good topic.

SUBJECT AREA VERSUS TOPIC

To begin to locate a speech topic, it is first necessary to understand the difference between a general subject area and a speech topic. A **subject area** is a general area of knowledge such as communication, college life, sports, or organic chemistry. A **topic** is a specific facet or aspect of a subject area. The subject of communication could be narrowed down to many topics for a public speaking class, such as: "Overcoming anxiety," "Communication on a first date," or "Improving communication in parent–child relationships." For organic chemistry, a speech topic could be: "What's in our drinking water here in Central City?" The subject area of Hana's speech was immigration. Based on analyzing her audience's needs and interests, the aspect of immigration she could focus on might be: "The impact of increased immigration on college life in the United States."

5.4 A SUBJECT AREA is a general area of knowledge such as college life, communication, sports, or organic chemistry.

5.5 A TOPIC is a specific facet or aspect of a subject area.

5.6 MASS APPEAL SUBJECT AREAS are those most people probably will find of some interest, such as historical subjects, critical issues and controversial subjects, and widely accepted principles.

Several general types of subject areas have potential for what we might call **mass appeal**; most people probably will find them of some interest. For instance, researchers have found over time that historical perspectives on a topic have proven effective in speech classrooms.[7] From a general subject in U.S. history like the civil war, you could choose a topic with appeal to the local audience, such as: "The impact of the civil war on our community." If your audience is mostly females, you could choose the general subject area of women's rights and consider one particular historical figure like Susan B. Anthony. In the 1800s, women in the United States had few legal rights and did not have the right to vote. Susan B. Anthony gave a speech about her arrest for casting an illegal vote in the presidential election of 1872, based on being a woman. She was tried and then fined $100 but refused to pay. The challenge with this or any historic topic is focusing it so it seems relevant to your contemporary audience. You could ask the students listening to the Susan B. Anthony speech whether they voted in the last election; and if so, were they fined $100?

Another type of subject area that has stood the test of time is speeches on critical issues, also referred to as controversial speech subjects.[8] While the analysis of a current critical issue or controversial topic could satisfy Carnegie's three criteria—you know or could learn a lot about it, you care about it, and you want to talk about it—giving such a speech is challenging. As a speaker you need to delve deeply into all sides of the controversial topic and present all you learn respectfully and without bias. You need to include the various dominant perspectives or ways of looking at the topic. Also, as with historic speeches, you need to consider whether the issue is relevant to your listeners. Hana's speech about immigration has the potential for being a controversial topic because not everyone sees the issue in the same way.

A last type of subject area that may work for you comes to us from a hundred years ago. In 1919, an anonymous author offered tips on selecting speech topics in one of the few national communication journals being published at that time. In Box 5.1, the author suggests selecting a topic based on a widely accepted principle, such as: "Valuing freedom and democracy." The language and wording definitely sounds like it was written a long time ago, but the advice still holds true today.

Box 5.1: 100-Year-Old Advice on Topic Selection

About 100 years ago, an anonymous author advised selecting a subject based upon a widely accepted principle, one most audience members probably would agree with. Given it was 1919, there is no mention of mass media or the Internet!

How to Select a Subject for a Speech: Lesson 164

When you are in doubt on what subject to speak, select one that is based upon a widely accepted principle. This gives you three advantages:

1. You will be at harmony with most of your hearers.
2. You will have a broad field on which to speak.
3. You will have a subject of commanding importance.

Here are some directions on finding subjects. You should note topics suggested by the following:

1. Current events
2. Recent speeches
3. Recent books
4. Recent plays
5. How men (or women) express differences of opinion
6. Recent demands of labor
7. Recent plans for public improvement
8. Recent plans for national development
9. Foreign relations
10. New educational plans

Source: How to select a subject for speech. (1919, Oct). *Quarterly Journal of Speech Education, 5*(4), 392–399.

PERSONAL RESOURCES

Often students in public speaking classes struggle with choosing topics, because they don't think their own experiences and interests are significant enough to talk about with a public audience. But as Dale Carnegie tells us, a good topic is one that appeals to you and, because you're interested in it, you'll prepare and present a better speech. To thoroughly explore your own experiences and interests for a possible topic, marketing experts recommend using personal brainstorming to spark creativity and inspiration. This means thinking imaginatively about your own interests and writing down everything that comes to mind that you do and like. Then examine the list for a subject area of interest and a topic within it. You also could use this brainstorming technique by talking with a group of your classmates to come up with possible topics. You may think your personal background is not of interest to others, but other students may see your life experiences differently.

Besides searching your own mind and experiences for a topic, there are other resources that may suggest a possible topic. Browse through newspapers, magazines, and books at the local bookstore or library. If a topic catches your eye and strikes you as interesting, chances are that others will find it interesting as well. Or look for a topic idea by talking with friends and family about current events taking place locally, nationally, or internationally, and watch the news on TV for events that may suggest a topic.

INTERNET AND DATABASES

If you're still out of ideas, you could try using the Internet to find a topic. Go to any of the websites on the Internet that includes what is called an **idea generator**. These sites help you explore various subject areas as well as actual topic ideas. An easy-to-use website that contains an idea directory is located at: http://www.lib.odu.edu/libassist/idea/index.php. At this site, you can search any one of these main categories or subject areas: Arts & Humanities (history, literature, religion, etc.), Business & Public Administration, Education, Engineering & Technology, Health Sciences, Physical & Biological Sciences, Psychology, Social Sciences (criminal justice, women's studies, etc.) Sports, or Recreation & Leisure. For each subject area, there are hundreds of topic ideas provided. Figure 5.1 shows the list of possible topics provided for the social sciences subject area on this website.

5.7 AN IDEA GENERATOR is a website that helps you explore various subject areas as well as actual topic ideas.

If you're still unsure of topics your listeners will find appealing, take a look at this website: http://www.famous-speeches-and-speech-topics.info/speech-topics/index.htm. It lists different types of speeches and then the top topics for each speech type. You will find 100 topics for persuasive speeches, 100 for informative speeches, 50 each for demonstration speeches, funny speeches, interesting speeches, and tribute speeches, and 25 of what they call "fun speech topics." Finally, you could use your school library's research databases; click on the Wordlist, Subject Guide, Index, Thesaurus, or Visual Search (in EBSCOhost databases) for topic ideas. Enter a word or phrase to see an array of related or more specific subjects.

These websites and databases provide many more topics than you possibly could use, literally an abundance of possible subjects and topics. Take the time to peruse them and find a topic that appeals to you and you can get excited about. Trust your intuition, but then check it out with your course instructor and other students in the class before finalizing a choice of topic. Whatever topic you choose, it must be adapted for the particular audience and speaking occasion.

ADAPTING TOPIC TO AUDIENCE AND OCCASION

To adapt a topic competently, you decide on an approach to it that will appeal to your listeners and that will be sensitive to any constraints in the particular speaking situation and occasion. Chapter 4 provided details about conducting audience analysis in general. Given the importance of this step to the success of your speech, we start here with a quick review of the audience analysis process as it relates to adapting a topic to an audience.

Figure 5.1: Finding a Speech Topic Using an Idea Generator

At idea generator websites, you explore an array of subject areas and possible speech topics for each subject area. Here's an example of a list of topics that fall under the subject area of social sciences. You'll find ideas you may not think of without this kind of help.

abortion
abuse in nursing homes
abuse, ignored
Affirmative Action
airport searches of passengers and bags
Al-Qaeda
American consumerism
Animal rights
Arab-Israeli relations
baby "dumping"
Barbie doll's influence
birth control Borstal system
bracelets to support causes
capital punishment as a deterrent
Catholic priests and sexual abuse
charity scams
childproof handguns
CIA
civility in the cell phone era
computer crime
conspiracies
couch surfing
crack houses
curfew for teenagers
death penalty
digital divide
domestic violence
drug rehabilitation in prisons
drug use in pregnancy: prosecute?
drunk drivers & MADD
elections—unusual outcomes
embedded reporting
equal rights in employment
equitable access to the Internet
espionage
fads
families
famine
female genital mutilation
fetal rights
forensic evidence

foster homes
fraud
free speech on the Internet
gangs
gender stereotypes in film
gender-neutral language
glass ceiling (women vs. men, salary gap)
globalization
gun control
hate groups
hobo life in America
Holocaust survivors
homeland security
homeless
human gene map—social implications
human sterilization
humor
identity theft
illegal drug use
international terrorism
Internet
Internet addiction
interracial adoptions
Iraq War
Ku Klux Klan
latch key children
laughter
legalization of marijuana
lesbian & gay marriages
lesbian & gay parenting
lethal injection vs. electric chair
literacy
lobbyists
lotteries
love in cyberspace
"makeover" phenomenon on TV
marriage, history of
massacres on campus
military tribunals
military uniforms
missile defense

nepotism
nuclear warfare
nudists
nursing homes, abuse
off-track betting
organized crime
parenting
partial-birth abortion
Patriot Act
peace movement
plagiarism
plea bargaining = justice?
polygamy & polyandry
pornography
poverty
prisons—build more?
prisons: do they create criminal personalities?
privacy rights
prostitution
Puerto Rico: independence?
puppy mills
racial profiling
radical feminism
raising children
"rave" phenomenon
reality TV programs
religious symbols in public places
riots
rituals
same sex parents adopting
scams
seat belt use
serial killers
sexual harassment
Should Quebec be independent?
single-parent families
slavery
social networking
sodomy laws
stalking
stereotypes
support groups

Continued on next page

Continued from previous page

surrogate mothers	U.S. budget balancing	witness protection program
taboos	undercover FBI agents	women in combat
Taliban	underground railroad	women in non-traditional roles
talk shows	Utopia	women in WW II
terrorism tactics & effects	violence in sports, on TV, etc.	women suffrage
torture as punishment	voting procedures—problems	work/life ratio
troubled Northern Ireland	welfare reform	working poor
tsunami: effects & reactions	"whistle-blowers"	

Source: Retrieved from http://www.lib.odu.edu/libassist/idea/index.php.

ADAPTING TO THE LISTENERS

You first consider the listeners' personal demographics and cultural and psychological characteristics. Demographics include the listeners' ages, household types they live in, occupations, income, and education levels. Cultural characteristics include the groups they were born into—sex, race, ethnicity, region or country of origin; and, the groups they grew up in—religious, political, and other clubs or organizations. Psychological characteristics include the listeners' needs and motivations and their beliefs, attitudes, and values.

An advantage of adapting your topic to these characteristics of your audience is that it will help you limit and focus what you'll cover in the speech. If the topic seems too broad, think about what the audience really needs or wants to know about it. Also consider the level of explanation necessary for them to understand it. Finally, consider how much background description you'll need to include in order for them to appreciate the topic. Even experienced speakers often fail to narrow and focus their topics and therefore the content of their speeches might seem too broad. They think each tiny bit of information is so critical they need to pack it all in.

Hana's possible speech about immigration at the beginning of this chapter is an example of a subject area that needs to be narrowed and focused as a speech topic, and then adapted to her particular audience. Using immigration as a key word in an idea generator, Hana comes up with eight possible topics:

1. Immigration issues and arguments
2. Illegal immigration
3. Immigration services
4. U.S. immigration
5. Immigration history
6. Immigration forms
7. Immigration law
8. Immigration statistics

Of these eight topics, Hana may settle on the fourth one as a speech topic and talk about: "Her personal experiences with U.S. immigration." Then the challenge is adapting the topic in an interesting way for Angelique, Zak, Richard, Kumar, Mario, LaTisha and her other classmates. She realizes Frank Dance is right that she needs to decenter and move away from her self-centered view of the immigration topic.[9] To get that done, Hana decides to conduct an informal classroom poll asking open-ended and closed questions to ascertain the audience's attitudes, knowledge, and interest in immigration.[10] Then she will need to adapt the topic to the occasion and speaking situation and narrow it to any time constraints.

ADAPTING TO THE OCCASION AND NARROWING TO TIME CONSTRAINTS

Adapting a topic competently to the **public speaking occasion** includes considering any factors that will affect how you narrow and focus the topic such as time constraints, the actual physical situation, and the speaking event itself.

A common mistake public speakers make is failing to narrow their speech topic enough, which results in a speech that contains too much information and is way too long. When the speech is presented, the speaker has to race through to cover everything. Beyond fitting in the time limit, narrowing the topic also simplifies the preparation process. A speech topic that isn't narrow enough is difficult to research because it's unmanageably broad. However, when you present your speech,

5.8 THE PUBLIC SPEAKING OCCASION includes any factors that will affect how you narrow and focus the topic such as time constraints, the actual physical situation, and the speaking event itself.

if it's narrow and focused, your listeners will find it easier to understand and follow. On the other hand, a poorly narrowed and focused speech topic tends to sound like the speaker is rambling aimlessly on and on. You narrow a topic by getting more and more specific about what you will cover until it reaches a manageable level, and you're certain it can be covered adequately in the time allot-

Figure 5.2: Narrowing a subject area and topic to conform to time limits

Hana may have narrowed her speech topic in the following manner.

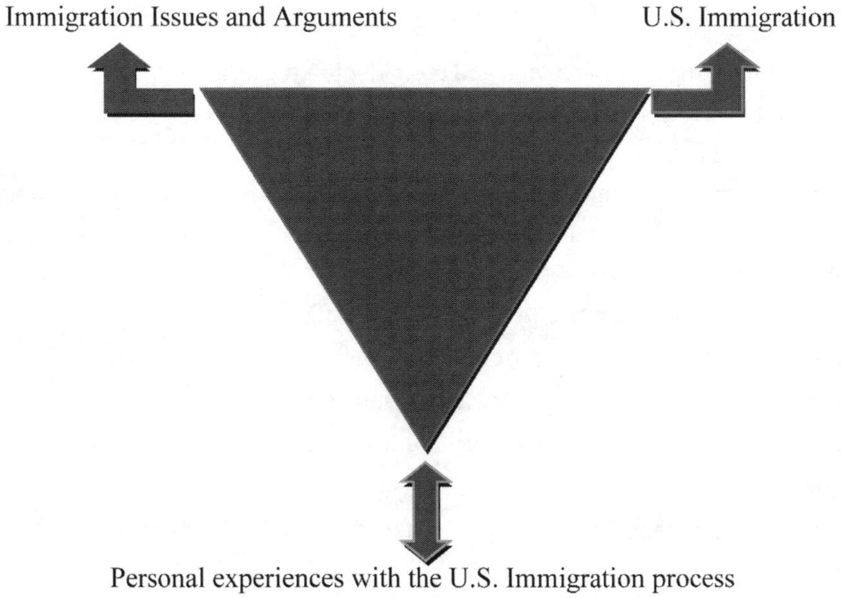

Immigration Issues and Arguments   U.S. Immigration

Personal experiences with the U.S. Immigration process

ted. Figure 5.2 shows how Hana could narrow her topic so it's not too broad and she can present it in the allotted amount of time.

In addition to time limits, you also need to consider how the actual physical situation (the place where the speech is presented) may impact your speech and its topic. If you are presenting in a large auditorium, a topic requiring a display of photographs of Hana's family going through customs would not work. If the room you present in has low-quality technology support, you may not want to develop your topic in a way that requires extensive use of video clips from YouTube. A later chapter focuses specifically on the use of technology in your presentations.

Finally, you should consider the speaking event itself and what is appropriate for that particular occasion. Right now, you probably are speaking in a public speaking class. In the future, you may be called on to present briefings or trainings at work or a few remarks to commemorate a special event like toasting the happy couple at a wedding or honoring someone with a eulogy at a funeral service. Needless to say, what is appropriate and how to focus your topic will be affected by the differences in these speaking events. The last chapter of this book provides more guidelines for speaking at work and at special occasions. For now, remember that how you adapt and focus your topic needs to work well given the time constraints, the physical situation, and the speaking event itself. While this may seem like a lot of attention to detail, details gone awry will ruin the very best of speeches.

This chapter emphasized the importance of what often is a neglected public speaking competency: Choosing and narrowing a topic appropriately for the audience and occasion. In Chapter 6, we will consider the next preparation competency: Communicating the thesis/specific purpose of your speech to the audience.

Things To Do: Competency One

Review this *Things To Do* list for choosing and narrowing a topic for your next speech. Have you done the following?

1. Started with a general subject area and then identified a topic in it. ☐
2. Considered a topic you know well, care about, and have a strong desire to tell the audience about. ☐
3. Considered a topic with mass appeal—such as a historical, critical issue, or controversial topic. ☐
4. Considered a topic that draws on your own personal experiences. ☐
5. Used an idea generator on the Internet to find a topic. ☐
6. Adapted the topic to the listeners' demographics. ☐
7. Adapted the topic to the listeners' cultural characteristics. ☐
8. Adapted the topic to the listeners' psychological characteristics. ☐
9. Narrowed the topic to the time constraints. ☐
10. Considered the impact of the situation on how you develop and present the topic. ☐

CHAPTER SUMMARY

Choosing, narrowing, and adapting a topic effectively results in a speech being well received by the audience. The Roman orator, Cicero agreed and wrote about five canons for public speaking: invention, arrangement, style, memory, and delivery. Invention calls for discovering or inventing what you will say creatively—the content of your speech. Arrangement focuses on how you arrange or organize what you say in your speech. Similarly, Dale Carnegie emphasizes speaking on the right topic as key to a successful speech. He says identifying the right topic should be based on knowing the topic well, caring about it, and having a strong desire to talk to the audience about it. Suggestions for choosing a good topic start with  understanding the difference between a general subject area and a speech topic and being aware of several types of subjects with mass appeal: historical, critical issues and controversial subjects, and subjects based on a widely accepted principle. Personal resources for finding a topic include exploring your own experiences and interests, browsing newspapers, magazines, and books, or talking with friends and family about current events. Other sources of subject and topic ideas are websites on the Internet with idea generators and databases in school libraries. After choosing a topic, then it must be adapted for the particular audience based on the listeners' personal demographics and cultural and psychological characteristics. The topic also needs to be narrowed to fit time constraints and adapted to the occasion including the actual physical situation and the speaking event itself.

KEY TERMS

The key terms below are defined in this chapter and presented alphabetically with definitions in the Glossary at the end of the book.

- canons of public speaking
- invention
- arrangement
- subject area

- topic
- mass appeal
- idea generator
- public speaking occasion

BUILDING COMPETENCE ACTIVITIES

INDIVIDUAL ACTIVITIES

1. Use the brainstorming techniques described in this chapter to identify a possible speech topic for an informative speech. Do the same thing for a possible speech topic for a persuasive speech.
2. Search the Internet and visit one of the websites containing an idea generator. Identify one subject area and a topic in that subject area that fits Carnegie's three pieces of advice for choosing a speech topic. The section about speech topics at Speechmaster.com is a good start point on the Internet for researching and finding a speech topic electronically. Go to: http://www.speechmastery.com/speech-topics.html.

3. On the Internet, visit this website that lists 14 questions to ask yourself in order to discover a personal experience speech topic. Answer the questions and see what speech topic you come up with. Go to http://www.speech-topics-help.com/personal-experience-speech-topics html.

4. Talk with your family members about their opinions of current events and develop a list of three speech topics for your next speech.

5. When speeches are next presented in class, evaluate how effectively each student chose, adapted, and narrowed his or her topic for the speech to the audience and situation.

GROUP ACTIVITIES

1. In groups of three to four students, use the brainstorming techniques described in this chapter to identify a possible speech topic for each student for an informative speech. Do the same thing for a persuasive speech.

2. With a partner, visit a website on the Internet containing an idea generator. Have each person identify one subject area and a topic in that subject area that fits Carnegie's three pieces of advice for choosing a speech topic. Critique the other person's choice of a topic.

3. In groups of three to four students, have each student identify a possible topic for the next speech assignment. Then determine an approach to each topic, adapting it based on audience analysis of the class.

4. When speeches are next presented in class, after the speeches meet with a group of three to four students to evaluate how effectively each student chose, adapted, and narrowed his or her topic for the speech to the audience and situation. Develop a list of recommendations for everyone in the group regarding this public speaking competency.

COMPETENCY CHECKPOINTS AND SELF-ASSESSMENT TOOL

Here is what you need to know and be able to do in order to competently select a topic for a speech. Determine your level of competency and whether you are ready to proceed to the next chapter. Give yourself one point for each checkpoint you answer satisfactorily.

COMPETENCY CHECKPOINTS	NUMBER OF POINTS
KNOWLEDGE 1. Explain why choosing a topic is an important competency when preparing a speech. 2. Describe Dale Carnegie's approach to identifying the right topic for a speech. 3. What is the difference between a subject area and speech topic? 4. What are the main considerations when adapting a speech topic to a particular audience and situation?	
SKILLS 1. Identify several different sources of topic ideas you could use to help find a good speech topic. 2. Locate several websites on the Internet you could use to help find a good speech topic. 3. Develop a list of possible speech topics that would be appropriate for your public speaking class.	

ETHICS AND CREDIBILITY 1. What would an ethical approach to a controversial speech topic entail? 2. What would an unethical approach to a critical issues topic entail? 3. Does adapting a speech topic to a particular audience reflect on the credibility of the speaker? How so?	
TOTAL CHECKPOINTS (OUT OF A POSSIBLE TEN POINTS)	

ENDNOTES

1. Menzel, K.E. & Carrell, L.J. (1994). The relationship between preparation and performance in public speaking. *Communication Education, 43,* 17–26.

2. Pearson, J.C., Child, J.T., & Kahl, D.H. (2006). Preparation meeting opportunity: How do college students prepare for public speeches? *Communication Quarterly, 54*(3), 351–366.

3. Kauffeld, F.J. (1997). Rhetorical invention and the speaker's selections of arguments. *Argument in a time of change, Tenth SCA/AFA Conference on Argumentation,* 35–39.

4. Carnegie, D. (1936). *How to win friends and influence people.* New York: Simon and Schuster.

5. The Dale Carnegie approach to public speaking. (2005, June 4). *The Toronto Star,* p. D-11.

6. Brilhart, J. (1957, November). What shall I talk about … ?. *Today's Speech, 5*(4), 19–20.

7. Bohlken, R. (1971). A petition for prescribed speech subjects in public speaking class. *Speech Teacher, 20*(3), 215–217.

8. Hugenberg, L.W. & O'Neill, D.J. (1987). Identifying critical issue speech topics utilizing the nominal group technique. ERIC #ED280091.

9. Dance, F. & Zak-Dance, C. (2007). *Voice, speech, and thought.* Dallas, Texas: Fountainhead Press, pp. 38–44.

10. Yook, E.L. (2004). Any questions? Knowing the audience through question types. *Communication Teacher, 18*(3), 91–93.

6

DEVELOPING A PURPOSE AND THESIS STATEMENT: COMPETENCY TWO

- **Developing the General Purpose, Specific Purpose, and Thesis Statement**
  - General Purpose
  - Specific Purpose
  - Thesis Statement
- **Writing the Thesis Statement**
- **Using the Thesis to Prepare**
- **Positioning the Thesis in the Speech**

"If you can't write your message in a sentence, you can't say it in an hour."
Dianna Booher, author and lecturer, b. 1948

• • •

Hana and Angelique were glad to learn about the basics of public speaking, like start-
ing with choosing a topic based on audience analysis. Angelique told Hana she thought
it was like learning the basics of skiing before she could take off like a hotdog down
the slope. Hana didn't quite get the analogy to a hotdog since learning to ski was not
a priority in her native country, China. Nonetheless, both students agreed they would
do a better job and be less nervous if they carefully narrowed and focused their speech
topics for the next informative speech. Hana asked her friend: "So what's next? I'm talk-
ing about my family's immigration to the United States. What's your topic?" Angelique
decided on non-Western rhetoric as a topic thinking it would appeal to the culturally
diverse group of students in the class. She would focus the topic on Eastern rhetoric
in countries like China and Japan. Having a friend like Hana would give her firsthand
insights and maybe a few examples. Angelique replied to Hana: "If you really think
we should follow the four preparation competencies in order, then our next step is to
develop a purpose and thesis statement for our speeches. According to this chapter,
the audience should understand the specific purpose of your speech within the open-
ing few sentences." Hana wondered to herself if that kind of directness was always a
good idea. The two friends decided to review the chapter one more time to be sure
they understood what to do about the thesis statement.

• • •

Hana and Angelique are to be commended for not rushing through the speech preparation process. It's very tempting to get something down on paper right away that you'll actually say in your
speech. But these two students realize that the people who developed the four preparation competencies know what they are doing. Both appreciate the importance of developing a speech purpose and communicating a thesis to listeners. However, Angelique agrees with communicating the
thesis/specific purpose to audience members early in the speech, but Hana does not. A comparison of the rhetorical heritage of the Eastern to Western rhetoric may explain their different reactions. As Chapter 2 told us, Western rhetoric—Angelique's tradition—highly values direct verbal
expression. By comparison, Eastern rhetoric—Hana's tradition—values indirectness. That explains
why Angelique favors positioning the thesis early in the speech so listeners know exactly what to

expect, and Hana is not sure about that approach. This chapter clarifies what a thesis is and where you should put it in the speech.

Based on what you learn in this chapter, you will be able to *communicate the thesis/specific purpose in a manner appropriate for the audience and occasion*. This is Competency Two and it includes the ability to:

- Develop a general purpose, specific purpose, and thesis statement for your speech that is exceptionally clear and identifiable.
- Use the thesis to help prepare the rest of the speech.
- Position the thesis most effectively in the speech.

DEVELOPING THE GENERAL PURPOSE, SPECIFIC PURPOSE, AND THESIS STATEMENT

Once you're satisfied with your speech topic, the next step in preparing any speech is to clarify what you hope to accomplish by speaking. All successful speeches are built around a clear purpose because, if you aren't clear about your purpose, you won't be able to achieve it. In addition, if you fail to develop a clear purpose and present a clear and identifiable thesis, your listeners won't understand what your speech is all about.[1] We begin our discussion of this competency by describing each of these elements—the general purpose, specific purpose, and thesis statement—and how they work together.

> 6.1 THE GENERAL PURPOSE is the overall goal of the speech, for example, to entertain and amuse the audience, to commemorate an occasion, or the more common general purposes are to inform or to persuade.

GENERAL PURPOSE

Speeches can have any one of several general purposes. The **general purpose** is the overall goal of the speech, for example, to entertain and amuse the audience, to commemorate an occasion, or the more common general purposes—to inform or to persuade. These general purposes were referred to in Chapter 2 as speech types. To reiterate, an informative speech has the purpose of communicating something new or a new perspective to an audience and moving listeners to greater understanding. If your purpose is to inform, you know you've achieved it when audience members understand the facts and information you present. A persuasive speech has the purpose of influencing an audience's attitudes, beliefs, values, or behaviors. If your purpose is to persuade the listeners to agree to do something or change their opinions, you know you've achieved it when they take the desired action or change their minds.

In the majority of public speaking classes, most of the speeches you present will have either the general purpose to inform or to persuade. Angelique's topic, non-Western or Eastern rhetoric, and Hana's topic, her family's immigration to the United States both sound like speeches to inform. But even though we are discussing these two purposes or types of speeches as if they are distinctly different from one another, that is not the case; most speeches are not purely informative, nor purely persuasive. To achieve the general purpose of an informative speech, you have to persuade the audience that you know what you're talking about. To accomplish the general purpose of a persuasive speech, you usually inform the audience using facts and evidence to support your argument.

SPECIFIC PURPOSE

Just as every speech has a general purpose, so too, every speech has its own **specific purpose,** which is a statement of the desired end result or response the speaker would like from the audience. As a speaker, you hope to have a specific effect on the audience. The specific purpose is whatever you want the audience to know, do, or feel, as a result of your speech. Angelique's speech about Eastern rhetoric provides an example. Notice that this specific purpose is written as a single infinitive statement summarizing exactly what the speech will achieve: An infinitive statement starts with "to...."

> **6.2 THE SPECIFIC PURPOSE is a statement of the desired end result or response the speaker would like from the audience.**

> To inform the audience about the contributions of Eastern rhetoric to our understanding of effective public speaking.

As this example illustrates, a good specific purpose is clear, realistic, and audience focused. Because it's clear, it can guide your work throughout the entire preparation process, letting you know exactly what to research and what to include in your speech. By being realistic, it limits your speech to what can be accomplished in the amount of time allowed. And, by being audience focused, it describes the exact response you want from the audience. If you have a problem deciding on the specific purpose for your speech, ask yourself the questions posed in Box 6.1.

THESIS STATEMENT

Building on the specific purpose, the next step is to formulate a thesis statement for your speech. The **thesis statement** is the central idea or claim of your speech, which you will say out loud to the

---

Box 6.1: Developing the Specific Purpose

Ask yourself these questions about your speech topic in order to develop a clear specific purpose.

- Why am I giving this speech?
- How can the audience benefit from what I have to say?
- What specific response do I want from the audience?
- If it's an informative speech, what do I want the audience to learn?
- If it's a persuasive speech, why do I want them to agree with me?

Write your answer down right here, as an infinitive statement, and then evaluate it by asking the next set of questions. _____

_____

_____

- Is this purpose reasonably clear and easy to understand?
- Does it include benefits for the audience?
- Is it realistic in terms of the expectations for the speaking assignment?
- Does it put limits on what I'll cover?

Source: Retrieved from http://www.unc.edu/depts/wcweb/handouts/speeches/html (August 9, 2009).

audience when you actually deliver the speech. It is the bottom line—the one main thing you want the audience to remember. At the heart of every effective speech is one important idea or message the audience should remember when your speech is done. It is written as a simple, declarative sentence (or two), and it restates the speech purpose clearly and relevantly for the particular audience. While you may formulate a thesis statement early in the speech development process, it is likely that you'll revise and reword it as you research your topic.

....
6.3 THE THESIS STATEMENT is the central idea or claim of your speech, which you will say out loud to the audience when you actually deliver the speech.

Angelique's speech about Eastern rhetoric illustrates how the thesis builds on and extends the specific purpose of a speech. In the following introductory paragraph for the speech, the actual thesis statement is italicized.

> During this class, we are all called upon to present the best speeches we possibly can and we are all in the same boat—looking for good advice wherever we can find it. *Today, I would like to make all of you aware of the unique and rich contributions of Eastern rhetoric to our understanding of how to present highly effective public speeches.*

On a less serious note, one author likens what he calls "the dreaded thesis statement" to his underwear.[2] He says that a thesis, like his underwear, "cannot be too brief. It has to be loose enough to hold a big idea, yet snug enough to keep him in focus….a thesis statement is a big idea boiled down to a single sentence." Let's now consider some simple steps for producing such a thesis statement.

WRITING THE THESIS STATEMENT

Writing the thesis statement is a useful part of preparation, because it helps clarify and organize possible main ideas or main points for the speech itself. Below are the steps to follow in order to transform the specific purpose of your speech into an effective and useful thesis statement:

1. First, examine the specific purpose you developed for your speech and list eight to ten main points you think would help to accomplish it. Obviously, even eight points are way too many for a short speech, but if you brainstorm lots of ideas, you won't overlook any important ones.
2. Look at the resulting list and combine related points and delete any that don't seem essential to accomplishing the purpose. Try to narrow the eight to ten points down to a minimum of two and a maximum of five main points, depending on the length of your speech.
3. Look at the two to five main points and compose a single declarative sentence that relates the points to each other and summarizes what you'll say in the speech. Phrase this thesis carefully, because it will set the tone for your speech and determine the reaction you'll get from the audience.

To clarify the speech preparation steps covered so far, Box 6.2 contains two examples of subject area, topic, purpose, and thesis statement.

Box 6.2: Understanding Topic, Purpose, and Thesis Statement

These two examples illustrate how students like you moved from a general subject area for a speech to having a clear thesis statement.

HANA'S SPEECH

1. Subject Area: Immigration

   Narrowed Topic: Personal experiences with U.S. immigration

   General Purpose: To inform

   Specific Purpose: To inform the listeners about how the immigration process works and its impact on college students in the U.S.

   Thesis Statement: Given the increasing number of international students and students emigrating to the U.S. from other countries, it is useful for all students at U.S. colleges and universities to be aware of the immigration process these students and their families have experienced.

ANGELIQUE'S SPEECH

2. Subject Area: Rhetoric and public speaking

   Narrowed Topic: The value of Eastern rhetoric to speakers in Western cultures

   General Purpose: To inform

   Specific Purpose: To inform the listeners about the contributions of Eastern rhetoric to our understanding of effective public speaking

   Thesis Statement: Today, I would like to make all of you aware of the potentially rich contributions of Eastern rhetoric to our understanding of how to present highly effective public speeches.

USING THE THESIS TO PREPARE

Developing the thesis statement definitely gets the speech preparation process off to a good start. Following the three steps for writing a thesis statement helps to decide on the main points and subpoints for your speech, and it suggests how you may want to organize the main points. In Box 6.3, Angelique's informative speech about Eastern rhetoric is used to illustrate this development process.

When you know your main points and subpoints, you also know what aspects of the speech topic need the most research. You can decide which main and subpoints will be informed by your own experiences and you can develop a research plan for the other main points. You will quickly realize that having a thesis and main points saves you time and energy by focusing your search for support materials. If you go to any library or electronic databases or the Internet with only a speech topic, or even worse with only a general subject area, you will be overwhelmed by the vast amount of information available on any topic. By contrast, with a thesis and main points in hand, you are able to zero in on what's relevant and ignore what is not. More advice on researching and finding support materials is presented in Chapter 7.

As you begin to research your main points, you may discover new information that suggests thinking differently about the thesis statement or how to organize the main points. An article or interview with an expert on your topic may cause you to rethink your approach to the topic. Suppose, for instance, Angelique finds a story about a U.S. diplomat in China who modified her rhetoric to be respectful of her Chinese counterparts. As a result, the diplomat was able to negotiate a policy agree-

Box 6.3: Writing the Thesis Statement and Starting to Prepare Your Speech

The specific purpose of Angelique's speech is to inform the audience about the contributions of Eastern rhetoric to understanding effective public speaking. Here are eight possible main points for the speech with an indication of how they resulted in two main points and a thesis statement for the speech.

ANGELIQUE'S EIGHT POSSIBLE MAIN POINTS

1. Why she became interested in non-Western rhetoric.
2. A description of Eastern rhetoric and its basic concepts.
3. A comparison of Eastern rhetoric to Western rhetoric.
4. Some examples of Eastern rhetoric.
5. What happens when Western rhetorical strategies are used in Eastern cultures.
6. What happens when Eastern rhetorical strategies are used in Western cultures.
7. How Western rhetoric could make use of concepts from Eastern rhetoric.
8. What benefits listeners might gain by incorporating Eastern rhetorical strategies in their speeches.

MAIN IDEA/MAIN POINT 1
The nature of Eastern rhetoric compared to Western
- Subpoint: A description of Eastern rhetoric and its basic concepts (2).
- Subpoint: A comparison of Eastern rhetoric to Western rhetoric (3).
- Subpoint: Examples of what happens when Eastern rhetorical strategies are used in Western cultures and Western rhetorical strategies are used in Eastern cultures (4, 5, and 6).

MAIN IDEA/MAIN POINT 2
How to use Eastern rhetorical strategies beneficially in speeches presented in Western cultures
- Subpoint: How Western rhetoric could incorporate concepts from Eastern rhetoric (7).
- Subpoint: What benefits speakers would gain by incorporating Eastern rhetorical strategies in their speeches (8).
- Subpoint: A call for listeners to try using some Eastern rhetorical strategies in their next speeches.

THE RESULTING THESIS STATEMENT

"Today, I would like to make all of you aware of the potentially rich contributions of Eastern rhetoric to our understanding of how to present highly effective public speeches."

ment others had failed to produce. Angelique might want to revise her main points and subpoints to ensure she has enough time to tell this story. So the lesson is to be open to revising the thesis statement until you are completely satisfied with it. It is far better to rethink a solid thesis or central idea, than to try to create a speech from scratch out of a random array of bits and pieces of information.

POSITIONING THE THESIS IN THE SPEECH

Think back to the story at the beginning of this chapter and Hana's concern about presenting the purpose and thesis statement within the opening few sentences of her speech. As you know, a Western approach to rhetoric says this is a good idea and an Eastern approach says it may not always be well advised. Obviously, we need some general guidelines for positioning and presenting the thesis to the listeners. Two factors affect the question of how and when to present the thesis—cultural preferences of the audience and their level of agreement or disagreement with the topic.

Regarding cultural preferences, as we already mentioned, a predominantly Western audience may expect the speaker to communicate a specific purpose and thesis statement in a clear and identifiable manner early, preferably in the introduction. Angelique's thesis, as written, would work fine:

> Today, I would like to make all of you aware of the potentially rich contributions of Eastern rhetoric to our understanding of how to present highly effective public speeches.

By comparison, a predominantly Eastern audience might prefer the thesis statement to be understated and presented more tentatively. Angelique could reword her thesis in this way:

> Today, I will describe the rhetorical strategies of two cultures—the West and the East. We will look at how public speakers like you might benefit from considering the use of some Eastern rhetorical strategies in your speeches.

This rewording of Angelique's thesis also could work if she thinks the audience may disagree somewhat with her central idea. When an audience is favorably disposed to a topic and central idea, presenting the thesis directly and early in the speech is all right. But if the audience is not favorably disposed to a central idea, then a less direct approach is often more effective. The speaker can forecast the thesis and central idea in the introduction but cannot take a strong stand until a case has been built by presenting the main and subpoints. If Angelique learns her audience doesn't favor cultures learning from one another, she could use the reworded and more tentative approach to her thesis.

....
6.4 THEME REINFORCERS are the points a speaker presents throughout the speech to support and reinforce the central idea they are trying to get across.

Finally, we need to think about effectively reinforcing the thesis or central idea throughout the speech. **Theme reinforcers** are the points a speaker presents throughout the speech to support and reinforce the central idea they are trying to get across.[3] The thought here is to return at the end of each main point to the theme you introduced in the thesis statement. Of course, you don't repeat the same exact words over and over; rather you restate the thesis as it relates to the particular main point. By continually restating the main idea, it is more likely the listeners will understand and appreciate the thesis and its relationship to each main point. Take a look again at Table 6.3 and Angelique's main points. Main point 1: The nature of Eastern rhetoric compared to Western. Her reinforcer could be: Given this comparison of Eastern and Western rhetoric, it's clear each culture could contribute some insights about effective public speaking to the other. Main point 2: How to use Eastern rhetorical strategies beneficially in speeches presented in Western cultures. Her reinforcer could be: Given these possible benefits, borrowing some rhetorical strategies from Eastern rhetoric may serve all of us quite well, not only here in this class, but whenever we present speeches in the future.

Angelique and Hana successfully developed good thesis statements for their speeches. In this chapter, you learned about the benefits of developing a clear specific purpose and thesis statement for any speech. If you follow the recommendations for writing a thesis, you will have main points and subpoints outlined and ready to go. Then you can proceed to Chapter 7 and learn about researching and gathering support materials for your next speech.

Things To Do: Competency Two

Review this *Things To Do* list for developing a specific purpose and thesis statement for your next speech. Based on the topic you have chosen, have you done the following?

1. Developed a specific purpose for the speech that is presented as an infinitive statement ☐ and is clear, realistic, and audience focused.
2. Written a thesis statement built on the specific purpose that tells the audience what ☐ you want them to know, understand, and remember when your speech is done.
3. Clarified the main points and subpoints as a result of writing the thesis statement. ☐
4. Developed a research plan based on the main points and subpoints. ☐
5. Determined the most effective positioning of the thesis in the speech based on the cul- ☐ tural preferences of the listeners and their level of agreement or disagreement with the central idea in the thesis.
6. Prepared theme reinforcers for each main point in the speech. ☐

CHAPTER SUMMARY

Three elements are critical to accomplishing Competency Two effectively: the general purpose, specific purpose, and thesis statement. The general purpose is the overall goal of the speech, for example, to entertain and amuse, to commemorate, or the more common general purposes in most public speaking classes, which are to inform or to persuade. The specific purpose is a statement of the desired end result or response the speaker would like from the audience. A good specific purpose is written as an infinitive statement and is clear, realistic, and audience focused. Building on the specific purpose, the thesis statement is the central idea or claim of your speech, which you say out loud to the audience when

you actually deliver the speech. The thesis statement is written as a simple, declarative sentence (or two) that restates the speech purpose for the audience. Writing the thesis helps to clarify and organize possible main ideas or main points for the speech itself. Knowing the main points and subpoints for the speech helps in searching for support materials for the speech. Based on new information from that research effort, sometimes the thesis statement or main points are revised. Cultural preferences of the audience and their level of agreement or disagreement with the topic affect positioning of the thesis in the speech and how it is presented to the listeners. Theme reinforcers are used throughout the speech to support and reinforce the central idea the speaker is trying to get across.

KEY TERMS

The key terms below are defined in this chapter and presented alphabetically with definitions in the Glossary at the end of the book.

- general purpose
- specific purpose

- thesis statement
- theme reinforcer

BUILDING COMPETENCE ACTIVITIES

INDIVIDUAL ACTIVITIES

1. When speeches are next presented in class, evaluate how effectively each student developed a purpose for the speech and presented a thesis statement.
2. Attend a public speech or presentation (it could be a lecture in another class), and see if you can identify the speaker's specific purpose and thesis. Were these two elements clear and identifiable?
3. Go to either one of these websites: http://www.wfu.edu/~louden/Political%20Communication/ Class%20Information/SPEECHES.html or http://www.csus.edu/indiv/k/kiddv/ComsSites/ speeches.html; both contain an array of public speeches. Choose a speech and identify in the speech the specific purpose and thesis statement. Write a short evaluation of how effectively these elements were presented. Include whether the speech contained theme reinforcers for the main points.

GROUP ACTIVITIES

1. When speeches are next presented in class, after the speeches, meet with a group of three to four students to evaluate how effectively each student developed a purpose for the speech and presented a thesis statement. Prepare a list of recommendations for everyone in the group regarding this public speaking competency.
2. With one or two other students, attend a public speech or presentation (it could be a lecture in another class in which you are all enrolled). Have each student individually identify the speaker's specific purpose and thesis. Compare notes after the lecture to see if you came up with the same purpose and thesis.
3. Form groups of three to four students and go to either of these websites: http://www.abacon. com/pubspeak/histsit.html, or http://www.mhhe.com/socscience/comm/new-home/; both contain an array of public speeches. Have each group member select a different speech and try to identify in the speech the specific purpose and the thesis statement. Compare how effectively these elements were presented in each speech. Include whether the speech contained theme reinforcers for the main points.
4. Choose a partner and have each student come up with a possible topic for the next speech assignment. Exchange topics and have each student go through the three steps for writing a thesis statement for the topic. Evaluate each other's work and provide feedback about it.

COMPETENCY CHECKPOINTS AND SELF-ASSESSMENT TOOL

Here is what you need to know and be able to do in order to competently develop a specific purpose and thesis statement for your speech. Determine your level of competency and whether you are ready to proceed to the next chapter. Give yourself one point for each checkpoint you answer satisfactorily.

COMPETENCY CHECKPOINTS	NUMBER OF POINTS
KNOWLEDGE 1. Define and describe the role of a general purpose and specific purpose in a speech. 2. Define and describe the role of a thesis statement in a speech. 3. Outline three steps to writing a thesis statement.	
SKILLS 1. Choose a possible topic for your next speech and develop a specific purpose for the topic. 2. Using that specific purpose, write a thesis statement for the topic using the three steps presented in this chapter. 3. Using the main ideas, the main points produced by writing the thesis, develop a research plan for the speech. 4. Using the main ideas and main points, write theme reinforcers for each main point in the speech.	
ETHICS AND CREDIBILITY 1. What would an ethical approach to developing a specific purpose call for a speaker to consider? 2. What would an ethical approach to developing a thesis statement call for a speaker to consider? 3. How could the development and presentation of a clear thesis statement reflect on the credibility of a speaker?	
TOTAL CHECKPOINTS (OUT OF A POSSIBLE TEN POINTS)	

ENDNOTES

1. Haluska, J.C. (2006). In defense of the formula essay. *Academic Questions, 20*(1), 46-55.

2. Frank, S. (2005, Jan.). I'll show you my underwear (or how to tackle the dreaded thesis statement). *Writing, 27*(4), 14–17.

3. Kelly, M. (2009). *Putting all the pieces together: Effective speech writing.* Retrieved from http://712educators.aboutcom/ cs/speeches/a/speechwriting_2/htm.

7

RESEARCHING AND SUPPORTING YOUR SPEECH: COMPETENCY THREE

- **Gathering Information**
  - Objective and Subjective Information
- **Types of Support Materials and Evidence**
  - Definitions and Descriptions
  - Facts and Statistics
  - Examples
  - Stories
  - Testimonies and Quotations
- **Using the Library and Electronic Databases**
  - Reference Books
  - Newspapers and Periodicals
  - Government Documents
- **Using the Internet**
- **Using Human Sources**
  - Personal Observations and Experiences
  - Informational Interviews
- **Evaluating and Citing Sources**
  - Using Critical Thinking to Evaluate Sources
  - Selecting and Using Support Materials
    That Enhance your Credibility
  - Citing Sources Correctly and Avoiding Plagiarism

"Say not always what you know, but always know what you say." Claudius Ptolemaeus, a Roman citizen, mathematician, and poet, c. AD 90–c.168

• • •

On the third day of the public speaking course, a speaker from the school library presented a lecture on using the library and its resources to gather support for the second round of informative speeches. The most helpful part was when she asked about the students' speech topics and then went into academic and business databases on the computer connected to the library to research the topics. She helped Hana find articles on immigration directly linked to her thesis statement and Angelique wanted sources on non-Western rhetoric. Then Kumar got his turn. He was good at research but was having trouble choosing among the articles on his topic—the influence of pop music on cultures around the world. Some of the support materials he found about the globalization of popular music were from questionable websites and he wasn't sure if those were ok to use. Plus, he didn't know how to reference the websites in his speech or speech outline. He knew it wasn't ethical to use any outside information without giving credit for it, but he was unsure how to do that in a speech or on his speech outline. The librarian talked with him about evaluating print and electronic sources and avoiding plagiarism when you speak publicly. She said Chapter 7 in the textbook would be a great resource for answering all of Kumar's questions.

Box 7.1: Kumar's Thesis Statement and Main Points

Based on preliminary research, Kumar identified these main points and a thesis for his speech.

MAIN IDEA/MAIN POINT 1:
POPULAR MUSIC IS BECOMING INCREASINGLY GLOBAL AND MULTICULTURAL.
- Subpoint: The emergence and influence of global media
- Subpoint: The globalization of pop music as a result of global media technology
- Subpoint: The influence worldwide of pop music on other cultures

MAIN IDEA/MAIN POINT 2:
GLOBAL POP MUSIC'S POTENTIAL TO PROMOTE MULTICULTURAL UNDERSTANDING
- Subpoint: How influential pop music is on young people
- Subpoint: How exposure to the music of other cultures promotes multicultural understanding
- Subpoint: Opportunities for bringing people together based on the globalization of pop music

THE RESULTING THESIS STATEMENT
"Popular music is highly influential around the world. In fact, pop music and all it represents have the capacity to become the stimulant and glue to bring people together and encourage multicultural understanding among cultures."

• • •

Kumar's topic is a good one and his questions for the librarian were just as good. He already had a thesis statement and two main points (see Box 7.1), and he knew from Chapter 6 how to use the main points to help gather information and find the right support materials. But this can be a challenge for anyone, because of the vast amount of information available these days on practically any topic. In fact, some say we are living in *an information explosion.* That may be true given all the resources available in libraries, to say nothing of what's at our fingertips on the Internet. As a result, choosing among all the articles, facts and figures, and websites related to your main points may seem like a daunting task. This chapter promises to organize this challenge for you and make it manageable.

Based on what you learn in this chapter, you will be able to: *provide supporting materials (including electronic and non-electronic presentational aids) appropriate to the audience and occasion.* This is Competency Three and it includes the ability to:

- Find and use support material, exceptional in quality and variety.
- Find and use support material that unquestionably enhances the clarity of your speech.
- Link the supporting material clearly to the thesis of your speech.
- Use support material that decidedly enhances your credibility as a speaker.

GATHERING INFORMATION

You've chosen a topic and developed a purpose and thesis statement for your speech. Now you need to do some research to find the right support materials for each main point. Developing this competency will help you present more effective speeches in many different environments. You may find yourself presenting a briefing or training program on the job. As one communication professional tells us, for such programs to be successful, you need to have experience translating research meaningfully for non-expert audiences.[1] Let's get started with one suggestion that will simplify this competency for you. When you research and gather information, you're looking for two sorts of support materials—objective and subjective—both are essential to a good speech and add variety and interest to it.

OBJECTIVE AND SUBJECTIVE INFORMATION

Speakers gather **objective information** from sources such as research studies, reference books, and resources housed in libraries or obtained from the Internet. Objective information is called that partly because it exists in the form of an object, like the information in a book, and because it has been researched and made available by reputable and objective authorities. Quotations, definitions, facts, figures, and statistics all qualify as objective information. For objective information in Kumar's speech, he could use some statistics on the extent to which pop music and pop musicians have become superstars in countries other than their own.

7.1 OBJECTIVE INFORMATION is from sources such as research studies, reference books, and resources housed in libraries or obtained from the Internet.

7.2. SUBJECTIVE INFORMATION is information speakers recall from their own experiences or obtain from observing or interviewing someone else.

Subjective information is information that speakers recall from their own experiences or obtain from observing or interviewing someone else. This type of information can take the form of personal opinion or the testimony of a reliable source. Examples, anecdotes, or stories are all subjective information that can be used to make objective facts more real and relevant. For subjective information, Kumar could tell a personal story about his appreciation of cultures other than his native India, as a result of exposure to pop music.

But how much objective and how much subjective information should you include in your speech? A good suggestion to follow is the "30/70 rule" developed by Dance & Zak-Dance.[2] Devote about 30 percent of your speech to objective information that's new to your audience—hard facts and data. Then assign the remaining 70 percent of your speech to material that will be more memorable to your listeners and will draw them in—subjective stories and real-world experiences. Though somewhat difficult to adhere to, this rule is based on the notion that most people can only take in a limited amount of objective, new information at one time, perhaps two to three main ideas. Limiting the amount of objective information you present will keep your audience paying attention and help them retain what you say.

Dance's advice is reinforced by an article in *PR Week*: "A truly memorable speech becomes so partly because it strikes exactly the right balance between content and entertainment."[3] To achieve this balance, we are advised to use an outline of the main and subpoints of the speech and mark each piece of support and information with a highlighter; use one color for humorous comments, examples, and stories (subjective support) and another color for statistical information, facts and figures (objective support). You will instantly see if you have specific types of information bunched together or if you go too long without any entertaining or subjective material. Your goal in using this technique is to quickly grasp where you may need to do more research or rearrange, add, or subtract specific types of content and support materials.

TYPES OF SUPPORT MATERIALS AND EVIDENCE

Your main aim with this competency is to find and use a variety of high-quality support materials, all clearly linked to the thesis of your speech. The objective and subjective information may take a variety of forms. The following forms or types of support materials are useful in any speech, whether informative or persuasive. The most frequently used types of objective support materials are definitions and descriptions and facts and statistics.

DEFINITIONS AND DESCRIPTIONS

Clarity in any speech is achieved in part by providing definitions and descriptions. In Chapter 1, you learned that the meaning of any word varies from one person to another. Such variations in meaning can result in two problems, and either could cause the audience to misunderstand key concepts in your speech. First, different members of the audience may interpret common and familiar words in different ways. To avoid that happening, if a familiar word is serving as a key term in your speech, provide a simple and concise definition of it, so your listeners know exactly what you're talking about. Words like abortion, affirmative action, or welfare need to be defined. Use a dictionary to determine the most acceptable definition for the key term, and include it toward the beginning of your speech. Second, uncommon terms that are new or unfamiliar to the listeners also must be clarified. That can be accomplished by defining the new word or term, and providing a description of it.

The word immigration is fairly common but may mean different things to different people. Some people think of immigration as the system that made the United States strong in the early 20th century. Others associate the term with the presence of illegal immigrants in the United States today. Hana should provide a simple definition of immigration toward the beginning of her speech to ensure all audience members understand the concept of immigration as she intends it. For example, the *American Heritage Dictionary* defines the verb, immigrate, as meaning, "To enter and settle in a country or region to which one is not native." *Roget's Thesaurus* provides an even simpler definition: "Departure from one's native land to settle in another." By presenting one of these simple definitions, Hana would clarify exactly what she is talking about in her speech, and what she is not talking about.

FACTS AND STATISTICS

Another way to provide objective support for any main point in your speech is to present facts and statistics. A **fact** is an individual piece of information that listeners could verify for themselves if they wanted to. To be effective, a fact should be highly relevant to the speech topic, and it should contain enough evidence that it can stand on its own as a solid piece of objective information. Since facts need to be verifiable, they ought to come from very reliable and respected sources of information, for instance articles published in academic journals or well-respected newspapers or magazines. Statistics are a type of fact frequently used to bolster any argument in a speech.

Statistics are numerical summaries of facts, figures, and research findings that provide pictures of data about people, ideas, or patterns of behavior. There are two types of statistics you can use as support in your speech: descriptive and inferential. **Descriptive statistics** describe or present pictures of what whole groups of people do, think, or are like. They summarize the behaviors or attitudes of everyone in the group. **Inferential statistics** make inferences or draw conclusions about larger groups of people based on learning something about a smaller sample of people, selected out of the larger group. Selecting the right sample out of the larger group, who accurately represent the larger group, is key to good inferential statistics. Many research studies published in academic

7.3 A FACT is an individual piece of information that listeners could verify for themselves if they wanted to.

7.4 STATISTICS are numerical summaries of facts, figures, and research findings that provide pictures of data about people, ideas, or patterns of behavior.

7.5. DESCRIPTIVE STATISTICS describe or present pictures of what whole groups of people do, think, or are like.

7.6. INFERENTIAL STATISTICS make inferences or draw conclusions about larger groups of people based on learning something about a smaller sample of people, selected out of the larger group.

journals make use of inferential statistics and those studies are considered very reliable sources of information. Kumar would need to be very selective about the sources he uses, but he could use statistics to paint a picture of the increase in pop music consumption worldwide over recent years. A visual depiction of the statistics would be most effective (see Figure 7.1).

If you use statistics, select your figures carefully and don't overwhelm the audience with numbers. More is not necessarily better—in fact, it can be confusing. If you need to present a lot of numbers, provide a simple interpretation of the statistics, perhaps in the form of an electronic (slides or

Figure 7.1: Using Statistics to Support a Main Point in a Speech

Based on global ticket sales, Kumar found these statistics about the popularity of various pop music stars around the world.

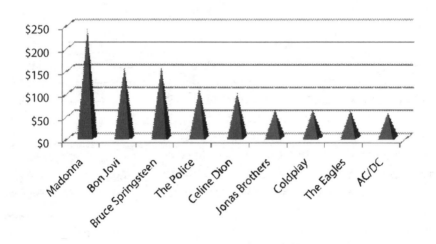

Global Pop Music's Potential to Promote Multicultural Understanding: 2008 Global Sales from Pop Musicians Tours

Source: *Global ticket sales in 2008 in millions of dollars* (2009). Retrieved from http://www.industryfinest.com/blogs/celebrities-blog/madonna-leads-2009-list-of-music-money-makers.html

PowerPoint) or nonelectronic (flip chart or poster) presentation aid. Charts and graphs often help to present statistics more clearly.

Also consider simplifying and strengthening your statistical evidence by combining it with a strong example. The example makes a situation or event real and personal, and statistics indicate that the example is widespread.

That said, never use statistics or examples in any way that would misrepresent the truth or lead your listeners to faulty conclusions. For instance, you may discover some statistical evidence that could be manipulated to appear to support your claim, while in reality, it does not. Such use of inaccurate or misleading statistics would be highly unethical.

In addition to using definitions, descriptions, facts, and statistics, other more subjective types of support materials are examples, stories, testimonies, and quotations.

EXAMPLES

A simple but effective form of support is the example. An **example** is a specific item, person, or event that helps to explain or illustrate an idea, clarify a difficult concept, or make anything you say more interesting or real to the audience. A competent speaker carefully plans the use of powerful examples, realizing that one strong example is more effective than several inadequate ones. You can choose between using real examples or hypothetical ones. A hypothetical example is something that hasn't actually happened but could happen, which can be just as effective as a real example. In using a hypothetical example, you ask your listeners to imagine a situation related to the speech topic. For instance, in Hana's speech on immigration, she could say: "Imagine how you would feel if, when you started this class, it was the first time you had ever set foot on a college campus in the United States." Even though examples are effective, it is unethical to use an example to prove a point, if you know it's an isolated incident that is not true on a larger scale. That kind of misrepresentation is as bad as distorting statistics to support your argument or main point.

> **7.7 AN EXAMPLE is a specific item, person, or event that helps to explain or illustrate an idea, clarify a difficult concept, or make anything you say more interesting or real to the audience.**

STORIES

When you tell a **story**, which is actually just a long example, it serves the same purpose—to illustrate an idea, clarify a concept, or make a point more interesting or real. The ability to tell a good story is one of the most valuable skills a public speaker can have—it fuels a speech with energy and engages the audience in its action. A story grabs the audience's attention. However, a story that is either poorly told or not relevant to the content of your speech can negatively impact your credibility. To avoid that situation, choose your story carefully, be sure it's relevant and don't include it just to fill up time or amuse the audience. Keep the story short and concise, and help your listeners relate to it by describing real people and events. Create a mental picture of the action that takes place in the story by describing what happened or what someone actually did.

> **7.8 A STORY is just a long example, it serves the same purpose—to illustrate an idea, clarify a concept, or make a point more interesting or real.**

> **7.9 NARRATIVE THEORY says people are essentially storytellers and storytelling is one of the oldest and most universal forms of human communication.**

A good argument for using stories is provided by what is referred to as **Narrative Theory**. A narrative *is* a story, and this theory says people are essentially storytellers.[4] Storytelling works, in part, because it is one of the oldest and most universal forms of human communication. Long before people could write things down, they told each other stories in order to pass their history on from one generation to the next. Narrative Theory goes on to tell us that two things make for an effective and believable story. A good story has coherence—it seems to work and hang together for those who hear it. A good story has fidelity—it rings true for the listeners. If a story you tell has coherence and fidelity, it will help enliven and illustrate the meaning and significance of a key point in your speech. Hana's personal immigration experience would work well as a story in her speech.

TESTIMONIES AND QUOTATIONS

Two more valuable forms of support make use of someone else's words to support the ideas in your speech. **Testimony** utilizes the opinion of an expert or the account of an event by a witness to it. A **quotation** is another person's exact words. Either or both of these techniques can be used to provide authoritative evidence in support of your claim, when your own credibility with the listeners isn't as impressive as it needs to be. For a testimony or quotation to be effective, choosing the right source is imperative. Find experts or people who hold respected positions in the subject area you are speaking about, preferably someone your listeners know of. You can use a person who is not highly expert, if he or she has had an experience that is relevant to your speech topic. You can use a person who is not well known if you tell the audience why the individual's opinion is important.

> **7.10 TESTIMONY utilizes the opinion of an expert or the account of an event by a witness to it.**
>
> **7.11 A QUOTATION is another person's exact words.**

In Angelique's speech about non-Western rhetoric, she could use a testimony or direct quotation from a scholar with expertise in Eastern rhetoric to support one of her main points. Hana could use a quote from an expert on immigration. Kumar could locate a quote by a pop music icon known to other students in the class, who has said something about the impact and value of globalizing pop music. For instance, Kumar knows that Bono of U2 is an internationally known musician. After searching the web, Kumar found a relevant quote from Bono stating "Music can change the world because it can change people."[5]

There are many possible sources or places where you could look for the types of support materials just described. Your first inclination may be to "Google" your topic and see what you come up with. That approach to researching your main points probably will yield a list of thousands of different websites. Like Kumar in our opening story, you may not be able to discern credible sources on the Internet from those less credible. So we suggest you begin your search right in your own school library. Following that research effort, you will be better informed and can search the Internet more discriminately.

USING THE LIBRARY AND ELECTRONIC DATABASES

The best place to start researching your main points is the library on your campus. While you may choose to access the library and its databases electronically, that is far different from casting a broad net about your topic on the Internet. You will find the librarian, as in our opening story, is capable of pointing you to a variety of sources of information that can be accessed in printed form as well as in thousands of computerized databases.[6]

> **7.12 A COMPUTERIZED DATABASE is a collection of information, searched from a computer terminal, which contains abstracts/ summaries or full-text versions of documents and publications or indexes to information that is located elsewhere.**

A **computerized database** is a collection of information, searched from a computer terminal, which contains abstracts/ summaries or full-text versions of documents and publications or indexes to information that is located elsewhere. Online databases include those that are housed in the library computer system itself as well as databases that are accessed using the Internet. Most college or academic libraries provide lists of all the computerized databases accessible from the library's computer terminals or from a computer located elsewhere if you have the proper password to gain access.

On its shelves and in its many computerized databases, your library has many objective resources for your speeches that include: reference books, newspapers and periodicals, and government documents.

REFERENCE BOOKS

The library contains many diverse reference works such as encyclopedias, dictionaries, directories, biographies, almanacs, statistical reports, and collections of quotations—a wealth of information at your disposal. Many if not most of these reference books are available in print and online.

Encyclopedias provide broad overviews of many subjects that can serve as starting points for research, because they cross-reference subjects and list additional readings and names of experts in a field. Single-volume encyclopedias such as *The Columbia Encyclopedia* and *The Random House Encyclopedia* provide quick but brief introductions to subject areas, while some useful multiple-volume encyclopedias are *The New Encyclopaedia Britannica* and the *Encyclopedia Americana*. There are also specialized encyclopedias covering particular subject areas like art, philosophy, religion, technology, and ethnic studies. For example, Kumar could support his point about the influence worldwide of pop music using a quotation he found in Baker's *Student Encyclopedia of Music*. A famous poet, Henry Wadsworth Longfellow, once said: "Music is the universal language of mankind."[7] This quotation would encourage the audience to begin thinking about the universal impact of music around the world.

Dictionaries not only help clarify unfamiliar terminology for you, the definition of a word, as mentioned earlier, can be useful in the speech itself. The 20-volume *Oxford English Dictionary* is available in print and online. Specialized dictionaries are available for technical and professional fields and can help you understand terms in a new subject area.

Directories contain information about various professions, special interest groups, and organizations. Frequently the listed organizations can provide valuable information for developing a speech or the name of a person who could be contacted to discuss your speech topic. For example, you could use the *Encyclopedia of Associations* to find the name of an organization whose members specialize in some aspect of your speech topic.

If you want information about a famous person, living or dead, you would check in a biographical reference book. *Who's Who in America* and *Who's Who in the World* are available separately in print and online in a database called *Who's Who on the Web*. Two indexes to biographical books, the *Biography Index* and *Current Biography,* don't contain information about famous people, but they do direct you to short biographies or whole books about famous individuals.

Almanacs are collections and compilations of statistics and other facts that summarize information about nations, politics, the labor force, natural phenomena, and so on. The *Statistical Abstract of the United States*, an annual publication of the Department of Commerce, is a collection of statistics about life, work, and government in the United States. Best known of the almanacs are the *Information Please Almanac* and the *World Almanac and Book of Facts.*

Books of quotations, organized by subject, topic, or source, could provide a clever or meaningful quote by a famous person to include in your speech. Most popular are *Bartlett's Familiar Quotations* and the *Oxford Dictionary of Quotations*. Libraries usually will have a wide selection of more specialized quotation books such as *The 637 Best Things Anybody Ever Said* by Robert Byrne and *The Guinness Book of Poisonous Quotes* by Colin Jarman.

NEWSPAPERS AND PERIODICALS

Newspapers and periodicals, by contrast to reference books, are good sources of current information about daily life—politics, crime, fashion, and the many events that shape and influence society. Past issues of these kinds of publications can be used to learn about historical perspectives on topics and events. This vast source of information includes daily, weekly, and other newspapers, as well as regularly printed and published periodicals. Periodicals include popular magazines, trade journals, business magazines, and academic journals.

Indexes to newspapers and periodicals can be searched by topic or key word to find articles and stories of relevance to your speech topic. Academic libraries subscribe to many different databases you can use to search for articles. These databases will identify articles in newspapers, magazines, and scholarly journals. Some popular general databases include *EBSCO Academic Search Premier*, *Infotrac Academic OneFile*, and *Wilson Web*. There also are specialized databases in subject areas like education or psychology, any of which can be searched by topic or key word. As suggested, most popular indexes are available in printed form and online. You also can go directly to some newspapers and periodicals on their websites on the Internet, *The New York Times*, for example.

GOVERNMENT DOCUMENTS

Most U.S. governmental departments and offices regularly collect and publish information and data to keep the public informed. The subjects covered in government publications are endless, ranging from college enrollment to the unemployment rate, to census data, population projections, and economic forecasts. Like other large sources of information, indexes and catalogues are available in the library to simplify the process of searching for the right government document.

All of this governmental information is in the public domain, which means it can be easily accessed on the Internet by visiting the website for the relevant government department, like the U.S. Bureau of Labor, or the Department of Education, Justice, or Labor. Also, the Government Printing Office publishes the *Monthly Catalog of United States Government Publications,* which is available online at http://catalog.gpo.gov. At the THOMAS website (http://thomas.loc.gov/), you will find the latest information on bills being debated and passed in Congress that may provide valuable information for your speech.

In summary, support materials derived from researching in the library are useful, because typically, they are viewed as reliable and relatively trustworthy. Using research he finds in the library, Kumar could support his point about the emergence and significant influence of global media by referring to the observations of authors de Block and Rydin.[8] They clearly state youth cultures are becoming increasingly global, as media exposure to different parts of the world is allowing young people to recognize, identify with, and adopt similar styles of music, fashion, graphics, and dance. By quoting these authors, Kumar is not making his claim alone; rather he is using the published remarks of the two authors to support his main point.

It is important to consider that some websites on the Internet may not be perceived as completely trustworthy when compared to the types of sources found in libraries. But the Internet is easy to access and does have plenty of good information. Let's now consider how to use it effectively.

USING THE INTERNET

Like the library, the Internet does afford access to many sources of objective and subjective information. If you use it wisely and selectively, the Internet can be a priceless resource for researching a speech, or it can be a frustrating waste of time. You may find exactly the right supporting information in minutes or you may find nothing of value and waste time in the process. Nevertheless, used effectively and efficiently, the Internet provides several avenues for researching your speech, including: e-mail and listservs, newsgroups, chat rooms, blogs, and websites on the World Wide Web.

E-mail is useful for communicating interpersonally with people who may be able to help you research your speech. Something about being online often brings out the best in people, and they go to great lengths to help others who are looking for information. Most college professors, for example, are more than ready to help students by providing new sources of information, copies of papers, or quotes and testimonies in their specialty area. If you locate an e-mail listserv of a group of people interested in the subject area or topic of your speech, you can send an inquiry about your topic to many people at once. To locate a relevant listserv, *CataList* at http://www.lsoft.com/catalist.html is an online catalog of listservs that is updated almost daily and contains a description and links to over 50,000 public lists—that means anybody can send a message to the list. Other useful compilations of listservs in specialty areas may be located on the Internet. Kumar could try to get some background information about music promoting multicultural understanding by contacting an e-mail listserv such as that of the North American World Music Coalition at http://worldmusic-coalition.org/.[9]

Also on the Internet, you can participate in a newsgroup, chat room, or blog where people are discussing your subject area or speech topic. By participating in an electronic discussion, you can ask questions in real time of potential experts in a field related to your speech topic. On the Internet, you will find websites that provide lists of bulletin boards, chat rooms, online-forums, news groups, and blogs on an unbelievable array of topics. For instance, Google Groups (http://groups.google.com/) provide search tools to help locate electronic discussion groups. You enter your topic and are instantly provided a list of websites where discussions related to that topic are happening and you can join in. The addresses of expert individuals, e-mail lists, and chat rooms also are available from associations or organizations interested in a subject or topic area. Visit the website of an organization to get those addresses. For example, the National Communication Association at www.natcom.org sponsors a public e-mail discussion list called CRTNET. You can send any question about communication by e-mail to that list, and it will go to thousands of experts and professionals interested in communication.

The World Wide Web on the Internet does provide access to an overwhelming number of websites, many of which may contain useful information of relevance to your speech topic. The web is seen as such a viable tool for information gathering for speeches that a debate program incorporates its use in a forensic event entitled "electronic extemporaneous speaking."[10] Students on both sides of a debate topic construct a 7-minute speech in 30 minutes and are given access to the Internet to help prepare their speeches. The event is said to have a positive impact on students' skills related to research, organization, critical thinking, and speaking.

When accessing the World Wide Web, there are, of course, a variety of search engines you can use with your Internet browser, such as google.com, ask.com, or yahoo.com. A search engine like Webcrawler.com claims to have spun together the strengths of those first three. What is important to remember is these search engines serve different purposes in disseminating information, so no one engine will find all available sites. To maximize your search, use the engine's Help icon for tips on conducting your search.

Finally, you can consolidate your library and Internet research efforts by accessing, on the Internet, many of the resources typically available in a library. Go to a website like the *Internet Library for Librarians* at http://www.itcompany.com/inforetriever/index.htm. In the "Ready Reference" section of this site, with one click, you can access almanacs, fact books and statistics, bibliographies, directories, encyclopedias, maps and travel, news and weather, as well as miscellaneous other support materials for your speech.

USING HUMAN SOURCES

As we discussed earlier in this chapter, not all of the support materials you use in your speech should come from published or online sources. We talked about using examples and stories to bring your speech to life and make it memorable. You can identify these types of support through personal observations and experiences and by conducting informational interviews.

PERSONAL OBSERVATIONS AND EXPERIENCES

Information gathered by observing others or describing your own experiences lends support and credence to any objective claim or idea you present. Besides, telling a story or providing an example is an effective way to relate to your listeners. In Hana's immigration speech, she could describe her observations of the good or bad experiences of other immigrants, including her own family. Similarly, she could talk about her own personal experience with the rigors of the immigration process in order to come to the United States. Kumar could enhance his speech with a personal account about coming to appreciate Western culture as a result of exposure to American pop music. He could tell about his trip from India to London with his family in 2005 and going to London's Hyde Park to watch a live concert with U2 and his favorite singer, Bono. He could describe the excitement of that concert and the impact it had on himself and the audience. Kumar remembered reading that an estimated one million people attended the Live 8 concerts, supporting the *Make Poverty History* campaign, in London, Paris, Rome, Philadelphia, Barrie (near Toronto), Berlin, Tokyo, Johannesburg, and Moscow. AOLmusic.com, a partner in the venture, reported more than five million people watched the concerts live online and they called it "The Day Music Changed the World." In all, an estimated one billion people across the globe watched the concerts either live, on TV, or via the Internet;[11] and he, Kumar, had been a part of that important event. What a great story for his speech.

In spite of the advantage of adding interest to your speech, when you use observations or personal stories, you need to do so in an ethical manner. That means presenting this form of evidence truthfully. Present the information objectively and don't infer that one or several isolated incidents are what would happen all of the time. Just because Hana's parents may have had an unfavorable experience, that is not a reason to believe or suggest that all immigrants to the United States will have a similar bad experience. In addition, a biased description of a personal experience potentially can offend the listeners and damage your credibility. You should not distort an event to serve your own purpose or use someone else's story or experience without giving them credit for it. Similarly, telling an inappropriate or offensive story is wrong, even if it's due to poor audience analysis on your part.

To come up with a story for your speech, think about your speech topic and ask yourself: "Have I done something, known someone, or witnessed something that relates to the topic in some way?" Tell the audience that story and because it's personal to you, you'll tell it well. But remember, any story represents your viewpoint and *only* your viewpoint, so the ethical thing to do is acknowledge that fact to your listeners.

INFORMATIONAL INTERVIEWS

Interviewing is an effective way to gather subjective information from an expert or from someone whose life experience relates to the thesis and main points of your speech. While you may think of interviewing in the context of looking for a job, an informational interview is an excellent way to gather testimony and relevant quotations for a speech. For example, Kumar could conduct an interview with a media expert, such as Edmund Thomas, owner of Gentle Rain Productions ™. When asked how the globalization of pop music represents an opportunity to promote multicultural understanding, Thomas responded: "Sometimes, the very first glimpse of a foreign culture is through music. Since music transcends language, it has the ability to break down barriers of communication. In this age of the World Wide Web, music is easily accessible. In no other time in history have cultures been so intermingled; music is the benchmark of each culture—its signature. And it is the vibrant, fresh, cutting edge expressions of youth through pop music that are the vanguards of multicultural expansion." This type of quote could support Kumar's main point that the globalization of pop music represents an opportunity to promote multicultural understanding.

Before you decide to use an interview to gather information, determine whether that method will provide the kind of support you need for your speech. Do you have sufficient objective information but need the opinion of an expert or the testimony of someone experienced in your topic? If so, consider whether you can arrange an interview with a person who will be a reputable source of information. After you've identified a candidate to interview, then contact the interviewee by phone, e-mail, or in a letter. Introduce yourself and your speech topic; if the person agrees to be interviewed, offer a choice of several ways for the interview to occur, including in person, by phone, or by e-mail; then choose a mutually satisfactory time. If the interviewee has little time to be interviewed or is geographically far away, consider conducting the entire interview by e-mail. It could be less time-consuming and garner excellent results, particularly if the interviewee is a notable expert who agrees with your position on the topic.

Preparation is the key to a successful interview, so carefully plan what you'll ask and how you'll ask it. Asking good questions is the best way to ensure you end up with useful stories for your speech.[12] Develop interview questions ahead of time, rank ordering them from the information you need the most to that which you need the least. This is an important step, since you may not have enough time to ask all the questions you prepare. Draft questions that explore aspects of your topic that the interviewee knows about and can respond to with relative ease. Include open-ended questions, which are those that the interviewee cannot answer with a simple yes or no; and prepare several follow-up questions for each open-ended question. Submit your interview questions ahead of time, if the interviewee would prefer.

During the interview itself, be prepared to skip questions if the discussion moves in a direction you didn't expect. Above all, be flexible, polite, and respectful of the interviewee's time. Let the interviewee do the talking, and intervene only to keep the interview on track. Tape record the interview or take careful notes of what is said. But ask for permission to tape the interview, if you want to do so. Before you end the interview, don't forget to thank the interviewee for the valuable information he or she has shared with you.

Review your notes as soon as possible after the interview, looking for themes or major ideas to use as support material in your speech. If the interviewee was well spoken or colorful, look for a meaningful quote that will enliven your speech. But be sure to ask for permission to use the quote.

EVALUATING AND CITING SOURCES

By now, you should have a pretty good idea of possible sources of support materials for the main points of your speech. You also may need some general advice on using the materials you've found effectively and appropriately in your speech. Most public speaking students face challenges similar to what Kumar described in the opening story. You need to know how to evaluate critically whether a source is appropriate and worth using—particularly if you found it on a website. You need to understand how the use of certain sources may affect your credibility as a speaker, and you need to be able to cite the sources correctly and avoid plagiarism.

USING CRITICAL THINKING TO EVALUATE SOURCES

When gathering support materials for your speech, using critical thinking, as defined in Chapter 2, is crucial. This type of **evaluative thinking** involves weighing evidence, assumptions, and ideas based on sound reasoning and logic. That is precisely what you must do as you research your speech. You continuously make critical evaluative judgments about what information to include and how to logically use it in your speech. That means returning again and again to your main points and deciding which piece of support material—quotation, statistic, story, or academic article—will best support which main point.

7.13 EVALUATIVE THINKING involves weighing evidence, assumptions, and ideas based on sound reasoning and logic.

As you gather information, you examine each piece of evidence and make a critical and reasoned decision about its potential role in your speech. Each bit of supporting material you include needs to serve a valuable function in your speech by proving a point, clarifying an idea, or making your speech memorable to the audience. If you state a fact, tell a story, or show an overhead of some statistics, that piece of information or evidence ought to have a clear reason for being in your speech. Given the many sources of information available, in print and electronic form, you must approach the entire research process using these critical and evaluative thinking skills to your best advantage. Box 7.2 provides specific suggestions for thinking critically when researching and preparing your speech.

Box 7.2: Critical Thinking and Researching Your Speech

Researchers have learned that critical thinking and communication are inextricably intertwined.[1,2] They found a positive impact on students' critical thinking abilities, on public speaking and debate, and problem-based discussion. As students learned more about communication, their critical thinking skills improved.

Critical thinking has advantages for you as a public speaker. A critical thinker evaluates information before forming judgments. As you prepare a speech, you research support materials, examine the evidence, and then form opinions about it. As a result, you become well informed on the topic. When hearing your evidence, the listeners will believe you know what you're talking about and that you examined the topic with an open mind. Your well-informed judgments will promote respect from the audience and enhance your credibility. Furthermore, thinking critically while you research your speech enables you to present your ideas with more confidence, because you can support your claims and defend your opinions.

Here are some "do's" and several "don'ts" for improving your critical thinking skills:

DO's:

1. Be open to new ideas but research the necessary information to verify those ideas.
2. Seek to understand new ideas by examining all the information and evidence.
3. Consider all ideas, whether your own or someone else's, from different viewpoints.
4. Probe and examine assumptions by questioning and challenging them.
5. Understand the difference between a fact and an opinion—you can verify a fact but not an opinion.
6. Explore contradictions and differences in opposing viewpoints.
7. Weigh all the evidence before forming a judgment.
8. Draw conclusions only after examining all alternatives and possibilities.

DONT's:

1. Accept unsupported claims or assertions.
2. Rush to judgment and form an opinion without examining the evidence.
3. Assume all information posted on the Internet is authoritative and reliable.

Sources: [1]Allen, M., & Berkowitz, S. (1999). A meta-analysis of the impact of forensics and communication education on critical thinking. *Communication Education, 48*(1), 18–30;

[2]Sellnow, D D., & Ahlfeldt, S. L. (2005). Fostering critical thinking and teamwork skills via a problem-based learning (PBL) approach to public speaking fundamentals. *Communication Teacher, 19*(1), 33–38.

An important part of critical evaluation for a researcher and public speaker is investigating and verifying the authenticity of any source, before including it in a speech.[13] In this regard, the Internet poses the biggest problem because it lacks the controls of traditional publishing outlets; anyone can post anything they want on a web page. Therefore, information presented as factual could actually be only someone's opinion. Evaluate any website based on the information presented on its home page and what you can learn about the authors or developers of the site. What are their credentials and are they qualified to speak as experts on the topic of the site? Is the information on the site objective or does it appear to be a biased viewpoint on the topic? Is the information accurate, when you compare it to similar information on the same topic from other sources? Is it current and is there an indication of when it was posted or updated? As you use these questions to evaluate a website, understand that sites containing the most valuable information for your speech may not be those with the most graphics and visual appeal. Because graphics load slowly and take more time for people to access, sites that are information intensive sometimes use fewer graphics.

Further, the Internet poses one more problem—people can present themselves any way they want online. A person who sounds like an expert in a chat room may lack the credentials to qualify as an expert. The problem in using the Internet is that scholarly resources do abound there, but they are presented right along with unfounded, inaccurate, and out-of-date claims and information.[14]

Guidelines for evaluating electronic sources of information are available on the web itself. One particular site provides a comprehensive list of the many other evaluation sites, all of which discuss how to assess the merits of electronic information (http://www.vuw.ac.nz/staff/alastair_smith/evaln/evaln.htm). If you visit this site, you will see that the amount of information on the Internet about evaluating websites is overwhelming. At a minimum, keep the five simple criteria presented in Box 7.3 in mind before using any website as support material in your speech. A last suggestion for evaluating research sources in general comes to us from an author writing for Harvard University's management newsletter.[15] This writer provides tips for evaluating research and says we should ask other people not involved to evaluate the quality of our research efforts. That means when you have added the support materials to the main points for your speech, let another person, even another student in the class, react to the argument and logic of what you have created.

***

Box 7.3: Five Criteria for Evaluating Websites

If you are considering using support materials from a website in your speech, take a minute to examine the site using these five basic criteria.

1. Accuracy: Does the page list the author and institution that published the page and provide a way of contacting him/her?
2. Authority: Does the page list the authors' credentials? What type of domain does it come from—educational, nonprofit, commercial, government, etc.?
3. Objectivity: Does the page provide accurate information with limited advertising and is it objective in presenting the information?
4. Currency: Is the page current and updated regularly (as stated on the page) and are any links also up to date?
5. Coverage: Can you view the information properly or is some of it limited to fees, browser technology, or software requirements?

Source: *Five Criteria for Evaluating Websites* (2009). Retrieved from http://www.library.cornell.edu/olinuris/ref/webcrit.html

SELECTING AND USING SUPPORT MATERIALS THAT ENHANCE YOUR CREDIBILITY

As you critically evaluate the use of support materials in your speech, you need to consider how the use of certain sources may affect your credibility as a public speaker. You make a variety of decisions while preparing to speak, which later may impact whether you are perceived by listeners as credible. If you choose support materials to use and make those decisions ethically, it's more likely the audience will see you as highly credible. We already discussed in Chapter 1 how ethical communication and speaker credibility are related to one another. A communicator who tries to communicate ethically typically is perceived by most people as reasonably credible. Recall, we said credibility means being perceived by others as both well intended and qualified and able to speak knowledgeably on the given topic. Obviously then, choosing the right support material is a matter related to ethics and credibility. The following two suggestions are simplified but could help you develop your own ethical code for speech preparation and selecting and using support materials in your speech.

- Don't allow the end to justify the means. Your end is to accomplish the purpose of your speech, to convince the audience of something or to persuade them to do something. How are you going to handle research and evidence that may not work in the best interest of accomplishing that purpose? What if some piece of information you discover contradicts or challenges one of your major points? If you conceal that information, you're suggesting the audience isn't capable of weighing all the evidence and making a good decision. So you are ethically responsible to present all viewpoints, openly and fairly, and to allow the listeners to form their own opinions. Honor all viewpoints, and don't conceal any evidence that counters your argument. Of course, even your detractors will expect you to argue strongly for your own position.
- Don't use numbers or statistics to mislead the audience about the truth. Numbers can be biased by the researchers who generate them or by the speaker who presents and interprets them. We usually believe what statistics say, and we perceive statistical studies as precise and reliable. Therefore, we can be more easily swayed toward a certain position, if that position is supported by numbers. If, however, during the research process you discover some numbers that contradict your position, you have an ethical responsibility to report that discovery. Again, it is unethical to knowingly use the persuasive ability of numbers to misrepresent reality.

Speech preparation that is ethical may appear complex. However, remember the simplified definition of ethical communication from Chapter 1. Ethical communication simply means sharing sufficient information with others so they can make fully informed choices and decisions. Isn't that what you would want others to do when communicating with you? A public speaker has an ethical responsibility to share information and relevant support materials with listeners to facilitate their freedom of choice and their right to form their own opinions. By doing so, audience members will respect you more and thus your credibility as a presenter is enhanced.

By now, you may think we have talked about every possible aspect of researching and supporting a speech. You are right, and we are almost done. The last thing you need to know is how to let the audience and the instructor know where you got your information.

CITING SOURCES CORRECTLY AND AVOIDING PLAGIARISM

Once you have critically evaluated and selected the best support materials for each main point in your speech, then you need to consider how to document your sources of information. Using information, data, or material without providing credit where credit is due is unethical and involves committing plagiarism. **Plagiarism** is the unauthorized use or close imitation of other people's ideas, thoughts, language, or words without acknowledging and citing their source.

7.14 PLAGIARISM is the unauthorized use or close imitation of other people's ideas, thoughts, language, or words without acknowledging and citing their source.

The best way to avoid plagiarism as a public speaker is simple. Any source that would require credit in a written paper should be acknowledged and given credit when you speak. In fact, you should identify and cite your sources whether you are quoting them directly or paraphrasing and summarizing someone else's work. The bottom line is you need to let your audience know exactly where you got your information for two reasons. By citing sources in your speech, the audience knows where the information came from so they can evaluate the credibility of each source and therefore the credibility of your speech. Plus, they can seek out more information on the topic if they want to know more—and that is a compliment to you. If you see students in the audience taking notes about your sources, know you have done a good job of this competency.

Specifically, in a spoken citation, you don't have to include full references for each source as you would in an academic paper; but, you do need to refer to each of your sources while speaking. Give the audience enough information about each source so they could find the information on their own. Present the source title, author, and date, but not page numbers or volume numbers as you

Table 7.1: How to Cite Sources in a Public Speech

Citing sources correctly and carefully is the best way to avoid committing plagiarism.

TYPE OF SOURCE	HOW TO CITE THIS SOURCE IN YOUR SPEECH
Direct quotations	"And, I quote…." Or "As (name the source) put it…."
Book	"According to Mary Smith, author of *Understanding Eastern Rhetoric*…." (Include book title and author)
Periodical (magazine or newspaper)	"*Newsweek* magazine recently wrote about…" "A *Washington Post* editorial examined this issue…." (Include magazine title and date)
Journal	"John Jones wrote in the Spring 2009 issue of *Communication Education* about…."(Include journal title, date, and author)
Website (an organization)	"The U.S. Immigration Office website provides details about…." (Include the title of the organization)
Website (news/magazine)	"CNN.com, on August 11, 2009, reported that…." (Include the title and date)
Interviews or lectures	Lin Wang, a Professor of Religion at University of Colorado, had this to say about…." Or "According to Lin Wang, a professor of Religion at …." (Include name and credentials of the source)

Source: *How to Cite Sources in a Public Speech*. (2009). Retrieved from http://writing.colostate.edu/guides/speaking/infomod/pop6c.cfm

would in a written citation. Box 7.3 provides examples of how to cite each of the most commonly used sources correctly in your speech.

In this chapter, you took another big step forward in the speech preparation process. In Chapter 5, we examined how to choose and narrow a speech topic, and Chapter 6 focused on developing a purpose for the topic and a thesis statement and main points for your speech. Now you understand how to gather objective and subjective information and support materials to help achieve the purpose of your speech and support its main and subpoints. We now proceed to Chapter 8, the last preparation competency, which involves organizing your support materials into a coherent and focused outline for presenting your next speech.

Things To Do: Competency Three

Review this *Things To Do* list for researching and supporting your next speech. Based on the thesis statement and main points you already developed, have you done the following?

1. Identified objective support materials for the main points that are of high quality and ☐ clearly linked to the thesis of the speech?

2. Identified subjective support materials for the main points that are of high quality ☐ and clearly linked to the thesis of the speech?

3. Used the library and its computerized databases to search for a variety of high-qual- ☐ ity support material?

4. Used the Internet to search for support materials and scrutinized any websites to ☐ ensure they will reflect favorably on your credibility as a speaker.

5. Evaluated critically the support materials you plan to include in your speech to ensure ☐ they are of high quality and you have a good balance of objective and subjective information.

6. Developed presentational aids for any complicated statistics? ☐

7. Prepared correct citations to document the use of any sources and support materials ☐ in your speech?

CHAPTER SUMMARY

Two sorts of information are essential to Competency Three: objective and subjective. Objective information is from sources such as research studies, reference books, and resources housed in libraries or obtained from the Internet. Subjective information is information speakers recall from their own experiences or obtain from observing or interviewing someone else. The 30/70 rule says to strive for 30% objective information and 70% subjective. The most frequently used types of objective support materials are definitions and descriptions, and facts and statistics. A fact is an individual piece of informa-

tion that listeners could verify for themselves if they wanted to. Statistics are numerical summaries of facts, figures, and research findings that provide pictures of data about people, ideas, or patterns of behavior. Descriptive statistics describe or present pictures of what whole groups of people do, think, or are like. Inferential statistics make inferences or draw conclusions about larger groups of people based on learning something about a smaller sample of people selected out of the larger group. Other more subjective types of support materials are examples, stories, testimonies and quotations. An example is a specific item, person, or event that helps to explain or illustrate an idea, clarify a difficult concept, or make anything you say more interesting or real to the audience. A story is a long example that serves the same purpose—to illustrate an idea, clarify a concept, or make a point more interesting or real. The use of a story or narrative can enliven and illustrate the meaning and significance of a key point in the speech. Two more valuable forms of support make use of someone else's words to support the ideas in your speech. Testimony utilizes the opinion of an expert or the account of an event by a witness to it, and a quotation is another person's exact words. There are many possible sources or places where you could look for the various types of support materials. In the library, you can search for support materials using computerized databases that provide collections of information, from a computer terminal. You also can search for support materials in reference books, newspapers and periodicals, and government documents. The Internet provides several avenues for researching your speech including e-mail and listservs, newsgroups, chat rooms, blogs, and websites on the World Wide Web. You can identify support materials like examples and stories through personal observations and experiences and by conducting informational interviews. After locating support materials for the main points in your speech, then you need to evaluate critically whether a source is appropriate and worth using—particularly if you found it on a website. This critical thinking involves evaluating evidence, assumptions, and ideas based on sound reasoning and logic. You need to consider how the use of certain sources may affect your credibility as a speaker, and you need to be able to cite the sources correctly and avoid plagiarism. Plagiarism is the unauthorized use or close imitation of other people's ideas, thoughts, language, or words without acknowledging and citing their source.

KEY TERMS

The key terms below are defined in this chapter and presented alphabetically with definitions in the Glossary at the end of the book.

- objective information
- subjective information
- fact
- statistics
- descriptive statistics
- inferential statistics
- example

- story
- Narrative Theory
- testimony
- quotation
- computerized database
- evaluative thinking
- plagiarism

BUILDING COMPETENCE ACTIVITIES

INDIVIDUAL ACTIVITIES

1. When speeches are next presented in class, evaluate how effectively each student uses subjective and objective information in her or his speech.

2. In the next lecture you attend, see if you can identify the various types of support materials the speaker uses. Try to come up with any other types of support materials that would have enhanced the presentation.

3. Visit the History Channel website at http://www.history.com/video.do?action=home and choose a historical speech from the audio or video archives. Write a short evaluation of how effectively the speaker used objective and subjective support materials in the speech.

4. Thinking ahead to your next speech topic, locate a website you potentially could use for support materials for the topic. Use the five criteria for evaluating websites presented in this chapter (Accuracy, Authority, Objectivity, Currency, and Coverage) and decide whether the site is worth using in your next speech.

GROUP ACTIVITIES

1. When speeches are next presented in class, after the speeches, meet with a group of three to four students to evaluate how effectively each student used subjective and objective support materials in the speech. Prepare a list of recommendations for everyone in the group regarding this public speaking competency.

2. With one or two other students, attend a public speech or presentation (it could be a lecture in another class in which you are all enrolled). Have each student individually develop a list and description of how the speaker or lecturer used support materials in the lecture. Compare your lists after the lecture and decide if the 30/70 rule was followed. Discuss how the speaker's use of support materials affected perceptions of speaker credibility.

3. Form groups of three to four students. Together visit the History Channel website at http://www.history.com/video.do?action=home and have each student choose a historical speech from the audio or video archives. After viewing the speech, have each group member identify and describe how the historical speaker used different types of support materials in the speech just viewed.

4. Choose a partner and have each student come up with a topic and a thesis statement and main points for the next speech assignment. Exchange what you have written and come up with two types of possible support material for each main point—one objective and one subjective.

COMPETENCY CHECKPOINTS AND SELF-ASSESSMENT TOOL

Here is what you need to know and be able to do in order to effectively research and support your speech thesis. Determine your level of competency and whether you are ready to proceed to the next chapter. Give yourself one point for each checkpoint you answer satisfactorily.

COMPETENCY CHECKPOINTS	NUMBER OF POINTS
KNOWLEDGE 1. Define objective information and provide three examples of objective support materials. 2. Define subjective information and provide three examples of subjective support materials. 3. Describe and evaluate the possible sources or places where you could locate support materials. 4. Explain the role of critical thinking in the evaluation of sources of support materials.	
SKILLS 1. Write out the thesis and main points for your next speech and identify two possible objective support materials for the main points. 2. Next, identify two possible subjective support materials for the main points. 3. Next, locate and evaluate two websites that could provide support materials for the main points. 4. Next, using your personal observations or experiences, identify an example or story you could use as support material for one of the main points.	
ETHICS AND CREDIBILITY 1. Examine the seven support materials derived from Skills 5–8 and determine whether sharing that information in your speech is an ethical and unbiased presentation of the topic. 2. Examine the seven support materials derived from Skills 5–8 and determine whether sharing that information will enhance your credibility as a public speaker.	
TOTAL CHECKPOINTS (OUT OF A POSSIBLE TEN POINTS)	

ENDNOTES

1. Bodie, G.D. (2008, April). Student as communication skills trainer: From research to "concept keys." *Communication Teacher, 22*(2), 51–55.

2. Dance, F. & Zak-Dance, C. (2007). *Voice, speech, and thought*. Dallas, Texas: Fountainhead.

3. PR Week (2007, February 26). *Choosing an event venue, speechwriting tips, more*, p. 29. Retrieved August 7, 2009, from PRWeek.com.

4. Fisher, W.R. (1984). Narration as a human communication paradigm: The case of public moral argument. *Communication Monographs, 52*, 347–367.

5. Bono (2009). Retrieved from http://www.brainyquote.com/quotes/authors/b/bono.html

6. Ringle, W.J. & Thompson, W.D. (1998). *TechEdge: Using computers to present and persuade*. Needham Heights, MA: Allyn & Bacon.

7. Kuhn, L., Schirmer-Thomson G. (1999). "Music." In *Baker's Student Encyclopedia of Music*.Retrieved from http://www.enotes.com/music-encyclopedia/music-3

8. de Block, L. & Rydin, I. (2006). Digital rapping in media productions: Intercultural communication through youth culture. In *Digital generations: Children, young people, and new media* (pp. 295–312). Mahwah, NJ: Lawrence Erlbaum.

9. North American World Music Coalition listserv (2009). Retrieved from http://worldmusiccoalition.org/

10. Voth, B. (1997). Catching a wave in the Internet surf: Electronic extemporaneous speaking. *Argumentation and Advocacy, 33,* 200–206.

11. King, J. (2005). *Live 8 global music concerts: Who was inspired to perform to the beat of fighting poverty in Africa? Rugged Elegance.* Retrieved from: http://www.ruggedelegantliving.com/a/003686.html.

12. Rowan, K.E. (1988, Winter). No-ideas students learn how to find, research stories. *Journalism Educator, 42*(4), 38–40.

13. Goldsborough, R. (July, 1999). Suggestions to help you survive workplace 'infoglut.' *Communication Briefings, 18,* 8a–8b.

14. McBride, K. & Dickstein, R. (1998, March 20) The Web demands critical reading by students. *The Chronicle of Higher Education,* B6.

15. Guensberg C. (2001). How to evaluate research. *Harvard Management Communication Letter, 4*(10), 12.

8

ORGANIZING AND OUTLINING YOUR SPEECH: COMPETENCY FOUR

- **Understanding Organization**
  The Importance of Organization
  Choosing and Using an Organizational Pattern
- **Planning the Main Parts of Your Speech**
  Introduction
  Body of the Speech
  Transitions
  Conclusion
- **Preparing an Outline**
  Working, Formal, and Presentational Outlines

"Only the prepared speaker deserves to be confident." Dale Carnegie, public speaking expert and author, 1888–1955

• • •

The second round of informative speeches in the public speaking course was spread out over two days. Angelique, Richard, and Hana presented on day one, but Kumar was scheduled for the second day. These four students had become fairly good friends. Right after class, they met at Jazzman's Cafe on campus to debrief about the first round of speeches. Grades would not be given back until all the informative speeches were done, so the students were guessing about their grades and evaluating their presentations. Hana and Angelique felt confident they aced the speech. "Angelique, the class really related to your speech on Eastern rhetoric," praised Hana. "Using the quotes from that international expert on Eastern rhetorical style worked well." "Same for you, Hana. Your personal story about going through immigration was a great open- ing attention getter," Angelique replied. Richard gently interrupted: "Enough of this mutual admiration...what about my speech? The class didn't seem to follow along, and I thought my organization of it was crystal clear. A couple students looked like they were drifting off by the time I got to my second main point. I don't know if it was the support materials I used, or I didn't organize it well enough." Kumar was quiet as he listened to his friends. His speech was next week, and he was confident in the support materials he had discovered. But he was not quite as confident about organizing and outlining what he would say. He had heard different cultures prefer different ways of organizing speeches. What if his approach doesn't work for the other students in the class? And, how much information should he put on his outline or note cards? One student who just presented had too much information with him, and he almost read the whole speech. Kumar decided to rely on what he had learned so far about com- petent public speaking. Maybe the recommendations about organizing and outlining in the textbook would point him in the right direction.

• • •

Kumar was right to be confident in the support materials he pulled together for his speech (see Table 8.1). He had used the suggestions in Chapter 7 and found good objective and subjective information for his main and subpoints. In addition, his two main points fully supported his thesis statement: "Popular music is highly influential around the world. In fact, pop music and all it represents has

Table 8.1: Sources of Support for Kumar's Thesis Statement and Speech

Kumar identified the following sources and support materials for his speech's main points and subpoints and then he used this information to develop an outline for his speech.

MAIN POINTS AND SUBPOINTS	SOURCES AND SUPPORT MATERIALS FOR EACH SUBPOINT
Main point 1: Popular music is becoming increasingly global and multicultural	
Subpoint: The emergence and influence of global media	de Block and Rydin's observations about the influence of global media and media exposure on youth cultures
Subpoint: The globalization of pop music as a result of global media technology	Statistics on the popularity of various pop music stars around the world Description of the Live 8 concerts as online video events with one billion people watching the concert live, on TV or the Internet
Subpoint: The influence worldwide of pop music on other cultures	Henry Wadsworth Longfellow's quote about music as the universal language
Main point 2: Global pop music's potential to promote multicultural understanding	
Subpoint: How influential pop music is on young people	Kumar's personal account about his family's trip to a Live 8 concert in London and how that influenced him and millions of others
Subpoint: How exposure to the music of other cultures promotes multicultural understanding	World Music Coalition email listserv comments about music promoting multicultural understanding
Subpoint: Opportunities for bringing people together based on the globalization of pop music	Quotation from Kumar's interview with media expert, Edmund Thomas, on the globalization of pop music breaking down communication barriers Bono quote saying music can change the world because it can change people

the capacity to become the stimulant and glue to bring people together and encourage multicultural understanding among cultures." While this is an inspiring thesis statement, Kumar now needs to organize his speech and develop useful outlines for planning and then presenting his speech. Using a simple and straightforward approach, this chapter will help you and Kumar address this next task.

Based on what you learn in this chapter, you will be able to: *use an organizational pattern appropriate to the topic, audience, occasion, and purpose.* This is Competency Four and it includes the ability to:

- Develop an exceptional introduction that clearly engages the audience in an appropriate and creative manner
- Plan an organizational pattern for the body of the speech that reflects superior clarity

- Use transitions to provide an exceptionally clear and logical progression within and between ideas
- Develop a conclusion that clearly reflects the content of the speech and leaves the audience with an undeniable message or call to action
- Prepare and use a working, formal, and presentational outline to facilitate the competent development and presentation of your speech

---

UNDERSTANDING ORGANIZATION

After gathering information and planning your support materials, the next step is to organize those materials clearly and logically and develop an outline of your speech. **Organizing** is the process by which you arrange your main points and support materials into a logical and effective pattern. If you have already developed a thesis statement and main points, you are well on the way to addressing this next task.

THE IMPORTANCE OF ORGANIZATION

The importance of organizing to public speaking competence cannot be overemphasized. Problems in organizing speeches have been around for a long time. Fifty years ago, a well-known communication scholar and teacher said problems speech students confront in organizing are the factors that most detract from the effectiveness of speeches.[1] In a more recent study, another communication researcher looked at what helps college students listen better to lectures and, interestingly, it is organization.[2] Titsworth explored the effects on students' note taking of two different types of cues or behaviors displayed by the lecturer, immediacy behaviors and organizational statements. Results of the study indicate that students record more details and key points when listening to lectures with prominent organizational cues. They pay more attention when listening to lectures in which a number of organizational pointers are provided by the speaker. This importance of organizing was reinforced by a writer for the Harvard Business School who is identified as a "public speaking champion." He advises those rising in corporate ranks that what audiences all too often see or hear in speeches in corporations and businesses is disorganization and the vagueness that comes from not organizing your material well.[3]

> **8.1 ORGANIZING is the process by which you arrange your main points and support materials into a logical and effective pattern.**

These types of studies and articles indicate how important good organization is to any public remarks. No matter how focused your thesis, no matter how intriguing your stories and statistics, if listeners can't follow the logic of your speech, it will not be effective. Think back to lectures or speeches you've attended that appeared disorganized to you. You may have been interested in the content of the speech, but you couldn't follow what the speaker was saying. In the opening story for this chapter, Richard may have had this problem but he wasn't sure why. You can avoid this problem by organizing your support materials using a clear organizational pattern.

CHOOSING AND USING AN ORGANIZATIONAL PATTERN

An **organizational pattern** is the structure of the speech that introduces and clearly supports the thesis and logically leads the audience through the main points to the conclusion. Put more simply, the organizational pattern is a blueprint for how you structure what you will say. When you organize your speech, you are fitting your thesis and support materials into a structure that has a definite form and shape that later you will make apparent to the audience. Sound organization guides you and the audience through all the points you want to cover, one at a time, and in a logical and meaningful sequence.

8.2 AN ORGANIZATIONAL PATTERN is the structure of the speech that introduces and clearly supports the thesis and logically leads the audience through the main points to the conclusion.

Figure 8.1: Basic Structure for a Speech Outline

When you organize a speech, you fit your main points and ideas into a basic structure for the speech that contains an introduction, body, and conclusion.

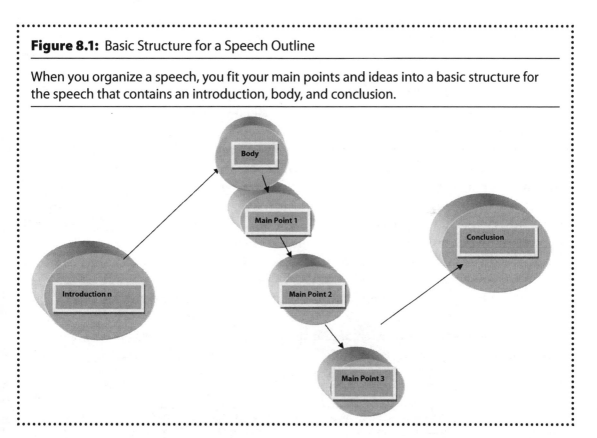

Typically, organizational patterns have three main parts. In the introduction, you briefly preview what your speech will be about. In the body, you develop and support your main points by describing and citing the support materials for all the subpoints. And in the conclusion, you briefly summarize and reinforce what you have said. This basic structure for any speech is illustrated in Figure 8.1. *Tell 'em what you're gonna tell em! Tell 'em! Then tell 'em what you said!* It is best to structure the body of the speech first and then develop the introduction and conclusion. Fortunately, if you followed the suggestions in Chapters 6 and 7 for developing a thesis, main points, and subpoints, then the body of your speech is almost done. Kumar's preliminary organization for the body is reflected in the description of his main points and support materials in Table 8.1.

Two thoughts about organizing are worth mentioning before we talk specifically about developing the introduction, body, and conclusion for your speech. First, we are recommending the use of a basic organizational pattern for speeches. However, later in Chapter 13, you will learn about specific ways to organize informative speeches: by category, time or space, comparison and contrast, or cause and effect. In Chapter 14, we discuss specific ways to organize persuasive speeches: by problem solution, motivated sequence, refuting the opponent, or comparing alternatives. For now, using the basic organizational pattern of an introduction, body, and conclusion will work fine for you. However, if you feel ambitious, jump ahead for more advanced ideas about organizing in Chapters 13 or 14.

Second, in our opening story, Kumar expressed a concern about cultural differences in organizing a speech. The basic structure for a speech in Figure 8.1 does have its roots in the rhetoric of Western culture. As we described in Chapter 2, this approach to organizing speeches dates back centuries to when Corax and Tisias trained Greek citizens to organize arguments for presentation in court. That centuries-old model contained a prologue, argument or proof, and epilogue, which obviously is quite similar to the basic organizational pattern we are recommending you use today. In Chapter 2, we also contrasted some basic concepts of the rhetorical heritages of Western and non-Western cultures. Western rhetoric values direct expression and logical and linear organization, moving clearly from point A to point B. Some non-Western cultures prefer a less direct and less linear approach to rhetoric and presenting your ideas to others.

Audiences in Japan may think a speaker who is direct and comes right out with one main point after another is aggressive and possibly impolite. Japanese audiences expect a speaker to go around the general topic and they are good at interpreting the speaker's hints in order to follow the line of reasoning. Speakers in China also may provide general background before they present each main point. The audience uses the background information to figure out where the speaker is heading. Indian or Hindi speakers also tend to avoid linear and straightforward organization of a speech. Indian audiences expect the speaker to branch off and then return to the main points, and they don't consider this disorganized or lacking in logic. Obviously, Kumar is right to be aware of cultural differences in how speeches are organized.

Clearly, no organizational pattern may be exactly right for all speeches in all situations and in all cultures. You do need to think about the particular audience and the cultural background of the listeners and how the organization of your speech may affect them. That concern aside, a basic approach to organizing should work well for you now. And the first task in developing an effective organizational pattern for your speech is to work on its three main parts.

PLANNING THE MAIN PARTS OF YOUR SPEECH

As Figure 8.1 shows, most speeches and speech outlines have three main parts: a beginning, middle, and an end—that is, an introduction, a body, and a conclusion. Those three parts of any speech will now be described and discussed in the order they occur when a speech is presented.

INTRODUCTION

The **introduction** orients the listeners to your speech and engages them in what will be said. When well-prepared and presented, the introduction builds rapport with the listeners, establishes the speaker's credibility, and sets the tone for the speech. The three main functions of the introduction are to: capture your listeners' attention; present your thesis and tell them why it is important; and preview what the speech will be about. To capture your listeners' attention, you can use any of several

8.3 THE INTRODUCTION orients the listeners to your speech and engages them in what will be said.

attention-getting devices: a startling statement, a question, a quotation, a personal experience or a story, or a reference or compliment to the audience or about the speaking occasion. As a quick aside, Box 8.1 offers suggestions for how *not* to introduce your speech; it also includes what not to do in your conclusion.

Box 8.1: How Not to Open and Conclude Your Speech

Try to avoid these pitfalls and potential disasters as you plan the introduction and conclusion for your speech

---

How Not to Open Your Speech

1. Don't open with a joke unless you are a really good joke teller.
2. Don't start with an apology of any kind.
3. Don't talk about yourself at the very start.
4. Don't tell the audience something they already know.

Why Not?

1. A joke that falls flat damages your credibility and sets you up for failure.
2. The listeners really don't want to start out by feeling sorry for you.
3. The listeners came to hear about your topic, not about you.
4. The audience doesn't want to be treated like they don't know much.

How Not to Conclude Your Speech

1. Don't introduce any new information in the conclusion.
2. Don't apologize or make excuses for anything you said or any other aspect of your speech.
3. When you start the conclusion, avoid phrases like "Now, in conclusion...." or "To conclude my speech for today, I would like to....."
4. When you've finished the conclusion, don't hem and haw, just stop talking or start taking questions.
5. Definitely, don't conclude by saying: "Well, I guess that's all I have to say."

Why Not?

1. The conclusion is intended to end the speech, not start something new.
2. Again, the listeners don't want to feel sorry for you. It makes them very uncomfortable.
3. The audience will know you're concluding without you saying so. Just begin your concluding remarks and they will get it.
4. Ending on a strong note leaves a good expression and enhances your credibility.
5. Phrases like this devalue the work you have put into preparing your speech.

Source: Henderson, J. (2007). How not to open your speech. *Directors & Boards, 31*(2), p. 20.

In Kumar's speech about the influence of pop music on multicultural understanding, he could start with the quotation he found on music as a universal language. Or he could consider opening on the following description of the pop music icon, Bono, which might better capture his listeners' attention:

> Paul David Hewson, most commonly known by his stage name Bono, is an Irish singer and musician, best known as the main vocalist of the Irish rock band, U2. Bono writes almost all U2 lyrics, and he often uses political, social, and religious themes. Outside U2, Bono is widely known for his tireless activism concerning social and political problems in Africa. He has cofounded several international organizations, such as *DATA*, which stands for Debt, AIDS, Trade, Africa. He has also helped to organize and perform in numerous benefit concerts, such as the 2005 *Live 8 concerts*. Bono, praised and criticized for his activism, has been nominated for the Nobel Peace Prize, granted an honorary knighthood by Queen Elizabeth II, and named Person of the Year by *Time* magazine. Bono is the only person to have been nominated for an Academy Award, Golden Globe, Grammy, and Nobel Peace Prize. These awards acknowledge how Bono uses his status as a pop music icon on behalf of others.[4]

The next part of the introduction is the thesis statement, the central idea or claim of your speech; it follows the attention getter in the introduction. In addition to stating the single most important idea of the speech, the thesis can include a statement of significance indicating why the speech is important to the audience. The audience will listen with greater attention if you say why the topic is important. In Kumar's introduction, he could stress the importance of the topic to the listeners by simply stating:

> Bono effectively uses pop music to create multicultural awareness and understanding of the plights and problems of people in other cultures. He is a good example of how popular music, which is highly influential around the world, can be used as the stimulant and glue to bring people together.

Most listeners would support the idea of bringing people together.

After you capture the listeners' attention and present the thesis, then you provide a preview of the content of the speech. The purpose of the preview is to indicate what the listeners can anticipate and what they should be listening for. The preview is literally a road map to the speech. Sometimes, the preview can specifically identify the main points of your speech, while other times, that isn't a good idea. If your speech is designed to build to a suspenseful conclusion, or if you first want to impress a hostile audience, you may not want to mention your main points quite so clearly in the preview. Here's the preview for Kumar's speech:

> We will begin today by looking at how popular music, as a result of global media, is becoming increasingly global and multicultural. Given this globalization of the music industry, it is evident that popular music has great potential for promoting multicultural understanding.

One final point before we end our discussion of introductions relates to the fact that cultures may differ in what they consider effective in an introduction. In an experimental study, 300 people in the Netherlands, France, and Senegal were asked about their appreciation of and response to three different introductions to a presentation about a mobile phone.[5] The study's results show that the three cultures differ with respect to the parts of an introduction they prefer most. The Dutch appreciated the overview most, while the French respondents preferred an ethical appeal in the introduction, and participants from Senegal preferred an anecdote or story that was included. The researchers concluded introductions that gain greatest attention in a tailored way for a particular culture are most likely to increase the audience's ability to listen.

BODY OF THE SPEECH

The **body of the speech** supports your central claim through the presentation of the main points. The **main points** are the key ideas that, taken together, support the thesis statement and prove the central claim of the speech. As you develop a thesis statement for your speech, you identify the main points for it and decide how to best organize those points. The organizational pattern you choose makes up the body of the speech and is an arrangement of the main points in the best possible way to accomplish the purpose of the speech. As you gathered your support materials for the main points, you may have planned to organize them in a particular way; you may rethink that organization of the body of the speech as you learn more about organizing. Logical patterns, based on how people think, are often used for informative speeches (Chapter 13). Psychological patterns, based on how people feel, work well for persuasive speeches (Chapter 14).

8.4 THE BODY OF THE SPEECH supports your central claim through the presentation of a series of main points.

8.5 THE MAIN POINTS are the key ideas that, taken together, support the thesis statement and prove the central claim of the speech.

TRANSITIONS

Within the body of the speech, **transitions**—words, phrases, or sentences—are used to indicate how the main points are related to each other; they're also used to connect the introduction to the body of the speech and the body to the conclusion. The three main functions of transitions are to: let the listeners know when you're ending one idea and moving on to the next; serve as an internal summary and tell the audience what you've covered so far; and, act as an internal preview to foreshadow your next point and tell the listeners what's coming next. A transition could be something as simple as saying: "Next, I'd like to describe..." (an internal preview); or "Having examined the problem of...., let's consider a solution...." (an internal summary). More sophisticated transitions can be developed once you have a completed outline for your speech, and you see where previews and summaries are most needed.

8.6 TRANSITIONS are words, phrases, or sentences that are used within the body of the speech to indicate how the main points are related to each other and they are used to connect the introduction to the body of the speech and the body to the conclusion.

CONCLUSION

The **conclusion** lets the listeners know the speech is ending and reminds them of your thesis and central idea. When well prepared and presented, the conclusion moves the listeners to understanding, if your purpose is to inform, or to action if your purpose is to persuade. The three main functions of the conclusion are to: review the content of the speech and summarize its meaning and purpose; refer back to the introduction and reinforce or restate the thesis statement; and, leave the audience with a final attention-getting message. Like the attention-getting device in the introduction, the final message or closing device can be a question, a short story, a quotation, or an inspirational appeal.

8.7 THE CONCLUSION lets the listeners know the speech is ending and reminds them of your thesis and central idea.

Here's a possible conclusion for Kumar's speech with each part identified as to its function:

- Review of the content of the speech: "Today we have examined how the emergence of global media has resulted in the globalization and multicultural nature of pop music. Given this globalization of the music industry, we then considered the potential for pop music to help promote multicultural understanding."
- Reinforcement of thesis: "On September 27, 2007, Bono received the Philadelphia Liberty Medal for his work to end world poverty and hunger. In accepting the Liberty Medal, Bono said, 'When you are trapped by poverty, you are not free. When trade laws prevent you from selling the food you grew, you are not free. When you are a monk in Burma barred from entering a temple because of your gospel of peace ... well, then none of us are truly free.' Bono donated the $100,000 prize associated with the Liberty Medal to an organization fighting HIV and AIDS in Africa. Bono and his philanthropic work are excellent examples of a new approach to bringing people together around the globe."
- Final message and appeal for understanding: "I hope now you better understand how popular music and pop musicians can become the stimulant and glue to encourage multicultural understanding among cultures."

As you plan and develop the introduction, body, and conclusion of your speech, you put them down on paper in a working, formal, and presentational outline of your speech. These are not three separate tasks. Rather, each one of the outlines grows out of the one that went before it.

PREPARING AN OUTLINE

An outline provides a structure for organizing everything you will say in your speech. When you consider speech structure, think about it as you would about a house. A well-constructed house is more than just a pile of bricks, boards, and nails held together haphazardly. Similarly, a good speech is more than just a jumble of your support materials—your ideas, facts, and figures. Rather, a competent speaker organizes the support materials into a well-structured outline of everything the speech is to cover. The outline is like an architect's drawings for how to build a house. Regardless of the speech, most outlines start with the basic structure presented earlier in Figure 8.1. Based on that simple structure, you'll make use of three types of outlines as you go through the process of preparing and then presenting your speech: a working outline, a formal outline, and a presentational outline.

WORKING, FORMAL, AND PRESENTATIONAL OUTLINES

A **working outline** contains most of the detailed information from your research efforts and is, in essence, a work-in-progress. You'll change it often as you experiment with different ways to organize the information you gathered by researching your topic. Since the purpose of the working outline is to help you plan your speech, it acts as a foundation for organizing and reorganizing your support materials and ideas into main points. Nobody sees your

8.8 A WORKING OUTLINE contains most of the detailed information from your research efforts and is, in essence, a work-in-progress.

working outline as it changes through time, but it ultimately serves as the base upon which you create a more formal outline.

A **formal outline** contains all of the information from the final version of your working outline, but it is organized and presented using a standard outlining format. The most common standard outline format makes use of an alphanumeric system in which main points are labeled with Roman numerals and subpoints with a consistent pattern of letters and numbers to indicate subordination of ideas. Indented headings and subheadings are used to indicate how the points in the outline relate to each other, with main points to the extreme left, and less important subpoints indented. Most word processing programs, like Microsoft's Word, have an outlining function that makes the development of a

> **8.9 A FORMAL OUTLINE contains all of the information from the final version of your working outline, but it is organized and presented using a standard outlining format.**

Figure 8.2: Standard Format for a Formal Outline

All speeches can be organized using this type of a standard outline format.

Speech Title: (Indicate the speech topic, pique curiosity, be concise)

General Purpose: (to inform, persuade, or entertain)

Specific Purpose: (infinitive statement indicating the goal of the speech)

   I. INTRODUCTION (written out in full sentences)
     A. Attention-getting or lead-in device
     B. Thesis statement (declarative sentence stating the central idea or claim of the speech and its significance to the audience)
     C. Preview of main points

  II. BODY (support materials that help accomplish the speech purpose, organized into 3–4 main points with subpoints for each main point)
     A. First main point (can be a complete sentence)
       1. Subpoint
       2. Subpoint
       *Transition to next main point (verbal or nonverbal)
     B. Second main point (can be a complete sentence)
       1. Subpoint
       2. Subpoint
       *Transition
  III. CONCLUSION (written out in full sentences)
     A. Review of main points
     B. Restatement of the thesis statement
     C. Closing device

---

formal outline much easier.

By developing a formal outline, you can visually examine what you've identified as main points and determine whether they're important enough to be major points. You can check whether you've covered enough but not too many subpoints under each main point, and you can review the logic

Figure 8.3: Kumar's Formal Outline

Using the standard outline format, Kumar developed this formal outline for his speech. See if you think it flows logically from one point to the next.

Speech Title: Pop Music and Globalization: What's the Link Between the Two?

General Purpose: To inform

Specific Purpose: To develop greater understanding of the potential positive influence of pop music on cultures around the world

I. INTRODUCTION
   A. Paul David Hewson, most commonly known by his stage name Bono, is an Irish singer and musician, best known as the main vocalist of the Irish rock band, U2. Bono writes almost all U2 lyrics, and he often uses political, social, and religious themes. Outside U2, Bono is widely known for his tireless activism concerning social and political problems in Africa. He has cofounded several international organizations, such as DATA, which stands for Debt, AIDS, Trade, Africa. He has also helped to organize and perform in numerous benefit concerts, such as the 2005 Live 8 concerts. Bono, praised and criticized for his activism, has been nominated for the Nobel Peace Prize, granted an honorary knighthood by Queen Elizabeth II, and named Person of the Year by *Time* magazine. Bono is the only person to have been nominated for an Academy Award, Golden Globe, Grammy, and Nobel Peace Prize. (Bono, 2009). These awards acknowledge how Bono uses his status as a pop music icon on behalf of others.
   B. Bono effectively uses pop music to create multicultural awareness and understanding of the plights and problems of people in other cultures. He is a good example of how popular music, which is highly influential around the world, can be used as the stimulant and glue to bring people together.
   C. We will begin today by looking at how popular music, as a result of global media, is becoming increasingly global and multicultural. Given this globalization of the music industry, it is evident that popular music has great potential for promoting multicultural understanding.
II. BODY
   A. Popular music is becoming increasingly global and multicultural.
      1. The emergence and influence of global media
         (de Block and Rydin's observations about the influence of global media and media exposure on youth cultures)
      2. The globalization of pop music as a result of global media technology
         (Statistics on the popularity of various pop music stars around the world and description of the Live 8 concerts as online video events with one billion people watching the concert live, on TV or the Internet)
      3. The influence worldwide of pop music on other cultures
         (Henry Wadsworth Longfellow's quote about music as the universal language)
         * Now you have a better understanding of the extent to which popular music is becoming global. Let's go on and consider how that globalization process can benefit people worldwide.
   B. Globally, pop music has the potential to promote multicultural understanding.
      1. How influential pop music is on young people
         (Kumar's personal account about his family's trip to a Live 8 concert in London and how that influenced him and millions of others)

Continued on next page

Continued from previous page

2. How exposure to the music of other cultures promotes multicultural understanding *(World Music Coalition email listserv comments about music promoting multicultural understanding)*
3. Opportunities for bringing people together based on the globalization of pop music *(Quotation from Kumar's interview with media expert, Edmund Thomas, on the globalization of pop music breaking down communication barriers and Bono quote saying music can change the world because it can change people)*
    * I hope I have made it clear how the globalization of pop music presents new opportunities for promoting multicultural awareness and understanding.

III. CONCLUSION
A. Today we have examined how the emergence of global media has resulted in the globalization and multicultural nature of pop music. Given this globalization of the music industry, we then considered the potential for pop music helping to promote multicultural understanding.
B. On September 27, 2007, Bono received the Philadelphia Liberty Medal for his work to end world poverty and hunger. In accepting the Liberty Medal, Bono said, "When you are trapped by poverty, you are not free. When trade laws prevent you from selling the food you grew, you are not free. When you are a monk in Burma barred from entering a temple because of your gospel of peace...well, then none of us are truly free." Bono donated the $100,000 prize associated with the Liberty Medal to an organization fighting HIV and AIDS in Africa. Bono and his philanthropic work are excellent examples of a new approach to bringing people together around the globe (Bono, 2009).
C. I hope now you better understand how popular music and pop musicians can become the stimulant and glue to encourage multicultural understanding among cultures.

of how your ideas are arranged and relate to one another. A standard outline format for preparing a formal outline is provided in Figure 8.2 to illustrate and clarify how you should outline your speech. If you want to see a completed formal outline, there's one for Kumar's speech about pop music presented in Figure 8.3.

Finally, you use the formal outline to produce a shorter, more concise outline to use when you present the speech. A **speaking or presentational outline** contains only enough information to remind you of what to say at a glance. You select out just enough information to remind you of what to say, though this outline may contain material like quotations that need to be read unerringly to the audience. This outline could take the form of a brief key word outline or some teachers suggest you put notes on one side of a group of 3" x 5" cards. Whether you use a key word outline or note cards, including too much information or detail will confuse you and cause you to lose your place in the speech. You might also fall into the trap of becoming **note dependent**—meaning you refer to your notes too often and lose contact with the audience when giving the speech. Also, if you rely too much on your presentational outline, you may end up reading the speech instead of presenting it. Figure 8.4 uses Kumar's speech to illustrate what a useful presentational outline should contain.

8.10 A SPEAKING OR PRESENTATIONAL OUTLINE contains only enough information to remind you of what to say at a glance.

8.11 NOTE DEPENDENT means you refer to your notes too often and lose contact with the audience when giving the speech.

Figure 8.4: Kumar's Presentational Outline

Using his formal outline, Kumar developed this presentational outline for his speech. It is a bit long as the conclusion is written out so Kumar presents the quotation accurately. He also may use the conclusion, exactly as written in his formal outline, when he actually speaks.

I. INTRODUCTION
- Paul David Hewson, stage name Bono
  ⊙ Main vocalist Irish rock band, U2
  ⊙ Writes U2 lyrics using political, social, religious themes
  ⊙ Activist on racial and political problems in Africa and worldwide
  ⊙ Cofounded international organizations, organized and played in benefit concerts
  ⊙ Many awards: Nobel Peace Prize nomination, honorary knighthood, *Time* magazine Person of Year; only person nominated for Academy Award, Golden Globe, Grammy, Nobel Peace Prize.
- Thesis: Bono uses pop music for multicultural awareness, understanding plights and problems of others; a good example of how pop music brings people together globally.
- Preview: Pop music global and multicultural; pop music promotes multicultural understanding.

II. BODY
- Main Point: Pop music becoming global and multicultural.
  ⊙ Influence of global media—de Block and Rydin on influence of media on youth.
  ⊙ Globalization of pop music—show statistics on pop music stars' global popularity; and, one billion people watching Live 8 concerts.
  ⊙ Influence of pop music on other cultures—Longfellow quote on music as universal language.
    * Transition: Better understanding of global pop music; next, benefit to people worldwide.
- Main Point: Globally, pop music potential to promote multicultural understanding.
  ⊙ Pop music big influence on young people—Kumar's story about family trip to Live 8 concert.
  ⊙ Exposure to music promotes multi-cultural understanding—Comments from World Music Coalition email listserv.
  ⊙ Bring people together globally using pop music —quotes from media expert, Edmund Thomas and from Bono on music changing the world.
    * Transition: I hope it's clear—globalization of pop music promotes multicultural awareness and understanding.

III. CONCLUSION
- Review: Talked about emergence of global media and positive effects of globalization of pop music on multicultural understanding.
- On September 27, 2007, Bono received the Philadelphia Liberty Medal for his work to end world poverty and hunger. In accepting the Liberty Medal, Bono said, "When you are trapped by poverty, you are not free. When trade laws prevent you from selling the food you grew, you are not free. When you are a monk in Burma barred from entering a temple because of your gospel of peace...well, then none of us are truly free." Bono donated the $100,000 prize associated with the Liberty Medal to an organization fighting HIV and

Continued on next page

Continued from previous page

> AIDS in Africa. Bono and his philanthropic work are excellent examples of a new approach to bringing people together around the globe (Bono, 2009).
> - I hope now you better understand how popular music and pop musicians can become the stimulant and glue to encourage multicultural understanding among cultures.

The steps to competent speech preparation and organization presented in this chapter helped Kumar ace his speech, just like Angelique and Hana. Had Richard applied the guidelines of Competency Four, he would have been more successful as well. Like Kumar, Angelique and Hana, you now should be motivated to prepare a good speech; understand how to prepare a speech effectively; and possess the skills necessary to competent speech preparation. The next four chapters discuss the four competencies essential to presenting a speech.

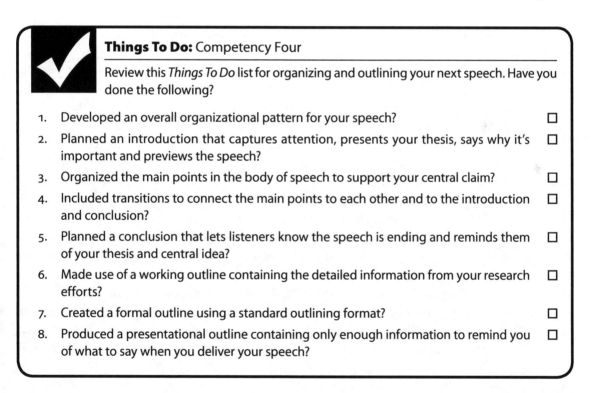

Things To Do: Competency Four

Review this *Things To Do* list for organizing and outlining your next speech. Have you done the following?

1. Developed an overall organizational pattern for your speech? ☐
2. Planned an introduction that captures attention, presents your thesis, says why it's important and previews the speech? ☐
3. Organized the main points in the body of speech to support your central claim? ☐
4. Included transitions to connect the main points to each other and to the introduction and conclusion? ☐
5. Planned a conclusion that lets listeners know the speech is ending and reminds them of your thesis and central idea? ☐
6. Made use of a working outline containing the detailed information from your research efforts? ☐
7. Created a formal outline using a standard outlining format? ☐
8. Produced a presentational outline containing only enough information to remind you of what to say when you deliver your speech? ☐

CHAPTER SUMMARY

After gathering support materials, the next step is to orga- nize those materials and develop an outline for your speech. Organizing is the process by which you arrange your main points and support materials into a logical and effective pat- tern. Sound organization has been proven critical to effective public speaking. It guides you and the audience through all the main points of the speech, one at a time, and in a logical and meaningful sequence. An organizational pattern is the struc- ture of the speech that introduces and clearly supports the the- sis and logically leads the audience through the main points to the conclusion. Typically, organizational patterns for speeches have three main parts: an introduction, body, and conclusion.

While a basic organizational pattern contains these three parts, you may organize informative and persuasive speeches using patterns specifically designed to accomplish these two purposes. Using the basic organizational pattern, the introduction orients the listeners to your speech and engages them in what will be said. The three main functions of the introduction are to: capture your listen- ers' attention; present your thesis and tell them why it is important; and preview what the speech will be about. The body of the speech supports your central claim through the presentation of a series of main points. The main points are the key ideas that, taken together, support the thesis statement and prove the central claim of the speech. Transitions are words, phrases, or sentences that are used within the body of the speech to indicate how the main points are related to each other, and they are used to connect the introduction to the body of the speech and the body to the conclusion. The conclusion lets the listeners know the speech is ending and reminds them of your thesis and central idea. The three main functions of the conclusion are to review the content of the speech and sum- marize its meaning and purpose, refer back to the introduction and reinforce or restate the thesis statement, and leave the audience with a final attention-getting message. While this basic approach to organizing should work well in general, a competent public speaker is aware of possible cultural differences and preferences for organizing speeches. As you plan and develop the introduction, body and conclusion, you put them down on paper in a working, formal, and presentational outline for your speech. A working outline contains most of the detailed information from your research efforts and is, in essence, a work-in-progress. A formal outline contains all of the information from the final version of your working outline, but it is organized and presented using a standard outline format. A speaking or presentational outline contains only enough information to remind you of what to say at a glance. By limiting the amount of information and detail on the presentational outline you avoid becoming note dependent. Note dependent means you refer to your notes too often and lose contact with the audience when giving the speech

KEY TERMS

The key terms below are defined in this chapter and presented alphabetically with definitions in the Glossary at the end of the book.

- organizing
- introduction
- main points
- conclusion
- formal outline
- note dependent

- organizational pattern
- body of the speech
- transitions
- working outline
- speaking or presentational outline

BUILDING COMPETENCE ACTIVITIES

INDIVIDUAL ACTIVITIES

1. When speeches are next presented in class, evaluate how effectively each student organized and outlined her or his speech. Determine whether the organizational "road map" was made clear to the listeners.

2. Attend a public speech or presentation (it could be a lecture in another class), and evaluate the introduction, body, and conclusion of the speech. Were the three main parts clear, logical, and creative?

3. Go to either one of these websites, both of which contain an array of public speeches: http://www.wfu.edu/~louden/Political%20Communication/Class%20Information/SPEECHES.html or http://www.csus.edu/indiv/k/kiddv/ComsSites/speeches.html. Choose a speech and evaluate the quality of the speaker's use of an organizational pattern. What type of pattern was used and was that use effective? Write a short evaluation of how effectively the speaker presented the three main parts of the speech—the introduction, body, and conclusion and whether transitions were used well.

4. Review Kumar's outlines presented in this chapter and decide if you think he used his support materials in the best possible way and if he organized the speech effectively.

GROUP ACTIVITIES

1. When speeches are next presented in class, after the speeches, meet with a group of three to four students to evaluate how effectively each student organized and outlined her or his speech. Prepare a list of general recommendations about organizing and outline to share with the class.

2. With one or two other students, attend a public speech or presentation (it could be a lecture in another class in which you are all enrolled). Have each student individually evaluate the speaker's introduction, body, and conclusion. Compare your individual evaluations after the lecture.

3. Form groups of three to four students and go to either of these websites both of which contain a big selection of public speeches: http://www.abacon.com/pubspeak/histsit.html, or http://www.mhhe.com/socscience/comm/new-home/. Have each group member select a different speech and try to identify the main points in the speech and describe the organizational pattern used. Compare how effectively each of the speeches was organized. Include whether the speech contained the use of clear transitions.

4. Choose a partner in the class and exchange your formal outlines. Evaluate and provide feedback to the other student about the clarity and logic of his or her formal outline.

COMPETENCY CHECKPOINTS AND SELF-ASSESSMENT TOOL

Here is what you need to know and be able to do regarding organizing and outlining your speech. Determine your level of competency and whether you are ready to proceed to the next chapter. Give yourself one point for each checkpoint you answer satisfactorily.

COMPETENCY CHECKPOINTS	NUMBER OF POINTS
KNOWLEDGE 1. Describe what speech organization is and why it is important. 2. What are the three main parts of a basic organizational pattern and what functions does each part serve in your speech? 3. How may cultural differences and preferences for organizing a speech be managed by a competent public speaker? 4. Explain how you use the three types of outlines to effectively prepare your speech.	
SKILLS 1. Use your main points and subpoints to develop an organizational pattern for the body of your next speech. 2. Use the detailed information from your research efforts to develop a working outline for your next speech. 3. Use the working outline to develop a formal outline for your speech based on the standard outline format provided in this chapter. 4. Use the formal outline to develop a speaking/presentational outline for your next speech.	
ETHICS AND CREDIBILITY 1. What would an ethical approach to organizing a speech call on you as a speaker to consider and do? 2. How will the use of an effective organizational pattern for your speech enhance your credibility as a speaker?	
TOTAL CHECKPOINTS (OUT OF A POSSIBLE TEN POINTS)	

ENDNOTES

1. Tompkins, P.K. (1959). Organizing the speech to inform. *Today's Speech, 7*(3), 21–22.

2. Titsworth, B. S. (2004) Students' notetaking: The effects of teacher immediacy and clarity. *Communication Education, 53*(4), 305–320.

3. Morgan, N. (2003). How to put together a great speech when you're under the gun. *Harvard Business School Publishing Corporation, 6*(9), p.3 Prod. #: C0309D-PDF-ENG.

4. Bono (2009). Retrieved from http://www.answers.com/topic/bono

5. Gerritsen, M. & Wannet, E. (2005, May). Cultural differences in the appreciation of introductions of presentations. *Technical Communication, 52*(2), 194–208.

PART THREE:
PRESENTING A SPEECH

In Part One of this textbook, you were introduced to communication in general and public speaking in particular. In Part Two, we focused on four critical competencies for preparing speeches well: finding a topic, developing a purpose and thesis statement, researching your speech, and organizing and outlining it. These four steps prepare you to deliver a great speech. High-quality presentations also result from the number of times you rehearse your speech before an audience and the amount and number of times you rehearse silently and out loud.[1] We already mentioned in Chapter 3 how important it is to practice ahead of time. Obviously, both preparing and practicing your speech will result in a much more effective delivery, the main topic addressed in this part of your book.

Cicero, the great Roman orator, often referred to the importance of style and delivery. A quick perusal of more recent writings about public speaking comes up with all sorts of benefits to be gained from being able to deliver a good speech. One speech expert tells us even when the content of a speech is kept the same, how it is delivered can make the speaker seem either powerful or powerless.[2] Another expert also calls our attention to the significant effects of speech style on whether a presentation is seen as a "powerless speech."[3] Corporate leaders are promised "power from the podium," if they follow the advice of their corporate speechwriters.[4]

If you want to "present like a pro," public relations experts say to improve your delivery: by watching and studying presentations of successful people, and take advantage of every opportunity to speak publicly.[5] State legislators also are identified as in need of "tips for a more powerful presentation," and they often are given practical guidelines for acquiring this *power* of public speaking.[6]

Do you notice a recurring theme in these writings and how-to hints? A public speech, if effectively delivered, can be a powerful tool for communicating with others. The lesson is clear. How you deliver a speech is an important part of public speaking competence. In Part Three, we now focus on the competencies essential to presenting your speech effectively and appropriately.

- Chapter 9: Communicating with Words: Competency Five
- Chapter 10: Communicating with Your Voice: Competencies Six and Seven
- Chapter 11: Communicating Nonverbally: Competency Eight

9

COMMUNICATING WITH WORDS:
COMPETENCY FIVE

- **Using Words and Language Effectively and Appropriately**
    - Clarity
    - Vividness
    - Appropriateness

"For one word a man is often claimed to be wise, and for one word he is often deemed to be foolish. We should be careful indeed of what we say." Confucius, Chinese philosopher and teacher of ethics, 550–478 BC

• •
• • •

Most of the students in the public speaking class were well prepared to present their informative speeches. Equally important, by rehearsing a few times with a small group of their classmates, they were feeling fairly confident about their presentation skills. Angelique was ready to talk about non-Western rhetoric, Hana about her immigration to the United States, and Kumar about the global influence of pop music. During rehearsals, they used the delivery competencies to give each other feedback and a little straightforward criticism. Kumar told Angelique, "The simple language and familiar words you use to describe rhetoric makes it easy to understand, though some of the terminology about Eastern rhetoric is new to me. Drawing mental images of the great Greek and Roman orators speaking to the masses bring your speech to life as I listen to it." Then Kumar turned his attention to Hana's speech. "Hana, the way you talk about going through immigration with your family is excellent. I got involved in the process with you and could really imagine what it was like being an immigrant coming to the United States. However, a little of what you say sounds a bit condescending, like you don't think we will understand your family's experiences." "That's not how I mean to come across, I'll work on that," Hana replied, and then added: "When I listened to your speech, I sort of got the same feeling, Kumar. Some of the language you use to describe globalization sounds like academic jargon you got from a book. Maybe you can simplify the wording to match the audience's understanding."

• •
• • •

The students' ability to reflect on how they use language is admirable and indicates how much they are learning about delivering a speech. The host of a late night TV show for many years, Steve Allen, agrees about the importance of choosing your words carefully whenever you speak publicly—at school, at work, and on TV.[7] Allen likens delivering speeches to making soup, claiming the chief ingredient determining the quality of any speech is words. He says key words are the steel girders holding together the content of the speech. They are the spider in the web, the hub in the wheel around which the entire speech revolves. Allen's simple advice is this: Select a few key words, build your speech around those words, and be sure to explain their meaning to the audience. Use everyday words, the language of the audience. Talk to others as you would like others to talk to you. In our opening story, Kumar gave Angelique similar advice about the words she used to describe Eastern rhetoric. Let's now explore exactly what it means to use words competently in a speech.

Based on what you learn in this chapter, you will be able to *use language appropriate to the audience and occasion of your speech.* This is Competency Five and it includes the ability to:

- Choose and use language that is exceptionally clear and enhances audience comprehension of the speech
- Choose and use language that is exceptionally vivid and enhances audience enthusiasm for the speech
- Choose and use language that is free of inappropriate jargon and that is non-sexist, non-racist, etc.

USING WORDS AND LANGUAGE EFFECTIVELY AND APPROPRIATELY

As Angelique, Hana, and Kumar's practice session illustrates, using language competently is essential to giving a good speech. By simply changing a few of the words they used, Angelique, Hana, and Kumar probably communicated far better with other students in the class. Plus, they became aware of using language competently, a public speaking skill that will last them, and you, a lifetime.

Competent language enhances any listeners' understanding and enthusiasm for a speech by the use of words that are clear, vivid, and appropriate. While most people could not deliver a speech like a polished politician, clarity, vividness, and appropriateness nonetheless are essential to all competent speakers.

9.1 COMPETENT LANGUAGE enhances any listeners' understanding and enthusiasm for a speech by the use of words that are clear, vivid, and appropriate.

CLARITY

The importance of clarity in communication was first mentioned in Chapter 1. We said language can and should be used to clarify the meaning of any spoken message. In the case of public speaking, **clear language** uses words in such a way that listeners understand and can easily comprehend the meaning of the speaker's message. If your listeners have to try to figure out what you mean, they'll be distracted from listen-

9.2 CLEAR LANGUAGE uses words in such a way that listeners understand and can easily comprehend the meaning of the speaker's message.

ing to the content of your speech. You achieve clarity by being sensitive to how the meanings of words vary from one person to another, and by using words that are concrete and familiar to your listeners.

Meaning. According to Chapter 1, words and nonverbal symbols mean different things to different people and different things in different situations. Since that is true, when you present a speech to an audience of twenty people, there are twenty opportunities for what you say to mean something different. If your listeners are not very diverse, it's more likely that they will interpret your words in a similar manner, while a more diverse audience may result in more varying interpretations of the message. In either case, since words communicate powerful but different meanings for people, good speakers choose their words carefully to ensure their meaning is clear.[8]

For example, if Hana refers to herself as a member of a minority group and by that she means she is one of only a few students on campus who have immigrated to the United States, that meaning might not be clear. A word like *minority* can be varyingly interpreted. Some of the students in the audience may interpret minority group to mean Hana is Chinese or she is a female. If Hana continues to talk about her experiences as a member of a minority group without saying what she means—that she is an immigrant—the audience might be confused and her speech would lack clarity. One effective way to achieve clarity is by using concrete words.

Concreteness. To help your listeners interpret your words as you intend them, you should use words and phrases that are more concrete rather than abstract. A **concrete word** refers to something specific your audience can visualize, such as a specific object, person, or place. In contrast, an abstract word is more general and describes something less able to be immediately visualized by the listeners. The more concrete your words are, the more precise the word picture will be that they bring to mind for your listeners. If your words are too abstract, there will be too much room for misinterpretation and a lack of clarity. In Kumar's speech about the influence of pop music, talking about a rock musician like Bono of U2 is an example of the simple use of concreteness. Most students would immediately visualize Bono with his dark glasses at a large rock concert, whereas, talking about pop musicians in general would be too abstract to visualize.

> ....
> **9.3 A CONCRETE WORD refers to something specific your audience can visualize, such as a specific object, person, or place.**

Familiarity. In addition to using concrete language to achieve clarity, it's also helpful to use words with which your listeners are familiar. While every field of knowledge has its own jargon and specialized or technical terms, the use of unfamiliar words clouds rather than clarifies any speech. In the same way, slang or the use of words or phrases only known in a particular region or by a particular group of people also will lead to misunderstandings.[9] The everyday expressions that some of your listeners understand immediately may have little or no meaning to others. A phrase such as "it's raining cats and dogs" or "the ball is in your court" may be easily understood by many people in the United States but confusing to people from other countries or cultures. Similarly, listeners from the West or North in the United States may not understand expressions widely used in some other region of the country. The same holds true for people from different age or social groups. Some of Kumar's classmates, for instance, may know a lot about popular music, and others may not be at all familiar with it.

When you express yourself using clear and familiar language, you help the audience understand and relate to your message. In an age of information overload, most audiences don't have the time or the desire to decipher a speaker's message, if that speaker uses techno-speak, double-speak, or even "I made it up so I sound smarter than you-speak."[10] The speaker who uses techno-speak, double-speak, or even "I made it up so I sound smarter than you-speak," misses the opportunity to clearly and powerfully communicate the message. Also, while it may be tempting to use elaborate and impressive language, you run the risk of mispronouncing or misusing a fancy word and appearing to want to impress the audience.

To achieve clarity, a competent speaker chooses his or her words carefully, pays attention to the meaning of words, and uses words that are concrete and familiar. By being aware of how you say what you say, a side benefit is that you'll avoid being redundant and repetitive. If you make a point clear the first time, there is no need to repeat it in a variety of ways in order for your listeners to understand. Plus, you'll be able to pay more attention to using vivid language that will enliven your speech for your listeners.

VIVIDNESS

Vivid language promotes enthusiasm for a speech by bringing the speaker's message to life and moving the audience emotionally. It makes a speech memorable and its main points engaging and real for the listeners. The great Roman orator, Cicero, said that real style in public speaking is achieved primarily through the speaker's use of language. The kind of style Cicero was referring to will add great impact to your speech. In fact, researchers have found the powerful use of language affects perceptions of a speaker's dynamism, status, and credibility as well as the listeners' attitudes toward what the speaker is recommending.[11,12]

In the chapter on researching for your speech, we discussed how stories and examples can get the audience involved in the main points of your speech and bring it to life. The vividness and style recommended by Cicero can be incorporated in how you tell a story or provide an example. You accomplish this through the use of two very effective language techniques: imagery and figures of speech.

Imagery is the creation of visual pictures and other sensory experiences through description. When listeners can almost see, feel, taste, smell, or hear something, they're much more likely to be impressed by it and remember it. For example, when Hana described leaving China to come to the United States, she probably drew mental and emotional pictures of the event for her listeners. She may have talked about her feelings as she approached the door to the immigration office with her parents and how nervous she felt sitting in the back of the room on the first day of the public speaking class. She might have included vivid descriptions of how her family reacted to the immigration experience as well.

In addition to imagery, there are six figures of speech—simile, metaphor, analogy, the rhetorical question, alliteration, and repetition—any and all of which will bring the style Cicero talked about to your speech. These **figures of speech** are ways of saying things that help listeners to visualize, identify with, or really think about the points you're trying to make.[13] You probably use these techniques in everyday conversation without realizing it, but their intentional use in a speech is quite effective.

A **simile** is an explicit comparison that compares two unlike things by using the words *like* or *as*. Hana could have used a simile by saying: *Most of us experience anxiety at one time or another, but for me, stepping on to U.S. soil was like a Broadway star stepping on stage for the first time on opening night.* Here are a few more examples of similes:

He's as big as a house. You eat like a bird. The winner of the race ran like greased lightning.

9.4 VIVID LANGUAGE promotes enthusiasm for a speech by bringing the speaker's message to life and moving the audience emotionally.

9.5 IMAGERY is the creation of visual pictures and other sensory experiences through description.

9.6 FIGURES OF SPEECH are ways of saying things that help listeners to visualize, identify with, or really think about the points you're trying to make.

9.7 A SIMILE is an explicit comparison that compares two unlike things by using the words *like* or *as*.

A **metaphor** implies a comparison between two dissimilar things, but it does so without using the words *like* or *as*. Here's an example:

> Communication apprehension can either be the anchor that weighs you down or the shoulder you stand on to reach new heights in public speaking.

An **analogy** is an extended simile or metaphor that asks the listeners to accept the fact that things that sound alike in most respects will be alike in the respect being discussed. Here's an example:

> Overcoming public speaking anxiety is like taking a journey to an unknown place. The first step is always the hardest and perhaps a bit scary. But as you move along and become familiar with the new terrain, your anxiety subsides. And when you reach your destination, you think it wasn't so hard getting there after all. As you look back on the journey of taking this public speaking class, I assure you of this. You will hardly recall the anxious feelings you experienced at the onset of our shared journey.

A **rhetorical question** is one that is asked for effect rather than to elicit an answer. When you ask a rhetorical question in your speech, you're inviting your listeners to answer silently to themselves and then continue thinking about the question as you provide an answer to it. This figure of speech is frequently used as the attention-getting device in the introduction to a speech. Here are two ways Angelique or Kumar could use a rhetorical question to start their speeches:

> If you could learn to use a few public speaking strategies borrowed from Eastern rhetoric, and if that use would significantly improve your next speech, would you want me to tell you about these strategies?

Most of you probably have enjoyed pop music in one form or another but have you ever thought about the amazing influence of pop music on cultures around the world?

Alliteration is the repetition of the same consonant sound in a series of words or phrases that draws attention to your words and helps your listeners remember what you said. When you use alliteration, the sounds add a subtle but memorable dimension to what you have said. Hana could use alliteration this way to make her speech more vivid:

> The profound angst, anxiety, and anguish my family experienced when faced with the challenge of emigrating from our native China to the United States is hard to describe, though I will try to do so today.

Repetition is when the speaker repeats the same word or phrase several times in the same or various sections of a speech. This repetition helps to emphasize or tie several ideas together so your audience remembers and understands the connections you've made. It also helps to reinforce your

9.8 A METAPHOR implies a comparison between two dissimilar things, but it does so without using the words *like* or *as*.

9.9 AN ANALOGY is an extended simile or metaphor that asks the listeners to accept the fact that things that sound alike in most respects will be alike in the respect being discussed.

9.10 A RHETORICAL QUESTION is one that is asked for effect rather than to elicit an answer.

9.11 ALLITERATION is the repetition of the same consonant sound in a series of words or phrases that draws attention to your words and helps your listeners remember what you said.

9.12 REPETITION is when the speaker repeats the same word or phrase several times in the same or various sections of a speech.

point and make it memorable. A speech by the 1960s civil rights leader, Martin Luther King—his famous *I Have a Dream* speech—is full of repetition. Here is but one example:

> Go back to Mississippi, go back to Alabama, go back to South Carolina, go back to Georgia, go back to the slums and ghettos of our northern cities, knowing that somehow this situation [discrimination based on race] can and will be changed.

By now you may be thinking vivid language and style are just for public speaking experts like Martin Luther King, but that's not the case. Anyone can use vivid language in a speech, simply by planning ahead. You can use a simple simile or metaphor to illustrate any subpoint you want to make. You can write out a rhetorical question or several sentences ahead of time that use alliteration or repetition. If you choose to use a simile or metaphor, try to personalize it for the audience by using personal pronouns like you, us, we, or let's. For instance, it would be more effective to say: *Most of us experience opening-night jitters during our first speeches* rather than *many students experience anxiety during their first speeches.* Look over the summary in Table 9.1 of the six types of figures of speech and decide which one or two of them you could use to make your next speech more vivid and the listeners more enthusiastic.

APPROPRIATENESS

In Chapter 1, you learned about appropriate communication in general. We said you need to be aware and respectful of the norms and expectations for communicating in any situation, and you need to communicate sensitively and respectfully with everyone involved. This call for communicating appropriately is particularly important when giving a speech, and the admonition to *choose your words carefully* is particularly relevant to public speaking. Because you are presenting to a number of different people in any audience, it may be more difficult to use language that will be considered appropriate by all the listeners. In a public speaking situation, **appropriate language** is language

9.13 APPROPRIATE LANGUAGE presents information in a way that respects and treats all audience members as equals without being condescending or using biased language and stereotypes.

Table 9.1: Figures of Speech

You could use one or more of these six figures of speech to encourage enthusiasm for your speech and make it more vivid and memorable for the audience.

FIGURE OF SPEECH	DESCRIPTION	CONSIDER HOW YOU COULD USE IT!
Simile	Compare unlike things using *like or as*	
Metaphor	Compare dissimilar things but don't use *like* or *as*	
Analogy	An extended simile or metaphor	
Rhetorical question	A question asked for effect, not to elicit an answer	
Alliteration	Repeat a consonant sound in a series of words or phrases	
Repetition	Repeat a word or phrase in a section or several sections of the speech	

that presents information in a way that respects and treats all audience members as equals without being condescending or using biased language and stereotypes. Let's explore these challenges to the use of appropriate language in a speech.

Condescending Language. To be respectful and treat your listeners as equals, you adapt what you say to their knowledge of your topic, while avoiding the use of **condescending language** that speaks down to them. If your audience is unfamiliar with the topic, you provide details about what they may not understand, but you do so without setting yourself up as the only expert on the topic. If information is presented in a condescending manner, you risk the audience members not listening to what you have to say. Any casualness with technical jargon and other information will communicate disrespect and negatively impact your listeners' attitude toward your message and you as a speaker. Rather than enhancing your credibility, the presentation of information in a condescending manner will harm it. In our opening story, Kumar found Hana's description of her family's immigration experience to be a little bit condescending, as if the audience probably wouldn't understand it. Hana no doubt took that advice and reworded her description in order to connect more with her listeners.

On the other hand, you don't want to go to an extreme to build rapport with the audience by presenting information in a way that isn't comfortable for you. Instead, present your speech in your own words, at a level the audience will understand. One expert in rhetoric refers to this as finding *conversational common ground* with the audience.[14] To do this, you consider the knowledge you share with the listeners and use that information base as a starting point for how you talk about the topic. You talk like you would normally and provide details to facilitate your listeners' further understanding of what you are saying.

9.14 CONDESCENDING LANGUAGE is when you speak down to people rather than respecting and treating them as equals and adapting what you say to their knowledge of your topic.

9.15 BIASED LANGUAGE is when you use words or phrases that derive their meaning from stereotypes, based on gender, race, ethnic group, age, or disability.

Biased Language. Another way to use language appropriately is to avoid the use of words or phrases that derive their meaning from stereotypes based on gender, race, ethnic group, age, or disability. Most people know to avoid overt racial slurs but may carry with them certain stereotypes that will influence what they say in a manner that may be offensive to others. A subtle bias in language could unintentionally offend or insult an individual listener or some subgroup in the audience. By contrast, unbiased language serves to bring audiences together and encourages open discussion of even the most controversial topics. In Kumar's speech about the global influence of pop music, he needs to be mindful to avoid stereotyping when talking about different countries and cultures. When he refers to Bono of U2's activist work concerning social and political problems in Africa, he should avoid sounding patronizing and talking about two cultures of *haves* and *have not's.*

One particular type of **biased language** to pay attention to and avoid using in your speeches relates to gender. Gender-biased language can result from something as simple as using male pronouns more often than female ones. Referring to *him* more often than *her* may suggest that the speaker respects men more than women. Gender bias also results from using words that designate certain occupations or professions as male and others as female. You can change that by making a few substitutions in the words you use to designate certain jobs, such as saying: flight attendant rather

Table 9.2: Avoiding Gender-Biased Words and Phrases

Simple changes in language will help you become a gender-neutral public speaker.

1. Replace phrases that contain man or woman with gender-neutral terms.	
INSTEAD OF:	**SUBSTITUTE:**
Policeman	Police officer
Manpower	Labor force
Waitress	Wait person or server
Workman	Laborer
2. Restructure sentences to eliminate sexist language.	
INSTEAD OF:	**SUBSTITUTE:**
The fabric in the dress is manmade.	The fabric in the dress is synthetic, not natural.
What are the average man-hours it will take to do the job?	How many hours will it take to do the job?
When will a new chairman be assigned to the job?	When will someone be appointed to the chair's position?
3. Use plurals to avoid gender specific pronouns.	
INSTEAD OF:	**SUBSTITUTE:**
When a staff member arrives, tell him to sit in the front row.	As staff members arrive, tell them to sit in the front row.
A public speaker should plan the handouts he will use ahead of time.	Public speakers should plan the handouts they will use ahead of time.
4. Mention women first as often as men.	
INSTEAD OF:	**SUBSTITUTE:**
Men and women experience public speaking anxiety in the same way.	Women and men experience public speaking anxiety in the same way.
He or she will help us out.	She or he will help us out.

Source: Detz, J. (2002) *How to write and give a speech,* 2nd ed. New York: St. Martin's Press.

than stewardess; fire fighter rather than fireman; chairperson rather than chairman; and, humanity rather than mankind. Remember, doctors, politicians, astronauts, and executives can be male or female, so avoid language that assumes a gender bias in any role. Moreover, rather than refer to someone as a *woman lawyer* or a *male nurse,* leave off the gender descriptor, unless it's really necessary to understand your point. Table 9.2 provides specific suggestions from a public speaking expert for using gender-neutral language in your speech.

The guidelines for avoiding gender-biased language apply equally to other types of bias. Stereotypically pairing certain professions or occupations with certain races or ethnic groups or remarking on the race or ethnic background of a person in a certain profession is a form of subtle language bias. For example, to refer to an African American doctor may somehow communicate

Box 9.1: Clear, Vivid, and Appropriate Language

You want to choose words and use language to promote understanding and enthusiasm for your speech, while avoiding saying anything that could offend or insult your listeners.

Clear language promotes understanding and comprehension of the meaning of the speech.
- Be sensitive to variations in meaning.
- Use concrete rather than abstract words.
- Use familiar words.

Vivid language promotes enthusiasm, brings the message to life, and moves the audience emotionally.
- Incorporate imagery to create visual pictures for the listeners.
- Incorporate a couple of figures of speech to help listeners visualize, identify with, or think about your main points.

Appropriate language respects and treats listeners as equals and avoids biased language and stereotypes.
- Adapt language to listeners' knowledge base and avoid being condescending.
- Avoid biased words or phrases based on stereotypes about gender, race, ethnic group, age, or disability.

that an African American doctor is an unusual occurrence. Fortunately, this type of bias is rapidly disappearing as society is becoming more diverse in every way. However, without intending to do so, this type of language can subtly offend some of the listeners in your audience. So leave off the reference to ethnicity or race when mentioning a person's profession. A good rule to follow is that unless your audience needs to know the gender, race, ethnicity, or even the age of the person you're talking about, omit that information from your speech. Likewise, leave out references to a person's disability unless that information is relevant. Eliminate from your speech any words or phrases that categorize people based on stereotypes or patronize people in any way.

Like Hana, Angelique, and Kumar you now know how to incorporate clarity, vividness, and appropriateness in your speeches. By developing a few well-planned and effective phrases or sentences that draw mental pictures and evoke emotions, you can improve your speech immensely. By carefully wording and writing out these parts of your speech ahead of time, you will ensure that you say them just as you intend. Box 9.1 summarizes the key ideas about using clear, vivid, and appropriate language to help you with this competency in your next speech.

CHAPTER SUMMARY

The first delivery competency relates to how you use language and communicate with words when speaking publicly. Competent language enhances any listener's understanding and enthusiasm for a speech by the use of words that are clear, vivid, and appropriate. Clear language uses words in such a way that listeners understand and can easily comprehend the meaning of the speaker's message. You achieve clarity by being sensitive

> **✓ Things To Do:** Competency Five
>
> Review this *Things To Do* List for choosing words and using language when you deliver your next speech. Have you done the following?
>
> 1. Reviewed your speech outline and included the use of clear language and words that □ will help the listeners understand the meaning of your message?
> 2. Chosen words that are more concrete rather than abstract? □
> 3. Chosen words that are familiar to your listeners rather than jargon or specialized terms □ or unfamiliar slang or regionalisms?
> 4. Reviewed your speech outline and included the use of vivid language and words that □ will promote enthusiasm for your speech and move the audience emotionally?
> 5. Planned to use some imagery to create visual pictures in the minds of the listeners? □
> 6. Planned to use several figures of speech to help listeners visualize, identify with, or □ think about your main points?
> 7. Checked over your speech to ensure it is free of any condescending language? □
> 8. Checked over your speech to ensure it is free of any biased language? □

to how the meanings of words vary among people and by using words that are concrete and familiar to your listeners. A concrete word refers to something specific that your audience can visualize, such as a specific object, person, or place. By contrast, an abstract word is more general and describes something less able to be immediately visualized by the listeners. The use of unfamiliar words, jargon, specialized or technical terms, or unfamiliar slang clouds rather than clarifies the meaning of any speech. Vivid language promotes enthusiasm for a speech by bringing the speaker's message to life and moving the audience emotionally, using imagery and figures of speech. Imagery is the creation of visual pictures and other sensory experiences through description. Figures of speech are ways of saying things that help listeners to visualize, identify with, or really think about the points you're trying to make. There are six figures of speech—simile, metaphor, analogy, the rhetorical question, alliteration, and repetition—any and all of which will bring style to your speech. Appropriate language presents information in a way that respects and treats all audience members as equals without being condescending or using biased language and stereotypes. To be respectful and treat your listeners as equals, you adapt what you say to their knowledge of your topic, while avoiding the use of condescending language. Condescending language is when you speak down to people rather than respecting and treating them as equals and adapting what you say to their knowledge of your topic. Biased language is when you use words or phrases that derive their meaning from stereotypes, based on gender, race, ethnic group, age, or disability. One important type of biased language to pay attention to and avoid in your speeches is gender-biased language.

KEY TERMS

The key terms below are defined in this chapter and presented alphabetically with definitions in the Glossary at the end of the book.

- competent language
- concrete words
- clear language
- vivid language

- imagery
- simile
- analogy
- alliteration
- appropriate language
- biased language

- figures of speech
- metaphor
- rhetorical question
- repetition
- condescending language

BUILDING COMPETENCE ACTIVITIES
INDIVIDUAL ACTIVITIES

1. When speeches are next presented in class, evaluate how effectively each student used words, focusing on the clarity, vividness, and appropriateness of students' language.
2. Attend a public speech or presentation (it could be a lecture in another class), and evaluate the speaker's use of clear, vivid, and appropriate language.
3. Go to either one of these websites, both of which contain an array of public speeches: http://www.wfu.edu/~louden/Political%20Communication/Class%20Information/SPEECHES.html or http://www.csus.edu/indiv/k/kiddv/ComsSites/speeches.html. Choose a speech and evaluate the quality of the speaker's use of clear, vivid, and appropriate language. Write a short evaluation of her/his use of language including both strengths and opportunities for enhancement.

GROUP ACTIVITIES

1. When speeches are next presented in class, after the speeches, meet with a group of three to four students to evaluate how effectively each student used words, focusing on the clarity, vividness, and appropriateness of students' language. Prepare a list of general recommendations on using language competently to share with the class.
2. With one or two other students, attend a public speech or presentation (it could be a lecture in another class in which you are all enrolled). Have each student individually evaluate the quality of the speaker's use of clear, vivid, and appropriate language. Compare your individual evaluations after the lecture.
3. Form groups of three to four students and go to either of these websites both of which contain a big selection of public speeches: http://www.abacon.com/pubspeak/histsit.html, or http://www.mhhe.com/socscience/comm/new-home/. Have each group member select a different speech and evaluate the quality of the speaker's use of clear, vivid, and appropriate language. In the group, compare how effectively each speaker used language with a focus on clarity, vividness, and appropriateness.
4. Choose a partner in the class and rehearse your next speech together. Provide feedback to the other student focusing specifically on the competent use of words and language. Include strengths and opportunities for enhancement in your feedback.

COMPETENCY CHECKPOINTS AND SELF-ASSESSMENT TOOL

Here is what you need to know and be able to do regarding the competent use of words and language. Determine your level of competency and whether you are ready to proceed to the next chapter. Give yourself one point for each checkpoint you answer satisfactorily.

COMPETENCY CHECKPOINTS	NUMBER OF POINTS
KNOWLEDGE	
1. Describe what competent language is and why it is important to public speaking.	
2. Explain how you use clear language competently.	
3. Explain how you use vivid language competently.	
4. Explain the appropriate use of language and how to avoid condescending or biased language.	
SKILLS	
1. Review what you plan to say in your next speech and eliminate any abstract or unfamiliar words or phrases and substitute more concrete and familiar terms in their place.	
2. Examine your next speech and determine how you might bring it to life using imagery of some kind.	
3. Examine your next speech and locate two to three subpoints where you could use a figure of speech effectively. Write out the figures of speech and add them to your presentation outline.	
4. Analyze your next speech to ensure all of the information you plan to present is not condescending and is free of bias in any form.	
ETHICS AND CREDIBILITY	
1. Identify a competent speaker's ethical responsibility with regard to using language and words that are clear, vivid, and appropriate.	
2. Describe how the use of language and words that are clear, vivid, and appropriate could enhance your credibility as a speaker.	
TOTAL CHECKPOINTS (OUT OF A POSSIBLE TEN POINTS)	

ENDNOTES

1. Menzel, K. E. & Carrell, L. J. (1994). The relationship between preparation and performance in public speaking. *Communication Education, 43*(1), 17–27.

2. The perils of powerful speech. (2007, June). *Negotiation,* p. 12.

3. Fragale, A.R. (2006, Nov). The power of powerless speech: The effects of speech style and task interdependence on status conferral. *Organizational Behavior and Human Decision Processes, 101*(2), 243–261.

4. Mckenna, T. (2007, March 12). The power from the podium. *PR Technique,* p. 14.

5. Marken, G.A. (2006). [Review of the book *Present like a pro,* by K.E. O'Conner], *Public Relations Quarterly, 51*(3), 2.

6. Detz, J. 2007, July/August). Tips for a more powerful presentation. *State Legislatures, 33*(7), 72–73.

7. Allen, S. (1986). *How to make a speech.* New York: McGraw-Hill.

8. Braud, G. (2007, Jan/Feb). What does that mean? *Communication World, 24*(1), 34, 37.

9. Khodarahmi, S. (2007). I hear what you're saying. *Communication World, 24*(1), 11–12.

10. Braud, G. (2007, Jan/Feb). What does that mean? *Communication World, 24*(1), 34, 37.

11. Haleta, L. L. (1996). Student perceptions of teachers' use of language: The effects of powerful and powerless language on impression formation and uncertainty. *Communication Education, 45,* 16–28.

12. Sparks, J.R., Areni, C.S. & Cox, K.C. (1998). An investigation of the effects of language style and communication modality on persuasion. *Communication Education, 65,* 108-125.

13. Holcomb, C. (2007, Winter). "Anyone can be president: Figures of speech, cultural forms, and performance. *Rhetorical Society Quarterly, 37*(1), 71–96.

14. Horton, W.S. & Gerrig, R.J. (2005, July). Conversational common ground and memory processes in language production. *Discourse Processes, 40*(1), 1–35.

10

COMMUNICATING WITH YOUR VOICE: COMPETENCIES SIX AND SEVEN

- **Using Your Voice Effectively and Appropriately**
    Rate
    Pitch
    Volume
    Public Voice and Private Voice
- **Using Your Voice Correctly**
    Pronunciation and Articulation
    Grammar

"Be still when you have nothing to say; when genuine passion moves you, say what you've got to say, and say it hot." D. H. Lawrence, English novelist, poet, playwright, essayist, and literary critic, 1885–1930

. . .

Right after Richard finished his persuasive speech, the instructor asked the class to comment on two things: what Richard said and how he said it. Most of the feedback was fairly good regarding what he said—the content of the speech was relevant, how he organized it made the information easy to follow, and his use of evidence was interesting and supported his thesis. The student comments stopped at that point because they didn't know what else to say or what else the instructor wanted them to notice about Richard's speech. It seemed pretty good to most of them. The instructor, with a quick apology for his use of slang, surprised the students by saying: "It ain't what you say, it's how you say it that makes the difference. You were able to appreciate the content of what Richard said because of how he spoke. But you didn't even notice how effectively he used his voice and how correctly he articulated his message." The instructor went on: "Richard did a fine job of bringing a conversational feel to his speech. He used what is sometimes referred to as a transparent delivery—you didn't notice it. Instead, his message is what you noticed." Angelique and Hana exchanged a quick glance and Kumar made a mental note: "Note to self...read Chapter 10 again in the textbook and practice what the book calls using a public voice as opposed to a private voice when you give a speech."

. . .

Richard's public speaking instructor calls our attention to two public speaking competencies that typically go unnoticed when they are done well but detract from a speech if done poorly. The two competencies focus on using your voice effectively and appropriately, and correctly. When you don't speak correctly, the audience notices right away. In a seminal article on this topic, a well-known communication scholar underlines the importance of these competencies. Barnett Pearce states that how you use your voice, vocal cues, and vocal delivery style affects not only your credibility as a public speaker, but also the listeners' change of attitude toward the topic of the speech.[1] So Angelique, Hana, and Kumar are smart to think about their vocalic delivery skills before they present their persuasive speeches, which do have the purpose of changing listeners' attitudes. Another communication writer talks about the importance of verbal skills for sales people.[2] Good verbal skills affect customers' perceptions of the quality of customer service they receive from sales people. Students also are advised their oral communication skills will compel audiences to listen, thus making sure they receive the full message being presented.[3] Richard obviously compelled other students to listen, based on how he used his voice.

Think about the many lectures you have attended during your college years. We are sure you will agree that *how* the professor says what he or she says significantly affects whether you pay attention. Let's now consider exactly how you can use your voice effectively, appropriately, and correctly to enhance the vocalic delivery of your next speech.

Based on what you learn in this chapter, you will be able to *use vocal variety in rate, pitch, and intensity to heighten and maintain interest in your speech.* This is Competency Six and it includes the ability to:

- Speak at a well-paced rate, pause silently, and avoid vocalized pauses
- Vary the pitch of your voice to enhance what you say
- Use volume and a public voice effectively so everyone in the audience can hear you

Also, as a result of what you learn in this chapter, you will be able to *use pronunciation, grammar, and articulation appropriately.* This is Competency Seven and it includes the ability to:

- Pronounce and articulate words and sounds clearly
- Use correct and appropriate grammar when you give your next speech

USING YOUR VOICE EFFECTIVELY AND APPROPRIATELY

The words you say are communicated to the audience by the sound of your voice. The instructor in our opening story stated a very popular and true communication axiom—a self-evident truth—*It isn't what you say but how you say it that counts*! As a competent speaker, you need to become aware of how you use your voice and strive for variety and contrast. When you present a speech, **vocal**

10.1 VOCAL VARIETY is used to heighten and maintain audience attention and interest in your message.

Box 10.1: Practicing Vocal Variety

Note: An effective public speaker varies the rate, pitch, and volume of the voice when delivering a speech. Use this exercise to develop your comfort level with the three types of vocal variety.

Read this statement in the different ways described below.
"Now is the time for all good people to come to the aid of their country."

1. Read the statement very fast, then very slow, and then at a moderate rate. Allow for inflection and emphasis of various words. How comfortable are you with a moderate rate?

2. Read the statement in a high-pitched voice and then in a low-pitched voice. Try to read it at what you think is an optimal pitch for your voice. Is that the pitch you typically use when you present a speech?

3. Read the statement very loud, very soft, and then using a volume you think would work best when delivering a public speech. How comfortable are you with that volume level?

variety is used to heighten and maintain audience attention and interest in your message. You can vary the rate (fast versus slow), pitch (high versus low), and volume (loud versus soft) of your voice. Before we discuss each of these three aspects of using your voice effectively, first try (you can try it with a friend in your class) the vocalic exercise in Box 10.1.

RATE

Rate is the speed at which a speaker delivers a speech. As mentioned in the chapter on listening, most people speak at around 200 words per minute, but listen about three times faster. A good

10.2 RATE is the speed at which a speaker delivers a speech.

public speaker varies this rate, sometimes talking fast and sometimes slower, but always speaking at a rate the audience can understand. Although you don't want to aim for a specific rate of speech, you can adjust your rate to the topic of the speech. A serious subject deserves a slower and more deliberate rate, while less serious subject matter can be delivered a bit faster. Experienced speakers also vary their rate based on the mood they want to create, for example, talking faster creates a sense of excitement. But beginning speakers often tend to talk too rapidly because they're nervous, which makes it difficult for listeners to absorb what is being said. By the same token, a speaker who talks too slowly will bore listeners and give them time to shift their focus away from the speech. And when a speaker delivers a speech at the same rate throughout, it sounds monotonous and the listeners also may tune out.

The key to avoiding these problems is variety in rate. To vary your rate, you can change the length of the silent pauses that fall naturally between words, phrases, or sentences.[4] Even while speaking fairly quickly, a silent pause can be used to emphasize a point and allow your listeners a moment to think about it. Pauses also act as transitions from one thought to the next, letting the listeners know you've completed one idea and you're moving on to another.

One benefit of pausing silently is that it helps you reduce your use of **vocalized pauses**, which are those meaningless sounds a speaker utters during moments of silence. The goal here is to speak

10.3 VOCALIZED PAUSES are the meaningless sounds a speaker utters during moments of silence.

smoothly and fluently by minimizing the amount of distracting filler words (you know, like, kind of, sort of), and filled pauses (uh, uhm, ah, and uh) in your speech. These are the demons capable of distracting listeners and interrupting the flow of an otherwise good speech. These fillers, which usually result from nervousness, affect how listeners perceive you, and they send a nonverbal message of uncertainty and indicate that you are not certain what to say next.[5]

One research study provides a good example of how some speakers tend to use what they call disfluencies.[6] Rather than saying "the candle" or "the chair," they say "theee uh candle" or "theee uh chair." If you have ever viewed a speech by President John Kennedy, he tended to use this type of disfluency quite often when he spoke publicly. Other communication researchers say these fillers do serve useful functions, particularly in interpersonal relations and interactions.[7] Such fillers can let the other person know it's her or his turn to talk; they also can be used by listeners to signal they are paying attention and comprehend the speaker's message. Two other researchers see a useful cross-cultural function of fillers. They say they are used when speakers encounter trouble formulating the right word when communicating across diverse languages.[8]

While these functions may be useful in some situations, public speaking is not the right context for allowing distracting sounds to appear in your speech. An easy way to learn to substitute a silent pause for a vocalized pause or filler is to record yourself giving a speech. Once you become aware of what vocalized pauses you tend to use, you can train yourself to pause silently and take a quick breath instead. When giving your speech, a good way to remember to pause silently is to do so at the end of each main point. The pause gives listeners a chance to reflect on what has been said and it signals you are moving on to the next main point. Dr. Barbara Swaby, a very effective public speaker, tells us she uses this technique whenever she speaks publicly. Swaby presented an exemplary convocation speech that is annotated in the appendix to this book. When she submitted the manuscript of her speech, Swaby had highlighted each place where she wanted to pause silently.

PITCH

Pitch is the highness or lowness of the speaking voice. All speakers have a natural pitch at which they usually speak, though one researcher found people tend to vary their habitual pitch depending on the speaking context.[9] For instance, pitch may vary depending on whether we are speaking in public, with a peer, or with a parent or spouse. In public, competent speakers intentionally try to achieve a more effective pitch by varying and adjusting it to a slightly lower or slightly higher timbre.[10] This change in pitch is called an **inflection**. Inflections of the voice reveal the emotional content of the message and tell the listeners whether a speaker feels strongly about a topic, or is asking a question. Raising your pitch at the end of a sentence, for example, indicates that a question is being asked. Sometimes inexperienced speakers do this at the end of their speeches, even when they don't intend to ask a question.

> **10.4 PITCH is the highness or lowness of the speaking voice.**
>
> **10.5 INFLECTION is a change in vocal pitch that reveals the emotional content of the message or tells listeners the speaker is asking a question**

When a person speaks publicly, anxiety may cause the vocal pitch to rise to a squeak, giving away the nervousness the person is feeling. It's hard to listen to a speaker with such a continuously high-pitched voice, but equally distracting is a speaker who uses a monotone pitch and stays in a narrow, unchanging pitch range for an entire speech. The speaker's voice then has a droning sound most listeners find very boring. By varying your pitch, you can maintain your listeners' attention and emphasize important points in your speech. Experienced speakers determine an optimal pitch for their particular voices and vary it with control when speaking publicly. When you are rehearsing your next speech, consider recording it and listen for the habitual pitch pattern you tend to use. Decide if it's optimal and make any adjustments in pitch during the practice session. Record your speech again and see if the pitch is more effective.

VOLUME

Volume is the intensity, the loudness or softness, of the speaker's voice. Competent public speakers vary their volume based on the size of the audience, the size of the room, and the amount of background noises they may be speaking against. Being heard is so important that experienced speakers often arrive early for speaking engagements to test out audio equipment and acoustics to be sure everyone will be able to hear without straining. They speak loud enough so everyone can hear them, but they are also careful not to overpower the

> **10.6 VOLUME is the intensity, the loudness or softness, of the speaker's voice.**

listeners with a booming or loud voice. When a speaker's volume is too loud, the listeners may feel their space is being invaded, making the speech an unpleasant experience.

People who are new to public speaking often don't talk loud enough or they let their voices quietly fade out at the end of a thought. A lack of confidence may account for some of this lack of volume, but one public speaking expert has another explanation.[11] In an article for teachers on how to perfect their vocal techniques, a professor of English tells us the structure of the English language often puts important information at the end of sentences. Therefore, it is important for public speakers to maintain a consistent voice level and volume from the beginning to the end of sentences. This professor says most of us tend to speak the opening words of a sentence vigorously and then wind up saying the last few words using a much quieter volume. This comes naturally because we expel our breath as we speak, so it's difficult to maintain the same volume level. If you're chatting with a friend, a dip in volume might not matter, but when speaking in public, maintaining vigor and volume is critical, particularly given that important information is at the end of sentences.

Again, when you rehearse your next speech, record it. Listen for whether your voice tends to trail off and fade away toward the end of sentences or main points. Think about how you can begin to project your voice in order to gain and maintain listeners' attention.

Box 10.2 summarizes the key ideas to remember and apply for using your voice effectively and appropriately. As a public speaker, you can use vocal variety most effectively by developing your public voice.

PUBLIC VOICE AND PRIVATE VOICE

A **public voice** is a voice that makes use of increased variety in rate and pitch and increased volume, so your words are easily heard and understood by the entire audience. Your private voice is

---

Box 10.2: Using Rate, Pitch, and Volume Effectively and Appropriately

By varying the rate, pitch, and volume of your voice, you can maintain the listeners' attention and interest in what you're saying.

RATE
- Sometimes talk rapidly and sometimes slowly, but always speak to be understood.
- Talk slower and more deliberately for a serious speech topic.
- Talk faster for less serious subject matter.
- Use silent pauses to transition from one main point to the next.
- Avoid vocalized pauses.

PITCH
- Adjust pitch to slightly lower or higher timbre.
- Use inflections to reveal emotional content.
- Don't raise pitch at the end of a sentence, except to ask a question.

VOLUME
- Vary volume but speak loud enough to be heard.
- Don't overpower listeners with a loud voice.
- Develop your public voice for presenting speeches.

the one you use in interpersonal conversations, or even in self-reflection or when thinking out loud. While your private voice seems quite natural, you need to become accustomed to a louder public voice for giving speeches, even though it may sound strange at first.

> **10.7 A PUBLIC VOICE makes use of increased variety in rate and pitch and increased volume, so your words are easily heard and understood by the entire audeince.**

To achieve a public voice, you need to experiment with giving your speech using the full variety in rate, pitch, and volume of which your voice is capable. As you do that, use your voice to call attention to important parts of your speech. The faster and louder you say something, the more emotion and excitement you assign to it. By slowing down, dropping your pitch, or decreasing your volume, you can call attention to an idea in a more subtle way. In spite of these suggestions for using your voice effectively, the ultimate decision about how to use your voice appropriately is based on the audience and situation in which the speech is being presented. What works in one situation may not be appropriate somewhere else. In the opening story for this chapter, Richard obviously struck a fine balance between effectiveness and appropriateness and used variety in rate, pitch, and volume successfully.

USING YOUR VOICE CORRECTLY

In addition to paying attention to vocal variety, competence results from speaking correctly. The failure to do so can have several negative results for you as a public speaker. First, your listeners may not understand what you're saying if, for example, you mispronounce a word. Second, an error will call attention to itself and distract the listeners from your message. Third, errors in speech will damage your credibility as a speaker. Consequently, a competent speaker pronounces words correctly, articulates speech sounds clearly, and uses correct grammar.

Figure 10.1: Use a Public Voice When You Speak in Public

A public voice, rather than private voice, helps to ensure your speech is easily heard and understood by all listeners in the audience, even those in the back row. You don't want to sound like a megaphone, but you do want everyone to hear what you have to say.

Pronunciation means stressing and accenting the right syllables in a word. **Articulation** is shaping individual speech sounds correctly, so they combine to produce an understandable word. **Grammar** is the rules and structure for putting words together in sentences.

PRONUNCIATION AND ARTICULATION

Most speakers try to pronounce words correctly and carefully. However, most people grow up pronouncing words like others around them; plus, regional and ethnic dialects affect pronunciation patterns. As a result, without knowing it, many familiar words are frequently mispronounced. Library may be said out loud as *lyberry*. Government is *guvermint*. Ask is *ax*. Just is *jist*. Get is *git*. If you have any doubt about how to pronounce a word, look it up in the dictionary and see which syllables should be accented in order to pronounce the word correctly. If you plan to mention a person's name in your speech, be sure you know how to pronounce it before you speak. Saying "I don't know how to pronounce this name" detracts from your credibility and makes a statement about poor preparation on your part.

Besides pronunciation problems, speakers frequently fail to articulate speech sounds correctly. Most people know that *awtuh* should be *ought to*. They know the right way to pronounce it, but they may not bother to articulate it correctly. On the other hand, clear and correct articulation supports and enhances your credibility. Common articulation problems are errors of: omission, substitution, addition, and slurring.

Omissions are saying sounds incorrectly because of leaving out and not saying part of a word. The most common omissions are word endings, like when the *ing* at the end of a word becomes *in*. Working becomes *workin* and speaking becomes *speakin*. Sometimes parts are omitted from the middle of a word as well as the end of it. Listening becomes *lis-nin*. Another form of omission is when a speaker doesn't pronounce the consonants at the end of words, like *d's* and *t's*. Grand becomes *gran* and an appointment becomes an *appointmin*.

Substitutions are when the speaker replaces part of a word with an incorrect sound. At the beginning of a word, the *d* sound may be substituted for the *t* sound. The result is that people say *dese*, *dem*, and *dose* instead of these, them, and those. Sometimes the ending of *th* is substituted by just *t*, and the word with becomes *wit*. **Additions** occur when a speaker adds extra parts to a word. An athlete becomes an *athalete*; regardless becomes *irregardless*.

Slurring, running sounds and words together, is another common articulation problem, perhaps one of the most common. It's caused by the speaker saying two or more words at once or overlapping the end of one word with the beginning of the next. Pairs of words that end with of or to often are slurred together: sort of becomes *sorta*; want to becomes *wanna*. To avoid such slurring in a public speech, alternative phrasing can be used. Instead of saying *alotta* something, it's more effective to refer to many, quite a few, or an array of.

10.8 PRONUNCIATION means stressing and accenting the right syllables in a word.

10.9 ARTICULATION is shaping individual speech sounds correctly, so they combine to produce an understandable word.

10.14 GRAMMAR is the rules and structures for putting words together in sentences.

10.10 OMISSIONS are saying sounds incorrectly because of leaving out and not saying part of a word.

10.11 SUBSTITUTIONS are when the speaker replaces part of a word with an incorrect sound.

10.12 ADDITIONS occur when a speaker adds extra parts to a word.

10.13 SLURRING, is when a speaker runs sounds and words together.

In common parlance and everyday conversations, these wrong ways of pronouncing words and articulating sounds may be commonplace. But if anybody has ever asked you—"What did you say?"—chances are you just mispronounced a word or slurred your speech. That may work in most conversations because you have an opportunity to say it again; however; in public speaking, the listeners can't interrupt and ask what you said. Besides, if you pronounce words correctly and articulate clearly, that effort will reflect favorably on you as a public speaker. Think about newscasters and how carefully they say what they say, out of respect for viewers. As a public speaker, you have the same responsibility to your listeners. Our advice remains the same. Record a rehearsal of your speech and pay attention to your pronunciation and articulation patterns.

GRAMMAR

Finally, correct language calls for avoiding grammatical errors. If listeners are distracted by a mistake in grammar, their attention turns from what you are saying to the grammatical error. If you commit an error in grammar, it calls into question your authority as a speaker and thereby damages your credibility. The listeners will think, perhaps wrongly so, that you don't know enough about the topic to talk about it correctly.

Most people pay close attention to the grammatical structure of sentences when they are writing, but they are less careful about grammar when they speak. The typical kinds of errors people make are simple things like the erroneous use of the verb to be: *All of them was there* is incorrect. All is a plural noun so should take the plural form of the verb. *All of them were there* is grammatically correct. These following pronouns are singular and should be used with singular verbs: each, every, everyone, everybody, anyone, anybody, and none.

> Wrong: Each of the boys are wearing a hat.
> Correct: Each of the boys is wearing a hat.

It may be helpful to remember that words like everybody, everyone, and none are contractions of every body, every one, not one, and therefore are used with singular verbs. The pronoun in this list that sounds most strange is none. *None of us uses this pronoun correctly* is correct.

Less obvious but equally offensive is the incorrect use of pronouns such as self, me, and I. Self is a pronoun used to reflect on a noun or another pronoun to add emphasis. *I myself accept the invitation to speak* is correct. *Richard and myself accept the invitation* is wrong; it should be *Richard and I accept the invitation.* I and me also can be the subject or object of the sentence. When used as the subject in a sentence, I is correct; and when used as the object in a sentence me is correct. *Thanks for inviting Richard and I* is wrong; *Thanks for inviting Richard and me* is correct. *Richard and me accept the invitation* is wrong; *Richard and I accept the invitation* is correct.

Subject–verb agreement errors happen when a word is confusing in regard to its plural and singular forms. *Data* and *media* are good examples. Datum and medium are the singular form of these nouns; data and media are the plural forms. So the correct subject–verb agreement would be: *The data from the study are interesting; the media were expected to wait until the speaker arrived.* Incorrect use would be: *The data is interesting* and *the media was expected to wait.*

Box 10.3 summarizes the key ideas to remember and apply in order to use your voice correctly. As a public speaker, you need to pronounce words and articulate sounds clearly and use grammar correctly. Such attention to correctness is guaranteed to reflect favorably on your credibility as a public speaker. In addition, paying attention to proper speech may have another benefit for you

Box 10.3: Using Correct Pronunciation, Articulation, and Grammar

By speaking correctly, you ensure the listeners understand what you say. Errors distract from your message and reflect negatively on your credibility.

PRONUNCIATION

- Pronounce words correctly
- Avoid regionalisms and dialect
- Look up words ahead of time that you can't pronounce

ARTICULATION

- Articulate speech sounds correctly
- Avoid the errors of omission, substitution, addition, and slurring

GRAMMAR

- Use correct grammar
- Avoid the wrong use of the *to be* verb and the pronouns *self, me,* and *I*
- Use correct subject–verb agreement for problem words like *data* and *media*

outside the public speaking classroom. Grammatically incorrect speech reflects a low level of professionalism in the workplace. In fact, some businesses are retaining speech coaches to help rising stars with speech flaws.[12]

Richard, in the opening story, mastered the two competencies discussed in this chapter. Hana, Angelique, and Kumar, no doubt, will follow their instructor's advice to pay attention to *how you say what you say*. Now that you are aware of the importance of using your voice effectively, appropriately, and correctly, Chapter 11 will focus on nonverbal communication and the competent delivery of your next speech.

Things To Do: Competencies Six and Seven

Review this *Things To Do* List for using your voice effectively, appropriately, and correctly when you deliver your next speech. Have you done the following?

1. Reviewed your speech outline and decided where you could vary the rate at which you speak and where you will pause silently? ☐

2. Reviewed your speech outline and identified where you could vary and adjust the pitch of your voice to emphasize a point? ☐

3. Reviewed your speech outline and determined where an increase or decrease in volume could be used effectively? ☐

4. Planned to make use of your public voice in such a way that all listeners in the audience can easily hear what you have to say? ☐

5. Examined your speech to ensure it is free of any grammar errors that would reflect negatively on your authority and credibility as a speaker? ☐

CHAPTER SUMMARY

The first and second delivery competencies focus on using your voice effectively and appropriately, and correctly. Whenever you present a speech, vocal variety is used to heighten and maintain audience attention and interest in your message. You should try to vary the rate, pitch, and volume of your voice. Rate is the speed at which a speaker delivers a speech. To avoid problems in rate, like talking too rapifdly, too slow, or at the same rate throughout the speech, you can pause silently to emphasize a point or use silent pauses as transitions from one thought to the next or between main points. A benefit of consciously using silent pauses is they help you reduce your use of vocalized pauses, the meaningless sounds a speaker utters

during moments of silence. Pitch is the highness or lowness of the speaking voice. While all speakers have a natural pitch, competent public speakers vary and adjust their pitch to a slightly lower or slightly higher timbre, which maintains listeners' attention and emphasizes main points. A change in pitch, an inflection, can reveal emotion or tell listeners the speaker is asking a question. Volume is the intensity, the loudness or softness, of the speaker's voice. Competent speakers vary their volume based on the size of the audience and the room, and the amount of background noises. Maintaining a consistent voice level and volume from the beginning to the end of sentences is better than letting your voice fade out at the end of a thought. A public voice makes use of increased variety in rate and pitch and increased volume, so your words are easily heard and understood by the entire audience. In addition to vocal variety, it is important to use your voice correctly. That means pronouncing words correctly, articulating speech sounds clearly, and using correct grammar. Pronunciation involves stressing and accenting the right syllables in a word. Articulation is shaping individual speech sounds correctly, so they combine to produce an understandable word. Common articulation problems to avoid are errors of omission, substitution, additions, and slurring. Omissions are saying sounds incorrectly because of leaving out and not saying part of a word. Substitutions are when the speaker replaces part of a word with an incorrect sound. Additions occur when a speaker adds extra parts to a word. Slurring is when a speaker runs sounds and words together. Correct language also calls for avoiding grammatical errors. Grammar is the rules and structures for putting words together in sentences. Grammatical errors distract listeners, call into question your authority as a speaker, and damage your credibility.

KEY TERMS

The key terms below are defined in this chapter and presented alphabetically with definitions in the Glossary at the end of the book.

- vocal variety
- vocalized pauses
- inflection
- public voice
- articulation
- omissions

- rate
- pitch
- volume
- pronunciation
- grammar
- substitutions

- additions
- slurring

BUILDING COMPETENCE ACTIVITIES

INDIVIDUAL ACTIVITIES

1. When speeches are next presented in class, evaluate how effectively each student used her or his voice to enhance the delivery of the speech. Focus on rate, pitch, volume, and correctness including grammar.
2. Attend a public speech or presentation (it could be a lecture in another class), and evaluate the speaker's use of vocalic variety.
3. Go to either one of these websites, both of which contain an array of public speeches: http://www.wfu.edu/~louden/Political%20Communication/Class%20Information/SPEECHES.html or http://www.csus.edu/indiv/k/kiddv/ComsSites/speeches.html. Choose a speech and evaluate the quality of the speaker's use of voice, considering both vocal variety and correctness. Write a short evaluation of her/his use of the voice including both strengths and opportunities for enhancement.
4. Practice your next speech, standing up in front of a mirror. Include vocal variety (rate, pitch, volume) and a public voice in your delivery and evaluate the results.

GROUP ACTIVITIES

1. When speeches are next presented in class, after the speeches, meet with a group of three to four students to evaluate how effectively each student used her or his voice to enhance the delivery of the speech. Focus on rate, pitch, volume, and correctness including grammar. Prepare a list of general recommendations on using the voice competently to share with the class.
2. With one or two other students, attend a public speech or presentation (it could be a lecture in another class in which you are all enrolled). Have each student individually evaluate the quality of the speaker's use of voice, considering both vocal variety and correctness. Compare your individual evaluations after the lecture.
3. Form groups of three to four students and go to either of these websites, both of which contain a big selection of public speeches: http://www.abacon.com/pubspeak/histsit.html or http://www.mhhe.com/socscience/comm/new-home/. Have each group member select a different speech and evaluate the quality of the speaker's use of voice, considering both vocal variety and correctness. In the group, compare how effectively each speaker used vocal variety.
4. Choose a partner in the class and rehearse your next speech together. Focus particularly on the use of vocal variety (rate, pitch, volume) and a public voice. Provide feedback to the other student, focusing specifically on vocal delivery. Include strengths and opportunities for enhancement in your feedback.

COMPETENCY CHECKPOINTS AND SELF-ASSESSMENT TOOL

Here is what you need to know and be able to do regarding using your voice effectively and appropriately, and correctly. Determine your level of competency and whether you are ready to proceed to the next chapter. Give yourself one point for each checkpoint you answer satisfactorily.

COMPETENCY CHECKPOINTS	NUMBER OF POINTS
KNOWLEDGE 1. Describe vocal variety and how a speaker uses it to heighten and maintain audience attention and interest in a speech. 2. Explain how you can use rate most effectively in your speech. 3. Explain how you can use pitch most effectively in your speech. 4. Explain how you can use volume most effectively in your speech. 5. Identify some of the most common problems public speakers face when trying to use their voices correctly.	
SKILLS 1. Review what you plan to say in your next speech and identify where you will use silent pauses. 2. Examine your next speech and determine where you might use variety in rate, pitch, or volume to emphasize a main or subpoint. 3. Practice and become more accustomed to the use of your normal voice as a public voice.	
ETHICS AND CREDIBILITY 1. Identify a competent speaker's ethical responsibility with regard to using the voice effectively, appropriately, and correctly. 2. Describe how the effective and correct use of your voice will enhance your credibility as a speaker.	
TOTAL CHECKPOINTS (OUT OF A POSSIBLE TEN POINTS)	

ENDNOTES

1. Pearce, B.W., (1971, Summer). The effect of vocal cues on credibility and attitude change. *Western Speech, 35*(3), 176–184.
2. Levin, R.P. (2005, Nov). The value of verbal skills. *Proofs, 88*(5), p. 74.
3. Gutgold, N.D. (2005, Sept). Teaching students to give successful paper presentations. *North Dakota Journal of Speech & Theatre, 18*, 44–48.
4. Rendle-Short, J. (2005, Apr). Managing the transitions between talk and silence in the academic monologue. *Research on Language & Social Interaction, 38*(2), 179–218.
5. Lange, P.G. (2008, Apr). An implicature for um: Signaling relative expertise. *Discourse Studies, 10*(2), 191–204.
6. Arnold, J., Fagnano, M., & Tanenhaus, M. (2003, Jan). Disfluencies signal theee, um, new information. *Journal of psycholinguistic research, 32*(1), 25–36.
7. Ward, N. (2006). Non-lexical conversational sounds in American English. *Pragmatics & Cognition, 14*(1), 129–182.
8. Hayashi, M. & Yoon, K. (2006). A cross-linguistic exploration of demonstratives in interaction: With particular reference to the context of word-formulation trouble. *Studies in Language, 30*(3), 485–540.
9. Zraick, R., Gentry, M., Smith-Olinde, L., & Gregg, B. (2006, Dec). The effect of speaking context on elicitation of habitual pitch. *Journal of Voice, 20*(4), 545–554.
10. Wolff, M. (1998). Perfect pitch. *Success, 45* (8), 18.
11. Lang, J.M. (2007, May 4). Perfecting your vocal technique. *Chronicle of Higher Education, 53*(35), C2–C3.
12. Lubin, J.S. (2004, Oct 5). To win advancements, you need to clean up any bad speech habits. *Wall Street Journal, Eastern Edition, 244*(67), p. B1.

11

COMMUNICATING NONVERBALLY:
COMPETENCY EIGHT

- **The Importance of Nonverbal Cues and Public Speaking**
- **Types of Nonverbal Messages**
    Physical Appearance
    Body Language
    Facial Expression and Eye Contact
- **Culture and Nonverbal Communication**
    Transparent Delivery

"The most important things are the hardest to say, because words diminish them." Stephen King, American author of horror novels, b. 1947

. . .

On the first day of persuasive speeches, the students were surprised to see a new student in class. Their instructor said Vanden had transferred to their campus from out of town and already had taken the first half of a similar public speaking course on his former campus. Angelique and the other students were a little surprised. "I'm just curious to see Vanden's speech today," observed Richard. Kumar added: "He may do a good job, but the emphasis today is on how we use nonverbal cues to relate to the audience. We're supposed to pay attention to all kinds of things. We need to use nonverbal communication to make contact and create rapport with the listeners, to say nothing of supporting our credibility nonverbally. That's a tall order for someone new to the class. We have an advantage, because we already know each other." At that point, the speeches started and Vanden volunteered to go first. The students sat back, ready to evaluate the nonverbal behaviors of their new classmate.

. . .

Vanden's speech went well. He and the other students in the class showed they were able to use nonverbal cues, the subject of Competency Eight, effectively and appropriately. The importance of this competency is stressed in an article on leveraging the power of nonverbal communication:

> No matter how knowledgeable a speaker and how sophisticated his [her] audience, speeches rest on a primitive aspect of communication. Humans experience basic and visceral reactions to signals they receive from human beings. It's the reason people conduct their most important business in person; they know instinctively to rely on the clues evolution has provided to help them make decisions concerning other people's honesty and trustworthiness. In other words, people are paying careful attention to nonverbal communication. How comfortable a speaker is in his [her] own skin, how he [she] stands and moves, how he [she] looks at others in the room, his [her] tone of voice, even the clothes he [she] wears, together, these variables constitute a constant flow of data running underneath whatever the speaker is saying.[1]

This good advice was intended for businesspeople to help them increase their credibility, authority, and persuasiveness in the minds of listeners. It applies equally to any public speaker, and it calls attention to the importance of the content of this chapter.

Based on what you learn in this chapter, you will be able to use physical behaviors and nonverbal communication that support your verbal message. This is Competency Eight and it includes the ability to make audience contact, create rapport, establish and maintain credibility, and indicate the formality level of the speaker's relationship with the listeners. These goals are achieved by:

- Managing your physical appearance effectively and appropriately
- Using body language, including posture, body movement and use of space, and gestures
- Using facial expression and eye contact

THE IMPORTANCE OF NONVERBAL CUES AND PUBLIC SPEAKING

A very prolific communication researcher, Judee Burgoon, provides a practical lens for thinking about how to use nonverbal cues when you speak publicly, whether in class, at work, or anywhere else. Burgoon talks about how people use communication to relate to one another, primarily in interpersonal relationships. She asserts that a lot of this relating happens nonverbally.[2] Burgoon's ideas about relating to others nonverbally apply equally to public speaking. When you speak publicly, in many ways, you are building a relationship with the audience. As in interpersonal communication, much of this relationship building in public speaking occurs nonverbally. Based on Burgoon's ideas about relating to others, you should ask yourself these sorts of questions about public speaking: How can I make contact, create common ground, and develop a sense of rapport with listeners nonverbally? How can I establish and maintain my credibility as a speaker using various nonverbal techniques? How can I use nonverbal cues to make a statement about how formal or informal my relationship is with the listeners in the particular public speaking situation?

These are big questions and the answers lie in the fact that there are many nonverbal cues public speakers can use to present themselves and relate effectively to their listeners. Table 11.1 outlines the relationship building functions a public speaker should try to achieve, and it indicates which nonverbal cues would help most to accomplish each function.

In our opening story, Vanden probably took Burgoon's advice in order to relate to the new students he had just met. We will now explore exactly how each type of nonverbal cue works and how you can use each cue to relate to the audience and enhance the delivery of your next speech.

TYPES OF NONVERBAL MESSAGES

In Chapter 1, we said verbal symbols are the words we use when we communicate using language, spoken or written; and nonverbal symbols are the crucial messages and cues we use to support and enhance the spoken message. Like Burgoon, we think these nonverbal cues have a large impact on how people react to messages. Despite that impact, frequently we are unaware of the messages we're sending nonverbally. Public speakers, in particular, tend to get tunnel vision and forget what their bodies are doing and the messages they are sending. The following nonverbal cues are most important to you as a public speaker: physical appearance, body language including posture, body movement and use of space, facial expression, and eye contact.

PHYSICAL APPEARANCE

Think about the initial impression you'll make on your listeners, when you stand up and walk to the podium or lectern. These first impressions are shaped, for the most part, by your **physical appearance**. This includes your clothing, shoes, jewelry, hair style, and even hair adornments. All

Table 11.1: Relational Functions and Nonverbal Cues

Here is a summary of the nonverbal cues you can use to enhance your ability to relate to your listeners.

NONVERBAL CUES	RELATIONAL FUNCTIONS OF EACH NONVERBAL CUE
Physical Appearance	Establish and maintain credibility Indicate whether the speaking situation is formal or informal
Posture, Body Movement, and Use of Space	Indicate a degree of formality Enhance your credibility Make audience contact Develop rapport with listeners
Gestures	Make audience contact Communicate openness and involvement with listeners
Facial Expressions	Make audience contact and develop rapport Let the audience know your feelings about the speech topic
Eye Contact	Make audience contact Develop rapport

these nonverbal cues influence what the audience thinks of you, even before you begin to speak. They also make a statement about how formal or informal a speech you are about to present. Even more important, your appearance is a key factor in establishing and maintaining your credibility as a speaker.

1.1 PHYSICAL APPEARANCE shapes first impressions and includes your clothing, shoes, jewelry, hair style, and even hair adornments.

You want to present yourself in the best possible light, without manipulating your appearance in any way that would seem artificial to the audience or make you uncomfortable. In general, avoid trying out a new hairstyle or outfit when you give your speech. A new hairstyle can go wrong or take too much preparation time, and you may not feel completely comfortable in new clothes. Feeling relaxed but attractive is the best appearance to put forward to any audience.

When thinking about your appearance and the impression you want to make, consider the results of a study of fashion in the classroom.[3] The study investigated the effects of clothing on students' perceptions of their instructors. Three styles of attire were compared: formal professional (business suits, dress shoes, etc.), casual professional (pants suit, casual dress), and casual (faded jeans, t-shirt, flannel shirt). The more formal the attire, the greater the increase was in the ratings of instructor competence. If that holds true for instructors in the classroom, the same approach can work for you. Another more recent study found that the formality of attire of student speakers positively affected ratings of speaking competence, regardless of the sex/gender of the speaker.[4] If you want to be perceived as competent, dress somewhat more formally but still comfortably for yourself.

BODY LANGUAGE

You're dressed to impress and there you sit, waiting to present your first speech. When it's your turn, stand up straight, hold your head up, and walk with confidence to the front of the room. A confident walk conveys a sense of self-assuredness and an air of confidence. Further, by acting self-assured, you will actually begin to feel more confident. All these bodily, nonverbal cues will help in building a relationship with the audience. **Body language** includes your posture, body movement and use of space, and gestures.

Posture. After arriving at the lectern, relax but maintain an alert body posture, with your shoulders held up and in line with your hips and knees. This posture will communicate that you're in control and ready to speak. **Posture** for a public speaker is defined as a position of your bodily parts that communicates your attitude and sense of self to the audience. For instance, if you slouch and lean on the podium or lectern, your posture communicates a lack of confidence and enthusiasm. By maintaining a more erect posture, you introduce a degree of formality, which indirectly can enhance your credibility. Another benefit of well-aligned and upright posture is it optimizes the function of your voice.[5] You can control the pitch and resonance of your voice, which enhances your overall vocalic delivery of the speech. A technique experienced public speakers use to maintain an upright body posture is this: They picture a small balloon pinned to the shoulders that lightly pulls them up and keeps them in an upright but relaxed position. Give it a try and see how it works for you.

11.2 BODY LANGUAGE includes your posture, body movement and use of space, and gestures.

11.3 POSTURE is defined as a position of your bodily parts that communicates your attitude and sense of self to the audience.

11.4 BODY MOVEMENT refers to how a public speaker stands and walks during the speech.

11.5 GESTURES are natural movements of the hands and arms that reinforce what is said, emphasize important points, and make presentations more interesting to watch.

Body Movement and Use of Space. During your speech, you should move about purposefully, not unconsciously, in the speaking space and area. **Body movement** in public speaking refers to how you stand and how you walk. By moving with purpose, you can emphasize a transition or focus the audience's attention on an important point you want to make. For instance, if you're about to tell a story, move closer to the audience while telling the tale and then back to your notes, as you conclude it. By moving toward the audience or from one side of the speaking area or lectern to the other, you decrease the distance between you and the listeners. This movement helps to maintain more sense of audience contact, and it creates rapport between the speaker and the listeners.

If you're using a presentation aid, it's effective to walk over to it and point to part of it as you discuss it. While it's effective to move purposefully to make a point or call attention to an aid, moving about aimlessly signals nervousness. Pacing, letting your body rock unconsciously from one foot to the other, or fiddling with objects on the lectern distracts listeners from what you're saying and communicates anxiety. So only use body movement intentionally and try to become aware of any unconscious body movements that may distract your listeners from your message.

Gestures. Whether standing or moving, competent speakers keep their hands and arms free and relaxed, so they are ready to incorporate natural movements or gestures into their presentations. **Gestures** are movements of the hands and arms used to reinforce what is said, emphasize important points, and make presentations more interesting to watch. Since most people gesture naturally when speaking one-on-one, gesturing when presenting a speech will make the presentation seem more natural and relaxed.

Gestures communicate openness to the audience and a sense of involvement. A small gesture communicates less involvement, while a larger gesture, within reason, communicates greater involvement. Most speakers gesture with their arms somewhere between their waist and shoulders, but the most important thing to do is to gesture in a way that's natural for you and matches the content of what you're saying. Here are a few hints for gesturing naturally:

- Vary your gestures from one hand to the other and sometimes gesture with both hands at the same time. Many speakers use their dominant hand more, leaving the other arm hanging like a limp dishrag.
- When you aren't gesturing, let both arms relax and drop your arms to your sides naturally.
- If you feel unsure about what to do with your hands, rest them lightly on the lectern at any time during your speech. This will help you appear much more in control of what you're saying.
- Try to hold your gestures longer when speaking publicly than you do in normal conversation, avoiding quick or jerky movements.
- Don't clasp your hands for too long in front or in back of you, as this will keep you from gesturing.
- Avoid gesturing in a way that may appear artificial to the audience. If you feel your gestures are contrived, they will almost certainly appear that way to the audience.

Finally, check out the advice in Box 11.1 for businesspeople on using gestures to become more authentic. The writer has an interesting idea about why public speakers shouldn't force themselves to gesture in a way that is not natural for them.[6] He is a strong advocate for businesspeople rehearsing before delivering their speeches, if they want to connect with their audiences intellectually and emotionally.[7] That's good advice for any public speaker.

FACIAL EXPRESSION AND EYE CONTACT

Closely related to body language are facial expression and eye contact, two more nonverbal cues you can use to your advantage as a public speaker. Like body language, these nonverbal cues also help you relate to the listeners more directly.

Facial expression is the vehicle you use to communicate emotion and how you feel about what you're saying to the audience. Your facial expression reflects the mood or tone of your speech but sometimes may reveal mixed feelings. If you don't believe in your claim, your facial expression will reveal your

> **11.6 FACIAL EXPRESSION is the vehicle you use to communicate emotion and how you feel about what you're saying to the audience.**

doubt. If you're nervous, your facial expression may be too strained, and you won't appear enthusiastic about the topic. Instead, try to have your facial expression match and reflect the content of your speech. If it's on a lighthearted topic, your facial expression should reflect lightheartedness. If your topic is serious, look serious. Moreover, try to avoid either a deadpan expression—no feeling at all—or a smile pasted on your face.

A gender difference in how people display feelings on the face is important to note. Research indicates that men and women use facial expressions differently when speaking.[8] Women express more emotion on their faces and smile more, even if they're unhappy or the message is not worth smiling about. If a woman is presenting a speech on a serious topic and smiles too much, that would be confusing to the audience. Another problem results when a female speaker displays too much emotion on the face, which can be distracting to the listeners. By contrast, men tend to limit the amount of emotion they display on their faces, such that listeners are not be able to tell how male speakers feel

Box 11.1: Advice for Becoming an Authentic Speaker

Nick Morgan has been a communication coach for businesspeople for more than two decades. He has a unique explanation for why some speakers' body language and gestures fail to create rapport and inspire enthusiasm in the audience. Morgan says recent brain research shows natural, unstudied gestures express emotions or impulses a split second before our thought processes have turned them into words. Therefore, the timing of rehearsed gestures will always be a little bit off and the audience will pick up unconsciously on the timing being off. When we rehearse any specific type of body language or nonverbal cues, we use them incorrectly during the actual speech—slightly after speaking the words they are associated with. As a result, listeners feel something is wrong because, during natural conversation, body language emerges before the associated words. A public speaker, who has rehearsed her or his body language too much, comes across as artificial and lacking in authenticity and genuineness.

So what's a speaker to do? Morgan says to demonstrate your authenticity, don't rehearse your body language. Yes, rehearse the content of your speech; but, during the rehearsal, allow your body language and gestures to occur naturally. Morgan goes on to say you should keep these four goals in mind when you rehearse your speech:

- Be open to your audience
- Connect with your audience
- Be passionate about your topic
- Listen to your audience's feedback nonverbally

When you rehearse with these goals in mind, you'll genuinely experience these feelings when delivering your speech. Plus, your body language will emerge at the right moment and match your verbal message. As a result, your listeners will know you're for real.

Source: Retrieved from http: //hbr.harvardbusiness.org/2008/11/how-to-become-an-authentic-speaker/ib.

about what they're saying. The way to get around these gender differences is simply to match your facial expression to the content of your speech. Whether you are a man or a woman, use facial expressions appropriate to your topic, and be sure your face communicates and reflects how you feel about what you are saying.

11.7 EYE CONTACT is a tool the public speaker uses to promote a sense of involvement with audience members and to gauge audience reaction to the speech.

Eye contact is a tool the public speaker uses to promote a sense of involvement with audience members and to gauge audience reaction to the speech. In North America, eye contact also communicates honesty, openness, and respect for others. On the other hand, if you avoid making eye contact with listeners in an audience of North Americans, they may perceive you as nervous at best or deceitful at worst.

To get better at using eye contact as a public speaker, mentally divide your audience into four quadrants, like a window with four panes. Look directly at and speak to at least one person in each quadrant at some point during the speech. Don't just gaze in their direction but actually stop and make eye contact with a specific member of the audience seated in each quadrant. Not only will this develop rapport and communicate interest and involvement to the entire audience, you also can check to see how the audience is reacting to your speech. If they're losing interest, you can speed up or talk a little louder to regain their attention. Or if it's appropriate to do so, you can invite audience participation by asking questions about their opinion of what you're saying.

It should be quite clear by now that nonverbal communication is a critical part of public speaking competence. All these nonverbal cues are summarized in Box 11.3 and will help you relate effectively to the listeners during your next speech. However, to use these nonverbal cues appropriately, you need to be aware of the impact of culture on how your nonverbal messages may be interpreted.

CULTURE AND NONVERBAL COMMUNICATION

In any communication situation, including public speaking, we all need to be aware of how nonverbal messages may be varyingly interpreted because of cultural differences. In Chapter 4, we thoroughly discussed the impact of such differences on public speaking and listening. Box 11.3 describes a communication approach that honors various cultures in any audience, so diversity enhances rather than distracts from your delivery. The box describes an approach to communication called multicodality.[9] **Multicodality** suggests a competent speaker retains his or her unique way of using words and nonverbal cues, while incorporating some of the unique communication patterns of the listeners into what is said and done—a technique researchers call *code-switching*. See what you think of the recommendations of these intercultural scholars.

By now you may need some kind of a guideline to help make decisions about using all the nonverbal communication skills just described. Knowing how to avoid pitfalls and blunders—what not

---

Box 11.2: Nonverbal Cues and Public Speaking

Here is a summary of the nonverbal cues you can use to support and enhance your verbal message with a few hints for using each type of cue.

APPEARANCE
- Modify your appearance to make a good first impression.
- Don't do so in a way that looks artificial or makes you uncomfortable.

POSTURE, BODY MOVEMENT, AND USE OF SPACE
- Walk confidently.
- At the lectern, relax but maintain an alert body posture.
- Move about in the speaking area voluntarily and purposefully.
- Avoid pacing, body rocking, or fiddling with objects.

GESTURES
- Make use of both hands and gesture naturally.
- Relax and drop arms to your sides when not gesturing.
- Rest hands lightly on the lectern.
- Hold gestures longer.
- Don't clasp hands in front or back of you.

FACIAL EXPRESSIONS
- Use your face to communicate how you feel about your speech.
- Let your facial expression reflect the mood and tone of the speech.
- Avoid a deadpan expression.
- Match your facial expression to what you're saying.

EYE CONTACT
- Use eye contact to communicate interest and involvement to the audience.
- Use it to gauge how the listeners are reacting to your speech.

to do nonverbally—is thought of in the business world as a very necessary bit of knowledge.[10] In our diverse global economy, you likely will be called on to present speeches or trainings to multicultural audiences. Using a transparent delivery will help you decide what you should do, or not do, when presenting such speeches.

> **11.8 MULTICODALITY calls for retaining your unique way of using words and nonverbal cues, while incorporating some of the unique communication patterns of the listeners into what you say and do.**

TRANSPARENT DELIVERY

Dr. Frank Dance, a national expert in public speaking, offers a useful recommendation for using verbal and nonverbal presentation skills most effectively.[11] Dance coined the phrase **transparent delivery**, which means presenting a speech in such a way that the audience doesn't focus on elements of the delivery but instead pays full attention to the message. Instead of noticing your hand gestures or how you move around, the audience notices and pays attention to the content of your message—thus the delivery itself becomes transparent.

To achieve a transparent delivery, watch yourself present a speech on videotape. Examine how you use all the various presentation skills and think about how they will impact the audience's reac-

---

Box 11.3: Advice on Becoming Multicodal—What's That?

Intercultural communication experts agree communicating with people of different cultural backgrounds than your own can be challenging. Difficulties and misunderstandings may arise from differences in how the communicators of diverse backgrounds use verbal and nonverbal communication. In a public speaking situation, problems with nonverbal communication can be particularly challenging. First of all, the number of listeners of different cultural backgrounds, who use nonverbal cues differently, may be great. Second, we typically know when we miscommunicate using spoken language, but we often don't when we miscommunicate using nonverbal cues and symbols. Given these realities, a competent public speaker needs to look for ways to bridge the differences among people and build rapport and understanding in a respectful way with culturally different and diverse audiences.

One approach to communicating across differences, called *multicodality,* can help. Multicodality is similar to being multi-lingual, in that speakers retain their own unique way of using words and nonverbal cues, while learning to use some of the words and cues of their listeners. Widely studied by scholars in linguistics, communication, and sociology, researchers refer to this as *code-switching.* This means you switch from your own way of encoding a verbal or nonverbal message and encode the message in ways diverse listeners in the audience will find appealing.

A public speaker who is multicodal would first become familiar with any distinctive verbal or nonverbal cultural codes or patterns of the listeners in the audience. Then those codes or patterns could be used in the speech to build rapport and communicate an awareness and value of the listeners' culture. That said, it's important to note that public speakers should not forsake their own way of communicating to embrace the code of the listeners, nor should they overuse the other code in an insincere or condescending manner. Rather, aspects of the listeners' nonverbal cues or codes should be incorporated within the speaker's message to communicate interest and respect. While you may not need to use multicodality in a public speaking class right now, many jobs and careers are taking people to all ends of the globe and into cultures with which they may not be familiar. Remember this communication technique as it may serve you well one day.

Source: Retrieved from http://www.colorado.edu/ling/CRIL/Volume19_Issue1/paper_NILEP.pdf

11.9 TRANSPARENT DELIVERY means presenting a speech in such a way that the audience doesn't focus on elements of the delivery but instead pays full attention to the message.

tions to your speech. If the use of certain words helps to clarify and create interest in your speech, then use those words. If increasing the volume of your voice encourages the listeners to pay attention to you, then increase your volume. If a slurred way of speaking might cause audience members to wonder what you're saying, work on your articulation. If a certain gesture calls attention to itself and not to a point you want to make, don't gesture in that way. If your facial expression or the way you make eye contact is distracting, change those behaviors. In sum, do what enhances your speech and avoid anything that interferes with its effective delivery. Everything about your presentation should draw the audience's attention to understanding what you say and retaining the message of your speech. In the opening story for this chapter, Vanden apparently used all the delivery competencies well and achieved a transparent delivery.

In Part Three, you learned about the competencies essential to presenting your speeches most effectively and appropriately. In Chapter 9, we focused on communicating with words, in Chapter 10, communicating with your voice, and in this chapter, communicating nonverbally. You are now invited to join your friends—Vanden, Hana, Angelique, and Kumar—to think about applying the preparation and presenting competencies to public speaking in different situations. The first chapter in Part Four is about using presentation aids, traditional and electronic. This is a public speaking challenge you really need to understand and master.

CHAPTER SUMMARY

The importance of nonverbal communication to public speaking is emphasized by an awareness of how nonverbal cues can help a speaker build a relationship with the audience. In addition to supporting the verbal message, nonverbal cues help you make audience contact, create rapport, enhance credibility, and indicate how formal a relationship you will have with the listeners. Speakers achieve these goals by managing their physical appearance and effectively using body language, facial expression, and eye contact. Physical appearance, including clothing, shoes, jewelry, hair style and hair adornments, shapes first impressions, indicates how formal a speech to expect, and establishes and maintains a speaker's credibility. You should use physical appearance somewhat formally but without feeling uncomfortable. A competent speaker also uses body language, including posture, body movement and use of space, and gestures, to convey a sense of self-assuredness and confidence to the audience. Posture is a position of your bodily parts that communicates your attitude and sense of self to the audience. An erect posture indicates a degree of formality, enhances credibility, and optimizes your use of your voice. Body movement refers to how a public speaker stands and walks during the speech. Moving with purpose helps you emphasize transitions and important points, maintain contact, and create rapport with the audience. Moving aimlessly or pacing in the space signals nervousness and distracts listeners from the speech. Gestures are natural movements of the hands and arms that reinforce what is said, emphasize important points, and make presentations more interesting. As a competent speaker, you are advised to use gestures in a natural and relaxed manner that matches the content of what you are saying. Closely related to body language is facial expression and eye contact. Facial expression com-

Things To Do: Competency Eight

Review this *Things To Do* list for using nonverbal communication effectively, appropriately, and correctly when you deliver your next speech. Have you done the following?

1. Thought ahead to your next speech and decided how to use physical appearance to create a favorable first expression and enhance your credibility? ☐

2. Reviewed your speech outline and identified where you could use body movement to emphasize transitions or main points? ☐

3. Reviewed your speech outline and determined how you might use natural gestures to reinforce what you say and make your presentation more interesting to the audience? ☐

4. Thought about how you will use facial expression to communicate your feelings about the content of your speech and eye contact to promote a sense of involvement with the audience? ☐

5. Considered whether you could overcome any cultural differences that may be present in the audience by using a bit of code switching? ☐

6. Practiced your speech to ensure you are using a transparent delivery? ☐

municates emotion and how the speaker feels about what is said to the audience. Most important, you should use sufficient facial expression to communicate feelings that are appropriate to the topic of your speech. Eye contact is a tool the speaker uses to promote a sense of involvement with audience members and to gauge audience reaction to the speech. Failing to use eye contact may result in being perceived as nervous or even deceitful. In using any of these nonverbal cues, your awareness of how their meanings may vary because of cultural differences of audience members is important. These differences can be bridged through the use of multicodality and code switching, which involves retaining your unique way of using words and nonverbal cues while incorporating some of the unique communication patterns of the listeners in what you say. Finally, a transparent delivery will help you present a speech so that audience members don't focus on elements of the delivery but instead pay full attention to your message.

KEY TERMS

The key terms below are defined in this chapter and presented alphabetically with definitions in the Glossary at the end of the book.

- physical appearance
- posture
- gestures
- eye contact
- transparent delivery
- body language
- body movement
- facial expression
- multicodality

BUILDING COMPETENCE ACTIVITIES

INDIVIDUAL ACTIVITIES

1. When speeches are next presented in class, evaluate how effectively each student used nonverbal cues to enhance the delivery of the speech. Focus on strengths and missed opportunities to use nonverbal communication to the student's advantage.

2. Attend a public speech or presentation (it could be a lecture in another class). Evaluate the speaker's use of nonverbal cues to make contact and create rapport with the audience, and establish and maintain credibility.

3. Go to either one of these websites, both of which contain an array of public speeches: http://www.wfu.edu/~louden/Political%20Communication/Class%20Information/SPEECHES.html or http://www.csus.edu/indiv/k/kiddv/ComsSites/speeches.html. Choose a speech and evaluate the quality of the speaker's use of nonverbal cues. Write short evaluations of her/his use of nonverbal cues to make contact and create rapport with the audience, and establish and maintain credibility.

4. Practice your next speech, standing up in front of a mirror. Include in the delivery any nonverbal cues you deem appropriate to enhance the delivery of the speech. Evaluate the results with a focus on what worked and what did not.

GROUP ACTIVITIES

1. When speeches are next presented in class, after the speeches, meet with a group of three to four students to evaluate how effectively each student used nonverbal cues to enhance the delivery of the speech. Focus on strengths and missed opportunities and prepare a list of general recommendations on using nonverbal communication competently to share with the class.

2. With one or two other students, attend a public speech or presentation (it could be a lecture in another class in which you are all enrolled). Have each student individually evaluate the quality of the speaker's use of nonverbal cues in the presentation. Compare your individual evaluations after the lecture.

3. Form groups of three to four students and go to either of these websites both of which contain a big selection of public speeches: http://www.abacon.com/pubspeak/histsit.html, or http://www.mhhe.com/socscience/comm/new-home/. Have each group member select a different speech and evaluate the quality of the speaker's use of nonverbal cues. In the group, compare your evaluations.

4. Choose a partner in the class and rehearse your next speech together. Focus particularly on the use of nonverbal communication in the delivery of the speech. Provide feedback to the other student and strengths and opportunities for enhancement in your feedback.

COMPETENCY CHECKPOINTS AND SELF-ASSESSMENT TOOL

Here is what you need to know and be able to do regarding nonverbal communication and presenting a speech. Determine your level of competency and whether you are ready to proceed to the next chapter. Give yourself one point for each checkpoint you answer satisfactorily.

COMPETENCY CHECKPOINTS	NUMBER OF POINTS
KNOWLEDGE	
1. Explain why nonverbal communication and using nonverbal cues well is important to delivering a speech competently.	
2. Define and describe the role of physical appearance in delivering a speech competently.	
3. Define and describe the role of body language, including posture, body movement, use of space, and gestures, in delivering a speech competently.	

4. Define and describe the role of facial expression in delivering a speech competently.
5. Define and describe the role of eye contact in delivering a speech competently.
6. Describe the roles of multicodality and of a transparent delivery in public speaking competence.

SKILLS

1. Examine the outline for your next speech and determine which of the nonverbal cues described in this chapter will most enhance the delivery of the speech.
2. Practice your next speech, incorporate appropriate nonverbal cues, and decide whether you are able to use a transparent delivery effectively.

ETHICS AND CREDIBILITY

1. What would an ethical approach to using nonverbal cues in a speech call on a speaker to consider?
2. How would a competent speaker use nonverbal cues to most effectively enhance her or his credibility?

TOTAL CHECKPOINTS (OUT OF A POSSIBLE TEN POINTS)

ENDNOTES

1. Genard, G. (2004, Spring). Leveraging the power of nonverbal communication. *Harvard Management Communication Letter, 1*(2), 3–4.
2. Burgoon, J.K. &Hale, J.L. (1984).The fundamental topoi of relational communication. *Communication Monographs, (51)*3, 193-214. (see also: Burgoon, J. K., Birk, T., & Pfau, M. (1990). Nonverbal behaviors, persuasion, and credibility. *Human Communication Research, 17*, 140-169. Burgoon, J. K., & White, C. A. (1997). Researching nonverbal message production: A view from interaction adaptation theory. In J. O. Greene (Ed.), *Message production: Advances in communication theory* (pp. 279–312). Mahwah, NJ: Lawrence Erlbaum. Burgoon, J. K., Buller, D. B., & Woodall, W. G. (1996). *Nonverbal communication: The unspoken dialogue* (2nd ed.). New York: McGraw-Hill. Burgoon, J. K., & Le Poire, B. A. (1999). Nonverbal cues and interpersonal judgments: Participant and observer perceptions of intimacy, dominance, composure, and formality. *Communication Monographs, (66)*2, 105–124.
3. Morris, T., Gorham, J., Cohen, S., & Huffman, D. (1996). Fashion in the classroom: Effects of attire on student perceptions of instructors in college classes. *Communication Education, 45*, 135–148.
4. Sellnow, D.D. & Treinen, K.P. (2004). The role of gender in perceived speaker competence: An analysis of student peer critiques. *Communication Education 53*(3), 286–296.
5. Wilson Arboleda, B.M. & Frederick, A. L. (2008). Considerations for maintenance of postural alignment for voice production. *Journal of Voice, 22*(1), 90–99.
6. Morgan, N. (2008, Nov). How to become an authentic speaker. *Harvard Business Review, 86*(11), 115–119.
7. Morgan, N. (2004, Winter). Preparing to be real. *Harvard Management Communication Letter,1*(1), 3–5.
8. Borisoff, D., & Merrill, L. (1998). The *power to communicate: Gender differences as barriers. 3rd Ed.* Prospect Heights, IL: Waveland.
9. Auer, P. (Ed.) (1998*). Code-switching in conversation: Language, interaction, and identity.* London: Routledge.
10. Avoiding nonverbal blunders. (2000, September). *Harvard Management Communication Newsletter, 3*(9), p. 7.
11. Dance, F.E.X. (July, 1999). Successful presenters master the art of being transparent. *Presentations*, p. 80.

PART FOUR: SPEAKING IN DIFFERENT SITUATIONS

A Final Note from the Author to the Reader of This Textbook!

In the Introduction to Part One of this book, I encouraged you to enjoy the process of becoming a more confident and competent public speaker. I hope it has gone well and you have benefited from learning to get up on your feet and give a speech competently and confidently. You started out in Part One with a general introduction to studying communication and public speaking. In Part Two, we focused on four basic competencies for preparing speeches and in Part Three on four competencies for presenting speeches. You are almost done! In Part Four, we apply what you have learned about preparing and presenting to how you give speeches in these different situations:

- Chapter 12: Using Presentation Aids
- Chapter 13: Speaking to Inform
- Chapter 14: Speaking to Persuade
- Chapter 15: Speaking at Work and on Special Occasions

This is my last personal note to you. If you would like to tell me about any exciting experiences you have giving speeches, contact me directly at smorreal@uccs.edu. It would be a pleasure to hear from you.

Cordially,

Dr. Sherry Morreale

12

USING PRESENTATION AIDS

- **Understanding Presentation Aids**
  Types of Speech Aids
- **Presenting with Speech Aids**
  Unprojected Speech Aids
- **Presenting with Projected Computerized Aids**
- **Suggestions for Using all Presentation Aids**

"I'm a great believer that any tool that enhances communication has pro-found effects in terms of how people can learn from each other." Bill Gates, Chairman of Microsoft, business magnate and philanthropist, b. 1955

. .
. . .

Students in the public speaking class were given a choice about what kind of presen-tational or visual aid they would use for their final informative speeches. The instructor described an array of types of aids, but she didn't sound overwhelmingly enthusias-tic about using PowerPoint for the informative speech: "PowerPoint, while an impor-tant skill, is not your only option for a presentation aid. Communication scholars are debating whether the use of computerized speech presentations is always a good thing. Some say PowerPoint makes for attractive and dynamic presentations, but oth-ers say it can result in monotonous speeches, one boring slide after another with too much information and too many bulleted items on each slide." Kumar, Richard, and Angelique met with a few other students right after class, which they now did every week. Kumar typically reads the textbook chapter ahead of time, and he shared his thoughts about presentation aids: "There are a lot of different types of speech aids described in Chapter 12. We don't have to rely on PowerPoint, if the result could be a boring speech." Angelique took issue with Kumar's negative attitude about using PowerPoint: "I think using PowerPoint slides works well. It's a popular approach to presenting in the real world, and we need to be able to use it effectively. Used right, it will strengthen our speeches, if our slides are simple and clear. They can organize what we say, so the audience doesn't get lost. Of course, we shouldn't let the PowerPoint detract from our ability to make audience contact nonverbally." LaTisha settled the argument about what type of speech aid to use: "Hey, this isn't show and tell. We're not back in grade school. Let's all read Chapter 12 and figure out the best aid for each of our speeches. We need to know how to do this right."

. .
. . .

These students are thinking seriously about how to use presentation aids to enhance the delivery of their speeches. You should as well. Presentation aids, professional in appearance and effectively used, can help make your speeches more appealing and easier to follow, whether you're presenting in your public speaking class, at work, or at a major international conference.[1] One communication author tells us presentation aids help increase the number of listeners you reach with your speech, because they address the diverse learning styles of audience members.[2] Another author says visual aids are vitally important, because they are capable of promoting interest, clarity, and retention by audience members of information you present in your speech.[3]

However, another researcher adds a cautionary note about using computerized speech aids.[4] Dale Cyphert says students need to understand exactly what makes a visual aid effective, particularly the use of a presentation technology like PowerPoint. He says public speaking is entering what he refers to as *the age of electronic eloquence*. Therefore, students need to be able to fully and effectively integrate visual (PowerPoint) and verbal messages (what they say) in order to engage in effective civic participation in the media age. Cyphert's opinion about the 21st century being dominated by electronic communication makes sense. This chapter covers the fundamentals for using presentation aids competently, by addressing these topics:

- What a presentation aid is and its purpose in your speech.
- The types of speech aids from which you may choose.
- How to present using un-projected speech aids?
- How to present using a projected computerized speech aid, like PowerPoint.

UNDERSTANDING PRESENTATION AIDS

A highly valuable form of support material you can and should prepare ahead of time is varyingly referred to as a speech aid or a presentation aid. A **presentation aid** is anything other than your spoken words that assists in illustrating or supporting the content of the speech. Visual aids are the most popular type, but other speech aids you may not have considered are aural (hearing) aids, like music. A student valedictorian once effectively incorporated music throughout her graduation speech.[5] She picked three different songs to represent the graduates' elementary, middle, and high school years and played them softly, while she went through memories of those past years. She ended with a song of hope and left students thinking about what they had to look forward to in the future.

In addition to adding interest and excitement to a speech, as this valedictorian did with music, presentation aids are useful when you need to clarify a difficult concept, present a complex idea, or demonstrate a process the audience would have difficulty understanding. As the following description of different types of aids illustrates, there is a speech aid to accomplish any of these goals.

> **12.1 A PRESENTATION AID is** anything other than your spoken words that assists in illustrating or supporting the content of the speech.

TYPES OF SPEECH AIDS

Your choice of a speech aid is only limited by your imagination, creativity, and how much time you are willing to spend preparing it. Your first thought, like the students in our opening story, is probably to use a computerized program like PowerPoint. But if you decide to use a nonelectronic speech aid, there are many types to choose from including objects and models; diagrams and drawings; pictures and photographs, maps; charts and graphs; and tables and lists.

Objects, including models, are useful visual aids when you want to show your listeners what something looks like

> **12.2 OBJECTS, including models,** are visual aids you can use to show your listeners what something looks like or how it works.

or how it works. A New York Yankees baseball cap could be used in a speech about the record for hitting homeruns. A set of gardening tools would be helpful if you're explaining aspects of horticulture and cultivating different types of flowers. If you use an object of any kind, be sure it's large enough that all audience members can see it but small enough so you can conceal it until the point in your speech when it becomes relevant. To avoid distracting the audience from what you're saying, only show the object when you're actually talking about it. In cases when the object you would like to use is too large and cumbersome to bring in or too small for the listeners to see clearly, you can show your audience a model rather than the object itself. Architects, for example, provide models of buildings when they present their ideas to clients. If you want to talk about the solar system and how planets relate to one another, a scaled-down model would make a good visual aid.

12.3 A DIAGRAM OR DRAWING is a visual aid used to explain how something appears or operates.

12.4 A PICTURE OR PHOTOGRAPH is a visual aid used when a more realistic depiction of a person, a place, or an object is needed in your speech.

12.5 A MAP is a useful visual aid when you want to pinpoint a location or highlight a geographical area.

12.6 A CHART OR GRAPH is a visual aid for presenting statistics that helps to clarify relationships among numbers and reveals any trends or patterns.

If you prefer not to create a model, you can use a **diagram** or **drawing** to explain how something appears or operates. These types of aids are particularly useful for explaining particular points or steps in a process or simplifying and clarifying relationships. If you want to explain how a car engine works, a diagram will help the listeners follow your explanation of the steps in that process. If an architect wanted to show a client the façade of a building, a drawing would work well. Diagrams and drawings help listeners understand ideas that words alone can't adequately describe. But the aid must depict the thing it represents both clearly and accurately.

If your speech would be enhanced by a more realistic depiction of a person, a place, or an object, then a **picture** or **photograph** will be helpful. The realism of a picture or photo can bring an idea or a concept to life more effectively than a diagram or drawing. A painting of the snow-capped peaks of the Colorado Rockies would decidedly enhance a speech about a ski vacation. A photograph of the face of a young child would humanize a request for a contribution to a charity benefiting children in developing countries. Appeals on TV for contributions to such organizations often use photographs to good advantage. The picture or photograph needs to be large enough for all the members of the audience to see, and it should be cropped or framed to eliminate any distracting details.

When you want to pinpoint a location or highlight a geographical area, you can use a **map** as a visual aid. Maps also can help you talk about concentrations of people or industries, weather patterns, landmarks, or transportation routes. In business settings, visual maps often are used to show the structure of the corporation, or how sales and profits are realized across the country or around the globe.[6] If your speech is about a historical period, a map of what the world or area looked like at that time will make an intriguing visual aid.

When you're planning to present statistics or a series of numbers to support a point in your speech, you need a visual aid that will help your listeners easily grasp the meaning of the figures. Putting statistics into a **chart** or **graph**, as discussed in Chapter 7, will clarify the relationships among the numbers and reveal any trends or patterns. Among the most frequently used charts and graphs are line graphs, bar graphs, and pie charts. A few examples are provided in Figure 12.1.

Figure 12.1: Using Graphs and Charts in Informative Speeches

In these examples, the same information is presented using two types of graphs and a pie chart. Which one do you think is most effective?

Line Graph

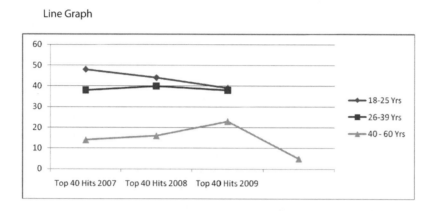

Pie Chart

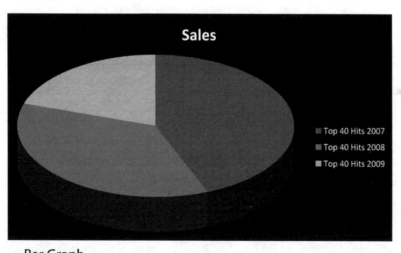

Bar Graph

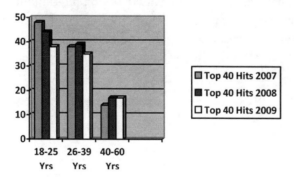

A line graph is used to show changes over time or the relationship of two or more sets of numbers. Because line graphs are simple to read, you can show the patterns of change in more than one

series of numbers without confusing the audience. A bar graph portrays numbers as rectangular bars, making a series of numbers even easier to read and understand. You can use a bar graph to compare two or three sets of numbers or to show trends. When you want to portray numbers as parts of a whole, you can use a pie chart. Each slice of the pie represents one part of the whole. Most of the time, it's best to put the largest slice of the pie at twelve o'clock and arrange the other slices clockwise in descending order of size.

When you want to organize, summarize, and then present detailed information, you use a table. **Tables** are all-text visual aids in which numbers or words are arranged in a grid of columns and rows. The advantage of a table is that by using short phrases for headings and minimizing text entries, you can include a lot of data in a small space. Articles in academic journals frequently present the results of research studies in table form. In a speech aid, you can use color in a table to focus your audience's attention on specific information. For instance, if you want the audience to examine the numbers presented for certain years, you could highlight those in a different color. Technical communication experts say background colors in slides should contrast with the colors used in a table or graph and cool colors like blue and green are better than warm colors like red or orange.[7] But avoid confusing the audience by including too much color in any table, which could be distracting.

12.7 TABLES are all-text visual aids in which numbers or words are arranged in a grid of columns and rows.

12.8 LISTS are all-text visual aids that can communicate a lot of information in a simple way.

Like tables, **lists** are all-text visual aids that can communicate a lot of information in a simple way. You can use lists to tell the audience at a glance which items are most important, by arranging the items in ascending or descending order of importance. Of course, sometimes the items on your list are of equal importance, in which case you arrange them in the order that you prefer to talk about them. Lists are most effective if you keep them short and to the point.

PRESENTING WITH SPEECH AIDS

Once you've chosen the type of aid to use, next you decide how you will present it. For example, you may want to use a table of statistics and you could present it to the audience using a flip chart or by incorporating it in a slide show. You can choose among a variety of presentation methods including unprojected speech aids that don't require the use of electricity to present or computer developed and presented visual aids that are now the most popular speech aid of all. Let's first consider the advantages and disadvantages of the various unprojected aids and how to present with each to best advantage.

UNPROJECTED SPEECH AIDS

Unprojected aids, including the chalkboard or whiteboard, flip charts and poster boards, and handouts, are among the easiest to use. Their advantages include they are inexpensive, unbreakable for the most part, and can be used in lighted rooms for ease of note taking. Their disadvantages

12.9 UNPROJECTED AIDS are easy to use and include the chalkboard or whiteboard, flip charts and poster boards, and handouts.

include they can be cumbersome, hard for large groups to see, and may cause the speaker's back to be to the audience. Here are some suggestions for using each of the unprojected aids competently:

Chalkboard/Whiteboard
- Write any material you can on the board before beginning your speech and, if possible, cover it up until needed.
- Remember to face the audience, not the chalk or whiteboard.
- Write legibly and simply and make sure the writing is visible to audience members in the back of the room.

Flip Charts/Posters
- Decide where you'll position and display the flip chart or poster ahead of time.
- Don't block the audience's view of the chart or poster and don't face it while you're speaking.
- Conceal material and then reveal it as you discuss it.

Handouts
- Use handouts to help the listeners follow or recall your main points, but don't let them take over your presentation.
- Wait to distribute your handouts until the end of your speech, so reading them won't distract audience members.
- If information on the handouts is essential to understanding your speech, distribute them ahead of time before you start to speak.
- If you use a computerized presentation, distribute handouts containing the computer slides ahead of time. Then the audience members can listen to you rather than writing down everything off each slide.

PRESENTING WITH PROJECTED COMPUTERIZED AIDS

Nobody would argue that the most popular form of projected visual aid is the **computerized presentation**. This method of presenting allows you to use a computer to display slides, photographs, drawings, diagrams, maps, charts, tables and lists, and video clips and other resources available directly from the Internet. The advantages of this type of speech aid are as follows: computerized presentations are useful for organizing and focusing speech content; they can be dramatic and colorful and are easier for members of large groups to see; plus, they can create a desired mood or effect for your speech. Disadvantages are: the possibility of malfunction or breakdown; they are not easily used in a lighted room; and, the slides may become the focus of attention rather than the speaker and the speech.

The use of computerized presentations is growing at a rapid rate in both business and education. Of the various software programs available for presenting speeches, Microsoft's PowerPoint dominates. Since it is readily available on the desktops of all those using Microsoft Office Suite, it is the software program of choice for the vast majority of public speakers. In

12.10 A COMPUTERIZED PRESENTATION allows you to use a computer to display slides, photographs, drawings, diagrams, maps, charts, tables and lists, video clips and other resources available directly from the Internet.

fact, an estimated 30 million PowerPoint presentations are given every day and that number, since 2001, has been on the rise.[8]

Despite the popularity of PowerPoint, the use of this computerized public speaking program has both defenders and detractors.[9] Proponents say it improves retention, persuasion, learning and motivation, and instructor credibility. Opponents say, while PowerPoint is an indispensable business skill, the slides often have a detrimental effect on dialogue and interaction.[10] For example, on one college campus, the Dean removed computers from all lecture halls and challenged professors to "teach naked," which means without the use of any machines or technology.[11] More than anything, the Dean wanted to discourage the use of PowerPoint, contending class time should be reserved for discussion and challenging debates and talks with professors.

The consensus of the critics is the use of programs like PowerPoint causes speakers to prepare presentations that take the life and vitality out of public speaking. They claim the use of these programs has debased rhetoric and public speaking to the level of an elementary school filmstrip. To support their claim, they ask us to imagine Martin Luther King's *I Had a Dream* speech or Abraham Lincoln's *Gettysburg Address.* If either speaker had presented with PowerPoint, would we still remember their landmark addresses today? Most of us might agree PowerPoint has its challenges. But we probably also agree it can be effective, even though many presentations and the slides they contain, are not what they should be.[12] Check out the list of challenges in Box 12.1, Thinking Outside the Box about PowerPoint.[13] By being aware of the challenges, you will be able to use any computerized presentation program to your advantage.

If you haven't used a computerized presentation software program before, an easy way to get started is with the tutorial assistant built into most programs. For example, PowerPoint contains a tutorial called AutoWizard, which will have you producing a presentation almost immediately. An array of other online tutorials also is available; just enter the term PowerPoint in any search engine. For additional instruction, computer centers on college campuses often provide free training in the use of software like PowerPoint.

The technical aspects of creating a computerized presentation are not the biggest challenge, as you can tell from the list in Box 12.1. Once you learn how to use it, the temptation is great to incorporate too many of PowerPoint's special effects in your presentation, which can be distracting to the audience. You run the risk of the computer-generated graphics becoming the focus of the presentation. Public speaking involves connecting in a personal way with listeners, as Judee Burgoon advised us in the chapter on using nonverbal cues. If the audience's attention is riveted on an impressive computerized presentation, they won't pay attention to you and your message. Therefore, you want to use this method of presentation effectively by not letting it take the place of you as a public speaker. The best way to use computerized presentation tools competently is to control both the quantity of information and the amount of action used in each slide. Think carefully about how complex and lively each slide will be. By preparing relatively simple visual graphics, you can talk to the audience when presenting the speech rather than reading off the slides.

Experts in public speaking offer these specific suggestions for using PowerPoint competently:

- One group of researchers challenges the conventional use of a single word or short phrase as the slide headline on PowerPoint slides. They say a short sentence headline, identifying the main idea or assertion of the particular slide, leads to a significant increase in listeners' retention of what was said.[14]
- Another author discusses how to develop an effective PowerPoint business presentation. He stresses PowerPoint can communicate ideas to the audience without boring them, but only if you avoid the use of what he calls *those dreadful bullet points.* Listeners know the speaker

needs to go through each bullet point before going on to the next slide, and they find the waiting process tedious at best.[15]

- Two more experts agree presenters shouldn't clutter their slides with visual effects that add little substance. Clip art and photography should be informative rather than just decorative. Also, the slides shouldn't be overly comprehensive. A good presentation covers only a few key or main points on the slides, and the speaker develops those points adequately when speaking.[16]

Box 12.1: Thinking Outside the Box about PowerPoint

You need to be aware of PowerPoint's 16 challenges, and then you will understand how to use any computerized presentation program competently.

---

1. PowerPoint can easily be abused. It's too easy to create slides. Because you can crank them out quickly, you make far more than are appropriate for the presentation.
2. It wastes time during the preparation stage. You can use up precious time tweaking a presentation.
3. It takes too much control away from the presenter. It's too easy to start the presentation with PowerPoint instead of starting with ideas and using PowerPoint to reinforce them.
4. It can make for ugly presentations. Most people are not trained in design. The computer puts tools in average hands that were once reserved only for artists. The result is ugly presentations.
5. It can actually impede attention. Audience members attend to the messenger—the bells and whistles—and not the message.
6. It too easily becomes a replacement for the presenter, not a reinforcement of what the presenter says. Instead of a visual aid for the speaker, the speaker becomes an audio aid for the slides.
7. PowerPoint sometimes masks the fact the presentation does not have enough intrinsic attention factors in itself.
8. It lends itself to unnecessary competition. Presenters, particularly students, become distracted with "dueling PowerPoints."
9. It does not lend itself to spontaneous discussions in the classroom or boardroom.
10. It is heavily scripted and is not a tool for discovery.
11. It does not handle text well. You end up reading what is written on the slide. A good rule for PowerPoint text is no more than seven lines of text on a slide and no more than seven words per line.
12. Presenters rely too much on the slides for structure. Clear structure should still be part of the verbal presentation, even with visual aids. The aids should reinforce the structure, not replace it.
13. Presenters fail to make their message memorable. They often rely too much on the visual slide and neglect repetition, examples, metaphors and other devices that make a message memorable.
14. Presenters fail to establish their own credibility, their most powerful appeal. They let the slides speak for them.
15. Speakers don't look at the audience and the audience doesn't look at the speaker; they look at the slides instead. Subtle nonverbal cues are lost such as eye-contact, posture, and gesturing to complement the verbal message.
16. Presenters tend to read off the slide, which results in a flat and uninspiring delivery.

Source: Kaminski, S.H. (2005). Retrieved from http://www.shkaminski.com/Classes/Handouts/powerpoint.htm

- A last piece of advice relates to how you present with PowerPoint. Do not read the words off the slides verbatim to the audience. This causes listeners to feel talked down to and they may become a little bored. To avoid this verbatim effect, paraphrase the words on the slide. For instance, if the slide reads "An Increase in Voter Registration," then say to the audience: "Our political party and the number of registered voters have grown impressively in this county over recent years."

By now you may think you know all there is to know about PowerPoint. But read Box 12.2 about a PowerPoint presentation game that is gaining worldwide attention—it's called *Pecha kucha*.[17]

We now conclude this chapter with a few general recommendations you may find useful, regardless of the type of presentation aid you decide to use.

Box 12.2: Practice PowerPoint with "Pecha Kucha"

Pecha kucha is a way to keep PowerPoint presentations short and focused by limiting them to 20 slides of 20 seconds each. That's 6 minutes, 40 seconds in all.

Pecha kucha is quite the rage in PowerPoint circles. The name comes from a Japanese term meaning chatter. Pecha Kucha Nights and contests are happening in cities around the world. The idea is to force the presenter to speak concisely, precisely, and clearly. Typically, Pecha kucha presentations are mostly images. The transitions from slide to slide are timed to 20 seconds, so the presenter can't extend the time.

How do you create a Pecha kucha presentation? Here are five easy steps to follow before you go to a contest in your home town.

1. Develop your speech outline, present or rehearse and time it to be sure you can present it in approximately six minutes, or a little more.
2. Create 20 slides that include a little text and large, striking images.
3. Write your script in the note pane of each slide, so that you know what you'll say for each slide. Recheck the timing.
4. Set the slides to advance after 20 seconds. Choose View and Slide Sorter and select all of the slides. On the Slide Sorter toolbar, click the Transition button or Animation. In the Advance Slide section, uncheck the *On Mouse* and check the *Automatically After* check box. In the Automatically After text box, enter 00:20.
5. Now practice the speech with the automated slides until you can deliver the presentation within 6 minutes and 40 seconds.

Source: Retrieved from http://www.ellenfinkelstein.com/powerpointtips/powerpoint_tip_stay_focused_pecha_kucha.htm

---

SUGGESTIONS FOR USING ALL PRESENTATION AIDS

Whether you plan to use PowerPoint or any other type of speech aid, remember these last suggestions while preparing it. Minimize the amount of detail you include in your visual display. Don't cram too much information onto any slide, handout, or flipchart page. For slides, use the **Seven by Seven Rule**, which limits each slide to seven lines down and seven words across. Be sure anything you put on any aid is clear, readable, and visible to all members of the audience. If you'd like to test the quality of the aid before you present with it, see if it passes the *nice* test.

N = Necessary to the speech and to supporting your thesis, not just an add-on

I = Impacts the audience in the way you intend

C = Clear and simple

E = Easily seen or heard by all audience members

If you decide to use a speech aid in your presentation, it's helpful to plan and prepare it carefully ahead of time and include it in at least one practice session, before you actually present with it. By doing this, you will answer several crucial questions you don't want to be asking yourself on the actual day of your presentation. For instance, you need to decide ahead of time where you'll set up and display the aid and where you'll stand relative to it. If you're using a projected image of some kind,

12.11 THE SEVEN BY SEVEN RULE limits each slide to seven lines down and seven words across.

experiment with standing next to the projected image or next to the lectern and your notes. Both of these locations are equally effective, but you need to choose which feels most comfortable to you. Also, experiment with either pointing to each item on the aid as you talk about it or just letting listeners read what is displayed for themselves. Practice with a pointer, electronic or not, if you plan to use one. Plan what you'll do with the pointer when it's not in use. Also practice with the clicker, if you use one to move from one slide to the next. An option for moving automatically from one slide to the next at timed intervals is available, but it limits how much time you can spend on each slide.

Box 12.3 provides yet more reminders for using a presentation aid well. Then in Box 12.4, a professional presenter tells a true story about what went wrong for her when using a presentation aid and how she graciously recovered.

Kumar, Richard, and Angelique used presentation aids effectively. Kumar opened and closed his speech about the influence of pop music with a CD playing one of Bono's latest songs about social activism. Richard included slides with bar graphs in his PowerPoint presentation indicating the significant increase in violent crimes in their community. Of course, he was careful not to let PowerPoint take over his presentation. Angelique's speech about non-Western rhetoric was enhanced by access-

---

Box 12.3: Suggestions for Competently Presenting with Speech Aids

The purpose of any presentation aid is to enhance, not distract from, your speech.

Follow these simple suggestions for the successful use of presentation aids:
Explain the aid briefly to the audience telling them what you're trying to achieve with it, before you talk about its contents.

- Speak to the audience, not to the visual aid. If you face the aid, the audience won't hear what you're saying.

- Use a pointer, a pencil, or a laser pointer, if you want to focus audience attention on the part of the aid you're talking about.

- If possible, cover up the sections of the aid you have yet to discuss. Reveal each section just as you begin to talk about it.

- Don't read the entire text of the aid to the audience, unless you want to emphasize a definition or description of something contained in it.

- Don't shuffle through handouts or fidget with any part of a speech aid while you're presenting. Instead, have the aid in order and positioned ahead of time and plan for how you'll pick it up and use it and what you will do with it when not in use.

Box 12.4: Presenting with a Speech Aid—A True Story

This speaker provides some advice about arriving early so you can consider any and all details for using the aid effectively.

Here is a great story about an "exciting experience" I had while giving a speech. I was conducting a training session for some employees concerning a new program. I was using a PowerPoint presentation. It was necessary for me to plug the projector into the wall in a way that meant that I needed to walk over the cord while presenting. I talk with my hands and walk around while I present. That day I was wearing short heels. I had failed to tape down the electrical cord, because I had travel delays in getting to the presentation site and the setup was hurried. Since I had done the setup, I felt that I knew where the cord was and could safely walk over it. Well, somewhere between excitedly talking with my hands and energetically walking around, I caught the heel of my shoe in the cord and fell to the floor. Because I was wearing a dress and fell "upstream" of the viewers, I quickly leapt up to avoid an unscheduled "show and tell" exhibition. I went right on as if nothing had happened and said, "I bet that you all just can't imagine what I might do for an encore." I assured them that I wasn't hurt and immediately proceeded to finish the session. I can't imagine how I was able to think so quickly on my feet (or off them as the case may be). I think the moral is: Always tape the cords down and carry a sharp wit with you at all times.

Source: An anonymous professional presenter in a real world organization

---

ing video clips on the Internet of non-Western speakers. All the students used speech aids that truly *aided* their speeches. Even their use of PowerPoint was impressive, reflecting they had learned to use the technology effectively. In the final three chapters of this book, you and these students will learn about speaking to inform, to persuade, and on special occasions.

CHAPTER SUMMARY

A valuable form of support material for any speech is a presentation aid, which is anything other than spoken words that assists in illustrating or supporting the content of the speech. Types of non-electronic aids are objects and models; diagrams and drawings; pictures and photographs, maps; charts and graphs; and tables and lists. Objects, including models, are used to show your listeners what something looks like or how it works. Only show the object when you are talking about it. A diagram or drawing is used to explain how something appears or operates. Be sure this type of aid depicts  the thing it represents clearly and accurately. If helpful to your speech, a picture or photograph can provide a more realistic depiction of a person, a place, or an object. Be sure the picture or photograph is large enough, so the entire audience can see it. A map is useful when you want to pinpoint a location or highlight a geographical area. A chart or graph helps to present statistics by clarifying relationships among numbers and revealing any trends or patterns. The most frequently used are line graphs, bar graphs, and pie charts. Tables are all-text visual aids in which numbers or words are arranged in a grid of columns and rows. The advantage of this aid is that you can include a lot of data in a small space. Lists are all-text visual aids that also can communicate a lot of information in a simple way. They can be used to tell the audience which items are most important by their order on the list, but keep lists short and to the point. Once you have chosen the type of aid to use, then you choose a presentation method for it, such as unprojected aids, not requiring electricity, or computer developed and presented visual aids. Unprojected aids are easy to use and include the chalkboard or whiteboard, flip charts and poster boards, and handouts. Their advantages include that they are inexpensive, unbreakable, and can be used in lighted rooms. Their disadvantages include that they can be: cumbersome, hard to see, and may cause you to turn your back to the audience. A computerized presentation allows you to use a computer to display slides, photographs, drawings, diagrams, maps, charts, tables and lists, video clips and other resources available directly from the Internet. The advantages of this aid include that it is useful for organizing and focusing speech content, dramatic and colorful, easy to see, and it can create a desired mood or effect for the speech. Disadvantages include malfunction or breakdown, not easily used in a lighted room, and, the slides may become the focus of attention rather than the speaker and the speech. Some critics claim the most popular computerized presentation program, PowerPoint, takes the life and vitality out of public speaking. However, most experts agree an awareness of the challenges to PowerPoint will help you use the program to your advantage. We are advised to control the quantity of information and amount of action used in each slide. By preparing relatively simple visual graphics, you can talk to the audience when presenting the speech rather than reading off the slides. The Seven by Seven Rule limits each slide to seven lines down and seven words across.

KEY TERMS

The key terms below are defined in this chapter and presented alphabetically with definitions in the Glossary at the end of the book.

- presentation aid
- diagram or drawing
- map
- tables
- unprojected aids
- Seven by Seven Rule
- objects
- picture or photograph
- chart or graph
- lists
- computerized presentation

BUILDING COMPETENCE ACTIVITIES

INDIVIDUAL ACTIVITIES

1. When speeches are next presented in class, evaluate how effectively each student used a speech aid to enhance the delivery of the speech. Evaluate the strengths and weaknesses of the speech aid and how it was included in the presentation.

2. Attend a public speech or presentation (it could be a lecture in another class). Evaluate the speaker's use of speech aids. If none was used, determine if the speech could have been better had the speaker used some type of speech aid. What type of aid should have been used?

3. Go to CuePrompter.com, which is a free teleprompter/autocue service. Your browser works like a teleprompter used by newscasters and no extra software is needed. Enter the full formal outline for your next speech and try delivering it using this speech aid. Evaluate the quality of your delivery using this aid.

4. Practice your next speech and include a speech aid to enhance the delivery of the speech. Evaluate the results with a focus on what worked and what did not.

5. Go to presentationzen.com, a blog on issues related to professional presentation design. A recent topic on the blog focused on "What is good PowerPoint design." Read or participate in the blog and come up with a short list of suggestions for improving how you use PowerPoint.

GROUP ACTIVITIES

1. When speeches are next presented in class, after the speeches, meet with a group of three to four students to evaluate how effectively each student used a speech aid to enhance the delivery of the speech. Evaluate the strengths and weaknesses of the speech aid and how it was included in the presentation. Prepare a list of general recommendations on using speech aids competently to share with the class.

2. With one or two other students, attend a public speech or presentation (it could be a lecture in another class in which you are all enrolled). Have each student individually evaluate the speaker's use of speech aids. If none was used, determine if the speech could have been better had the speaker used some type of speech aid. What type of aid should have been used? Compare your individual evaluations after the lecture.

3. Form groups of three to four students and go to CuePrompter.com, which is a free teleprompter/autocue service. Your browser works like a teleprompter used by newscasters and no extra software is needed. Have all students enter their full formal outlines for the next speech and try delivering the speeches using this speech aid. Compare your opinions of using this type of speech aid.

4. Choose a partner in the class and rehearse your next speech together using a speech aid. Provide feedback to the other student about how well the aid enhanced the delivery of the speech.

5. Form groups of four to five students. Visit the following website and read Box 12.2 describing the PowerPoint game called Pecha kucha. Run your own Pecha kucha contest. http://www.ellenfinkelstein.com/powerpointtips/powerpoint_tip_stay_focused_pecha_kucha.html.

6. With a partner from the class, go to presentationzen.com, a blog on issues related to professional presentation design. Read or participate in the blog and collaborate with your partner to come up with a short list of suggestions for improving how you use PowerPoint.

COMPETENCY CHECKPOINTS AND SELF-ASSESSMENT TOOL

Here is what you need to know and be able to do regarding presentation aids. Determine your level of competency and whether you are ready to proceed to the next chapter. Give yourself one point for each checkpoint you answer satisfactorily.

COMPETENCY CHECKPOINTS	NUMBER OF POINTS
KNOWLEDGE	
1. Explain what a presentation aid is and its purpose in a speech.	
2. Identify and describe the various types of speech aids.	
3. List and describe the advantages and disadvantages of using each of the un-projected speech aids.	

4. Outline the advantages and disadvantages of using a computerized speech program like PowerPoint.

SKILLS

1. Give an example of a speech that would be enhanced by the use of an object or model, a diagram or drawing, picture or photograph, map, chart or graph, or a table or list.
2. Give an example of a speech that would lend itself to the use of an unprojected aid such as the chalkboard or whiteboard, flip charts, and poster boards, or handouts.
3. Give an example of a speech that would be most effectively presented using PowerPoint.

ETHICS AND CREDIBILITY

1. Provide an example of the ethical use of speech aids.
2. Provide an example of the unethical use of speech aids.
3. How can a speech aid, well-chosen, developed, and presented, enhance your credibility as a speaker?

TOTAL CHECKPOINTS (OUT OF A POSSIBLE TEN POINTS)

ENDNOTES

1. Jacobs, J.L. Keep attendees awake: Writing effective presentations for international conferences. *CHEST*, 134(1), 204–206.
2. Sellnow, D. (2005). *Confident public speaking* (2nd ed.). Belmont, CA: Wadsworth.
3. Metcalfe, S. (2004). *Building a speech* (5th ed.). Belmont, CA: Wadsworth.
4. Cyphert, D. (2007). Presentation technology in the age of electronic eloquence: From visual aid to visual rhetoric. *Communication Education, 56*(2), 168–192.
5. Kelly, M. (2009, July). *Putting all the pieces together: Effective speech writing*. Retrieved from: http://712educators. about.com/cs/speeches/a/speechwriting_2.htm
6. O'Mara-Croft, B. (2008). Every picture tells a story. *Communication World, 25*(5), 22–25.
7. MacKiewicz, J. (2007). Perceptions of clarity and attractiveness in PowerPoint Graph Slides. *Technical Communication, 54*(20, 145–156.
8. Parker, I. (2001, May 28). Absolute PowerPoint: Can a software package edit our thoughts? *The New Yorker*, pp. 87–93.
9. Cyphert, D. (2007). Presentation technology in the age of electronic eloquence: From visual aid to visual rhetoric. *Communication Education, 56*(2), p. 170.
10. Cyphert, D. (2004). The problem of PowerPoint: Visual aid or visual rhetoric? *Business Communication Quarterly, 67*(1), 80–84.
11. Young, J.R. (2009, July 24). When computers leave classrooms, so does boredom. *The Chronicle of Higher Education, LV*(42), p. A1.
12. Doumont, J. (2005). The cognitive style of PowerPoint: Slides are not all evil. *Technical Communication, 52*(1), 64–70.
13. Kaminski, S.J. (2004). PowerPoint presentations: The good, the bad, and the ugly. Retrieved from http://www.shka-minski.com/Classes/Handouts/powerpoint.htm
14. Alley, M., Schreiber, M., Ramsdell, K., & Muffo, J. (2006). How the design of headlines in presentation slides affects audience retention. *Technical Communication, 53*(2), 225–234.
15. Wei, N. (2007). Making effective PowerPoint Presentations. *Pollution engineering, 39*(10), p. 23.
16. Heath, D. & Heath, C. (2008, Nov). Presentation pep talk. *Fast Company, 130*, 87–88.
17. *Pecha kucha*. Retrieved from Ellen Finkelstein.Com. http://www.ellenfinkelstein.com/powerpointtips/powerpoint_tip_stay_focused_pecha_kha.htm (See also http://www.pecha-kucha.org/ for information about contests in many cities around the world)

13

SPEAKING TO INFORM

- **Understanding the Informative Speech**
- **The Importance of Informative Speaking**
- **Types of Informative Speeches**
    Informative Objectives—Describing, Explaining, Instructing
    Informative content—Objects, Processes, Events, People,
        Issues, Concepts
    Integrating Informative Objectives and Speech Content
- **Organizing an Informative Speech**
    By Category
    By Time or Space
    By Comparison and Contrast
    By Cause and Effect
    Choosing an Organizational Pattern for Informing
- **Challenges to Credible and Ethical Informative Speaking**
    Inappropriate Topic
    Faulty Information
    Poor Organization
- **Overcoming Challenges and Motivating Listeners to Learn**

"The two words, information and communication, are often used inter-changeably, but they signify quite different things. Information is giving out; communication is getting through." Sydney J. Harris, American journalist and author, 1917–1986

• •
• • •

Final speeches in the class would be worth 150 points so the students were a bit anxious about the assignment. To make matters worse, the instructor announced they could make the speech informative or persuasive—it was their choice. In the student meeting after class, Zak and Vanden tried to explain the difference between speaking to inform and speaking to persuade to their classmates. Both Zak and Vanden work full time at the same company and are part-time students. Van provided this advice: "Zak and I present trainings at work all the time on using the new technology sent to us from the national office. Those trainings are definitely informative and I think informative speeches are the easiest to give. You don't have to change anybody's mind about anything." Zak begged to differ: "I think our trainings are persuasive. We need to convince our co-workers to use the new software, whether they like it or not." Kumar interrupted the debate, so they could move on to a discussion about presenting their final speeches well: "My speech about pop music and globalization is a good example of a speech that's both informative and a little persuasive. First, I inform the audience about how widespread pop music is around the world. Then I try to persuade them about the positive influence of pop musicians on social problems like hunger in other countries. The important thing I learned from reading Chapter 13 is you need to decide whether your speech is primarily informative or primarily persuasive, because that affects how you organize the body of the speech; I think my speech is mostly informative." Once again, the students at the meeting were impressed with Kumar's understanding of the speech assignment. They got to work figuring out the objectives for their final speeches, most of which were informative, and how to organize them most effectively. They could see the 150 points for final speeches well within their grasp.

• •
• • •

As these students approached their final speeches, they considered the challenge of informative speaking carefully. They took the advice of one communication researcher who reported on ways public speakers can effectively present complex topics in explanatory or informative speeches.[1]

Rowan tells us that listeners may not understand new and complex ideas in speeches for three reasons. The information in the speech may be confusing, because it involves difficult concepts or language, structures or processes that are hard to envision, or ideas that are difficult to understand or hard to believe. In all of these cases, Rowan suggests first analyzing the informative topic to discover what aspects of it will be most difficult for your listeners to understand. Based on that analysis, you then choose the most effective way to organize the major points in your speech to simplify and clarify the ideas that are hardest to understand.

Rowan's straightforward advice is enhanced in this chapter by discussing the following key ideas for preparing and presenting an effective informative speech. Like Kumar, by the time you are done with this chapter, you will be able to:

- Distinguish between informative and persuasive speaking and explain why informative speaking is important
- Describe the three objectives of informative speeches—to describe, explain, or instruct
- Describe the six types of informative speeches based on their content—objects, processes, events, people, issues, or concepts—and offer guidelines for using each type
- Explain the five ways to organize an informative speech—by category, time, space, comparison and contrast, or cause and effect—and offer suggestions for choosing and using each informative organizational pattern
- Understand and address three challenges to credible and ethical informative speaking

---

UNDERSTANDING THE INFORMATIVE SPEECH

As mentioned in Chapter 2, the purpose of speaking to inform is to communicate new information or a new perspective on a topic to an audience, and bring listeners to greater understanding or insight. The information you present may range from the intangible, like understanding the law of gravity, to very tangible, like how to change a flat tire or prepare for a job interview. Whether the speech is intended to explain a complex issue or concept, like Rowan told us how to do, or instruct the audience about how to do something, like Zak and Van do at work, either way, it's considered informative.

Some public speaking experts do say all speeches are inherently persuasive. According to this perspective, whenever you present information, you're attempting to persuade the audience that the information is true; therefore, all informative speaking is persuasive, to some extent. Other experts take the position that all human communication basically is informative, because it involves sharing information, creating, sending, and receiving messages. They say we are living in "the Information Age," "the Information Society," and, we are traveling "the Information Highway." In this information economy, the most precious resource is the ability to attend to and make sense of information.[2]

This debate aside, subtle distinctions can be drawn to clarify what an informative speech is by contrast to a persuasive one. The topic of an informative speech is usually less controversial than that of a persuasive speech. Furthermore, an informative speech is not intended to directly influence the reactions of the listeners; rather, its intent is to expand knowledge and understanding of the topic of the speech. The general purpose of informing is to help the audience understand, not necessarily agree with or take action on, what we say.

THE IMPORTANCE OF INFORMATIVE SPEAKING

Developing your ability to give an informative speech may be one of the most important public speaking competencies you'll learn, because you will use those skills frequently in this information age. The majority of us now earn our living by handling information in some way and conveying it to one another. Therefore, informative speaking is definitely a crucial aspect of most people's work lives. Obviously, a professor's lecture is an informative speech, but businesspeople also are frequently called upon to present information. In the profit and non-profit professional world, informative speaking can take the form of a briefing that summarizes large amounts of information, a report of progress on projects and activities, or a training that provides instructions about how to carry out a task or assignment. In giving any of these informative speeches, the goal is to promote understanding of the information presented and encourage the audience to retain a significant amount of it. Clearly, it is important to learn to present information effectively and that starts with an awareness of the different types of informative speeches.

TYPES OF INFORMATIVE SPEECHES

Informative speeches can be categorized based on two factors: the speech's objective and its content. The objective is what the informative speech is intended to achieve. The type of content refers to what the speech contains. For example, a speech about gravity is intended to explain (its objective) a process (its content).

13.1 INFORMATIVE SPEECH OBJECTIVES— speaking to describe, explain, or instruct—emphasize audience knowledge or ability, what the audience should know or be able to do by the end of the speech.

INFORMATIVE OBJECTIVES—DESCRIBING, EXPLAINING, INSTRUCTING

Three possible **objectives for an informative speech** are speaking to describe, explain, or instruct. These are general objectives for the speech, similar to the general purpose discussed in Chapter 6, but they are tailored to informative speaking. They emphasize audience knowledge or ability—what the audience should know or be able do by the end of the speech.

Descriptions are used when listeners are unfamiliar with the topic of the speech and need new information in order to understand it. If you want the listeners to become aware of and remember something new, your objective is to describe or provide a picture of it. If your speech is about a vacation to an exotic or unfamiliar place, you will need to describe what it's like there, perhaps by contrast to more familiar places. If you want to introduce a new product line to your sales force, you will describe what it is and its advantages over older products. Your informative objective for that speech could be stated like this:

13.2 DESCRIPTIONS are used when listeners are unfamiliar with the topic of the speech and need new information in order to understand it.

Sales force members will understand and be able to describe four advantages of the new product line compared to last year's products.

13.3 EXPLANATIONS clarify something already known but not well understood or they explain how something works.

Explanations clarify something already known but not well understood, or they explain how something works. If you want the listeners to understand why something exists or how it operates or occurs, your objective is to explain it. For example, if your speech is about public speaking anxiety, the other students are probably familiar with what it is, but they would appreciate an explanation of why they have it and what can be done about it. If your speech is about an increase in violent crimes, like Richard's in Chapter 4, you could explain why the problem exists and what should be done about it. To further clarify the distinction between an informative and persuasive speech, if you take a position on how to combat crime or drug use, your speech becomes more persuasive. A purely informative objective for this speech would be:

> The audience will be able to explain the underlying causes of the increase in violent crimes in the community as well as three strategies to combat the increase.

Instructions are useful when the objective is to teach the audience something or tell them how to use it. If you want the listeners to be able to apply what is presented, you provide instructions. In a classroom speech, if you want the other students to be able to use a particular method for reducing public speaking anxiety, you need to provide instructions for applying that method. If a new product available through your company needs to be demonstrated in order to sell it, then instructions in its use should be provided in an instructional speech. Here's an informative objective for that speech:

13.4 INSTRUCTIONS are useful when the objective is to teach the audience something or tell them how to use it.

13.5 INFORMATIVE SPEECH CONTENT is based on what the speech is primarily about—objects, processes, events, people, issues, or concepts.

> Each sales person will understand how to use the new product and be able to perform the six steps essential to its use by customers.

To appreciate the importance of this first step—clarifying the objective of your informative speech—consider what is emphasized in the advanced program of *Toastmasters International*, which trains some high-level employees in organizations.[3] The fast track of this program stresses how important it is to identify your objective, but the labels for the informative objectives are a bit different. *Toastmasters* give advice for a demonstration talk, a fact finding report, and an abstract concept speech. Regardless of labels, these coaches say to start with a clear objective and then think about the actual content of the speech.

INFORMATIVE CONTENT—OBJECTS, PROCESSES, EVENTS, PEOPLE, ISSUES, CONCEPTS

In addition to categorizing informative speeches based on what they try to achieve, they also can be categorized based on their **informative speech content**, what they are primarily about. The six categories for informative speeches based on content are speeches about objects, processes, events, people, issues, and concepts.

An **object speech** is usually about something tangible that can be seen, touched, or otherwise experienced through the physical senses, such as a car, a computer, a place, or even a monument of some kind, like the Vietnam Memorial or the World War II Memorial, both of which are in Washington,

13.6 AN OBJECT SPEECH is usually about something tangible that can be seen, touched, or otherwise experienced through the physical senses.

DC. Objects also can be things that can't be touched like the software program in a computer or the music on an iPod. Typical objects that could serve as a speech topic might be an historical site and its architecture, a famous painting or sculpture, a musical composition or a literary work, or a city or country's tourist attractions.

When preparing an object speech, it's particularly important to decide what your listeners really need to know in order for you to accomplish the objective of your speech. What they need to know will be based on what they already know about the object. You'll lose their attention if you cover details with which they are already familiar and since most objects are multifaceted, it's pointless to try to cover everything in one short speech. Instead, think about what the audience already knows and relate new information about the object to what is already known.

A **process speech** is about a system or sequence of steps that lead to a result or change taking place, such as the steps involved in applying for a student loan, shopping for a new car, or using a new computer program. The steps involved in communicating with children or people from another culture could all be process speeches with an instructional objective to help listeners learn how to communicate better with people unlike themselves. A process speech also could describe a process listeners may never actually engage in—like how election campaigns are conducted.

13.7 A PROCESS SPEECH is about a system or sequence of steps that lead to a result or change taking place.

13.8 AN EVENT SPEECH describes something that has occurred, such as an historical event or something noteworthy that has happened.

When giving a process speech, it's essential that the listeners are able to follow the steps in the process as you describe them. At the beginning of the speech, provide an overview or preview of the entire process, the big picture. Then as you get to each step in the process, mention how it fits into that big picture. If the process involves many steps, group some of the steps into logical phases or stages. At the end of each phase or stage, review the step you just covered and remind the audience of where you are in the overall process. When you've covered the entire process, summarize the steps and their relationship to the big picture. This kind of preview and summary are important in all informative speeches, but even more so with a process speech that may be more difficult to follow. To make a complicated process as clear as possible, use good visual aids to help listeners follow along, as you move from one step to the next.

An **event speech** describes something that has occurred, such as an historical event: the election of the first black president in the United States or something noteworthy that has happened in your community or elsewhere—a catastrophe like Hurricane Katrina in New Orleans or the oil spill along the Gulf coast. An event speech also could describe something you did yourself or that happened to you—like your experience visiting an impressive place for the first time or the day you got or lost a job. Hana's speech about her family's immigration to the United States is a typical event speech.

Events are similar to processes in that both focus on something that occurs or takes place, but an event speech describes and focuses more on the nature of the event itself rather than the how-to steps that get a process done. Of course, an event speech could include a description of the steps that led up to the event taking place. For instance, when John F. Kennedy was assassinated in Dallas in 1963, the steps leading up to the event would be important to include.

Another approach to an event speech would be to discuss its significance in time. Did the event mark a turning point in history or in your life? Or if the event was a negative one, what could have been done to prevent it, and what lessons have been learned as a result? Whatever approach you take, discuss the event fairly. Avoid letting personal biases affect your presentation of any data or facts involved in the event. To misrepresent what took place, or the effects the event may have had, would be unethical and therefore not competent.

A **speech about people** describes a person in much the same way an object speech describes an object. The idea of this type of speech is to paint a picture of a person that intrigues the listeners because of the details you include about him or her. The person can be a notable figure from history, a contemporary person of interest to the audience, or even someone you know—a relative, a friend, or a role model. The speech clarifies who the person is and presents information about him or her that is relevant and of interest to the audience.

If presenting a speech on a historical figure, you might include the person's special achievements, places he or she lived, or interesting facts about the individual the listeners might not have easy access to. You can pick almost any period in history and find a person with an interesting life story, but be sure you present the person in the context of their own time. Contemporary standards for behaviors may be different than the prevailing standards when the person was alive, and that would need to be made clear to your audience. If you choose to talk about a contemporary figure, focus on aspects of the person's life that would represent new and intriguing information to the audience. If you talk about someone you know personally, clearly state why that person's life or activities are relevant to your audience.

13.9 A SPEECH ABOUT PEOPLE describes a person in much the same way an object speech describes an object.

An **issue speech** examines a debatable topic from various points of view, such as global warming, immigration to the United States, abortion, or the "right to die." By presenting both sides of an issue in an unbiased way, a speech is informative. But as we said earlier, if you take a position on either side of the issue, the speech becomes persuasive—the topic of Chapter 14.

13.10 AN ISSUE SPEECH examines a debatable topic from various points of view.

13.11 A CONCEPT SPEECH is about abstract ideas—theories, principles, or values.

Maintaining objectivity is the biggest challenge to presenting an issue speech. Remain as objective as possible, presenting both sides of the issue equally and fairly. Be sure to research all perspectives thoroughly and try to cite the same amount and kind of evidence for each side. Give the same amount of time to each argument you present, and include examples, visual aids, and other support materials equitably. If your audience can't tell which side of an issue you favor at the end of the speech, then you have presented it ethically and credibly.

A **concept speech** is about abstract ideas—theories, principles, or values—such as the theory of relativity, the nature of ethical communication, freedom of speech or of the press, or human rights. Concepts typically are intangible, although their existence can spawn tangible results and actions. While freedom is an intangible concept, the actions of freedom fighters in an oppressive dictatorship are tangible statements about the concept of freedom.

Delivering a concept speech can be challenging, because each listener is likely to understand the concept somewhat differently. This problem of conceptual misinterpretation is a result of people from different countries or cultures assigning meaning varyingly to concepts. For example, the words "freedom," "peace," and "democracy" are understood by people in capitalist nations to mean one thing, but these concepts are interpreted differently by people in Communist nations. Moreover, within the same country or culture, concepts also may be varyingly interpreted by different listeners in your audience.

Therefore, when a concept is introduced, be sure to clarify its meaning in the context of your speech to ensure that it is understood as you intend. In addition, when you describe the concept, don't suggest that your description is the only correct view. Rather, present it as a talking point for promoting understanding between you and the listeners. Finally, because concepts can be broad, be sure to limit your focus and let the audience know what aspect of the concept you'll be covering.

INTEGRATING INFORMATIVE OBJECTIVES AND SPEECH CONTENT

Each of the six types of speeches based on content (object, process, event, people, issue, and concept) could be developed to achieve one or more of the three objectives (describe, explain, instruct). For instance, a speech about an object could simply *describe* the object, or it could *explain* how the object works, or it could *instruct* the listeners in how to use the object. That said, each type of content speech does lend itself more frequently to one of the three objectives. For example, an object speech is more often descriptive than explanatory or instructive. Table 13.1 rank orders the most likely objectives for each type of content speech.

Table 13.1: Integrating Types of Content Speeches and Possible Objectives

Each of the six types of informative speeches based on their content is more likely to lend itself to one of the three objectives more than the other two. For each type of content speech, the objectives are listed indicating which objective works best most of the time for that type of speech.

TYPE OF SPEECH	MOST LIKELY OBJECTIVE FOR THE SPEECH TYPE
An object speech	1. Describe 2. Explain 3. Instruct
A process speech	1. Explain 2. Describe 3. Instruct
An event speech	1. Describe 2. Explain
A people speech	1. Describe 2. Explain
An issue speech	1. Explain 2. Describe
A concept speech	1. Describe 2. Explain

ORGANIZING AN INFORMATIVE SPEECH

The principles of speech organization discussed in Chapter 8, while important for all speeches, are especially helpful for achieving the objective of an informative speech. Since the goal often is to communicate an abundance of new or complex information, good organization is essential for the audience to understand what is presented and not be overwhelmed by it. Furthermore, informative speeches are frequently about complicated or multifaceted topics. Understanding that kind of information is challenging unless the speech is well organized and easy to follow. Healthcare reform in the United States is but one example of such a topic. Despite numerous public speeches in 2010 about reforming healthcare, people often were heard to say they just didn't understand the proposed legislation in Congress.

The five possible **organizational patterns for an informative speech** are by category, time, space, comparison and contrast, and cause and effect. Despite the fact these five organizational patterns are most often used for informative speaking, several of them clearly could be used to make up the body of a persuasive speech. Cause and effect, for example, is frequently recommended for both informative and persuasive speeches.

BY CATEGORY

Organization by category divides information about a subject and topic into subgroups or subtopics. This structure is advantageous when your topic naturally clusters into subtopics or lists of items you want the listeners to understand or know how to do. Various aspects of an object or a person, steps in a process, or dimensions of a concept are subtopics that can be effectively organized by category. If you are describing a new bookkeeping system in an office, the presentation could be organized by category.

A. A description of the concepts and components of the system
B. Capabilities of the system
C. Limitations of the system
D. Future applications of the system using technology

13.12 INFORMATIVE SPEECH ORGANIZATIONAL PATTERNS include by: category, time, space, comparison and contrast, and cause and effect.

13.13 ORGANIZATION BY CATEGORY divides information about a subject and topic into subgroups or subtopics.

13.14 ORGANIZATION BY TIME is used to describe changes or developments in any situation or circumstance, either historical—linked to actual dates—or sequential—related to a sequence of steps that occur or are performed over time.

One problem with categorical organization is that the subtopics may sound unrelated, especially if you don't provide clear transitions, as you move from one category to the next. Also, you take the chance of boring the audience and sounding like you're droning on and on, from one category to the next. To avoid this problem, structure an introduction that builds a case for the importance of your topic at the beginning of your speech, and use a visual aid to help your listeners stay with you. A list or diagram on a flip chart would be helpful to guide listeners through your discussion of the categories.

BY TIME OR SPACE

Organization by time is used to describe changes or developments in any situation or circumstance. It can be historical—linked to actual dates or sequential—related to a sequence of steps that occur or are performed over time. A historical structure would work well, if you're describing an event such as a war or the founding and development of your college or a company in your community. If you want to describe the development and decline of the labor movement in the United States, a historical structure might be as follows:

A. 1792–1929: Labor unions grew to be a powerful economic force in the United States.
B. 1930–1950: Union membership grew in 30s and 40s and began to decline in the 50s
C. 1960–present: Membership has continued to decline; labor unions are searching for a foothold in the Information Age economy

Two problems can occur if you organize a speech historically. First, the audience may not think something that happened a long time ago is relevant to them. If that's the case, demonstrate the relevance of the speech topic to their lives today early in the speech. Second, you'll bore the audience if your speech is little more than a recounting of dates and times. To avoid that problem, include precise dates only to provide a context for appreciating the significance of the event, and make the particular time in history memorable using lively and colorful examples of life at that time.

A sequential time structure is effective in describing the steps that make up a process. If you are a financial advisor, you could sequentially describe how the stock market ebbs and flows for a client. A topic like the steps a student takes over time to choose a college to attend could follow this sequential pattern:

A. Gather information on schools that offer the desired major
B. Investigate scholarships and financial aid available
C. Apply to top three choices and await acceptance notification
D. Visit the campuses where accepted, meet with faculty and advisors, and make a decision

Organization by space organizes information based on the positioning of objects in physical space or relationships between locations. This structure works well when you want the listeners to visualize the arrangement of objects, locations, or distances. For example, if you're describing what your home is like, or the architectural design of a building

13.15 ORGANIZATION BY SPACE organizes information based on the positioning of objects in physical space, or relationships between locations.

or a mall, you would structure your speech around the layout of the building. Space organization would also work well to describe the best places to visit in a major city. A speech about New York could be organized like this:

A. Start in the heart of Manhattan at Times Square and Broadway
B. Tour upper Manhattan and key sights
C. Tour lower Manhattan and key sights
D. Ride the Staten Island ferry
E. Visit Brooklyn and the boroughs or suburbs of New York City

The main problem with space organization is being sure the listeners follow along and can visualize the spaces you are describing. Providing a map, layout, or diagram of the spaces, will help to solve that problem.

BY COMPARISON AND CONTRAST

Organization by comparison and contrast is used to describe or explain how a subject is similar to or different from something else. Comparison means pointing out the similarities, while contrast points out the differences. This structure works well if the subject of the speech can be easily related to something the audience already knows about and understands. It's also useful when significant similarities or differences between the subject of discussion and something else will help the audience understand and appreciate the subject.

13.16 ORGANIZATION BY COMPARISON AND CONTRAST is used to describe or explain how a subject is similar to or different from something else.

For example, comparison and contrast would be good for describing a visit to another country. You could first describe how the country is similar to one the listeners are familiar with, and then how the country and its people and customs are dissimilar. A speech about the United States and China could compare the two countries in this way:

A. Similarities: Warmth and hospitality of the people; highly industrialized; large concentrations of population in big cities

B. Differences: Political systems; more rapid building and development in China; stricter adherence to cultural traditions in China

One problem when using comparison and contrast is structuring the speech so the listeners know whether you're talking about a similarity or a difference. You could present all the comparisons followed by all the contrasts; then your speech would have two major points, one covering similarities and other covering differences. Or you could select important aspects of the subject and talk about the similarities or the differences of each aspect of the subject. The China and United States speech is simply organized around ways the two countries are the same (comparison) and ways they are different (contrast).

BY CAUSE AND EFFECT

Organization by cause and effect examines why something happens (the causes) and what happens as a result (the effects). This structure is good for understanding an event or an action of an individual, an organization, or an institution. It is also useful for describing a controversial issue, because it can illustrate connections between the issue and its conse-

13.17 ORGANIZATION BY CAUSE AND EFFECT examines why something happens (the causes) and what happens as a result (the effects).

quences. A cause and effect speech could be used to describe significant historical events, such as women winning the right to vote and the effects over time on the electoral process of women voters.

Be aware you may want to reverse the order and describe the effects first and then their cause. This reverse approach is recommended when the audience is already interested in the topic and knows something about it. By calling attention to the impact of the effects first, you heighten interest in the cause before you discuss it. In Richard's speech about violent crime increasing in the community, the speech could be structured like this:

A. Statistics on the rise in violent crimes in the community (effect)

B. Story about an innocent victim of a violent crime (effect)

C. Amount of dollars needed by drug addicts to fund their addictions (cause)

D. Poverty due to increases in unemployment (cause)

Two cautions are in order when using cause and effect organization for your speech. First, be sure you are clear about whether you are speaking to inform or to persuade, since this organizational pattern lends itself to both general purposes. The informative speech about violent crime would become persuasive if you urged the audience to take some action about the situation. Second, be certain the situation you're describing is really causing the effects or results you present. Be careful to describe a causal relationship and not just a series of coincidences. In presenting this type of speech, an ethical speaker makes sure the audience fully understands what happened and why, by presenting the information about the causes and effects as accurately as possible.

CHOOSING AN ORGANIZATIONAL PATTERN FOR INFORMING

An informative speech has the basic parts discussed in Chapter 8—an introduction, body, and conclusion—but the body of the speech is organized by category, time, space, or whichever organi-

Table 13.2: Types of Speeches and Ways to Organize Them

The six types of content speeches lend themselves to certain organizational structures.

TYPE OF SPEECH	ORGANIZATIONAL STRUCTURES FOR EACH TYPE OF SPEECH
An object speech	By category: Use if aspects of the object you're describing naturally cluster into categories. By space: Use if aspects of the object can easily be visualized in a spatial relationship to one another.
A process speech	By time: Use if the process you're describing occurs sequentially over time or as a sequence of steps. By space: Use if the steps in the process can be easily visualized as connected to each other.
An event speech	By time: Use when an event or a series of events can be described as they occurred over time. By cause and effect: Use when the event can be understood by describing why it happened and what resulted.
A people speech	By category: Use when you want to describe various aspects, characteristics, achievements, or actions of a person. By comparison and contrast: Use to understand a person based on how she or he is either like or unlike someone else. By cause and effect: Use to understand the cause and effects of the person's actions or decisions.
An issue speech	By cause and effect: Use to promote understanding of an issue by presenting why the issue exists and what is happening as a result. By comparison and contrast: Use to provide insights into an issue, based on how it is like or unlike another issue. By category: Use to describe the main ideas that comprise the issue.
A concept speech	By category: Use to describe main ideas that comprise the concept. By comparison and contrast: Use to provide insights into an unfamiliar concept by describing how it is like or unlike something else.

zational pattern you decide is best. To choose the best structure for the body of your speech, first determine the type of speech you're presenting, based on its content (object, process, event, people, issue, or concept). Then consider the following natural relationships between these six types of speeches, based on their content, and the organizational structures.

1. An object speech is often best organized—by category or space.
2. A process speech—by time or space.
3. An event speech—by time or cause and effect.
4. A speech about people—by category, comparison and contrast, or cause and effect.
5. An issue speech—by comparison and contrast, cause and effect, or category.
6. A concept speech—by category or comparison and contrast.

The relationships between the types of speech and organizational patterns are further clarified in Table 13.2. After looking those over, we can consider several challenges to presenting your informative speech credibly and ethically.

CHALLENGES TO CREDIBLE AND ETHICAL INFORMATIVE SPEAKING

When an informative speech fails to be effective, the cause is usually one of three problems. The speaker chose an inappropriate subject or topic; faulty or inappropriate information was used to support the topic; or the speech was poorly organized. Any one of these three problems represents a challenge that will affect whether you are perceived as a credible and ethical public speaker.

INAPPROPRIATE TOPIC

The importance of careful topic selection was thoroughly discussed in Chapter 5. For an informative speech, you should choose a topic your listeners will easily relate to; you need to take responsibility for providing background information to help them appreciate and understand it. With regard to informative speaking, selecting a topic that isn't well suited for the particular audience and situa-

Box 13.1: Cultural Referents and Mindset of the College Class of Today

These 20 cultural referents help to describe what an audience in today's college classrooms may find of interest, or at least, what they know about and don't know about.

1. They don't remember when "cut and paste" involved scissors.
2. Most of them do not know how to tie a tie—or why they should bother.
3. Pay-Per-View television has always been an option.
4. Voice mail has always been available.
5. "Whatever" is not part of a question but is a response indicating disinterest.
6. They have always had the right to burn the flag.
7. For caffeine emergencies, Starbucks has always been around the corner.
8. Bill Gates has always been worth at least a billion dollars.
9. The Starship *Enterprise* has always looked dated.
10. Pixar has always existed.
11. If they have even heard of her, they think Aretha Franklin has always been in the Rock and Roll Hall of Fame.
12. Police have always been able to search garbage without a search warrant.
13. Scientists have always been able to see supernovas.
14. Snowboarding has always been a popular winter pastime.
15. Libraries have always been the best centers for computer technology and access to good software.
16. Digital cameras have always existed.
17. Time Life and Warner Communications have always been joined.
18. CNBC has always been on the air.
19. *America's Funniest Home Videos* has always been on television.
20. They have always been challenged to distinguish between news and entertainment on cable TV.

Source: Beloit College, 700 College St., Beloit, WI 53511. Retrieved from: http://www.beloit.edu/mindset/ 2009.php.

tion may happen for this reason: the topic may be one you are familiar with, so researching and preparing the speech appears easier. Plus, you may feel more confident talking about the topic because of your personal knowledge. When you base the topic for an informative speech only on your own interests without thinking about what would appeal to the listeners, the challenge will be far greater to make that topic appealing to the particular audience.

The challenge you face in a public speaking class is figuring out an appropriate informative topic based on good audience analysis. Your audience may be made up mostly of today's entry-level college students. Their knowledge about contemporary culture and the world, and their life experiences make choosing an informative topic a challenge. A list of cultural referents for today's college students is presented in Box 13.1.[4] If your informative topic relates to any of these cultural referents, then you must provide background information to familiarize the listeners with it. Also, Table 13.3 contains a list of possible topics for informative speeches, based on the type of content you may want to present—about an object, a process, or whatever you prefer. Use the list to identify a topic you like but also one of potential interest to your audience. Once you choose the topic, ask yourself: Is this informative topic really of interest to the audience? Can I present it in such a way that the listeners will find it interesting?

Table 13.3: Topics for Informative Speeches

Here's a list of possible topics for each of the six different content types of speeches. Note the object and process speech topics mostly are drawn from your own knowledge base and experience, so be sure to provide information to motivate listeners to care.

TYPE OF SPEECH	POSSIBLE TOPICS FOR EACH TYPE OF SPEECH
An object speech	Things you collect: books, stamps, antiques; an extraordinary place you've visited or know about: a town, city, state, or country; a new gadget: an i-phone, handheld computer, or household item.
A process speech	Things you do or know how to do: snowshoeing, skiing, hiking, traveling, refinishing furniture, cooking, saving money, spending, getting along with others, living in another country, planning your life.
An event speech	A local or national current event, a noteworthy event from history, an event that marked a turning point in history, an event that occurred in the life of a noteworthy person, a special event that occurred in your life.
A people speech	A contemporary or historical person of significance to the audience, someone you know or have known of particular interest.
An issue speech	Nuclear disarmament, health care policies and reform, immigration at U.S. borders, conservation laws and practices, violence in the media, grading systems, substance abuse and regulation, healthcare and policies, political and governmental policies or programs, abortion laws and practices, unions and strike policies, lifestyles or gay marriage.
A concept speech	Nuclear power, multiculturalism/diversity, the world eco-system, media literacy, ethical communication, theory of evolution, principles of communication, democracy, friendship, love.

FAULTY INFORMATION

Whether you choose an informative topic from your own base of knowledge and experience or from an analysis of your audience, another challenge is choosing the right information to make the speech as effective as possible. Three problems can occur in addressing this challenge—too much information, too little information, or the wrong information.

Information overload, including too much information in a speech, is a common problem for informative speakers. The speaker includes more information than is necessary to accomplish the objective of the speech, more than can be covered in the time allotted, or too much high-level information. Since you can easily access vast electronic databases of knowledge on literally every subject and topic, the temptation is great to overload your speech with everything you have learned—it all seems important. As a result, the audience can't absorb all you present in what is often a short period of time.

....
13.18 INFORMATION OVERLOAD, including too much information in a speech, is a common problem for informative speakers.

On the other hand, including too little information in an informative speech also can be a problem. This problem sometimes comes from assuming you already know enough about the subject or topic, so you don't need to research it. A lack of adequate research will result in not discovering some intriguing facts that would help achieve your objective and liven up your informative speech. You may end up presenting information your audience already knows about or that they find less than exciting.

Figuring out how much or how little information to include is important, but the quality of that information also is of concern. Chapter 7 covered the array of possible support materials you can use in any type of speech. But since most informative speeches are limited in terms of length, each minute is precious and should be used to present only information the audience will relate to and that will help accomplish the informative objective. Use your clearly stated objective and look at the information you plan to include. Ask yourself: Is this information really necessary? Is it critical to accomplishing my informative objective?

POOR ORGANIZATION

A third challenge to giving an effective informative speech is failing to organize your information so it is easily understood by the listeners. A common mistake new speakers make is not realizing how hard it is for listeners to follow and absorb a large amount of information in a short period of time. Because you become familiar with the content of your informative speech, you may not realize how overwhelming it may be when your listeners hear it for the first time. If they have to spend time trying to figure out the maze of new information you're presenting, your informative speech just won't be effective. While the temptation may be to impress the audience by presenting lots of information in a complex way, instead present a clear and uncomplicated informative message that is easily understood. Pare it down to what is simple, basic, and essential to accomplishing the informative objective.

In addition to presenting information simply, present it logically, so the listeners can easily follow your line of reasoning. Use any one of the informative organizational patterns to arrange the main parts of your speech in a logical order. And use clear transitional words and phrases between main points to help the audience stay with you. Ask yourself, before you speak: Will the listeners be able to easily follow along? Have I done everything I can to help them follow the logic of my presentation?

OVERCOMING CHALLENGES AND MOTIVATING LISTENERS TO LEARN

Competent informative speaking calls for choosing the right topic for the particular audience, supporting the informative objective with the right information, and organizing the information simply and logically. As a result of such careful preparation, audience members will find you knowledgeable and therefore credible. In addition, because you openly share the information with them, presenting it without bias, they will see you as an ethical public speaker. That said, no matter how carefully you prepare your informative speech, your listeners still may not be motivated to listen and to care about what you have to say.[5]

As a competent speaker, you, of course, use good delivery skills and nonverbal cues to encourage audience involvement—eye contact, moving toward the audience, gesturing as you speak. But there are other ways to address the challenge of motivating listeners to learn. One way to motivate your listeners to actually listen is to involve them in caring about the topic early in the speech. Figure out an aspect of the topic that would be meaningful or relevant to the audience and incorporate it into your introduction and stress its relevance in your thesis statement. Come up with an attention getting device, a story or a startling statistic, related to that aspect of your topic. You also could encourage them to get involved by asking them to do something related to your speech topic. It could be something quite simple. "How many of you know the music of Bono and U2? Raise your hands." If you're talking about a topic that lends itself to an informal mini-quiz and you have time for it, you could hand out a questionnaire with a few questions related to your topic. If you have plenty of time, you could make use of volunteers from the audience. Even if you only use one or two volunteers, other members of the audience will feel more involved in your speech as well. You could have them demonstrate a dance step, an exercise, or even point to areas on a map as you talk about them. Finally, if time allows, a simple way to encourage audience involvement is to conclude with a short question and answer period.

The advice outlined in this chapter will help you present your next informative speech more effectively. Like Zak, Vanden, and Kumar you will present an excellent speech to inform. The next chapter will introduce you to similar concepts but as they apply to persuasive speaking.

CHAPTER SUMMARY

Contrasting informative to persuasive public speaking reveals that the topic of an informative speech is less controversial, and an informative speech is not intended to directly influence the reactions of the listeners. The intent of an informative speech is to expand knowledge and understanding of the topic of the speech. Informative speeches are categorized based on the speech objective and content. The objective is what the informative speech is intended to achieve. The type of content refers to what the speech

contains. Informative speech objectives—speaking to describe, explain, or instruct—emphasize audience knowledge or ability, what the audience should know or be able to do by the end of the speech. Descriptions are used when listeners are unfamiliar with the topic of the speech and need new information in order to understand it. Explanations clarify something already known but not well understood, or they explain how something works. Instructions are useful when the objective is to teach the audience something or tell them how to use it. Informative speech content is based on what the speech is primarily about—objects, processes, events, people, issues, or concepts. An object speech is usually about something tangible that can be seen, touched, or otherwise experienced through the physical senses. A process speech is about a system or sequence of steps that lead to a result or change taking place. An event speech describes something that has occurred, such as an historical event or something noteworthy that has happened. A speech about people describes a person in much the same way that an object speech describes an object. An issue speech examines a debatable topic from various points of view. A concept speech is about abstract ideas—theories, principles, or values. Since the goal of an informative speech often is to communicate new and complex information, good organization is essential for the audience to understand what is presented and not be overwhelmed by it. Informative speech organizational patterns include category, time, space, comparison and contrast, and cause and effect. Organization by category divides information about a subject and topic into subgroups or sub-topics. Organization by time is used to describe changes or developments in any situation or circumstance, either historical—linked to actual dates— or sequential—related to a sequence of steps that occur or are performed over time. Organization by space organizes information based on the positioning of objects in physical space or relationships between locations. Organization by comparison and contrast is used to describe or explain how a subject is similar to or different from something else. Organization by cause and effect examines why something happens (the causes) and what happens as a result (the effects). Three problems may cause an informative speech to be ineffective. The speaker chose an inappropriate subject or topic; faulty or inappropriate information was used to support the topic, sometimes resulting in information overload; or, the speech was poorly organized. Any one of these three problems represents a challenge that will affect whether you are perceived as a credible and ethical public speaker. In addition to choosing the right topic, using the right information, and organizing the information simply and logically, a competent speaker also involves the listeners in order to motivate them to learn.

KEY TERMS

The key terms below are defined in this chapter and presented alphabetically with definitions in the Glossary at the end of the book.

- informative speech objectives
- explanations
- informative speech content
- process speech
- people speech
- concept speech
- category organizational pattern
- space organizational pattern

- descriptions
- instructions
- object speech
- event speech
- issue speech
- informative speech organizational patterns
- time organizational pattern
- information overload

- cause and effect organizational pattern
- comparison and contrast organizational pattern

BUILDING COMPETENCE ACTIVITIES

INDIVIDUAL ACTIVITIES

1. Make three columns on a piece of paper. Label your columns: Types of Informative Speeches, Speech Topic, and Organizational Pattern, from left to right. In column one, list the six types of informative speeches, based on content. In column two, come up with one speech topic that appeals to you for each type of speech. In column three, decide which organizational pattern would work best for each topic you listed.
2. Analyze the exemplary informative speech in the appendix at the end of this book. Determine how well you think it achieves its informative objective. What did the speaker do well to achieve that objective?
3. Attend an informative public speech or lecture. Identify the objective of the speech presented and evaluate how well the speaker achieves the objective. Analyze the speech based on the challenges to informative speaking presented in this chapter—choice of topic, use of information, and organization.
4. Watch the lead story on a local newscast and take notes of what the newscaster says about the story. Then evaluate the newscaster's presentation of the story as informative. Consider the informative objective, content of the story, and its organizational pattern.

GROUP ACTIVITIES

1. Form a small group of 4–5 students and choose any one of the topics presented in Table 13.4. Each student in the group should write the topic on a piece of paper and decide on an objective, content type, and organizational pattern for that topic. Compare and discuss each student's ideas.
2. Form groups of three to four students and attend an informative public speech or lecture. Have each student individually identify the objective of the speech presented and evaluate how well the speaker achieves the objective. Analyze the speech based on the challenges to informative speaking presented in this chapter—choice of topic, use of information, and organization. Compare and discuss your individual evaluations.
3. Form groups of four students and choose one of the topics listed in Table 13.4 under issue speeches. Form pairs and assign to the first pair the development of an informative objective and an outline using the comparison and contrast organizational method. The second pair should use cause and effect organization to develop an objective and outline for the topic. Compare the two outlines to see which organizational pattern worked best and discuss why. Then stay in the group of four students and discuss what types of support materials would help achieve the objective of each outline.

COMPETENCY CHECKPOINTS AND SELF-ASSESSMENT TOOL

Here is what you need to know and be able to do regarding informative speeches. Determine your level of competency and whether you are ready to proceed to the next chapter. Give yourself one point for each checkpoint you answer satisfactorily.

COMPETENCY CHECKPOINTS	NUMBER OF POINTS
KNOWLEDGE 1. What are the key differences between informative and persuasive speeches? 2. Why is the ability to present information and informative speeches particularly important right now? 3. List and describe the three objectives of informative speeches. 4. List and describe the six types of informative speeches based on their content. 5. Identify and explain how to use the five different organizational patterns for informative speeches.	
SKILLS 1. Provide an example of an informative speech and write out an objective for that speech. 2. Use the same example of an informative speech and indicate what type of content is appropriate for it. 3. Use the same example of an informative speech and indicate what organizational pattern should be used for it.	
ETHICS AND CREDIBILITY 1. Outline challenges to ethical informative speaking and indicate how a speaker may address the challenges. 2. Outline challenges to credibility when presenting an informative speech and indicate how a speaker may address the challenges.	
TOTAL CHECKPOINTS (OUT OF A POSSIBLE TEN POINTS)	

ENDNOTES

1. Rowan, K. E. (2003). Informing and explaining skills: Theory and research on informative communication. In J. O. Greene & B. R. Burleson (Eds.), *The handbook of communication and social interaction skills* (pp. 403–438). Mahwah, NJ: Lawrence Erlbaum. Rowan, K.E. (1995). A new pedagogy for explanatory public speaking: Why arrangement should not substitute for invention. *Communication Education, 44*, 236–250.

2. Lanham, R.A. (2006). *The economics of attention: Style and substance in the age of information.* Chicago: University of Chicago Press.

3. *Toastmasters International: The Advanced Communication Program.* Retrieved from www.toastmasters.org/

4. *Mindset of the College Class of 2009.* Beloit College, 700 College St., Beloit, WI 53511. Retrieved from: http://www.beloit.edu/mindset/2009.php.

5. Roberts, C. (March, 1998). Developing willing listeners: A host of problems and a plethora of solutions. A paper presented at the annual meeting of the International Listening Association. Kansas City, KS.

14

SPEAKING TO PERSUADE

- **Understanding the Persuasive Speech**
  The Importance of Persuasive Speaking
- **Types of Persuasive Speeches Based on Objectives**
  Objective One—To Reinforce Attitudes, Beliefs, and Values
  Objective Two—To Change Attitudes, Beliefs, and Values
- Objective Three—To Move to Action and Change Behaviors
- **Organizing a Persuasive Speech**
  By Problem Solution
  By Motivated Sequence
  By Refuting the Opponent
  By Comparing Alternatives
- **Challenges to Credible and Ethical Persuasive Speaking**
  A Hostile Audience
  Faulty Reasoning
- **Overcoming Challenges and Influencing Listeners to Change**
  Logical Appeals and Reasoning
  Emotional Appeals and Psychology
  Character Appeals and Credibility
- **The Ethics of Persuasive Speaking**

"Speech is power: Speech is to persuade, to convert, to compel. It is to bring another out of his bad sense into your good sense." Ralph Waldo Emerson, American essayist, philosopher and poet, 1803–1882

. . .

At the students' last meeting before final speeches, several of them said they thought their speeches probably were persuasive. The topics they chose could be considered controversial and they hoped to influence the reactions of their classmate to their speeches. Angelique knows other students in the class already have a positive attitude toward non-Western rhetoric based on their reactions to her first informative speech. She now wants to convince them of the importance of learning a lot more about presenting speeches in countries like China, Japan, India, and Africa. "Many if not most jobs now require interacting with people in other countries. We all need to know how speeches are presented in other cultures." Hana knows immigration policies are becoming a polarizing political issue in the United States. She wants to change the attitudes of some of her classmates toward this topic. "Negative attitudes toward immigrants need to change, given the increasing size of the immigrant population in the United States." As a police officer, Richard really wants to motivate his classmates to get out and do something about the rise in violent crimes right in their own communities. "We all need to work together to control violent crime. It's not just the job of law enforcement any more." Based on what they want to achieve in their speeches, Angelique, Hana, and Richard all think their topics for final speeches are persuasive. They decide to meet again to figure out the best way to develop and organize their speeches to accomplish their persuasive goals.

. . .

Persuasive speeches are a common occurrence in most public speaking classes, and these three students correctly identified their final speeches as persuasive. They know they want to influence how listeners react to their speeches, and they know they need to organize a persuasive speech differently than an informative one. They now need to heed the advice of a communication teacher, Robert Smith, who points out how important it is to tailor a persuasive message to the intended audience members.[1] This advice was first discussed in the chapter on audience analysis. Smith reminded us that persuasive speakers are much more likely to be successful if they carefully consider the attitudes, beliefs, and values of those they want to persuade, specifically with regard to their persuasive topic. This "receiver-oriented approach" to persuasion calls for careful audience analysis and using what Smith calls receiver-oriented persuasive strategies. You may be surprised to learn that if you don't follow this advice, some audience members may become even more opposed to your persuasive topic as a result of your speech. As you present the speech, the listeners who initially disagree with you will argue mentally for the rightness of their position. They will become even more convinced that they are right and you are wrong as a result of listening to your speech. This challenge is discussed in more detail later in this chapter when we talk about dealing with a hostile audience.

Smith's advice about receiver-oriented persuasion is enhanced in this chapter by considering the following ideas for preparing and presenting an effective persuasive speech. By reading this chapter, you will be able to:

- Define and describe persuasive speaking and explain its importance.
- Identify and provide guidelines for using each of the three types of persuasive speeches based on their objectives— to reinforce listeners' attitudes, beliefs, and values; change their attitudes, beliefs, and values; or move listeners to action.
- Explain and provide suggestions for using each of four organizational patterns for a persuasive speech—problem solution, motivated sequence, refuting the opponent, or comparing alternatives.
- Understand the challenges to credible and ethical persuasive speaking and how to overcome those challenges using logical, emotional, and character/credibility appeals.

UNDERSTANDING THE PERSUASIVE SPEECH

In Chapter 2, a persuasive speech was described as having the purpose of influencing the audience's attitudes, beliefs, values, or behaviors. Clearly then, Robert Smith is right about analyzing what your audience thinks and feels about your persuasive topic ahead of time. In Chapter 13, we discussed how a persuasive speech differs from an informative one. For example, the topic of a persuasive speech typically is more controversial. While persuasive speeches do differ somewhat from informative, the two share some qualities as well. Both types of speeches start out with a specific purpose, first try to gain the audience's attention and then present suitable information to accomplish the objective and specific purpose of the speech. Good organization also is crucial to both types of speeches. These similarities aside, it is necessary first to understand why the ability to speak persuasively is important.

THE IMPORTANCE OF PERSUASIVE SPEAKING

Discussions about the importance of persuasion date back many centuries. Persuasive speaking has long been considered an important aspect of social life. In Chapter 2, you learned about the famous Greek philosopher and writer, Aristotle. In his book, *The Rhetoric,* Aristotle wrote about the need for people to be able to discover what he called the available means of persuasion in any situation.[2] Aristotle addressed this need by identifying four social values for rhetoric and persuasion. First, it prevents the triumph of fraud and injustice. It is not enough just to know what is right; people must be able to argue effectively for what is right. Second, rhetoric and persuasion are an effective method of instruction for the public. It is not sufficient just to understand an argument; a speaker must also be able to instruct the audience in a persuasive manner. Third, persuasive rhetoric helps people to see and understand both sides of an argument. Public debates are examples of this usefulness of persuasion. Fourth, rhetoric and persuasion are a viable means of defense. According to Aristotle, just as a person needs to be able to defend himself or herself physically, he or she should be able to persuasively fend off verbal attacks.

Just as in Aristotle's time, the effective use of persuasive speaking skills continues to be the foundation of a free and open society. People still use persuasion in contemporary society to state their opinions publicly and examine various sides of important issues and make informed decisions. Whether at the local or national level—in legislatures, schools, businesses, or public meetings—people use persuasive speaking to debate and then set organizational and public agendas for their communities. In all of these situations, the speaker first needs to clarify the goal or objective of the persuasive speech.

TYPES OF PERSUASIVE SPEECHES BASED ON OBJECTIVES

As with informative speeches, persuasive speeches can be categorized based on the speaker's objective, the response the speaker hopes for from the audience. Based on the objective, the three types of persuasive speeches attempt to: *reinforce* the listeners' attitudes, beliefs, and values; *change* their attitudes, beliefs, and values; or *move the listeners to action*, which often involves changing behaviors. Any one of these objectives calls for figuring out your audience's probable reaction to your persuasive topic and developing your speech based on that information. Table 14.1 provides examples of some possible audience reactions to several persuasive topics.

This categorization system for persuasive speeches may be misleading in that it suggests the three types are discrete and unrelated to one another. In reality, the types of speeches sometimes overlap. You may find yourself presenting a speech that has more than one objective, for example, to change both the attitudes and the behaviors of your listeners. In the opening story, Richard's objective may have been to change the listeners' attitudes toward the increase of violent crimes but also their actions and behaviors. We will now examine the three types of persuasive speeches, based on objectives, more closely.

OBJECTIVE ONE—TO REINFORCE ATTITUDES, BELIEFS, AND VALUES

If the audience members are already favorably disposed toward your topic and position, then your objective is to reinforce that favorable response and encourage them to an even greater degree of commitment. A **speech to reinforce** is intended to influence listeners by strengthening their convictions and taking advantage of their tendency to seek out and attend to messages with which they already agree. Most listeners are more likely to pay attention to and remember information that supports or resembles their own attitudes and opinions. So by reinforcing your listeners' attitudes, beliefs, or values, you'll increase the likelihood that they'll pay attention and remember what you say.

This type of speech works well if there is a need to raise your listeners' consciousness about an issue or concern. They may already agree with your position but have no sense of urgency about the topic. In this case, you want to encourage them to care more about it. For example, if your audience

14.1 A SPEECH TO REINFORCE is intended to influence listeners by strengthening their convictions and taking advantage of their tendency to seek out and attend to messages with which they already agree.

Table 14.1: Attitudes, Beliefs, Values, and Behaviors and Audience Reactions

When preparing a persuasive speech topic, you must determine the audience's attitudes, beliefs, values, and possible behaviors. That information will help you develop a speech that's more likely to achieve your persuasive objective.

TOPIC/ISSUE	ATTITUDE	BELIEF	VALUE	BEHAVIOR
Contraception education in public schools	Favor parents and families managing sex education of children	It's the responsibility of families to encourage moral values	Morality and religious values are a family matter	Petition the school board to rule against sex education in schools
Capital punishment	Favor life sentences for those committing murder or other violent crimes	It's wrong to take another person's life	Sacredness of all human life even those who have committed violent crimes	Would vote against putting people to death by use of the electric chair or lethal injection
First Amendment rights	Favor no control or interference by the government in freedom of speech	Everyone has a right to express their opinions in any way they prefer	Individual liberty is most important in a free society	Would vote against any policy favoring control of content on websites and the Internet
Assisted suicide	Favor doctors assisting the terminally ill to end their lives	People have a right to control their own destiny	Freedom of choice is important regarding all life decisions	Would encourage the use of living wills that allow people to die as they choose

believes that governmental aid to education is (or is not) a good idea, your job would be to reinforce their current beliefs and influence them to pay more attention to the messages of political candidates who agree with your position. Angelique's objective for her persuasive speech is to encourage her classmates to care more about differences in ways speeches are presented, based on a speaker's country or culture of origin.

To reinforce listeners' attitudes and beliefs, provide them with additional information that supports their existing attitudes and what they already believe to be true. Reinforce their values by indicating your respect for what they hold to be right or important. However, you should not say you agree with the listeners, if you do not. Instead, by presenting your position while respecting their values, you build rapport and good will. This approach enhances your credibility as a persuasive speaker and helps to accomplish the objective of speaking to reinforce.

OBJECTIVE TWO—TO CHANGE ATTITUDES, BELIEFS, AND VALUES

If the audience's present attitudes, beliefs, and values are not to your liking—if they contradict or prevent you from achieving your own goals—then your objective is to change the listeners' present response to a more desirable one. A **speech to change** is intended to convince the audience to change what they like or dislike, what they hold to be true or untrue, or what they consider important or unimportant.

14.2 A SPEECH TO CHANGE is intended to convince the audience to change what they like or dislike, what they hold to be true or untrue, or what they consider important or unimportant.

In order to change listeners' attitudes—what they like or dislike—you have to first provide them with information that motivates them to listen to you and then try to modify or change their attitudes. You could accomplish this by reinforcing an attitude they already hold to get their attention and establish mutual understanding and then make your own point. For example, if you're presenting a speech against government regulation of the Internet to listeners who are politically conservative, you would want to reinforce their existing attitudes that are probably for less government regulation. If the audience is more liberal, you would reinforce their concerns about the loss of freedom of speech that might occur through increased governmental regulation. Then you would provide your argument against regulation.

Hana's stated objective for her persuasive speech is to change her classmates' attitudes toward immigration policies, but she could best accomplish that objective by changing their knowledge and beliefs about the topic. The best way to change listeners' beliefs—what they hold to be true or untrue—is to present them with solid facts and evidence from highly credible sources. Since beliefs are based on what people know, if you want to change beliefs, you need compelling evidence to counteract their previous experiences and knowledge. Information from credible sources, as well as your own credibility as a speaker, is essential to convince the audience that their current beliefs are not necessarily true and they should change them.

To change your listeners' values—what they consider important or unimportant—is to make a fundamental change in something that is very basic to each individual.[3] Because values are embedded in a person's self-concept, they are much harder to change than attitudes or beliefs. Therefore, success in changing listeners' values is rare, but appealing to values is an effective technique for influencing attitudes and beliefs.

OBJECTIVE THREE—TO MOVE TO ACTION AND CHANGE BEHAVIORS

If the audience's behaviors are not what you would like them to be, then your objective is to influence or change what the listeners do—their actions. A **speech to move to action** is intended to influence listeners to either engage in a new and desirable behavior or discontinue an undesirable behavior. If you give a speech and ask your listeners to vote for your candidate, buy a product, or start recycling their trash, you are asking them to adopt a new behavior. If your speech asks them to stop smoking or littering, the action you're recommending is one of discontinuance.

To change people's behaviors, it is important to realize that attitudes, beliefs, and values shape and direct behaviors. For example, you may hold a favorable attitude toward climbing the corporate ladder, believe that education is the best way to get a good job, and value professional success. As a result of these attitudes, beliefs, and values, you'll engage in behaviors such as trying hard to succeed at work, going directly from high school to college, or returning to college after several years in the work force.

14.3 A SPEECH TO MOVE TO ACTION is intended to influence listeners to either engage in a new and desirable behavior or discontinue an undesirable behavior.

Consequently, if you want to change people's behaviors—which is hard to do—you must demonstrate their current behaviors aren't consistent with their attitudes, beliefs, or values. Most people prefer to think they act according to what they believe and value. If you can demonstrate to your listeners that another set of behaviors is more consistent with their attitudes, beliefs, and values, your speech is more likely to result in at least some behavioral change.

Richard's stated objective for his persuasive speech is to motivate his classmates to change their behaviors and get involved in controlling the rise in violent crimes. Maybe he wants everyone to get involved in a *Neighborhood Watch* program in their community. To accomplish this objective, he first needs to change any complacent attitudes the audience members may have about violent crimes—*it's not my problem*—and he needs to use solid evidence to change what they believe to be true about the topic.

Once you, and Richard, have clarified your persuasive objectives, the next step is to determine the best way to organize your persuasive speech.

ORGANIZING A PERSUASIVE SPEECH

The general principles of speech organization discussed in Chapter 8 apply to the persuasive speech as well. An effective persuasive speech is carefully organized and structured to accomplish its objective.[4] There are four simple ways to organize a persuasive speech that will help to accomplish the objective of influencing the audience. The problem-solution pattern and the motivated sequence are the best known and most popular. Refuting the opponent or comparing alternatives are useful when it's necessary to take opposing arguments into account.

BY PROBLEM SOLUTION

Problem-solution organization first identifies a problem and then proposes a workable solution for the problem. This classic approach, first noted by the ancient Greeks, works well for presentations because it is easy for the audience to understand. Once listeners become aware of the problem, they naturally turn to thinking: how can we solve it? Then a solution shows up in the speech, right when they need it.

14.4 PROBLEM-SOLUTION ORGANIZATION first identifies a problem and then proposes a workable solution for the problem.

This organizational pattern is used to structure the body of the speech. You draft an introduction, body, and conclusion but cover only two main points in the body of the speech. Your first main point describes the problem and persuades the audience the problem must be overcome. The second main point proposes a solution to overcome the problem. An illustration of how to do this is provided in Figure 14.1.

Richard's speech could be based on using problem-solution organization. He could describe what he sees as a crucial problem in the community and then offer a constructive solution to it.

- Problem: Violent crimes are on the increase and the police department is not sufficiently funded to address this problem in our communities. No new police officers will be hired this year and, in fact, some patrol officers are expecting cutbacks in their hours.
- Solution: Get involved in the local *Neighborhood Watch* program in your community.

Figure 14.1: Problem-Solution Organizational Pattern for a Persuasive Speech

This organizational pattern for a persuasive speech is structured similarly to the standard outline format described in Chapter 8. But the main points in the body of the speech are organized as a problem and a solution.

I. INTRODUCTION
II. BODY
    A. First Main Point: The Problem
    B. Second Main Point: The Solution
III. CONCLUSION

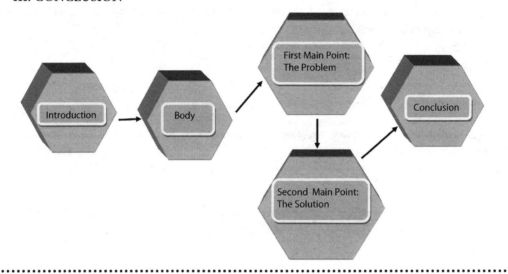

BY MOTIVATED SEQUENCE

An enhanced version of problem-solution organization has dominated the persuasion literature for years, since it was first introduced in 1935 by a professor at Purdue University, Alan Monroe.[5] The **motivated sequence organizational pattern** is a persuasive structure that moves through a sequence of five steps, designed to psychologically motivate and persuade listeners. This pattern is effective because it makes use of a natural sequential pattern of human thought: gaining the listeners' attention, convincing them of a need or problem, offering a solution to satisfy the need or solve the problem, and then helping them visualize the solution and take action relative to it.

Returning to the basic speech structure you learned about in Chapter 8, you present the attention step in your introduction, the need and satisfaction steps in the body of the speech, and the visualization and action steps in your conclusion. These five steps are outlined in Figure 14.2 and below are guidelines for developing your speech using this organizational pattern.

14.5 THE MOTIVATED SEQUENCE ORGANIZATIONAL PATTERN is a persuasive structure that moves through a sequence of five steps, designed to psychologically motivate and persuade listeners.

Step 1: *Get the audience's attention.*

In this first step, create interest in the topic of your speech and a desire on the part of your listeners to hear what you have

Figure 14.2: Motivated Sequence Organizational Pattern for a Persuasive Speech

The motivated sequence includes these five sequential steps: attention, need, satisfaction, visualization, and action.

I. INTRODUCTION
    A. ATTENTION: Grab the audience's attention and forecast the theme of the speech
II. BODY
    B. NEED/PROBLEM : Describe the problem or need, provide evidence of its importance, and relate it to the audience's desires and/or needs
    C. SATISFACTION/SOLUTION: Present a plan of action to address the problem or the need
III. CONCLUSION
    D. VISUALIZATION: Describe the results of the proposed plan or consequences of the audience's failure to change or to act
    E. ACTION: Summarize main ideas and call for the audience to change their beliefs or to act or react in the desired manner

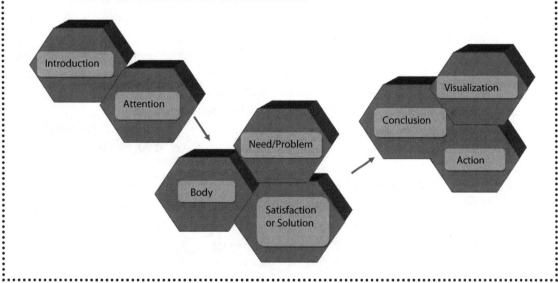

to say. Also provide a statement of the purpose of your speech and forecast the importance of the need or problem that will be the general theme of your speech.

Step 2: *Establish that a need or problem exists.*

In this step, describe and develop the need or problem by providing evidence of its existence and importance. Use examples, testimony, statistics, and other forms of support to emphasize the seriousness of the situation. Explain why the problem exists and relate it to the listeners by pointing out how it affects them. Motivate them to feel that a decision needs to be made or some action taken.

Step 3: *Propose a satisfying solution.*

This step is used to present a plan of action to meet the need or solve the problem that you established in the previous step. Explain to the listeners how your plan addresses the need or problem better than any other solution. To do this, you may have to demonstrate how your solution is superior to others.

Step 4: *Help the audience visualize the solution.*

This step helps the audience imagine the benefits of the solution you propose or the negative consequences of not adopting your solution. You ask your listeners to picture the proposed plan being implemented or what the world will look like if they fail to act.

Step 5: *Motivate the audience to take action.*

Finally, ask the audience to act on the solution you proposed to solve the problem. First summarize your main ideas as you would in any conclusion. Then clearly identify the specific action that is called for. If your objective is to change attitudes or beliefs, you try to motivate the listeners to reconsider their past positions and believe what you propose instead. If you want the listeners to change their behaviors, you urge them to take the specific actions you recommend to solve the problem.

Angelique's speech about public speaking in other countries could be based on using the motivated sequence and could be organized as follows.

- Attention: You may not know it now, but experts on the global economy tell us most careers in the 21st century will involve speaking or listening to presentations by international speakers from a wide array of different countries.
- Need: Suppose you find yourself at an international conference in China or selling your company's products in South Africa. Will you know how to present your remarks effectively and appropriately? Will you be able to understand a presentation by someone who puts their material together in a way that does not make sense to you at first?
- Satisfaction: Before you get that international job, you need to learn about public speaking in the countries that are now emerging as centers of global commerce: China, Japan, India, and Africa.
- Visualization: You will be head and shoulders above other employees, ready to jump on the next plane for Shanghai, Tokyo, New Delhi, or Cape Town.
- Action: I urge you to join me in the advanced public speaking class next semester, as we explore intercultural communication and public speaking.

BY REFUTING THE OPPONENT

Refuting the opponent organization dismantles your opponent's argument, in order to persuade the audience that your argument is superior. In using this type of organizational pattern, your goal is to convince the audience that the opposition's ideas are false, misinformed, or in some way harmful.

There are two basic approaches for refuting the opponent, either of which can be used as the main points to structure the body of your speech. The first is to convince the audience that the other argument is flawed—that there's something wrong with your opponent's line of reasoning. You examine his or her argument for any inconsistencies or errors in how evidence is presented or interpreted. The second approach is to convince the listeners that the actions recommended by your opponent will lead to undesirable results or consequences. You refute your opponent's argument by stressing its negative ramifications for your audience. Debaters use

14.6 REFUTING THE OPPONENT ORGANIZATION dismantles your opponent's argument, in order to persuade the audience that your argument is superior.

both of these persuasive approaches quite often. They try to find flaws in the opponent's argument and they stress its negative outcomes.

If you decide to use refuting the opponent, avoid engaging in personal attacks and stay strictly with the issues involved. Use solid evidence to criticize only your opponent's argument, because attacking a person can backfire and damage your own credibility. Moreover, mudslinging and personal attacks are unethical approaches to persuasion and therefore not competent.

Hana could achieve her objective to change her classmates' attitudes about immigration policies by refuting the opponents' arguments in either of these two ways.

- Those who are opposed to reforming immigration policies in the United States are ignoring several major flaws in the current policy.
- If the United States fails to reform our current immigration policies, the swelling population of illegal immigrants in this country will negatively impact the infrastructure in many states.

BY COMPARING ALTERNATIVES

Comparing alternatives organization first asks listeners to examine two or more alternatives, and then makes a strong appeal for the preferred choice. This organizational pattern is designed to convince the audience that among all the possible ways to solve a problem, there is but one choice that has significant advantages over the others.

To use this organizational pattern, you present a series of alternatives and provide reasons to reject each alternative, except the one you're persuading the audience to favor or adopt. You present all the other alternatives, and then the alternative you prefer last. Just as with refuting the opponent, you can use comparing alternatives to structure the body of your speech. You would then have several main points, each containing a different alternative, and ending with the presentation of your preferred choice.

Comparing alternatives is particularly useful if the listeners may be exposed to counter arguments from others. People presenting controversial policies can make good use of comparing alternatives. A manager at work may need to present a new personnel policy and expects some staff members to challenge it. Or a politician or legislator needs to present a new program and is aware there are alternative approaches for handling the situation. Speakers like these need to present the other alternatives, refute each, and leave only their proposal as the logical choice.

Hana's speech about immigration could also work as a comparing alternatives speech. She could present several different alternatives for changing U.S. policies about immigration, point out the flaws in each alternative, and then present the plan she favors as most workable.

14.7 COMPARING ALTERNATIVES ORGANIZATION first asks listeners to examine two or more alternatives, and then it makes a strong appeal for the preferred choice.

14.8 SOCIAL JUDGMENT THEORY says listeners' attitudes on any topic can be plotted on a continuum ranging from acceptance to rejection, with a non-committed attitude in the middle between those two positions.

Identifying the objective of your persuasive speech and choosing the most effective organizational pattern are crucial to influencing listeners' attitudes, beliefs, values, and behaviors. In addition, you need to be aware of and able to overcome several challenges to persuading in a credible and ethical manner.

CHALLENGES TO CREDIBLE AND ETHICAL PERSUASIVE SPEAKING

Persuasive speeches can represent a great challenge to any public speaker. As we said earlier in this chapter, some audience members may become more committed to their position as a result of listening to a speech that tries to change their minds. An early theory of persuasion has stood the test of time and gives a good explanation of this problem.[6] **Social Judgment Theory** says listeners' attitudes on any topic can be plotted on a continuum ranging from acceptance to rejection, with a non-committed attitude in the middle between those two positions. In the range or latitude of acceptance are positions on a topic or issue that individual listeners consider acceptable, including the one that's most acceptable. On the opposite end of the continuum lies the range or latitude of rejection and the positions individual listeners find objectionable, including the one that's most objectionable. Obviously the greater the latitude or range of rejection, the harder it will be to persuade the listeners to change. And if your position falls in the latitude of rejection for most listeners, you face an even greater challenge.

So your speech may fail for the same reason most persuasion fails—it's difficult to get people to change the attitudes, beliefs, values, and behaviors they have spent years developing. This difficulty may result from speakers failing to consider the hostility level of the audience or using faulty reasoning. Either of these problems represents a challenge that, unaddressed, could affect whether you are perceived as a credible and ethical public speaker.

A HOSTILE AUDIENCE

When presented with a persuasive argument, listeners often unconsciously engage in a form of *inner speech* or **counter-argument** that argues against the persuasive message being presented and for the listener's entrenched position or point of view. This silent counter-argument encourages listeners to build a case against your persuasive message rather than listening to the arguments you're presenting. Therefore, anticipating the audience's reactions ahead of time is crucial to giving a successful persuasive speech.

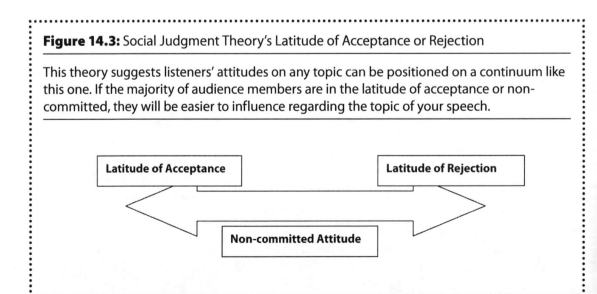

Figure 14.3: Social Judgment Theory's Latitude of Acceptance or Rejection

This theory suggests listeners' attitudes on any topic can be positioned on a continuum like this one. If the majority of audience members are in the latitude of acceptance or non-committed, they will be easier to influence regarding the topic of your speech.

Latitude of Acceptance

Latitude of Rejection

Non-committed Attitude

It is particularly important to consider your audience's position on your topic, when the majority of them strongly disagree with your position or have an unfavorable attitude toward you, your topic, or the particular situation. If you're facing such a hostile audience, that is a great challenge to effective persuasion. To deal with this challenge, you must anticipate all possible audience reactions to your speech and present your topic in a way that deals with, if not overcomes, audience hostility.

To manage counter-argument effectively, you want to try to prevent it from even getting started. One way to accomplish this is to present information in your speech so that it builds toward a positive response. If the audience's attitude toward your topic is negative, don't state a straightforward claim or thesis in your introduction, which will precipitate counter-argument. If you state a claim or viewpoint with which the listeners disagree, that could prejudice them against your message before they even hear your argument. Instead, use the thesis to forecast the general theme of your speech. Present neutral but valid information first and state your claim after the audience has heard your evidence.

14.9 COUNTER-ARGUMENT argues against the persuasive message being presented and for the listener's entrenched position or point of view.

If your goal is to persuade a hostile audience to change, you need to know the audience's attitude toward, information level about, and ego involvement in your topic. These factors, along with your own credibility as a speaker, will determine whether your persuasive message is likely to succeed. Consider the following three questions about your listeners as you prepare your persuasive speech.

1. Attitude: Are they friendly or hostile toward your position on the topic?
   If your listeners are hostile, use a balanced appeal. Reinforce the merit of their position on the topic, letting them know you respect their point of view. Tell them you'll be discussing several perspectives on the topic, and you plan to discuss the merits of each perspective. Present your speech using provisional and conditional language and don't directly attack or criticize their point of view. But while honoring their attitudes toward the topic, don't misrepresent your own position, which would be dishonest and unethical.

2. Information level: How much does the audience know about the subject area or topic? Are they well informed, somewhat informed, or misinformed?
   If your listeners are well informed, don't bore them or waste their time by telling them what they already know. Instead, establish your credibility on the topic and give them new information, before trying to persuade them to your way of thinking. If they're uninformed, link the new material to information they already know. And if they're misinformed, rather than criticizing or correcting them directly, present alternative ways of looking at the issue.

3. Ego involvement: How much do they care about the topic? To what degree are their egos tied up in it?
   If the listeners care a lot about the topic of your speech, their high level of ego involvement will make it particularly hard to persuade them. As soon as they realize your position is different from theirs, they stop listening and start creating counter-arguments reinforcing they are right and you are wrong. So if your listeners have a high degree of ego involvement in your topic, and if their position on it is quite different from yours, avoid overstating your case or explicitly stating your persuasive goal until after you have fully explained your position.

Several simple preparation techniques will help you deal with hostile audience reactions ahead of time and minimize negative reactions. First, pretend you're preparing a speech for the opposite side of the argument. For instance, if you're planning a speech that favors assisted suicide, do some library research examining the arguments of those who oppose it. This will alert you to the attitudes, beliefs, and values of an audience opposed to this topic. Second, have a friend or colleague listen to your speech and play devil's advocate. Ask this person to poke holes in your argument and tell you why they disagree with your position. With this feedback, revise your speech to build a stronger case to persuade a hostile, well-informed, and ego-involved audience.

FAULTY REASONING

In addition to the audience's hostile attitudes, another challenge to persuasion arises from speakers committing **logical fallacies**, which are errors in reasoning and logic that lead the listeners to false conclusions. These speakers are so intent on achieving their persuasive goals that they present evidence or information that is in error, unreasonable, or misrepresents the truth in some way. Whether intentional or unintentional, if fallacies in reasoning are detected, they reflect negatively on your credibility as a speaker and call into question your integrity and ethical standards.

Logicians have identified literally hundreds of logical fallacies to avoid, but the following common examples will give you an idea of the danger in failing to reason with integrity.

- **Ad hominem**: This fallacy occurs when a speaker attacks another person as opposed to the argument the person is making. Ad hominem is Latin for "to the man." Candidates in political campaigns commit this error in reasoning by attacking their opponents and failing to stick to the issues, sometimes in very subtle ways. For example, attacking the opponent and labeling him or her a left-wing liberal or a right-wing conservative would focus the audience's attention on the other person and not on her or his argument. Unfortunately, some candidates for public office have discovered that this approach to negative campaigning has a benefit. It works.

- **Non sequitor**: When a claim does not directly follow from the support material the speaker presents, this fallacy occurs. A non sequitor, literally, means that a statement does not follow from anything previously said. For example, a speaker discussing healthcare could discuss the benefits of nationalized health insurance, but would commit a non sequitor by concluding with a claim about what those benefits would mean for the defense industry.

- **Red herring**: This type of fallacy diverts the audience's attention from the real issue by presenting arguments or issues not relevant to the topic. The expression,

14.10 LOGICAL FALLACIES are errors in reasoning and logic that lead the listeners to false conclusions.

14.11 AD HOMINEM is a fallacy that occurs when a speaker attacks another person as opposed to the argument the person is making.

14.12 NON SEQUITOR is a fallacy that occurs when a claim does not directly follow from the support material that the speaker presents.

14.13 RED HERRING is a fallacy that diverts the audience's attention from the real issue by presenting arguments or issues that are not relevant to the topic.

14.14 SLIPPERY SLOPE REASONING occurs when a speaker suggests that because one event occurs, it automatically leads to a series of other undesirable events.

14.15 A STRAW MAN ARGUMENT occurs when the speaker attacks an entire argument by selecting a weak example or aspect of it, discrediting that example, and thus defaming the entire argument.

red herring, derives its meaning from the practice of dragging a smelly fish across a trail to divert the attention of hunting dogs. This technique might be used in a budget debate on a college campus about financial aid. A speaker could divert attention from financial aid issues by bringing up the red herring of insufficient funds for additional parking lots.

- **Slippery slope**: When a speaker suggests that because one event occurs, it automatically leads to a series of other undesirable events, this is called *slippery slope* reasoning. The speaker implies that if the listeners take one action, they are setting themselves up to slide down a slope from which there is no return. A legislator might say if Congress votes for one bill to crack down on illegal immigrants, then many other unnecessary reforms to U.S. immigration policies are bound to follow. Those other reforms may not automatically follow from passing one bill.

> **14.16 SWEEPING OR HASTY GENERALIZATIONS cluster ideas, people, or objects into one group and imply that all of the items in the group are the same, thus obscuring vital and relevant differences.**

- **Straw man argument**: With this type of logical fallacy, the speaker attacks an entire argument by selecting a weak example or aspect of it, discrediting that example, and thus defaming the entire argument. The speaker sets up a "straw man," which is easy to knock over. In a business or corporation, the personnel manager could say that the company should not be subject to affirmative action policies because women are already sufficiently represented in the work force. The issue of affirmative action is more complex than just female representation, so this would be the use of a "straw woman" argument.

- **Sweeping or hasty generalization**: Making generalizations that cluster ideas, people, or objects into one indiscriminate group, and implying that all of the items in the group are the same can obscure vital and relevant differences. A sweeping or hasty generalization results from moving to a conclusion too quickly and based on too few specific cases or examples. To say "athletes are bad students" is a sweeping generalization. If a speaker describes one basketball player who is a notoriously bad student and quickly generalizes to all players, that is a hasty generalization.

OVERCOMING CHALLENGES AND INFLUENCING LISTENERS TO CHANGE

Given you have anticipated your audience's reactions and constructed your persuasive argument effectively; you still need to do everything you can to motivate your listeners to change. You can address the challenges to ethical and credible persuasion by using one or more of three types of persuasive appeals. An **appeal** is a subtle technique or strategy a speaker uses to get the audience to accept his or her persuasive argument.

> **14.17 AN APPEAL is a subtle technique or strategy a speaker uses to get the audience to accept his or her persuasive argument.**

Current thinking on this topic is derived from the classical tradition of rhetoric, when in the 4th century B.C.E., Greek rhetoricians recommended persuasive speakers make use of *logos:* a form of logical appeals, *pathos:* emotional appeals, and *ethos:* or credibility appeals. Although there is some debate about which of these appeals are most effective—logic, emotion, or credibility—one expert, who developed a new model of persuasion, agrees that all three are effective, depending on the persuasive goal.[7]

LOGICAL APPEALS AND REASONING

A **logical appeal** is based on knowledge and reasoning, which involves how people think. It consists of presenting evidence and encouraging listeners to draw a conclusion based on that information. Logical arguments are particularly effective for audiences made up of people from Western or North American cultures; in these cultures, many people do prefer to make decisions based on examining evidence and information.

Logical arguments can be made in two ways—using deductive or inductive reasoning. **Deduction** is a process of reasoning in which a specific conclusion follows necessarily from a general principle that is often made up of a major and a minor premise. If the audience accepts the two premises as true, then they must also accept the specific conclusion as true.

Here's a classic example teachers of rhetoric often use to illustrate deductive reasoning:

> Major premise: *All of humanity is mortal.*
> Minor premise: *Socrates is human.*
> Specific conclusion: *Socrates is mortal.*

14.18 A LOGICAL APPEAL is based on knowledge and reasoning, which involves how people think.

14.19 DEDUCTION is a process of reasoning in which a specific conclusion follows necessarily from a general principle that is often made up of a major and a minor premise.

14.20 INDUCTION is a process of reasoning in which a general conclusion follows from the examination of a series of specific instances or examples.

Induction is a process of reasoning in which a general conclusion follows from the examination of a series of specific instances or examples. If listeners accept the specific instances or examples as true, then they must also accept the general conclusion as true. The more credible the specific examples, the more logical the conclusion will seem to the listeners. Using the classic example again, an inductive argument could come to a general conclusion in this way:

> Instance: *All women are mortal.*
> Instance: *All men are mortal.*
> General conclusion: *All human beings are mortal, including you and me.*

If you choose to use a logical appeal in your persuasive speech, the deductive or inductive premises, instances, and examples should be used to constitute the main points in the body of your speech.

EMOTIONAL APPEALS AND PSYCHOLOGY

An **emotional appeal** is based on psychology and passion, which involves how people feel. Despite what most people would like to think, they are not always logical. If your argument appeals to your listeners' emotions, it will get their attention and hold it. By reaching them emotionally and convincing them they should care about your topic, you will more likely achieve your persuasive goal. Direct mail requests or TV ads asking you to contribute to help the less fortunate— the homeless, the hungry, or helpless animals—frequently use emotional appeals in the form of dramatic photographs or heart-wrenching stories. To use emotional appeals effectively, you can appeal to any of a variety of your listeners' emotions, such as love, hate, sympathy, guilt, or even fear.

14.21 AN EMOTIONAL APPEAL is based on psychology and passion, which involves how people feel.

14.22 A FEAR APPEAL is based on changing listeners' attitudes or behaviors through the use of an anxiety-arousing message.

A **fear appeal** is based on changing listeners' attitudes or behaviors through the use of an anxiety-arousing message. This type of emotional appeal is useful in situations where you need to motivate the audience to pay attention and get more involved in your topic. A fear appeal is not inherently an ethical or unethical approach to persuasion. For example, health campaigns on anti-smoking or breast cancer often use fear appeals in an appropriate manner to convince people of the danger of the given health issue. In order for a fear appeal to be effective and ethical, it must include information that poses a real threat or danger to the listeners, and it must prescribe an effective action for handling the threat. That said, fear appeals should be used cautiously, realizing that too strong a fear appeal will backfire, particularly if the listeners are not provided information for dealing with the fear-inducing situation or problem.

Emotional and logical appeals can be used effectively together to accomplish the objective of a persuasive speech. Listeners typically respond to the emotional content of a speech first and then examine the logical evidence. So, combining emotion and logic, in that order, can be particularly effective in helping to accomplish your persuasive goal.

CHARACTER APPEALS AND CREDIBILITY

A **character appeal** is related to how listeners perceive the reputation, prestige, and authority of the speaker. If you establish the credibility of your sources of information and of yourself as a speaker, you are more likely to be believable and therefore persuasive. By contrast, if the audience disrespects or distrusts you, you'll have a harder time persuading them, regardless of any logical or emotional appeals you use. Worse yet, if you lack credibility, they may not even have an interest in what you have to say.

14.23 A CHARACTER APPEAL is related to how listeners perceive the reputation, prestige, and authority of the speaker.

Because their reputations precede them, some speakers, such as presidential candidates, are automatically perceived to be highly credible.[8] But how can a novice speaker establish credibility with an audience? Three factors influence whether you will impress your audience as being of high character and credible: expertise, trustworthiness, and charisma.

- Expertise: You need to be perceived by the listeners as someone who is competent and in command or knowledgeable of the subject of your speech. This kind of competence involves knowing the topic well, being prepared to talk about it, and bringing your own experience to the discussion. If you prepared your speech according to the guidelines in Part Two of this book, that preparation will be obvious to the audience and they will respect you as well informed on the topic. Or if you have experience relevant to the topic, for example, if they know you successfully stopped smoking, they'll more likely listen to your advice.
- Trustworthiness: You need to be perceived as a person of high character, so the listeners feel they can believe what you say. Character involves honesty and objectivity. Without a doubt, being an honest person who tells the truth will enhance your credibility, because sincerity and openness can quickly build the trust that is crucial to audience respect. In addition, you can demonstrate character by speaking objectively about your speech topic. Mentioning opposing viewpoints and quoting sources that challenge your position suggest to the audience you are open and honest and therefore deserving of their trust.[9]
- Charisma: Finally, you need to be perceived as a speaker with charisma, which means the audience finds you engaging, likable, and enthusiastic. All of the nonverbal cues for compe-

tent public speaking outlined in Chapter 11 will help you appear more energetic and there-fore more charismatic and credible.[10] Such a speaker is enthusiastic and therefore able to gain and hold the audience's attention. There have been many charismatic speakers in the world of politics—Bill Clinton, Ronald Reagan, and even dictators such as Hitler in Germany in the 20th century, or more recently Saddam Hussein in Iraq. Whether you agree with them or not, their ability to impress audiences was due in part to their personal charisma.

Some public speakers may use the three appeals—logic, emotion, and character—unethically and not in the best interest of those listening to their speeches. Given the importance of persuasive speaking skills in society, it is critical to understand ethical persuasion. As a public speaker, now and in the future, you will make ethical decisions about what to say and what not to say.

THE ETHICS OF PERSUASIVE SPEAKING

Sometimes persuasive speaking can be misunderstood and confused with coercion or manipulation, which are not ethical ways of influencing others. **Coercion** is a negative form of influence that occurs when a speaker per-suades others to act in a particular way out of fear of repri-sal, or by using force, or giving the listeners no choice but to cooperate. In Nazi Germany, some people were coerced by Hitler's speeches to betray their friends and family members who were providing safe havens for Jewish people. They were afraid that if they didn't cooperate, they themselves would be accused of disloyalty to the Nazi party.

14.24 COERCION is a negative form of influence that occurs when a speaker persuades others to act in a particular way out of fear of reprisal, or by using force, or giving the listeners no choice but to cooperate.

Manipulation is also a negative and unethical form of influence that is used to control people's actions or reactions in a devious or deceitful way. Political campaign speeches sometimes border on manipulation when they misrepresent an opponent's programs or positions on an issue. For exam-ple, a candidate for elected office might suggest that his or her opponent wants to end medical coverage or take away social security benefits from the elderly when that may not be the case.

14.25 MANIPULATION is a negative and unethical form of influence that is used to control people's actions or reactions in a devious or deceitful way.

By contrast to these unethical approaches, ethical public speaking leaves the decision about what to think or do up to the audience members. The speaker presents information, without coercing or manipulating the listeners, and allows them to make up their own minds. As a result, the persuaded listeners are more likely, in the future, to continue to hold the recommended attitudes or opinions and engage in the desired behaviors. When an audience member is coerced or manipulated into chang-ing, there is less commitment to the new opinion and less desire to continue the activity later on.

Building on the information about ethical communication first presented in Chapter 3, you now should be ready to deal with any challenges to ethical and credible public speaking you may face in the future. The advice provided in this chapter helped Angelique, Hana, and Richard present their persuasive speeches effectively and appropriately. Like these students, if you follow the guidelines provided here for preparing and presenting persuasive speeches, you too will influence your listen-ers and reinforce or change their attitudes, beliefs, values, and behaviors.

Beyond the public speaking class you are now in, you will have opportunities to speak publicly, at work and other special occasions and events—like in small groups, at public meetings, and even toasts at weddings. The final chapter of this book covers those kinds of opportunities.

CHAPTER SUMMARY

A persuasive speech is one that attempts to influence the audience's attitudes, beliefs, values, or behaviors. Because of its goal to influence, a persuasive speech is organized differently from an informative speech and takes a receiver-oriented approach by being more concerned with what the audience thinks and feels about the speech topic. Aristotle emphasized the importance of persuasive speaking skills that continue to be crucial for citizens in a free and open society. The three types of persuasive speeches, based on the speaker's objective, attempt to (1) reinforce the listeners' attitudes, beliefs, and values; (2) change attitudes, beliefs, and values, or (3) move the listeners to action. A persuasive speech can be organized in any one of four ways. Problem-solution organization first identifies a problem and then proposes a workable solution for the problem. The motivated sequence consists of five steps: attention, need, satisfaction, visualization, and action. Refuting the opponent organization dismantles the opposing argument. Comparing alternatives examines two or more alternatives and makes an appeal for the preferred choice. Challenges to persuasive speaking can result from an unawareness of the listeners' position on the topic or issue based on the continuum of acceptance versus rejection. The challenges include listeners engaging in counter-argument and speakers failing to consider the hostility level of the audience and using faulty reasoning. Faulty reasoning arises from a speaker using logical fallacies that lead listeners to false conclusions. To overcome these challenges, a competent speaker uses one or more of three types of appeals. A logical appeal is based on knowledge and reasoning, which involves how people think; it makes use of deductive or inductive reasoning to influence listeners. An emotional appeal is based on psychology and passion, which involves how people feel. A fear appeal tries to change listeners' attitudes or behaviors through the use of an anxiety-arousing message. A third type of appeal, character or credibility, is based on the listeners' perceptions of the reputation, prestige, and authority of the speaker. The speaker's perceived expertise, trustworthiness, and charisma affect perceptions of credibility. In using these skills, an ethical speaker avoids coercion or manipulation to influence an audience.

KEY TERMS

The key terms below are defined in this chapter and presented alphabetically with definitions in the Glossary at the end of the book.

- speech to reinforce
- speech to move to action
- motivated sequence
- comparing alternatives
- counter-argument

- speech to change
- problem solution
- refuting the opponent
- social judgment theory
- logical fallacies

- ad hominem
- red herring
- straw man argument
- appeal
- deduction
- emotional appeal
- character appeal
- manipulation

- non sequitor
- slippery slope
- sweeping or hasty generalizations
- logical appeal
- induction
- fear appeal
- coercion

BUILDING COMPETENCE ACTIVITIES

INDIVIDUAL ACTIVITIES

1. Make three columns on a piece of paper. Label your columns: Types of Persuasive Speeches, Speech Topic, and Organizational Pattern, from left to right. In column one, list the three types of informative speeches, based on content. In column two, come up with one speech topic that appeals to you for each type of speech. In column three, decide which organizational pattern would work best for each topic you listed.

2. Analyze the exemplary persuasive speech in the appendix at the end of this book. Determine how well you think it achieves its persuasive objective. What did the speaker do well to achieve that objective?

3. Attend a persuasive public speech or observe such a speech on TV or the Internet. Identify the objective of the speech presented and evaluate how well the speaker achieves the objective. Analyze the speech based on the challenges to persuasive speaking presented in this chapter—hostile audience and faulty reasoning. Did you observe the use of any of the logical fallacies?

4. Visit this website: http://www.speech-topics-help.com/good-persuasive-speech-topics.html with one other student. Choose a topic for a persuasive speech that appeals to you. Identify an objective for a speech on the topic and choose a persuasive organizational pattern that would work best for the speech. Develop the main parts of the speech based on the pattern you have chosen.

GROUP ACTIVITIES

1. Form groups of three to four students and attend a persuasive public speech or watch such a speech on TV or on the Internet. Have each student individually identify the objective of the speech presented and evaluate how well the speaker achieves the objective. Analyze the speech based on the challenges to persuasive speaking presented in this chapter—hostile audience and faulty reasoning. Did you observe the use of any of the logical fallacies? Compare and discuss your individual evaluations.

2. Form groups of three to four students. Analyze the exemplary persuasive speech in the appendix at the end of this book. Determine how well you think it achieves its persuasive objective. What did the speaker do well to achieve that objective?

3. Visit this website: http://www.speech-topics-help.com/good-persuasive-speech-topics.html with one other student. Each of you choose a topic for a persuasive speech that appeals to you. Collaborate to identify an objective for a speech on the topic and choose a persuasive organizational pattern that would work best for the speech. Develop the main parts of the speech based on the pattern you have chosen.

COMPETENCY CHECKPOINTS AND SELF-ASSESSMENT TOOL

Here is what you need to know and be able to do regarding persuasive speeches. Determine your level of competency and whether you are ready to proceed to the next chapter. Give yourself one point for each checkpoint you answer satisfactorily.

COMPETENCY CHECKPOINTS	NUMBER OF POINTS
KNOWLEDGE	
1. Explain how the key differences between speaking to inform and speaking to persuade affect how you prepare a persuasive speech.	
2. Why is the ability to present persuasive speeches important in a free and open society?	
3. List and describe the three objectives of persuasive speeches.	
4. Which of the three persuasive objectives may be hardest to achieve and why?	
5. Identify and explain how to use the four different organizational patterns for persuasive speeches.	
SKILLS	
1. Provide an example of a persuasive speech and write out an objective for that speech.	
2. Use the same example of a persuasive speech and indicate what organizational pattern should be used for it.	
3. Use the same example of a persuasive speech and identify your class' attitudes, beliefs, and values with regard to that topic.	
ETHICS AND CREDIBILITY	
1. Describe the challenges to credible and ethical persuasive speaking and explain why they occur.	
2. Indicate how a speaker may address the challenges to persuasive speaking.	
TOTAL CHECKPOINTS (OUT OF A POSSIBLE TEN POINTS)	

ENDNOTES

1. Smith, R.E. (2004). Recruit the student: Adapting persuasion to audiences. *Communication Teacher, 18*(2), 53–56.

2. Roberts, W. R., (Translator) (1954). *The rhetoric.* Aristotle. New York: The Modern Library.

3. Johannesen, R.L., Valde, K.S., & Whedbee, K.E. (2007). *Ethics in human communication, 6th Ed.* Long Grove, IL: Waveland.

4. Nick Morgan's Blog, Six Ways to Put Together a Persuasive Speech: Retrieved from: http://publicwords.typepad.com/nickmorgan/2009/06/six-ways-to-put-together-a persuasive-speech.html.

5. Monroe, A.H. (1935). *Principles and types of speech.* Glenview, IL: Scott, Foresman.

6. Sherif, C. W., Sherif, M. S. & Nebergall, R. E. (1965). *Attitude and attitude change.* Philadelphia, PA: W.B. Saunders.

7. Poggi, I. (2005). The goals of persuasion. *Pragmatics & Cognition, 2005, 23*(2), 297–336.

8. Johansson, M. (2008). Presentation of the political self: Commitment in electoral media dialogue. *Journal of Language and Social Psychology, 27*(4), 397–408.

9. Shockley-Zalabak, P.S., Morreale, S.P., & Hackman, M.Z. (2010). *Building the high trust organization: Five key dimensions of trust.* San Francisco: Jossey-Bass.

10. Gallo, C. (12/26/2007). The right amount of energy. *Business Week Online,* 11. Retrieved from http://www.BusinessWeekOnline.

15

SPEAKING AT WORK AND ON SPECIAL OCCASIONS

- **Presenting at Work**
    Understanding Speaking in 21st Century Organizations
    Types of Presentations in 21st century Organizations
    Technology-Assisted Presentations in Organizations
    Challenges to Technology-Assisted Presentations in Organizations
- **Presenting and Communicating in Teams**
- **Speaking to the Media**
- **Presenting on Special Occasions**

**"My father gave me these hints on speech-making: Be sincere...be brief...
be seated." James Roosevelt, oldest son of U.S. President Franklin D.
Roosevelt, 1907–1991**

• • •

*A group of students decided to get together a year after they completed the public
speaking course. They had become good friends and now they had a cause to celebrate. All of them had become better public speakers and, in fact, they had aced the
course. That was a surprise, given their anxiety at the start of the course about giving speeches. Angelique, Hana, Kumar, LaTisha, Mario, Richard, Vanden, and Zak
showed up for the reunion. A lot had happened to the students since they completed
the course, so they were anxious to catch up on everybody's news. Angelique had
graduated and gotten married: "You should have heard the wedding toasts, to say
nothing of how well I said my vows publicly to my new husband." Richard got a promotion to captain in the police force: "I'm surprised how confident I am now when I
speak to the group of officers now reporting to me." Kumar had traveled internationally and spoken to his extended family at a formal dinner and other events. Hana's
new job in a multinational company involves presentation using technology like video
conferencing and training webinars. Zak and Vanden are still working for the same
company, but their improved public speaking skills are helping them present better
trainings and instructional programs.*

• • •

Clearly, public speaking skills are lifelong skills. Like these students, you will find yourself speaking in many different professional and social situations. Where, in the future, do you think you will
make the most presentations? The answer to this question is at work.

At all levels in organizations and businesses, the ability to speak publicly is critical to accomplishing tasks with others and succeeding on the job. You will be presenting information using all
kinds of communication technology; you will often make recommendations and present project
updates to small and large groups. And, like Zak and Van, you will be presenting trainings and
providing instructions to others. At the management level, executives often study with communication coaches when they want to take their public speaking to the next level—for major keynote
addresses, financial reports, and critical presentations to boards of directors.[1] Leaders in organizations frequently find themselves challenged to communicate complex information with clarity and
ease—in meetings with global teams, leadership committees, and key customers and stakeholders.

Like speaking at work, speaking in social situations—from births, to weddings, to funerals—can be a challenge for any speaker. Whether you're congratulating the bride and groom or presenting or accepting an award, you need to know the right words to say and how to say them. If you are called upon to give a eulogy at a funeral, that may be one of the most difficult speaking assignments of all.

You already have the ability to prepare and present informative and persuasive speeches well. But in this chapter, we apply those skills specifically to speaking at work and on special occasions. After reading the chapter, you will be able to:

- Explain the nature of speaking at work and in 21st century organizations.
- Describe the three types of presentations that most often occur at work, based on their general purpose, and the various forms these presentations take.
- Outline the three more common types of web-based presentation technologies currently popular in organizations.
- Explain the nature of communication in teams in contemporary organizations, including how technology is used to convene meetings and how to present in a team.
- Identify challenges and ways to overcome challenges when organizations speak to the media.
- Describe and provide guidelines for the most frequent types of special occasion speeches.

PRESENTING AT WORK

Outside class, most of your public speaking probably will occur at work in an organizational setting. In most organizations, employees and managers often are called on to present information about which they are considered the company's experts. They may be asked to make recommendations on a policy or a course of action or provide instructions or trainings for other employees. In each of these situations, just as in the classroom, you need to learn as much as you can beforehand about the audience, their information or skills level regarding your presentation topic, and the physical situation or context. You may find yourself speaking to colleagues or peers at the same level in the company in a small conference room or presenting a new plan for running your entire department to high-level managers in an executive boardroom. These two contexts are quite different, so the two presentations will vary based on the audience and the goals you need to achieve as a speaker in the organization.

UNDERSTANDING SPEAKING IN 21ST CENTURY ORGANIZATIONS

Public speaking in today's organizations is very different as a result of two factors—globalization and technology. One expert states: "Our times are surely shaped by information and communication technology, partly because such technologies carry the essence of what is commonly referred to as the age of globalization: global reaches, fast pace, and knowledge as the main commodity."[2]

As a result of globalization, the presentations you give or participate in often may make use of global teleconferencing or videoconferencing. You may be communicating with groups of people scattered around the world, working in different time zones, and valuing different approaches to communicating. Understanding cultural differences in global presentations will become a critical competency for you. As a result of technology, rather than talking to coworkers face to face, you often will present information on web casts, which allow for one-way transmission from you as the sender to the receivers. Or you may present trainings for groups of coworkers using interactive webinars, which allow for two-way communication between the sender and receiver. Understanding the array of communication and cutting edge presentation technologies also will be a critical competency. Combining globalization and technology, you may find yourself presenting to an audience in one or several countries, as your technology-assisted presentation is translated into one or more languages. While this may sound like a unique situation, it is, in fact, the norm in many multinational organizations.

Researchers have not fully examined this impact of globalization and technology on public speaking in the contemporary workplace. In fact, advances in communication technology are moving so fast that researchers and teachers can't quite keep up with the changes. A simple example is the language used to describe some of the new communication technologies. The spellcheck tool in Microsoft Office Word does not yet include the term "webinar," which now is a common training tool in many organizations. Word's spellcheck suggests we must mean "seminar," not "webinar." As a competent communicator and public speaker, you need to stay ahead of the curve and learn as much as you can about the new opportunities for communicating publicly at work.

TYPES OF PRESENTATIONS IN 21ST CENTURY ORGANIZATIONS

Speeches and presentations in today's organization, like anywhere else, can be categorized based on these three purposes for speaking: to educate, to inform, or to persuade. **Educational presentations** teach others information and skills relevant to their jobs and the organization. Instructions and trainings are common examples. **Informative presentations** transmit knowledge from one organization member or unit to another or to others. Examples include briefings, status or progress reports, checkpoint meetings, and formal research investigations. **Persuasive presentations** attempt to influence problem solving or decision making in the organization. Included are recommendations to change policies or procedures of the organization, sales presentations, and resource requests. A presentation may have only one of these goals or it may have multiple purposes, such as informative and persuasive. For example, you may be informing coworkers about a new software database to which they have access, but you also are trying to persuade them to use the software enthusiastically.

Regardless of the purpose, the fact that presentations often are assisted by the use of technology affects how you present instructions and trainings (educational), briefings and status reports (informative), and policy and procedure recommendations (persuasive). Let's now look at some of these more common forms of organizational presentations and then the impact of technology on presenting them.

Instructions are educational presentations, provided by supervisors to one or several workers, outlining what must be done and how to do it, use it, or operate something. If a new reimbursement system is put in place, a supervisor may instruct those in her or

15.1 EDUCATIONAL PRESENTATIONS teach others information and skills relevant to their jobs and the organization.

15.2 INFORMATIVE PRESENTATIONS transmit knowledge from one organization member or unit to another or to others.

15.3 PERSUASIVE PRESENTATIONS attempt to influence problem solving or decision making in the organization.

15.4 INSTRUCTIONS are educational presentations, provided by supervisors to one or several workers, outlining what must be done and how to do it, use it, or operate something

his unit on using the system. By contrast, **trainings** are more formal events in which a professional consultant or presenter, who is an expert in an area, works with a group of people to teach them a new skill, job, or process. Contemporary organizations often offer trainings in job-related topics, such as using new equipment of all sorts, stress management, communication skills, or, working in teams.

Providing instructions or presenting a training is a challenge, because the speaker often knows far more about the topic than the trainees. The goal may be to present a new way of doing things to the trainees or coworkers. But precisely because the presenter is an expert, she or he may not realize how little the trainees know about the topic or their skill level. The result is that new information may be presented using language trainees don't understand. Those providing trainings in organizations in the use of new computer technologies sometimes fail to engage in audience analysis. Needless to say, Zak and Van used the audience analysis skills they learned in their public speaking class to develop better trainings for coworkers in their company.

Briefings are informative presentations on topics ranging from informal status or progress reports, to checkpoint meetings, to formal research investigations. These reports are a frequent occurrence in contemporary organizations, particularly technical companies. Because many organizations now use teams to get jobs done, briefings and reports within and between teams happen quite often. These checkpoint meetings often report on the progress of a given project or progress toward achieving a particular team or organizational goal. Briefings and reports are a challenge because the speaker doesn't need to start at the beginning of the project, each time it is presented. Rather the presenter summarizes the project at the beginning of the report and then describes where it is at presently. A competent presenter doesn't assume to know what the audience may remember since the last briefing; instead, he or she reviews and brings others up to speed without boring them or being repetitive. Obviously, a technology-assisted briefing, like a web cast, is particularly challenging because the speaker doesn't have access to the reactions and nonverbal cues of the listeners, as the briefing progresses.

Recommendations are persuasive presentations on topics ranging from minor issues such as changing a company procedure to major recommendations such as a company wide reorganization, a merger, or the introduction of a new product

15.5 TRAININGS are formal events in which a professional consultant or presenter, an expert in an area, works with a group of people to teach them a new skill, job, or process.

15.6 BRIEFINGS are informative presentations on topics ranging from informal status or progress reports, to check point meetings, to formal research investigations.

15.7 RECOMMENDATIONS are persuasive presentations, ranging from minor issues such as changing a company procedure to major recommendations such as a company wide reorganization, a merger, or the introduction of a new product line.

line. These persuasive presentations typically announce changes in organizational policies or protocols. But whenever change happens in an organization, it's best to anticipate that it will be challenged by some employees, if not many. Any change to standard operating procedure may be considered a negative occurrence. So a competent speaker expects to be challenged and considers ahead of time what questions will be asked during the presentation. Just as you would with a hostile audience for a persuasive speech, you address the listeners' concerns first and then present the recommended policy. Unlike traditional persuasive speeches though, you can spend less time establishing your own credibility, because you probably have ongoing relationships with others in the organization. That time would be better spent establishing the credibility of the new policy you are recommending.

TECHNOLOGY-ASSISTED PRESENTATIONS IN ORGANIZATIONS

Technology is truly everywhere in today's organizations. According to one group of researchers, the operation of a human organization requires the coordination of dozens of everyday tasks to ensure the smooth functioning of organizational activities, to monitor the status of activities, to gather information relevant to the organization, and to keep everyone informed.[3] These computer software researchers developed and are using a program called *Electric Elves* that monitors employees' workstations, computers, faxes, and mobile devices like cell phones and palm pilots, in order to organize routine tasks in the organization, 24 hours a day, seven days a week. This approach may sound a bit extreme, but it is an indicator of the role and influence of technology on every aspect of how people communicate in contemporary organizations. In Hana's new job in a multinational company, she found herself communicating and presenting with technology on a regular basis.

Even though presentations using technology are here to stay, organizational training is not abundant in the use of web casts, webinars, global teleconferences, and the like. As a result, these presentations often are not done well, and many of us just don't know how to use the technologies competently. The most important thing you can do is become aware of and be prepared to learn about their use in organizations. So let's first describe the more common types of web-based presentation technologies and then consider challenges to using presentation technologies competently.

Web cast presentations involve information and data transmission over the web that is one-way and does not allow interaction between the presenter and the audience. **Web conferencing** involves information and data transmission over the web that is two-way and allows interaction between the presenter and the audience. **Webinars** are web-based seminars, workshops, or trainings, transmitted over the web. Web casts and web conferences typically are informative or persuasive, or a combination of both, and webinars are focused on education or training.

....

15.8 WEB CAST PRESENTATIONS involve information and data transmission over the web that is one way and does not allow interaction between the presenter and the audience.

....

15.9 WEB CONFERENCING involves information and data transmission over the web that is two way and allows interaction between the presenter and the audience.

....

15.10 WEBINARS are web-based seminars, workshops, or trainings, transmitted over the web.

CHALLENGES TO TECHNOLOGY-ASSISTED PRESENTATIONS IN ORGANIZATIONS

Regardless of which of the presentation technologies you may be asked to use, understanding their functions and capacities, what they can and cannot do, and being comfortable with their use ahead of time is critical to an effective delivery. Like any presentation, personal preparation includes getting training from technology staff, or reading the manual if such staff members are not available. Rehearse using the technology, prepare presentation notes or an outline, and time the presentation using the technology itself, if possible.

Unlike other presentations, using technology offers its own unique set of challenges. For instance, failure to anticipate any complicated setup problems that may occur will reflect negatively on your credibility. The electricity goes off and you have no backup plan for media failure, and you didn't bring a hard copy of your presentation in case of such an emergency. Also, during a web cast or web conference, the visual aspect of the technology focuses attention on and magnifies any unconscious nonverbal habits, such as self-touch or moving aimlessly in front of the camera. What viewers notice and see about the speaker does distract from one's credibility. Inexperienced speakers sometimes even wander in and out of camera range without knowing it. Other speakers may forget to turn the microphone off when not speaking; sidebar conversations and noises in the speaker's location irritate listeners on the other end.

Another challenge relates to getting the distant audience involved in the presentation. Whether the web presentation is interactive or not, it's the speaker's responsibility to encourage and ensure listeners or trainees become involved in the subject being discussed.[4] There is nothing more boring than sitting on the other end of a web cast or web conference and not being invited to think about and contribute to the discussion. If the presentation is interactive, you need to include questions in your presentation that invite real responses from the listeners. Ask the distant audience for their ideas or critiques and allow time for their comments; be sure you have described the protocol for participating at a distance, such as identifying yourself before answering a question. If the presentation is a web cast and not interactive, include rhetorical questions that don't require actual answers; ask listeners to send you their thoughts electronically later on. If the distant audience is very large, you may need to ask for only a few responses and ask others to send their comments electronically.

A final word about technology-assisted presentations, particularly in organizations, is needed here. In Chapter 13, we discussed the advantages and disadvantages of computerized presentation aids, like PowerPoint. Some corporations now are discouraging the use of elaborate PowerPoint presentation because the preparation time takes workers away from their jobs. Elaborate "bells and whistles" effects, considered commonplace in PowerPoint presentations in the classroom and at face-to-face conferences, are discouraged in many organizations. Instead, PowerPoint presentations are kept simple and only used to organize and focus informative presentations or briefings. If other information is needed, the presentation is backed up by referring listeners to other technology sources or databases on shared servers.

In addition to being able to use technology to present in organizations, you also need to be familiar with communicating in face-to-face and virtual or geo-dispersed teams and giving team presentations. Richard, in our opening story, gained a promotion, perhaps in part because of his ability to speak with confidence to the team of officers in his unit of the police force.

PRESENTING AND COMMUNICATING IN TEAMS

A well-respected authority on organizational communication says the successful use of teams, in a variety of industries, is one of the fastest growing approaches to organization life.[5] A **team-based organization** is composed of a variety of teams with defined responsibilities, about which managers provide mostly indirect supervision. The growing number of team-based organizations is due, in part, to increased global competitiveness and a related need to reduce overhead and increase productivity. Other researchers report that, over the last fifteen years, these team-based organizations are proving to be more innovative and better able to share information than their more traditional counterparts.[6]

It is very likely you will spend at least part, if not all of your working time, working as a member of a team, virtual

15.11 A TEAM-BASED ORGANIZATION is composed of a variety of teams with defined responsibilities about which managers provide mostly indirect supervision.

or otherwise. And communication within and among these teams, including giving competent team presentations, will be crucial to the organization's success. Group or team presentations are somewhat different from individual presentations. Because more people are involved, the team has access to a variety of skills and resources for preparing and presenting that an individual presenter lacks. By the same token, it's a challenge to make a team presentation appear as one cohesive presentation and not a string of disconnected, individual speakers. Box 15.1 contrasts team presentations to individual speeches and gives advice for *presenting* effectively as a team. Another trainer gives us these eight tips for *preparing* a team presentation, if you are using PowerPoint.[7]

1. Create a game plan for preparing the presentation. Determine who will develop each section and build slides for that section. Start by discussing how many slides are needed and agree about the various sections needed and who will present which sections and which slides.

2. Ensure someone on the team is the presentation owner. Somebody has to take ownership of the final product, especially if everyone on the team is working on different sections and slides. That team member will be sent all sections and will be responsible for their ongoing integration into the "master" file.

3. Use the same template to avoid the need to reformat at the end of the preparation and development process.

4. Have someone, perhaps the presentation owner, choose the style, colors, fonts, etc. early on and tell other team members that they can emulate the same look and feel, as they develop their sections. Consistency is critical to producing a professional looking presentation and reducing effort needed to integrate the sections and slides later on.

5. Factor in extra time, if you have never worked with an individual on the team before. Not everyone's skill levels are the same, and the team needs to accommodate to all members.

6. Meet often enough to keep different sections in synch, but don't meet too often such that it impedes the process of completing the presentation.

7. Leave ample time to integrate all the sections and all the slides prior to the date for delivering the presentation.

8. Rehearse the presentation together *before* presenting in order to work out transitions, timing, and appropriate coverage of all sections.

But what about the challenge of communicating in virtual or geo-dispersed groups and teams?[8] A **virtual team** is a group of individuals, managers and other employees, organized and linked together by technology to work on short- or long-term projects. Organizations use virtual teams to link people with expertise in particular areas or specialties across geographical locations.

Technology has responded to the communication needs of these teams with three different types of electronic meeting support programs to help communicate and collaborate

15.12 A VIRTUAL TEAM is a group of individuals, managers and other employees, organized and linked together by technology to work on short or long term projects.

15.13 TELECONFERENCING includes meetings held through audio conferencing and videoconferencing systems.

15.14 COMPUTER CONFERENCING allows multiple participants to interact by contributing to an ongoing computer file accessible to all.

15.15 GROUP SUPPORT SYSTEMS supplement computer conferencing with information management capabilities, decision support tools, graphic displays, and meeting process management software.

Box 15.1: Effective Team Presentations in Organizations

With an awareness of how team and individual presentations differ, you can use the differences to your advantage.

What are the differences and possible advantages of team presentations?
- Variety is built in with different people planning and presenting.
- Different faces, paces, voices, and communication styles can complement each other…or distract! Build some consistency into what is said and how it's said.
- Greater expertise is available to develop and deliver the presentation.
- Presentation tasks can be managed better. One person can be responsible for the technology, another for timing and keeping the team on track, and others do more of the talking.
- Better audience involvement is possible. Team members can mingle during exercises, or if the presentation is online, some team members can develop interactive questions in the moment.
- At any point in the presentation, more people are available to answer questions.

How can you address the challenge of making it one team presentation and not a string of disconnected speakers?
- Plan the presentation around several key ideas or a main thesis just as you would for an individual speech. Use that thesis as the core for unifying elements in the presentation—not the number of speakers you have.
- Consider dressing somewhat similarly to convey a sense of coherence to the audience.
- Try for a similar presentation style rather than each person doing their own thing. If one speaker is wildly enthusiastic and the next speaker is calm and controlled, the contrast may be distracting.
- Consider using one person for the introduction and conclusion, another leads an exercise, another highlights research or monitors the presentation for possible questions.
- Use clear transitions as bridges to conclude one section and start another—you "tee up" the next speaker and then get out of his or her way.
- Practice ahead of time as a group and, if possible, in the room you will present in. Decide where everyone will stand or sit when not speaking. Time the presentation as teams often take more time to present than may be expected.

across time and space.[9] We have already touched on several of these, but here we are considering them purely as meeting technologies. **Teleconferencing** includes meetings held through audio conferencing and videoconferencing systems. **Computer conferencing** allows multiple participants to interact by contributing to an ongoing computer file accessible to all. **Group support systems** supplement computer conferencing with information management capabilities, decision support tools, graphic displays, and meeting process management software. These technologies allow for synchronous, simultaneous communication or asynchronous communication among workers in diverse time zones and locations. These systems are not as complicated as they may sound. For example, when you use a computerized group support system, members of your work team may be given a problem or task to examine individually. Everyone enters their recommendations in the system, then either the system or a human facilitator organizes the ideas in logical themes or categories. A summary of the recommendations is sent back to team members and they respond to the summary.

In the future, you could find yourself working in a geographically dispersed team and using one of the new meeting technologies. That doesn't mean you need to go out right now and learn all about them. It does mean you need to be aware of the rapidly changing technological environment in most organizations and be prepared to learn about and use any new technologies that come your way.

SPEAKING TO THE MEDIA

One last aspect of speaking at work, worthy of your consideration, is communicating with the media. This is a somewhat different presentation challenge, because the media are an external audience. Most of the presentational speaking discussed so far has been about internal audiences in organizations. Media relations experts tell us there are competing interests when you, as a representative of an organization, speak to the media. The interests of the organization sometimes clash with what the media want to know—what journalists refer to as the public's right to know. For instance, announcements to the media by a pharmaceutical company about harmful effects of a drug product may pit the company's interests against those of the public.

The best way to manage these competing interests is to speak to the media from the viewpoint of the public's best interest, not the organization's self-interest. It is important to tell the truth to the media and the general public and not distort the facts in any way. That said, don't try to cover too much information and with too much detail. The quotation at the start of this chapter applies here: "Be sincere...be brief...be seated!"

Other common mistakes you want to avoid when communicating with the media on behalf of your organization include the following:

- Failure to speak out in a timely manner, a lack of communication or action.
- Failure to listen to the public or the media's concerns and needs.
- A lack of openness and honesty about those concerns and needs.
- Trying to cover up for not knowing the answer to a question from the media. It is better to say, "I am not sure, but I'll get back to you."

If you find yourself speaking to the media on behalf of your organization, remember our definition of ethical communication as it will help you decide what to say or not say: *You have an ethical responsibility to share sufficient information with others so they can make fully informed choices about any matters of importance to themselves.*

PRESENTING ON SPECIAL OCCASIONS

We now turn our attention to a very different type of presentation. You may find you are asked to present a speech in your personal or social life. That certainly was Angelique's experience when she spoke publicly at her own wedding and Kumar's experience in India at a formal family dinner.

Typical special occasions where you may need to give a speech are luncheons, banquets, award ceremonies, birthdays, weddings, and funerals. At most of these events, you are usually a friend or an acquaintance of many of the members of the audience or a member of the same family. By comparison to speaking at work, presenting on special occasions and at special events may be somewhat

Box 15.2: Tips for Special Occasion Speaking

Here are some descriptions of the various types of speeches you may present on special occasions.

Emcees: The master or mistress of ceremony hosts an event. They welcome guests, plan and oversee the preparation, and introduce each speaker. They ask the audience to show their appreciation for each talk. They also may consult with others to decide upon the theme for the event and the order of presentations.

Convocation: This opening talk sets the stage for the event or conference. It is usual to have a poignant verse, story or pithy statement. This speaker confers with the emcee to ensure the presentation is consistent with the theme of the event.

Keynote address: This talk serves as the main attraction of an event. A commencement address on a college campus is filled with sage advice for students on using the principles they gleaned from their education.

Historian: This type of talk provides an overview of a topic of interest to the audience and relevance to the event. Highlights of key turning points, leaders, and major conflicts may be included. The historian often interviews people to get their reflections or memories about the topic.

Adjournment: This talk is like the convocation but it serves as the final fare-thee-well talk. It is valuable to coordinate the content of these two speeches.

Awards presentations: These are generally short talks that have some substance to them. The Academy Awards is one example of awards presentation and acceptance speeches. Notice that recipients on that show have just 45 seconds to speak, and the audience is often done listening before that time is up.

As an award presenter, try to be specific and descriptive in your explanations of the commendations that you offer the recipient. Have a tangible item to accompany that award (e.g., a certificate, a trophy, or a book). When you present the award, don't reveal the recipient's name until you've nearly completed the description. This builds a climax. In addition, do not reveal to the recipient that you are going to give that person an award. This usually is to be a surprise!

As an award recipient, generally strive to receive the award gracefully and modestly. Do not argue against the commendations and do share the praise you get with those who have assisted you (e.g., your partner, instructor, best friend, and/or dog).

Toast: Toasts are intended to thank a host, celebrate an occasion, or observe an anniversary of something special. Toasts should be upbeat, short, and well rehearsed. Not surprisingly, several alcohol distributors offer tips on toast making on their web sites on the Internet.

Entertainer: This light-hearted talk, often though not always, pokes fun at oneself or others. It's useful to share amusing recollections of personal experiences. At the Academy Awards, Jon Stewart, Ellen DeGeneres, Hugh Jackman, Alec Baldwin, and Steve Martin served as entertainers as well as emcees.

Source: Tips for Special Occasion Speaking. Retrieved from http://www.nvcc.edu/home/npeck/spd100/special.htm

more personal, perhaps even emotional. Such presentations often are intended to honor, welcome, or bid goodbye to a person or a group and that may be a touching event. As in other contexts, competence in social situations involves understanding the audience, the speaking situation, and what is expected of you.

Advice for giving special occasion speeches is abundant on the Internet. One website even allows you to customize your remarks for any occasion, from a Jewish bar mitzvah, to a birthday, retirement, wedding, or wedding anniversary. You answer questions and a speech building program instantly generates a customized special occasion speech for you.[10] You and the students in our opening story don't need the help of a computerized software program to develop a speech. But on a more serious note, here are several tips to remember that apply to all special occasion speeches. As a general rule, these speeches should be fairly brief. Talking too long or a lack of focus and clarity may suggest insensitivity to the needs and interests of the audience. Err on the side of brevity and prepare well ahead of time. No matter how short, plan and organize your special occasion speech in advance, and practice it until you can deliver it with confidence and enthusiasm. Box 15.2 provides specific recommendations for most of the special occasion speeches that you will be presenting in the future.

Your journey through a public speaking course and this textbook is just about over. As we advised you to do in the conclusion to any speech, we would like to revisit our introduction to this book. We promised you would grow as a communicator and public speaker and that would be a life enhancing experience. We close by saying we hope that happened for you, and we also sincerely remind you to stay in touch.

CHAPTER SUMMARY

Outside a public speaking class, you will be asked to present speeches at work and in social situations. Public speaking at work, in organizations in the 21st century, is influenced by globalization and technology. Three types of presentations at work are categorized based on their general purpose. Educational presentations teach others information and skills relevant to their jobs and the organization. Informative presentations transmit knowledge from one organization member or unit to another or to others. Persuasive presentations attempt to influence problem solving or decision making in the organization. The more common forms that these presentations take in contemporary organizations are instructions, trainings, briefings, and recommendations. Instructions are educational presentations, provided by supervisors to one or several workers, outlining what must be done and how to do it, use it, or operate something. Trainings are formal events in which a professional consultant or presenter, an expert in an area, works with a group of people to teach them a new skill, job, or process. Briefings are informative presentations on topics ranging from informal status or progress reports, to checkpoint meetings, to formal research investigations. Recommendations are persuasive presentations, ranging from minor issues such as changing a company procedure to major recommendations such as a company wide reorganization, a merger, or the introduction of a new product line. Technology-assisted presentations are frequent in organizations though organizational training in the use of presentation technologies is not abundant. The more common types of web-based presentation technologies, with which you should be familiar, are these: web cast presentations, which involve information and data transmission over the web that is one way and does not allow interaction between the presenter and the audience; web conferencing, which involves information and data transmission over the web that is two way and allows interaction between the presenter and the audience; and webinars, which are web-based seminars, workshops, or trainings, transmitted over the web. Included in challenges to using presentation and meeting technologies well is the use of

PowerPoint, which some organizations now say should not be filled with elaborate "bells and whistles." You also need to be familiar with team presentations and communication in face-to-face and geo-dispersed teams. Team-based organizations, those composed of a variety of teams with defined responsibilities about which managers provide mostly indirect supervision, are gaining in popularity. Organizations also are using virtual teams to link people with expertise in particular areas or specialties across geographical locations. A virtual team is a group of individuals, managers and other employees, organized and linked together by technology to work on short or long term projects. Technology also is being used to address the communication needs of these teams. Three different types of electronic meeting support programs are available. Teleconferencing includes meetings held through audio conferencing and videoconferencing systems. Computer conferencing allows multiple participants to interact by contributing to an ongoing computer file accessible to all. And, group support systems supplement computer conferencing with information management capabilities, decision support tools, graphic displays, and meeting process management software. Speaking to the media is a challenge for organizations because the interests of the organization sometimes clash with what the media want to know. In addition to speaking at work, communicating in teams, and speaking to the media, you also may be asked to present a speech on a special occasion, such as at a luncheon or a banquet, an awards ceremony, birthday, wedding, or funeral.

KEY TERMS

The key terms below are defined in this chapter and presented alphabetically with definitions in the Glossary at the end of the book.

- educational presentations
- persuasive presentations
- trainings
- recommendations
- web conferencing
- team-based organization
- teleconferencing
- group support systems

- informative presentations
- instructions
- briefings
- web cast presentations
- webinars
- virtual team
- computer conferencing

BUILDING COMPETENCE ACTIVITIES

INDIVIDUAL ACTIVITIES

1. Visit this website that provides tips for all different sorts of special occasion speeches: http://www.nvcc.edu/home/npeck/spd100/special.htm. Develop an outline for a speech for one of the sorts of speeches listed.

2. Think back on your own professional experiences in organizations and identify a presentation you attended. Decide if the presentation's general purpose was educational, informative, or persuasive and evaluate how well the presentation achieved its goal. Determine if the form of the presentation was an instruction, training, a briefing of some kind, or a recommendation. Write a one-page evaluation of the presentation.

3. Think back on your own professional experiences in organizations and identify a presentation you attended that was in some way technology assisted. Describe how competently or incompetently the speaker used the presentation technology.

4. Think back on your own social life and identify a special occasion speech you observed or presented yourself. Evaluate the presentation based on the suggestions for such speeches presented in this chapter. If there was room for improvement, what might the speaker or you have done more competently?

GROUP ACTIVITIES

1. With two or three other students, visit this website that provides tips for all different sorts of special occasion speeches: http://www.nvcc.edu/home/npeck/spd100/special.htm. Have each student choose a different sort of speech and develop an outline for that speech. Share the outlines with one another and compare and critique the speeches you have developed.

2. Form groups of three to four students. Have each student think back on his or her own professional experiences in organizations and identify a presentation each student has attended. Have each student describe that presentation; say whether its general purpose was educational, informative, or persuasive and report how well the presentation achieved its goal. Also have each student indicate if the form of the presentation was an instruction, training, briefing of some kind, or a recommendation.

3. Form groups of three to four students. Have each student think back on his or her own professional experiences in organizations and identify a presentation he or she attended that was in some way technology assisted. Have each student describe how competently or incompetently the speaker used the presentation technology.

4. Form groups of three to four students. Have each student think back on her or his own social life and identify a special occasion speech she or he attended or presented. Have each student evaluate the presentation based on the suggestions for such speeches presented in this chapter. If there was room for improvement, each student should say what the speaker (herself or his self) might have done more competently.

COMPETENCY CHECKPOINTS AND SELF-ASSESSMENT TOOL

Here is what you need to know and be able to do regarding speaking at work and on special occasions. Determine your level of competency and whether you are ready to proceed to the next chapter. Give yourself one point for each checkpoint you answer satisfactorily.

COMPETENCY CHECKPOINTS	NUMBER OF POINTS
KNOWLEDGE 1. Describe the three types of presentations that occur at work, based on their general purpose.	
2. Explain the impact of globalization and technology on public speaking in 21st century organizations.	
3. Identify and describe the more common forms of educational, informative, and persuasive presentations that occur in contemporary organizations.	

4. Regarding the more common web-based presentation technologies—web casts, web conferencing, and webinars—what are the challenges to competent presenting?
5. Clarify and describe team-based organizations and virtual teams.
6. How is technology facilitating communication and collaboration in geo-dispersed teams?

SKILLS

1. Provide an example of an educational, informative, or persuasive presentation in a real or hypothetical organization and outline how you would develop that presentation using some type of presentation technology.
2. Summarize a situation in a hypothetical organization in which you might need to speak to the media about and develop a strategy for communicating about the situation.
3. Give an example of a special occasion speech that might take place in your life and describe how you would present the speech.

ETHICS AND CREDIBILITY

1. What challenges to credible and ethical communication do competent communicators face when using technology to present or convene meetings in a 21st century organization?

TOTAL CHECKPOINTS (OUT OF A POSSIBLE TEN POINTS)

ENDNOTES

1. Executive Speaking, Inc. Retrieved from http://www.execspeak.com/?gclid=CLq7pIiFwJ4CFQghnAodXFV2pA

2. Drori, G. (2010). Globalization and technology divides: Bifurcation of policy between the "Digital Divide" and the "Innovation Divide." *Sociological Inquiry, 80*(1), 63–91.

3. Chalupsky, H., Gil, Y., Knoblock, C.A., Lerman, K., Oh, J., Pynadath, D.V., Russ, T.A., & Tambe, M. (2002). Electric elves: Agent technology for supporting human organizations. *Artificial Intelligence Magazine, 23*(2), 11–24.

4. Stephens, K.K. & Mottot, T.P. (2008). Interactivity in a web conference Training Context: Effects on trainers and trainees. *Communication Education, 57*(1), 88–104.

5. Shockley-Zalabak, P.S. (2009). *Fundamentals of organizational communication: Knowledge, sensitivity, skills, values (8th Ed.)* Boston: Pearson.

6. Hackman, M.Z. & Johnson, C.E. (2000). *Leadership: A communication perspective.* Prospect Heights, IL: Waveland.

7. Myerson, E. (2008, November 12). *8 tips for effective team presentations.* Retrieved from http://www.powerpoint-ninja.com

8. Timmerman, C.E. & Scott, C.R. (2006). Virtually working: Communicative and structural predictors of media use and key outcomes in virtual work teams. *Communication Monographs, 73*(1), 108–136.

9. Fulk, J. & Collins-Jarvis, L. (2001). Without meetings: Technological mediation of organizational gatherings. In *The new handbook of organizational communication: Advances in theory, research, and methods,* eds. F. Jablin and L. Putnam, 624–663. Thousand Oaks, CA: Sage.

10. Speech Builder Special Occasion Speeches. Retrieved from http://speeches.com/speeches/1/menu/demonstration/speech1.aspx?gclid=CMr7yeyTwJ4CFRafnAodxGtppA

APPENDIX

"If all my possessions and powers were to be taken from me with one exception, I would choose to keep the power of speech, for by it I could soon recover all the rest." Daniel Webster, American statesman and famous orator, 1782–1852

- Standard Outline Format for a Formal Speech
- Motivated Sequence Outline Format for a Persuasive Speech
- The NCA Competent Speaker Speech Evaluation Forms
- Annotated Speeches for Analysis and Discussion
  - An Exemplary Informative Speech
  - An Exemplary Persuasive Speech
  - A Special Occasion Speech
  - A Fictitious Student Speech

STANDARD OUTLINE FORMAT FOR A FORMAL SPEECH

Speech Title: (indicate the speech topic, pique curiosity, be concise)

General Purpose: (to inform, persuade, or entertain)

Specific Purpose: (infinitive statement indicating the goal of the speech)

I. **Introduction** (Written out in full sentences)
    A. Attention-getting or lead-in device
    B. Thesis statement (declarative sentence stating the central idea or claim of the speech and its significance to the audience)
    C. Preview of main points
II. **Body** (support materials that help accomplish the speech purpose, organized into 3–4 main points with subpoints for each main point)
    A. First main point (can be a complete sentence)
        1. Subpoint
        2. Subpoint
        * Transition to next main point (verbal or nonverbal)
    B. Second main point (can be a complete sentence)
        1. Subpoint
        2. Subpoint
        * Transition
III. **Conclusion** (written out in full sentences)
    A. Review of main points
    B. Restatement of the thesis statement
    C. Closing device

MOTIVATED SEQUENCE OUTLINE FORMAT FOR A PERSUASIVE SPEECH

Speech Title: (indicate the speech topic, pique curiosity, be concise)

General Purpose: (to persuade)

Specific Purpose: (infinitive statement indicating the goal of the speech)

I. **Introduction**
    A. **Attention**: Grab the audience's attention and forecast the theme of speech.
II. **Body**
    B. **Need/Problem**: Describe the problem or need, provide evidence of its importance, and relate it to the audience's desires and/or needs.
    C. **Satisfaction/Solution**: Present a plan of action to address the problem or the need.
III. **Conclusion**
    D. **Visualization**: Describe the results of the proposed plan or consequences of the audience's failure to change or to act.
    E. **Action**: Summarize main ideas and call for the audience to change their beliefs or to act or react in the desired manner.

The NCA Competent Speaker Speech Evaluation Form

Course: _____ Semester: _____ Date: _____ Project: _____
Speaker(s): _____

PRESENTATIONAL COMPETENCIES	RATINGS		
	UNSATISFACTORY	SATISFACTORY	EXCELLENT
Competency One: Chooses and narrows a topic appropriate for the audience & occasion			
Competency Two: Communicates the thesis/specific purpose in a manner appropriate for the audience & occasion			
Competency Three: Provides supporting material (including electronic and non-electronic presentational aids) appropriate for the audience & occasion			
Competency Four: Uses an organizational pattern appropriate to the topic, audience, occasion, & purpose			
Competency Five: Uses language appropriate to the audience & occasion			
Competency Six: Uses vocal variety in rate, pitch, & intensity (volume) to heighten & maintain interest appropriate to the audience & occasion			
Competency Seven: Uses pronunciation, grammar, & articulation appropriate to the audience & occasion			
Competency Eight: Uses physical behaviors that support the verbal message			
Summative Score			
General Comments			

The NCA Competent Speaker Holistic Speech Evaluation Form

Course: _____ Semester:_____ Date:_____ Project:_____
Speaker(s):_____

PRESENTATIONAL COMPETENCIES	RATINGS		
	UNSATISFACTORY	SATISFACTORY	EXCELLENT
PREPARATION AND CONTENT ☐ Chooses and narrows topic appropriately ☐ Communicates thesis/specific purpose ☐ Provides appropriate supporting material (includes presentational aids) ☐ Uses an effective organizational pattern			
PRESENTATION AND DELIVERY ☐ Uses language appropriately ☐ Uses vocal variety in rate, pitch, and intensity ☐ Uses appropriate pronunciation, grammar, and articulation ☐ Uses physical (nonverbal) behaviors that support the verbal message			
Summative Score			
General Comments			

ANNOTATED SPEECHES FOR ANALYSIS AND DISCUSSION

Exemplary Speeches from the Interstate Oratorical Society Contest

This national oratorical event produces published proceedings of outstanding speeches of college students from across the country, who participate in the annual competition. The first oratorical contest was held at Galesburg, Illinois on February 27, 1884. Contestants in the interstate contests have gone on to establish themselves meritoriously in a number of professions. While most of the speeches are persuasive, some do use an informative organizational pattern. Two of the highest-ranked, prize-winning speeches from the 2008 and 2009 events, one informative and one persuasive, are presented here in the appendix as fully annotated manuscripts.

Speech One: An exemplary informative speech presented by Kerri Simons, 2008
"Inflammatory Breast Cancer: Developing Awareness of a Silent Killer"

Speech Two: An exemplary persuasive speech presented by Hope Stallings, 2009
"Prosecution Deferred Is Justice Denied"

CONTEMPORARY PUBLIC SPEECHES

Speech Three: A special occasion speech adapted for this textbook
Convocation Speech, August, 2009, University of Colorado at Colorado Springs
Dr. Barbara Swaby

Speech Four: A fictitious student's speech developed for and featured in this textbook
"Pop Music and Globalization: What's the Link Between the Two?
Prepared by Kumar

AN EXEMPLARY INFORMATIVE SPEECH

Presented by Kerri Simons, Northern Illinois University
Coached by Judy Santacaterina
3rd Place in the 2008 137th Annual Contest of the Interstate Oratorical Association

"Inflammatory Breast Cancer: Developing Awareness of a Silent Killer"

This prize-winning speech is an example of speaking to inform as described in Chapter 13. It is mainly informative in organization in that it contains an introduction, three main points, and a conclusion. However, the speaker obviously also has a persuasive goal; so while it is structured as an informative speech, it is somewhat persuasive as well. The way it is persuasive is indicated by the use of a problem-solution structure. Annotations are presented at the end of the speech to help you appreciate how the speech is organized and makes use of various types of support materials. Read the speech and the annotations to see how the speaker, Kerri Simons, accomplishes her specific purpose, which is to develop greater awareness of Inflammatory Breast Cancer or IBC.

1. On July 31, 2007, *Good Morning America's* popular host, Robin Roberts, announced that she was diagnosed with breast cancer. She explained, "I did a self-breast exam and found something women everywhere fear: I found a lump."

2. Like millions of others, Roberts had heard the message time after time in one form or another; surrounded by a sea of pink ribbons, posters, billboards, and public service announcements ,all telling us the same thing: breast self-exams and mammograms can save lives, and fortunately for Roberts and millions of others that is true. In fact, according to the *American Cancer Society*, in the last 20 years breast cancer awareness campaigns have been able to increase survival rates of typical breast cancer by 20 percent.

3. Unfortunately, however, these same breast cancer awareness campaigns have completely ignored the most deadly and aggressive form of breast cancer: Inflammatory Breast Cancer or IBC. IBC is known as a very aggressive and deadly form of breast cancer but also a rare form. The National Cancer Institute states that only about five percent of all breast cancers are inflammatory, and while some of you may be thinking that that statistic is rather low, translated that means more than 9,000 people will be diagnosed with IBC just this year, and because five percent is anything but minimal for those 9,000 people and their families.

4. It's crucial that we first, understand exactly what IBC is and how it differs from other forms of breast cancer, second, discuss the two major causes, which are lack of awareness and misinformation, and finally explore some solutions that can increase awareness, and in turn, save the lives of those who suffer from this deadliest form of breast cancer.

5. Before we begin, it is crucial that we understand just what IBC is and how it differs from other forms of breast cancer. According to the National Cancer Institute, IBC tends to be diagnosed at a younger age when compared with non-IBC breast cancers, and it's important to note that like other types of breast cancer, while primarily found in women, IBC can also be found in men. Unlike other types of breast cancer, however, Inflammatory Breast Cancer almost always presents itself without a lump, making it undetectable by both mammograms and self-breast exams, explains breast cancer specialist Dr. Judy Gralow. Instead, according to the Mayo Clinic, IBC forms in sheets or nests, affecting the lymphatic system, which means the cancer quickly spreads from the breast to the lymph nodes and then to other parts of the body. The symptoms of IBC differ, as well. This type of breast cancer is called inflammatory because the breast often looks red, swollen, or inflamed. The American Public Health Association goes on to explain its other symptoms including intense itching or pain in the breast, ridges, or thickened areas of the skin, an inverted nipple, or a bruise that does not go away.

6. With such visible symptoms, it's surprising that IBC is such a silent killer, but as Lynn Hagerman, a chief executive officer for the Susan G. Komen Foundation points out, "so much emphasis on the lump increases the lack of awareness of other types of breast cancer, including IBC," which brings us to our next point of analysis: the lack of awareness.

7. The unfortunate reality is that both patients and their doctors are either unaware or misinformed regarding IBC. An *ABC National News* report on October 5, 2007, found that most people have never even heard of IBC before. Actually, none of the people interviewed had ever heard of Inflammatory Breast Cancer. Nancy Key, an IBC survivor, was one of those people. After her diagnosis she was dumbfounded. She explains, "How can I have something when I go to the doctor every year [to get mammograms], I do monthly self-exams, I don't even have a lump, yet I have the worst breast cancer there is?"

8. Tragically, patients like Nancy Key are not the only ones who have been conditioned to look for lumps; members of the medical community have been as well. In fact, a May 7, 2006 investigative report by KOMO TV of Seattle, Washington found that only one out of the four cancer centers in the Seattle area had ever heard of Inflammatory Breast Cancer. When told that her own cancer center's help line had no idea what IBC was Dr. Gralow responded, "Wow . . .which means I have some educating of my own staff to do." Sadly, Seattle is not the only place this lack of awareness is taking place; this is a nationwide problem.

9. New Yorker Kathryn Gordon explains, "I'm still angry that my life is being threatened by something I have never even heard of, and my doctor, who I consider a well-prepared woman, didn't have a clue either." Even if doctors do know about IBC, many are misinformed. A 25-year-old mother of three in Georgia went to doctor for swollen, painful breast. Two different doctors prescribed her two different antibiotics to no avail. Because no lump showed up on her mammogram, no biopsy was ordered, and the doctors kept telling her that she was too young to have breast cancer. Unfortunately, she's not the only case of misdiagnosis. People who share their stories on the IBC Support Group website have similar experiences. One woman's IBC was first diagnosed as spider bites. Another woman's doctor told her that in order for her pain and itching to stop, she needed to stop wearing an underwire bra. One man was misdiagnosed with three different things before even being tested for IBC.

10. In *The Star* on October 27, 2007, Dr. Massimo Cristofanilli, explains, "I see this all the time. By the time most doctors 'figure it out,' the cancer has already spread throughout the lymphatic system and to the major organs of the body, and by this stage, the cancer is very deadly." In other words, according to the Inflammatory Breast Cancer Research Foundation, when IBC is diagnosed, the cancer is already in stage 3-B or stage 4 cancer. There is no stage 5.

11. By now we should be aware that this abysmal lack of awareness and misinformation is robbing victims of that precious early diagnosis and a stronger chance of survival.

12. Fortunately, there are steps that each of us can take to help win this battle against Inflammatory Breast Cancer.

13. First, encourage your congress person to follow the lead of Senator Tim Jennings from New Mexico. Jennings proposed legislature to earmark $3.2 million for IBC research. As he points out, "this isn't a state issue, it isn't even a funding issue, this is a humanity issue."

14. Second, educate yourself, and if you may be experiencing some symptoms of IBC, advocate for yourself, because as we've seen, too many doctors are either unaware or misinformed regarding IBC.

15. And please, continue to get mammograms and do the monthly self-breast exam, and keep in mind, this does go for men, as well. Just don't narrow your search to the lump—look for redness, the inverted nipple, or the bruise that may not go away.

16. And consider asking your doctor about digital mammography, which is now being covered by most insurance companies. Digital mammography provides a three-dimensional view of the inner structures of the breast, and unlike traditional mammography, can detect Inflammatory Breast Cancer.

17. Finally, educate others because as Lani Barfield, an IBC advocate, points out, "just because it is not as common as non-IBC breast cancers, is not a good reason not to know about it." I have compiled an informational handout that I have passed out on my campus, and to my family and friends. I encourage each of you to take one after this speech and do the same. The number one way to win this battle is with knowledge.

18. Get the word out because this solution of awareness is simple, but more importantly, it's effective. Take, for example, the pink campaign by the Susan G. Komen Foundation. In the last 20 years, by promoting mammograms and breast self-exams, they have been able to boost the survival rate of typical breast cancer from 75 percent to 95 percent and in some cases, 97 percent. Right now, according to the Inflammatory Breast Cancer Research Foundation, IBC has a survival rate of only 40 percent, and *Reuters' Health* goes on to explain that the average survival time for IBC patients is only 2.9 years. Imagine what increased awareness could do for IBC.

19. Throughout this speech, we've learned what Inflammatory Breast Cancer is and how it differs from other types of breast cancer, we've discussed the lack of awareness and misinformation not only in patients, but in doctors and cancer centers, as well, and we have explored some extremely simple solutions. The most important solution? Awareness. In the last ten minutes, you have been given the most effective tool to win this battle: knowledge. Share it. For those 9,000 people. Share it.

"Inflammatory Breast Cancer: Developing Awareness of a Silent Killer"
Annotations of the Speech

1. Introduction—Attention Getter: The speaker opens with the straightforward announcement by a television personality on-the-air, Robin Roberts, who says she has breast cancer—something every woman dreads.
2. The speaker sets up her topic by reminding the audience of how familiar and effective the "pink" campaign by the American Cancer Society has been with pink ribbons and reminders of annual mammograms.
3. The thesis is presented here…*these same breast cancer awareness campaigns have completely ignored the most deadly and aggressive form of breast cancer, Inflammatory Breast Cancer or IBC.* After the speaker introduces her topic, she provides background as to its importance.
4. The speaker previews what she will cover during the speech and uses the preview as a transition to the body of the speech and her first main point.
5. Body of the Speech: This is the first main point, stated simply:…*it is crucial that we understand just what IBC is and how it differs from other forms of breast cancer.*
6. This sentence serves as a transition to the next main point:…*which brings us to our next point of analysis: the lack of awareness.*
7. The speaker supports her second main point about unawareness of IBC by first citing a source with whom most of us are familiar, ABC National News. Then she provides a second example of lack of awareness, a quotation from an IBC survivor.
8. The speaker continues to reinforce her second point by citing a credible source that discovered information hot lines for local cancer centers were unaware of IBC.
9. The speaker continues with more personal stories of misdiagnosis.
10. Here the speaker cites an official source, a newspaper that quotes a physician who describes how misdiagnosis of the disease can be fatal: *There is no stage 5.*
11. This sentence provides a transition to the speaker's final and main point three.
12. The speaker moves to her third main point:…*there are steps that each of us can take to help win this battle against Inflammatory Breast Cancer.*
13. The speaker, in a series of subpoints, details the steps to be taken as a solution to the problem already described. *First, encourage your congress person…*

14. The second subpoint: *second, educate yourself...*
15. The third subpoint:...*continue to get mammograms and do the monthly self-breast exam*
16. The fourth subpoint: *consider asking your doctor about digital mammography.*
17. The fifth subpoint: *educate others...*
18. Here the speaker issues a call for action on the part of her listeners by telling them they can save lives. This call is much like the visualization step when a speaker uses the motivated sequence; *Imagine what increased awareness could do for IBC.*
19. Conclusion. The speaker summarizes what the audience has learned about IBC and reiterates the discussion topics presented in her main points: understanding what IBC is, the lack of awareness on the part of the health community and the public in general, and need to share the message with others.

AN EXEMPLARY PERSUASIVE SPEECH

Presented by Hope Stallings, Berry College
Coached by Randy Richardson and Melanie Conrad
1st Place in the 2009 138th Annual Contest of the Interstate Oratorical Association

"Prosecution Deferred Is Justice Denied"

This prize-winning speech is an example of speaking to persuade as described in Chapter 14. The speech is mainly persuasive in organization in that it contains discernible persuasive steps based on the motivated sequence: attention, need (problem), satisfaction (solution), and a call to action step with some visualization included in it. The speech also uses information and evidence to illustrate the severity of the problem. Annotations are presented at the end of the speech to illustrate how the speech is organized and makes use of support materials. Read the speech and the annotations to see how the speaker, Hope Stallings, accomplishes her specific purpose, which is to develop awareness of the problem of deferred prosecution agreements and motivate listeners to become involved in political activism and encouraging awareness of the problem.

1. What do Morgan Stanley, Wachovia, Fannie Mae, Merrill Lynch, and AIG all have in common? You might say that they all contributed to the credit crisis in September, and according to the *Washington Post* of March 25, 2009, the ensuing $787 billion government bailout of big business. And you'd be right—partially. You see, these corporations have something else in common. In the past five years, each has been indicted on criminal charges like fraud. Never heard about the trial or verdict? That's because in spite of their fraudulent behavior, these corporations never went to court. They avoided media spotlight, investor scrutiny, and public outrage by entering into deferred prosecution agreements.
2. The *Record* of July 21, 2008 explains that deferred prosecution agreements allow corporations to avoid criminal convictions by paying a small fine out of court. In other words, these companies paid our government to ensure that we remain ignorant, and we have, right up to the collapse of our economy and our personal financial security.
3. In their current form, deferred prosecution agreements, or DPAs, are unethical, unjust, and flat out wrong. In this new day, we must work together with our new administration and new Congress to reform madness and reclaim justice.

4. To become a part of this reformation of DPAs, we first need to understand the details of deferred prosecution agreements; we'll then consider causes, and finally formulate solutions.

5. According to the *Mondaq News Alert* of April 22, 2008, a deferred prosecution agreement occurs when a prosecutor files an indictment for a company that has committed a crime, and that indictment is put on hold in exchange for a commitment by that company to reform and pay a fine. If the company meets the obligation listed in the agreement, the prosecutor, also called a corporate monitor, asks the judge to dismiss the indictment, and the company gets away without a criminal conviction. In a DPA, the government collects fines and then appoints a corporate monitor to impose internal changes with little to no Department of Justice guidelines.

6. *American Banker* of December 12, 2008 reports that DPAs are becoming unfortunately more common, as our now frail banking system means that banks and corporations that formerly might have been a target of criminal charges may now face the lighter load of a DPA. And the numbers agree. The *Corporate Crime Reporter* revealed on January 29, 2009 that between 2003 and 2009, there were 112 reported corporate DPAs, compared to only 11 between 1992 and 2001.

7. One hundred twelve might not seem like many, but consider the devastating impact that just one of these ineffective DPAs can have on our economy. The *Wall Street Journal* of March 27, 2009 reports that in 2004, insurance giant AIG avoided criminal charges for fraud by entering into a deferred prosecution agreement. AIG paid a $126 million fine and was appointed a corporate monitor, but in 2008, found itself under another federal investigation for the same thing; the *Wall Street Journal* says that this time, AIG's fraud contributed to its downfall in September's credit crisis. And AIG is not alone. Even household names such as American Express, Monster.com, Chevron, AmSouth Bank, KPMG, and Countrywide Financial have all avoided criminal convictions by entering into DPAs.

8. Or consider the case of Powers Fasteners, which entered into a DPA to avoid a manslaughter charge after the Boston Big Dig tunnel collapse. According to the *Washington Post* of December 18, 2008, Powers Fasteners agreed to pay $16 million and recall the faulty epoxy that caused the collapse. But that's cold consolation to the family of Milena DeValle, who was killed after being crushed by 26 tons of ceiling panels as a result of the epoxy. DPAs are allowing corporations to get away with murder. Literally.

9. Deferred prosecution agreements clearly run counter to our ideals of justice and fairness. We therefore need to understand why they occur, namely corporate corruption, government collusion, and public delusion.

10. The first cause of this problem is that corporations have abandoned ethical behavior in search of profit. The *Associated Press* reported on March 10, 2008 that though deferred prosecution agreements were originally designed to allow individuals, such as juveniles and first-time drug offenders, to reform without the stigma of a conviction, corporations started entering into DPAs about fifteen years ago for the same reasons: to avoid the scandal and revenue decrease associated with criminal charges. And if the corporation's executives pull the right strings, it will even get to choose its own corporate monitor in the DPA. According to the previously cited *Mondaq News Alert*, the corporate monitor is either appointed by the U.S. Department of Justice or selected by the corporation itself. Because this monitor acts as prosecutor, judge, and jury for the corporation with few guidelines, choosing a former employee, friend, or political ally for a corporate monitor often results in no internal changes and the indictment still being dropped.

11. The second cause is that the government is in collusion with Corporate America. The October 2008 issue of the *Metropolitan Corporate Counsel* reported that the post-indictment collapse of Arthur Andersen prompted U.S. Attorney General Larry Thompson to release the Thompson Memorandum, which made it easier for corporations to enter into DPAs. By encouraging corporations to enter into DPAs, the Department of Justice sought to save the economy from the results of another fraud scandal while cleaning out the court docket and staying friendly with big business. *Time Magazine* of March 30, 2009 states that Washington simply looked the other way in regards to corporate crime, allowing corporations to break rules without serious repercussions in order to make friends.

12. The final cause is public delusion. Since the collapse of Enron, we've been deluded into thinking that we've got it all covered. The events of the last few months have made tragically and abundantly clear that we do not. According to the *Associated Press* of April 7, 2009, deferred prosecution agreements didn't draw any attention until 2008 after it was disclosed that John Ashcroft had been secretly selected as a corporate monitor. With the Ashcroft assignment, DPAs finally made the news. But because it's difficult to explain deferred prosecution agreements without using legal or financial jargon, DPAs have not been widely discussed by the mainstream media that seeks to write on a fourth grade reading level. Additionally, the U.S. House of Representatives documents revealed on May 22, 2008 that some DPAs are never made public at all, and even Congress and the Department of Justice have difficulties counting just how many have occurred covertly in recent years.

13. Now that we understand the catastrophic impact of DPAs on our economy and personal economic well-being, we should be sufficiently angry to do something about it. I wish I could say that solutions come on three levels: corporate, governmental, and individual, but I can't. The fact is, we've hoped for too long that corporations could monitor themselves, and we've all felt the results of their failure to do so. Now is the time for the government to step in with the support of the people and change the current state of DPAs.

14. Though banishing corporate deferred prosecution agreements completely is a long-term solution, it is more practical for Congress to pass legislation altering DPAs and mandating that they be made public. Representatives Bill Pascrell and Steve Cohen are attempting to do just that through the Accountability in Deferred Prosecution Act. The *States News Service* of April 2, 2009 reveals that the Accountability in Deferred Prosecution Act of 2009 will regulate corporate deferred prosecution agreements in federal criminal cases. The bill will set guidelines ensuring an open and public process and will prevent corporations from choosing their own corporate monitor, which brings us to personal solutions.

15. We must become active in this fight for justice through political activism and encouraging awareness. Contact your congressional representatives in support of the Accountability in Deferred Prosecution Act of 2009. Without encouragement from us, the bill may not gain enough votes to pass the House and the Senate. Second, though it sounds cliché, we must spread awareness of this issue. Because the cause of public delusion can only be solved by awareness, and as long as we're apathetic about awareness of DPAs, the problems will continue. I challenge you to take two minutes—just two minutes—today to talk to someone else at this tournament about DPAs. Mention it to your friends or coworkers back home; contact your local media. I have compiled a fact sheet to help you to do just that; please take one after the round. Also, visit my website www.dangersofdpas.org, on which you can find the latest news about DPAs, examples of real-life DPAs, and links to contact your represen-

tatives in support of the Accountability in Deferred Prosecution Act. By taking small steps toward awareness now, we can ignite change.

16. So today, by understanding the problems, causes and solutions of corporate deferred prosecution agreements, we've learned how to become part of the reformation. We cannot let these corporate wrongdoings continue. AIG, Fannie Mae, and Merrill Lynch are institutions that we've trusted with our financial investments, and until the trust between institution and individual can be reestablished, we must invest in reforms that will end this shameful, unethical, and unjust practice of corporate deferred prosecution agreements once and for all.

"Prosecution Deferred is Justice Denied"
Annotations of the Speech

1. Introduction—Attention Getter: The speaker begins with a question in order to engage the listeners' attention and begins to describe the problem of failure to punish fraudulent behavior.

2. The speaker sets up his topic by giving a brief description of a deferred prosecution agreement (DPA) and how this practice contributed to the collapse of the economy.

3. The thesis presented here is how unjust/unfair DPAs are and issues a call to action.

4. This sentence provides a transition and preview from the introduction and attention getter to the main body of the speech, starting with the description of the problem/need.

5. Body of the Speech: This paragraph begins the first main point with a thorough description of the problem, a discussion and in-depth explanation of DPAs.

6. First subpoint:...*banks and corporations that formerly might have been a target of criminal charges may now face the lighter load of a DPA.* The speaker supports the first main point of how unjust/unfair a DPA is by citing official sources that address both the increase of DPAs and the evasion of criminal charges by corporations.

7. Second subpoint:...*devastating impact that just one of these ineffective DPAs can have on our economy.* The speaker supports his argument by again citing an official source (*Wall Street Journal*) that describes the impact of DPAs on the national economy.

8. Third subpoint:...*DPAs are allowing corporations to get away with murder.* The speaker hammers home the unfairness of DPAs by citing the *Washington Post* article of a DPA that covered up manslaughter charges.

9. Here the speaker provides a transition from the first point (how bad DPAs are) to the second main point, which is why DPAs occur. This transition also serves as theme reinforcer for the speech.

10. First subpoint: The speaker explains the first cause of the problem:...*corporations have abandoned ethical behavior.* This statement bolsters the first point that DPAs are unfair and unethical. And not only are DPAs unethical, corporations take it a step further by appointing their own monitors to evade any punishment.

11. Second subpoint: The speaker moves to the second cause of the problem:...*government is in collusion with Corporate America.* The speaker specifically mentions that the Department of Justice itself is working hand in hand with large corporations to establish DPAs. She cites *Time Magazine* to strengthen the scandalous connection between government and large corporations.

12. Third subpoint: The speaker explains the final cause of the problem:...*public delusion.* A quotation from the Associated Press is used to indicate governmental involvement in DPAs and that, because DPAs are difficult to explain in the press, they are not a major news topic.

13. The speaker now provides a transition from the problem (what it is and why it occurs) to the solution or satisfaction step of the persuasive speech. A preliminary description of the solution is included: *Now is the time for the government to step in with the support of the people and change the current state of DPAs.*

14. Here the speaker begins to describe a solution to the problem of DPAs—*it is more practical for Congress to pass legislation altering DPAs and mandating that they be made public.* The speaker describes the bill being proposed in Congress to defeat DPAs.

15. With this clarion call to action, the speaker gives the listeners concrete steps to take by urging them to call their congressional representatives and giving them a website to get more information. Note that the speaker includes negative visualization in this action step, that is, what will happen if the listeners fail to act:...*as long as we're apathetic about awareness of DPAs, the problems will continue.*

16. Conclusion: The speaker brings us full circle by reviewing what has been presented in the speech and making one final call to action. She reminds the listeners they have learned about *the problems, causes and solutions of corporate deferred prosecution agreements,* but they also have learned *how to become a part of the reformation.*

A SPECIAL OCCASION SPEECH

Convocation Speech, August 2009
University of Colorado at Colorado Springs
Dr. Barbara Swaby

This convocation speech is an excellent example of the special occasion speeches described in Chapter 15. It was presented at the 2009 convocation ceremony at the University of Colorado at Colorado Springs, a public event that initiates the new academic year. The speaker and author of the speech, Dr. Barbara Swaby, is a Professor of Education and President's Teaching Scholar at University of Colorado. The speech is structured informatively, using two main points, but it clearly has a persuasive purpose as well. If we had to write a purpose statement for Dr. Swaby, it might sound something like this: To motivate incoming freshmen to value their undergraduate educational experience and to work hard and appreciate the opportunity provided to them by their parents and the university. Annotations are presented at the end of the speech to show you how the speech was developed and organized. Read the speech and the annotations to see how Swaby tries to accomplish her purpose using support materials such as advice from a best-selling book, *The Last Lecture,* and a poem about choice written by a former U.S. poet laureate, Robert Frost.

1. Thank you Provost Bacon, for that most generous introduction. Chancellor Shockley, Provost Bacon, faculty, visitors, parents and students: I am honored to have been asked to share with you this afternoon. I wish both to welcome and to congratulate the freshmen class of 2009, the future graduating class of 2013. This event somewhat marks the beginning of your adult journey. I applaud you.

2. I have been asked to share with you some of the life lessons that have framed my journey and that also relate to Randy Pausch's book *The Last Lecture*, a book that was required reading for all incoming freshmen.

3. For those of you who are visitors and who may be unfamiliar with the book…very briefly… *The Last Lecture* is a book of life lessons written by Dr. Randy Pausch, a professor at Carnegie Mellon University. In 2006, he was diagnosed with deadly pancreatic cancer. He gave his last lecture, which shared his diagnosis and his life lessons with his students. The content of the book also became life lessons to be shared with his three very young children after his death. Dr. Pausch lost his battle with cancer in 2008. The book is a book about life and the courage to live it…and about the lessons that charted the life journey of this courageous and brilliant man.

4. First, a brief word to the parents of our freshman students. Eight years ago, I sat as you do now…as a parent of an incoming freshman…experiencing much of the same ambivalence— the same emotions that you most likely feel now. I assure you—as a parent—that you need not experience any more than the inevitable and unavoidable anxiety as you leave your sons and daughters in this our UCCS community.

5. UCCS will provide for your offspring an environment of physical safety, of varied academic, social and personal resources, dynamic academic opportunity and of open access to staff members, professors and administrators. The campus will indeed honor and promote the status of adulthood of its students…yet it also will make available a network of assistance and support options to all its students. Your sons and daughters are in the right place.

6. I wish this afternoon to direct my comments to the freshman class. I will identify two major themes or lessons from *The Last Lecture* which lessons have also been significant in my own academic journey. These themes are: Gratitude and Choice.

7. Lesson One: Gratitude

    Gratitude is certainly a robust and enduring theme of the book, *The Last Lecture*. It seems incongruous that this man—dying of cancer—should be so focused on gratitude. The dedication of his book reads: With thanks to my parents who allowed me to dream. His book ends with acknowledgements and thanks to his colleagues, family and students… and strewn throughout the book is that theme of gratitude.

8. There is a Chinese proverb that states: Those who drink the water must remember those who dug the well.

    Today more than ever, is a perfect time to reflect on this lesson…as you take a giant step toward adulthood. Each of you has made significant achievements in your relatively short life. I applaud you. You have completed successfully your high school experiences and have achieved well enough to earn a place in this academic community. This accomplishment is no insignificant achievement.

9. One million of your contemporaries dropped out of high school in 2008 and we anticipate another million in 2009. Only 71 percent of your peers graduate from high school within the traditional four-year span. You have put in your time. You have earned your space here. We congratulate you.

10. However, it is critical that you reflect on the many individuals who have made this reality possible for you, your family, teachers, administrators, mentors and friends…but most important, your parents. Most of you are here today as the direct result of the commitment, sacrifice, personal investment and reassurance of your parents.

    It is my hope and suggestion that you acknowledge their support and do so often.

In the Fall of 1964, I left my native country of Jamaica in the West Indies as a 15-year-old girl and joined the Freshman class of Tusculum College in totally segregated Greeneville, Tennessee. I will not take the time to remind you of the sociological and political realities of the Southern United States in 1964; Sufficient to say, I was the first and only black student on that campus and remained such for the following three years. But how did a 15-year-old girl from Jamaica end up in Greeneville, Tennessee?

I am so thankful that I learned what gratitude was very early: first from my esteemed parents, then from a series of unbelievable and incredible events which reinforced in me lessons of gratitude learned in my family.

11. Randy Pausch begins Chapter 4 of his book with the words:

"I won the parent lottery." I won that lottery as well. I am the youngest of three children. Our parents were both teachers and principals and my father was also a Presbyterian pastor. They lived their lives in complete commitment to their Christian faith…they demonstrated an unswerving dedication to the education of the poor and they devoted their lives in total to their family.

12. Of all the physical objects retained from my childhood, my most cherished is a small packet of letters written to me over the years by my parents. When my parents came to live with our family in 1997, my father presented me with a small package containing letters from both parents, several duplicated using carbon paper, completely unfamiliar to most of you…I am sure.

I wish to share with you a paragraph from a letter written to me by my father in November of 1964…three months after I began college. I quote:

"I recognize that you are now on your own and are submerged in the independence that you so desire. Please understand…this is meant to be a criticism! Nevertheless, let me remind you of a few imperatives as you enter college. Your mother was completely unprepared for your departure from home at such an early age. She is having a difficult time adjusting to your absence. It is my expectation that you will write to her more than sporadically, and show your appreciation for her investment in your upbringing and her enduring attention to your welfare. This I expect. You should do this out of extreme thankfulness…but if obligation needs to be your motivation, let it. It should be done."

13. This lesson of gratitude was reinforced in me by two incredible life events.

First: my entrance to college.

I completed my high school requirements and matriculated to college in 1963. Because I was only 14 years old, I spent the next year teaching in the elementary school at which my mother was the principal. I was also a pianist and was practicing for the upcoming national piano examinations. One Sunday morning there arrived in Church a visitor, not unlike the many individuals who visited our church each week. I had played for the morning services that Sunday. At the end of the service, my father called me and introduced me to this visitor….a Dr. Raymond Rankin, whom I assumed was a medical doctor. I was asked to perform one of the classical pieces required for the Grade 8 Nationals. I did…he commended me…and that I thought was that.

About three weeks later, I received a letter from the United States. It came from Tusculum College, the office of the President: Dr. Raymond Rankin…the same man for whom I had played the piano a few weeks prior. He offered me a four-year scholarship to Tusculum College. This complete stranger saw in me some potential and extended to me such extreme generosity with absolutely no guarantee that his investment would pay off.

14. Many believe the old adage…Lightning never strikes in the same place twice. Well for me, it did. Four years later, in 1968, I graduated from Tusculum and returned to teach at the schools of my parents. Not only did I have a full teaching load, but I also was the house mother of the boarding girls, girls who lived on campus throughout each semester. One evening, three years later in 1971, I was overseeing the evening homework period, when I became aware of a car very slowly driving down our driveway. Naturally, I went out to investigate. There I met a man, obviously an American, who introduced himself as Calvin Didier. He was visiting the island and had become hopelessly lost. In addition, his car had a flat tire. Of course, I invited him in and introduced him to my parents. Fortunately, we had a watchman on duty and because it was by then quite dark, I held a flashlight as the watchman changed this man's tire. He was very thankful…he had enjoyed meeting and speaking with my parents… said his goodbyes…and that was that…another experience in the catalogue of my memory. About one month later, I received a letter from The House of Hope Presbyterian Church in St. Paul, Minnesota, Rev. Calvin Didier, Senior Pastor. It read:

"The Women's Association of the House of Hope Presbyterian Church would like to offer you a scholarship to earn your masters degree at any university of your choice in the world. Lesson: Be ever prepared and responsive: You have no idea when opportunities will present themselves."

For me, lightning did indeed strike twice. That church backed me for seven years as I read for my masters and my PhD degrees. The major point that I want to make, however, is this: How does one show gratitude for one's entire academic experience? How does one show gratitude for a lifetime of support from one's parents?

15. Here is what I learned: I learned that giving is the most eloquent form of gratitude. Gratitude is best demonstrated by giving back, by paying forward.

Pausch says it well in his statement: "Go and do for others what someone did for you."

My work here at UCCS, my involvement in the LOGO Project which gives books to children, my commitment to providing hundreds of free reading evaluations each year to community children, my providing free reading clinics to children, all are directly linked to my enduring gratitude first to and FOR my parents, to Dr. Raymond Rankin, and Reverend Calvin Didier.

UCCS will provide you with a wide variety of opportunities to give back…to honor the gifts of your parents and families…by serving your peers, your colleges, your university, and your community. I encourage you to take advantage of one of these opportunities and allow yourselves to prove that giving indeed is the most eloquent form of gratitude.

16. Lesson Two: Choice

Forty-five years ago, almost to the day, I sat and listened to the president of our college deliver the convocation address to the incoming freshmen of 1964. It was then that I was introduced to the poem which has become my favorite poem in our language:

"Two roads diverged in a yellow wood. And sorry I could not travel both and be one traveler. Long I stood and looked down as far as I could to where it bent in the undergrowth. Then took the other.…as just…as fair.…and having perhaps the better claim. Because it was grassy and wanted wear. Though, as for that, the passing there had worn them really about the same. And both that morning equally lay in leaves no feet had trodden black. Oh, I left the first for another day. Yet knowing how way leads on to way, I doubted if I should ever come back. I should be telling this with a sigh somewhere ages and ages hence. Two roads diverged in a wood, and I? I took the one less traveled by...and that has made all the difference." Robert Frost: "The Road Not Taken": 1915

Well...welcome to that yellow wood, perhaps the most important and memorable experience of your life to this point.

This day is predominantly about choice.

The University of Colorado has chosen you to join our learning community.

You have chosen to accept the invitation. You have made the right choice.

BUT...this is a symbiotic relationship:

I am sure you have high expectations of us. No doubt, you expect exposure to new academic disciplines, viewpoints, cultures, passions, philosophies and conversations.

I have no doubt we will exceed your expectations.

Know, however, that we have equally high expectations of each of you. We hope you bring with you an uncontainable inquisitiveness and a boundless desire to learn.

We look forward to hearing your new perspectives in science, mathematics, music, art, education, English, engineering, business, technology and in all the other areas available on our campus.

We anxiously await learning about your unique perspectives. You all will add immeasurable richness to the texture of our university community.

17. The choices that you make...each and every one of them...will indeed create the blueprint of the life you will lead...the people you will eventually become. Shortly before my father's death, I asked him if there was anything specific he regretted in his life. His response was immediate. He said,

"I wish that I had understood fully very early in my youth...that every single action of my present...would become a thread in the permanent tapestry of my future."

In this large yellow wood, I would encourage you to embrace your power to choose and to recognize that the choices you make each and every day will indeed chart the course of your future.

18. Perhaps my very favorite quote from Pausch's book is this:

"You can't control the cards you are dealt: just how you play the hand."

Your choices are yours. This is the time for you to examine who you are, who you want to become, which of your family lessons...your family values...you will internalize...which you will choose to make your own. I trust you will play your hand well...with honor, integrity and courage.

19. I end with another paragraph from the freshman letter of my father: I quote:

"Your grades are of critical importance. In order to have an enjoyable, fulfilling and successful college experience, first you must ensure you remain in college. You have had years of academic practice: You should require few reminders of what it takes to achieve academic success. I exhort you to take the following behavioral suggestions: You are far away from home and must alone embrace your destiny by making these appropriate choices purposely.

- Attend all your classes.
- Sit in front of the class so that you will not be overcome by inattention.
- Be responsible for your own learning. Do your homework before you ask for assistance.
- Ask your professors for assistance whenever needed.
- You know what study and practice are: Apply the knowledge.
- Your health is important. Rest, eat properly, and stay active.
- Find an immediate opportunity to serve and practice generosity liberally.

- You are generally well mannered and pleasant. Make a distinct effort to raise "generally" to "predominantly."
- These choices will lead to good health, personal happiness, and academic success. Know however, that the choice remains yours."
- This advice given to me by my father…. I give with hope to each of you. I wish you all successful choices.
- On behalf of the administration, faculty, and staff of the UCCS community, once again I am delighted to welcome you to our university.

We look forward to a rewarding and enjoyable exchange with each of you.

Your college experience has now officially begun.

Convocatum est.

Thank you.

Convocation Speech, August 2009, University of Colorado at Colorado Springs
Annotations of the Speech

1. Dr. Swaby begins this speech, as most special occasion presentations often do, by acknowledging special guests and dignitaries and the freshmen class to whom she is speaking.
2. This sentence serves as a transition to introduce *The Last Lecture*.
3. Here, Swaby uses her introductory remarks to provide a framework for her speech by describing the book, *The Last Lecture*, and its author. This introduction accomplishes two goals—yes, it provides the framework for the two main points to be covered in the speech, but it also motivates the listeners to become intrigued by and involved in the advice she is about to provide to the freshmen class.
4. Realizing many parents of freshmen also are in the audience, here Dr. Swaby respectfully provides a few remarks for those listeners and sets the stage for emphasizing respect for parents, which she skillfully weaves throughout her entire speech.
5. Here Dr. Swaby reiterates her respect for parents by reassuring them the university is deserving of the opportunity to educate their children….*Your sons and daughters are in the right place.*
6. Swaby clearly introduces and previews the entire speech and her two main points, the two major themes or lessons from *The Last Lecture*: gratitude and choice.
7. The first main point and lesson from the book, gratitude, is expansively developed and supported with quotations from the book and personal and professional examples from Swaby's own life. Stories of her life lessons about gratitude are interwoven in the discussion using impressive and memorable examples.
8. Here the speaker chooses to use a proverb from another source to provide interest for her listeners while indirectly addressing respect for parents…*those that drink the water must remember those who dug the well.*
9. Dr. Swaby uses statistics to make a first subpoint to students that they are already extraordinary: *One million of your contemporaries dropped out of high school in 2008.*
10. In this sentence, she talks about gratitude to others and, most important, to parents. She provides a second subpoint, her own story of gratitude and respect for her parents.
11. Swaby now uses a quote from the book—*I won the parent lottery*—to both reinforce her theme of gratitude and provide a transition to her next story of the letters she received from her father.

12. She shares her story of letters she received from her father and his admonition to show gratitude toward her mother.

13. This statement is a clear transition to her third subpoint about two incredible life events that exemplify showing gratitude. The first is about a complete stranger who *saw in me some potential and extended to me such extreme generosity.*

14. Dr. Swaby expands the third subpoint by describing a second incredible life using the phrase: *For me, lightning did indeed strike twice.*

15. The speaker summarizes the entire first main point of her speech and what she learned about gratitude: *giving indeed is the most eloquent form of gratitude.*

16. The second main point and lesson from the book focuses on choice and uses a poem by Robert Frost to make the point about how important choices are in life. Swaby reads the poem, which is a short one. Then she personalizes the poem for the students by talking about the choice they made to start their undergraduate education.

17. She uses a quotation from her dying father and a quotation from *The Last Lecture* book to emphasize the importance of choice-making in the freshmen students' lives.

18. Dr Swaby circles back to tie-in *The Last Lecture* to her main point of choices by quoting Randy Pausch on choice: *You can't control the cards you are dealt; just how you play the hand.*

19. Swaby's conclusion is memorable as she quotes again from one of her father's letters. His advice to her provides some concrete suggestions for the students in the audience about making appropriate choices as freshmen. She encourages the student listeners to make good choices and she eloquently welcomes them to campus community...*Convocatum est.*

A FICTITIOUS STUDENT SPEECH

Pop Music and Globalization: What's the Link Between the Two?

By Kumar

The development and preparation of this fictitious student speech is described in Part Two: Preparing a Speech. A detailed outline, used to prepare this manuscript of the speech, is provided in Chapter 8. The speech is structured as an informative speech but clearly is somewhat persuasive as well. Annotations are presented at the end of the speech to help you appreciate how the speech is organized and makes use of various types of support materials. Read the speech and the annotations to see how the speaker, Kumar, tries to accomplish the specific purpose: to develop greater understanding of the potential positive influence of pop music on cultures around the world.

1. How many of you have ever heard of Paul David Hewson? A few of you? Good.

2. Well, Paul David Hewson, most commonly known by his stage name Bono, is an Irish singer and musician, best known as the main vocalist of the Irish rock band, U2. Bono writes almost all U2 lyrics, and he often uses political, social, and religious themes. Outside U2, Bono is widely known for his tireless activism concerning social and political problems in Africa. He has cofounded several international organizations, such as DATA, which stands for Debt, AIDS, Trade, Africa. He has also helped to organize and perform in numerous benefit concerts, such as the 2005 Live 8 concert. Bono, praised and criticized for his activism, has been nominated for the Nobel Peace Prize, granted an honorary knighthood by Queen Elizabeth II, and named Person of the Year by *Time* magazine. Bono is the only person to have been nominated for an Academy Award, Golden Globe, Grammy, and Nobel Peace Prize (Bono,

2009). These awards acknowledge how Bono uses his status as a pop music icon on behalf of others.

3. Bono effectively uses pop music to create multicultural awareness and understanding of the plights and problems of people in other cultures. He is a good example of how popular music, which is highly influential around the world, can be used as the stimulant and glue to bring people together.

4. We will begin today by looking at how popular music, as a result of global media, is becoming increasingly global and multicultural. Given this globalization of the music industry, it is evident that popular music has great potential for promoting multicultural understanding.

5. Popular music is becoming increasingly global and multicultural.

6. In fact a study done by de Block and Rydin in 2006 clearly shows the emergence and influence of global media. These authors observed how youth cultures are becoming increasingly global, as media exposure to different parts of the world is now allowing young people to recognize, identify with, and adopt similar styles of music, fashion, graphics, and dance.

7. As you can see by this slide, there are many internationally successful popular musicians. Madonna sold around $225 million dollars worth of music worldwide!

8. The advances that have been made in media technology have allowed the globalization of pop music to become a reality. For example, in July of 2005, it was estimated that 1 million people attended Live 8 concerts that were held to support the *Make Poverty History* campaign. These concerts were held all over the world—London, Paris, Rome, Philadelphia, Barrie (near Toronto), Berlin, Tokyo, Johannesburg, and Moscow.

9. AOLmusic.com was a partner in the venture and reported more than 5 million people watched the concerts live online. There were more than 175,000 simultaneous video streams registered, a third more than the previous biggest online video event! America Online called it "The Day Music Changed the World." In all, it has been estimated that 1 billion people across the globe watched the concerts either live, on TV, or via the Internet!

10. Henry Wadsworth Longfellow noted that "music is the universal language of mankind." The tremendous audience support for the Live 8 concerts reflects how universal music truly can be and how pop music is influencing other cultures worldwide.

11. Now you have a better understanding of the extent to which popular music is becoming global. Let's go on and consider how that globalization process can benefit people worldwide.

12. As I stated earlier, pop music has the potential to promote multicultural understanding.

13. I think this is especially true for today's younger generation. I personally came to appreciate Western culture more fully because of American pop music. I and my Indian family traveled from India to London in 2005 and we were fortunate enough to get to attend the Hyde Park Live 8 concert. It was amazing; I got to see U2 and my favorite singer, Bono. There were some other major stars, like Elton John, Pink Floyd and Madonna, who sang while she held the hand of a girl named Birhan Woldu. It was a news report about Birhan Woldu and others who were starving in Africa that was the catalyst for the Live 8 concert! It was pretty powerful and my whole family still remembers that day! That concert was an important event, and I feel the music was really directed more at my generation than my parents'—it impacted all of us, but it had the biggest influence on me and my siblings!

14. Based on my experience at the Live 8 concert, I believe exposure to music of other cultures can help to promote multicultural understanding and I am not alone.

15. On the World Music Coalition website and e-mail listserv, there are all manner of artists collaborating in an effort to promote multicultural understanding and appreciation; one blog

by WorldVillage talks about two artists, one Irish and the other Jewish, as forging a link of mutual admiration and common ground through their music!

16. I also spoke with local media expert, Mr. Edmund Thomas, who is the owner of Gentle Rain Productions in the United States. I asked Mr. Thomas how the globalization of pop music might represent an opportunity to promote multicultural understanding. He responded, and I quote, "Sometimes, the very first glimpse of a foreign culture is through music. Since music transcends language, it has the ability to break down barriers of communication. In this age of the World Wide Web, music is easily accessible. In no other time in history have cultures been so intermingled; music is the benchmark of each culture—its signature. And it is the vibrant, fresh, cutting edge expressions of youth through pop music that are the vanguards of multicultural expansion." Bono says that "music can change the world because it can change people."

17. I hope I have made it clear how the globalization of pop music presents new opportunities for promoting multicultural awareness and understanding.

18. Today we have examined how the emergence of global media has resulted in the globalization and multicultural nature of pop music. Given this globalization of the music industry, we then considered the potential for pop music to help promote multicultural understanding.

19. On September 27, 2007, Bono received the Philadelphia Liberty Medal for his work to end world poverty and hunger. In accepting the Liberty Medal, Bono said, "When you are trapped by poverty, you are not free. When trade laws prevent you from selling the food you grew, you are not free. When you are a monk in Burma barred from entering a temple because of your gospel of peace…well, then none of us are truly free." Bono donated the $100,000 prize associated with the Liberty Medal to an organization fighting HIV and AIDS in Africa. Bono and his philanthropic work are excellent examples of a new approach to bringing people together around the globe (Bono, 2009).

20. I hope now you better understand how popular music and pop musicians can become the stimulant and glue to encourage multicultural understanding among cultures.

Pop Music and Globalization: What's the Link Between the Two? Annotations of Kumar's Speech

1. Introduction—Attention Getter: The speaker begins with a question in order to engage the listeners' attention and show respect by acknowledging their response.

2. The speaker sets up his topic by informing the audience about the social and political activism of the influential musician, Bono; as well as the awards Bono received on behalf of his tireless efforts.

3. The thesis is presented here as the speaker ties the musician's use of music to the main thesis regarding how popular music can be used as the stimulant and glue to bring people of different cultures together.

4. This sentence provides a transition from the introduction into the main body of the speech by telling the listeners what will be discussed: the globalization and multicultural aspects of popular music and how it has potential to promote multicultural understanding.

5. Body of the Speech: This is the first main point. The speaker uses a simple and direct statement: *Popular music is becoming increasingly global and multicultural.*

6. First subpoint: *The emergence and influence of global media.* The speaker immediately supports his first main point by citing a credible source, a scientific study, which offers evi-

dence that youth cultures are becoming more global and identifying across cultures through music, fashion, graphics, and dance.

7. Second subpoint: *The globalization of pop music as a result of global media technology.* The speaker first gives information in graph form that reflects the worldwide popularity of several well-known pop musicians.

8. The speaker then provides an example to illustrate the second subpoint; he describes a recent historic worldwide music event—the 2005 Live 8 Concerts—which supports his claim that popular music, through global media, is reaching greater audiences than ever before.

9. A final citation of a credible source (AOL) regarding the 2005 Live 8 concerts, along with a direct quote, "the day music changed the world" taken from the source, is told to the listeners to strengthen the validity of the information just provided.

10. Third subpoint: *The influence worldwide of pop music on other cultures.* A quote by noted poet Henry Wadsworth Longfellow is used to enrich the understanding of the audience regarding how universal and influential pop music can be.

11. This is a transition sentence used to move from the first main point into the second main point of the speech. Note how the speaker briefly summarizes the first main point and then sets up the next point to be discussed.

12. Second main point: *Pop music has the potential to promote multicultural understanding.* Again the speaker keeps his main point simple and straightforward.

13. First subpoint: *Music can be used to promote multicultural understanding.* A personal narrative is used to illustrate the speaker's claim and also reinforce the information given in the introduction (about Bono) and the first main point (the 2005 Live 8 concerts) of the speech.

14. Transition to following subpoints: The speaker makes a claim that he is not alone in his experience regarding the multicultural understanding pop music can help provide.

15. Second subpoint: *How exposure to the music of other cultures promotes multicultural understanding.* The speaker cites a website and email listserv resources that support the promotion of multicultural understanding; one particular blog is referenced that gives a specific example of two musicians—one Irish and one Jewish—who are using their music to forge a link of mutual admiration and common ground.

16. Third subpoint: *Opportunities for bringing people together based on the globalization of pop music.* A personal interview with a local media expert is recounted, using a direct quote, to provide credible support for the speaker's statement that pop music may provide opportunities to promote multicultural understanding. This is followed by a powerful quote from Bono, another credible source, which aptly summarizes the speaker's second main point.

17. This sentence serves as a transition from the main body of the speech into the conclusion.

18. Conclusion: This first section briefly summarizes the main points of the speech by reiterating what information was considered—first, how the emergence of global media has resulted in pop music becoming global and multicultural in nature, and second, how pop music has the potential to promote multicultural understanding.

19. The speaker brings the speech full circle by quoting a powerful portion of the acceptance speech Bono gave when he received the Philadelphia Liberty Medal in 2007. By referring back to internationally renowned musician Bono, and his philanthropic work, the speaker summarizes all the information given in the speech in a memorable way.

20. The thesis is then clearly restated by the speaker as he expresses his hope that the audience better understands how popular music and pop musicians can become the stimulant and glue to encourage multicultural understanding among cultures.

GLOSSARY

AD HOMINEM is a fallacy that occurs when a speaker attacks another person as opposed to the argument the person is making.

ADDITIONS occur when a speaker adds extra parts to a word.

ALLITERATION is the repetition of the same consonant sound in a series of words or phrases that draws attention to your words and helps your listeners remember what you said.

ANALOGY is an extended simile or metaphor that asks the listeners to accept the fact that things that sound alike in most respects will be alike in the respect being discussed.

APPEAL is a subtle technique or strategy a speaker uses to get the audience to accept his or her persuasive argument.

APPROPRIATE COMMUNICATION means you are aware and respectful of the norms and expectations for communication behavior in the particular situation.

APPROPRIATE LANGUAGE presents information in a way that respects and treats all audience members as equals without being condescending or using biased language and stereotypes.

ARRANGEMENT focuses on how you arrange or organize what you say in a speech.

ARTICULATION is shaping individual speech sounds correctly, so they combine to produce an understandable word.

ATTITUDES are the listeners' psychological reactions, positive or negative, to another person, object, or concept.

AUDIENCE ANALYSIS is the process speakers use to determine facts and information about the listeners and the speaking situation and occasion that will influence reactions to the speech and how the speech is prepared and delivered.

BELIEFS are your listeners' convictions about reality, based on their cultural background, knowledge, and experiences in life.

BIASED LANGUAGE is when you use words or phrases that derive their meaning from stereotypes, based on gender, race, ethnic group, age, or disability.

BODY LANGUAGE includes your posture, body movement and use of space, and gestures.

BODY MOVEMENT refers to how a public speaker stands and walks during the speech.

BODY OF THE SPEECH supports your central claim through the presentation of a series of main points.

BRIEFINGS are informative presentations on topics ranging from informal status or progress reports, to check point meetings, to formal research investigations.

CANONS OF PUBLIC SPEAKING are invention, arrangement, style, memory, and delivery.

CATEGORY ORGANIZATIONAL PATTERN divides information about a subject and topic into subgroups or subtopics.

CAUSE AND EFFECT ORGANIZATIONAL PATTERN examines why something happens (the causes) and what happens as a result (the effects).

CHANNEL is the medium through which the message is sent (voice, e-mail, phone, newspaper, etc.)

CHARACTER APPEAL is related to how listeners perceive the reputation, prestige, and authority of the speaker.

CHART OR GRAPH is a visual aid for presenting statistics that helps to clarify relationships among numbers and reveals any trends or patterns.

CLEAR LANGUAGE uses words in such a way that listeners understand and can easily comprehend the meaning of the speaker's message.

COERCION is a negative form of influence that occurs when a speaker persuades others to act in a particular way out of fear of reprisal, or by using force, or giving the listeners no choice but to cooperate.

COGNITIVE MODIFICATION is a process that changes or modifies your unrealistic expectations and beliefs about public speaking.

COMMUNICATION is the process of managing messages and media for the purpose of creating meaning and promoting understanding.

COMPARING ALTERNATIVES organization first asks listeners to examine two or more alternatives, and then it makes a strong appeal for the preferred choice.

COMPARISON AND CONTRAST ORGANIZATIONAL PATTERN is used to describe or explain how a subject is similar to or different from something else.

COMPETENT COMMUNICATION is both *effective* and *appropriate* for the particular situation.

COMPETENT LANGUAGE enhances any listeners' understanding and enthusiasm for a speech by the use of words that are clear, vivid, and appropriate.

COMPETENT PUBLIC SPEAKING is both effective and appropriate for the particular rhetorical situation.

COMPUTER CONFERENCING allows multiple participants to interact by contributing to an ongoing computer file accessible to all.

COMPUTER-MEDIATED COMMUNICATION (CMC) is any human symbolic interaction through digitally based technologies.

COMPUTERIZED DATABASE is a collection of information, searched from a computer terminal, which contains abstracts/summaries or full-text versions of documents and publications or indexes to information that is located elsewhere.

COMPUTERIZED PRESENTATION allows you to use a computer to display slides, photographs, drawings, diagrams, maps, charts, tables and lists, video clips and other resources available directly from the Internet.

CONCEPT SPEECH is about abstract ideas—theories, principles, or values.

CONCLUSION lets the listeners know the speech is ending and reminds them of your thesis and central idea.

CONCRETE WORDS enhance any listeners' understanding and enthusiasm for a speech by the use of words that are clear, vivid, and appropriate.

CONDESCENDING LANGUAGE is when you speak down to people rather than respecting and treating them as equals and adapting what you say to their knowledge of your topic.

CONSTRUCTING MEANING involves assigning meaning to the speaker's message and mentally clarifying your understanding of it.

CONTEXT LEVEL refers to the number of people involved in the communication event and the distance between or among the communicators.

CONTEXTS OF COMMUNICATION are the life situations in which you communicate.

COUNTER-ARGUMENT argues against the persuasive message being presented and for the listener's entrenched position or point of view.

CREDIBILITY means being perceived by others as both well intended and qualified and able to speak informedly on the given topic.

CRITICAL THINKING is the process of evaluating evidence, assumptions, and ideas based on sound reasoning and logic.

CULTURAL BARRIERS encompass characteristics of listeners like race, ethnicity, gender, and age, may affect listening in significant but not obvious ways.

CULTURAL CHARACTERISTICS of importance can be divided into two groups your listeners belong to—groups they were born into and groups they grew up in.

CULTURE consists of the enduring patterns of thought, values, and behaviors that define a group of people.

DECENTERING involves moving away from your own center, a self-centered view of your topic and the world, and paying more attention to the diverse views of the audience members.

DEDUCTION is a process of reasoning in which a specific conclusion follows necessarily from a general principle that is often made up of a major and a minor premise.

DESCRIPTIONS are used when listeners are unfamiliar with the topic of the speech and need new information in order to understand it.

DESCRIPTIVE STATISTICS describe or present pictures of what whole groups of people do, think, or are like.

DIAGRAM OR DRAWING is a visual aid used to explain how something appears or operates.

DIALECTIC is a question and answer process and logical discussion used to examine all sides of an issue in search of the truth that was advocated by the Greek philosopher, Plato.

DIVERSITY means how much alike or unlike the members of any group of people may be in terms of their cultural background.

EDUCATIONAL PRESENTATIONS teach others information and skills relevant to their jobs and the organization.

EFFECTIVE COMMUNICATION means you are able to achieve the goal or purpose for which you are communicating.

EMOTIONAL APPEAL is based on psychology and passion, which involves how people feel.

ETHICAL COMMUNICATION means sharing sufficient and appropriate information with others such that they can make fully informed decisions about matters of importance to themselves.

ETHICS is a branch of philosophy that explores what constitutes good (or right) and bad (or wrong); and, how people decide whether a particular decision or activity is good or bad.

EVALUATIVE THINKING involves weighing evidence, assumptions, and ideas based on sound reasoning and logic.

EVENT SPEECH describes something that has occurred, such as an historical event or something noteworthy that has happened.

EXAMPLE is a specific item, person, or event that helps to explain or illustrate an idea, clarify a difficult concept, or make anything you say more interesting or real to the audience.

EXPLANATIONS clarify something already known but not well understood or they explain how something works.

EXTEMPORANEOUS SPEECH is carefully planned and prepared ahead of time and is delivered using a conversational tone of voice.

EYE CONTACT is a tool the public speaker uses to promote a sense of involvement with audience members and to gauge audience reaction to the speech.

FACIAL EXPRESSION is the vehicle you use to communicate emotion and how you feel about what you're saying to the audience.

FACT is an individual piece of information that listeners could verify for themselves if they wanted to.

FEAR APPEAL is based on changing listeners' attitudes or behaviors through the use of an anxiety-arousing message.

FIGURES OF SPEECH are ways of saying things that help listeners to visualize, identify with, or really think about the points you're trying to make.

FORMAL OUTLINE contains all of the information from the final version of your working outline, but it is organized and presented using a standard outlining format.

GENERAL PURPOSE is the overall goal of the speech, for example, to entertain and amuse the audience, to commemorate an occasion, or the more common general purposes are to inform or to persuade.

GESTURES are natural movements of the hands and arms that reinforce what is said, emphasize important points, and make presentations more interesting to watch.

GOAL SETTING is a process for alleviating anxiety that provides a structured plan for changing your communication and public speaking behaviors.

GRAMMAR is the rules and structure for putting words together in sentences.

GROUP SUPPORT SYSTEMS supplement computer conferencing with information management capabilities, decision support tools, graphic displays, and meeting process management software.

IDEA GENERATOR is a website that helps you explore various subject areas as well as actual topic ideas.

IMAGERY is the creation of visual pictures and other sensory experiences through description.

IMPROMPTU SPEECH is delivered with minimal preparation, usually with little or no time to plan and develop your talk.

INDUCTION is a process of reasoning in which a general conclusion follows from the examination of a series of specific instances or examples.

INFERENTIAL STATISTICS make inferences or draw conclusions about larger groups of people based on learning something about a smaller sample of people, selected out of the larger group.

INFLECTION is a change in vocal pitch that reveals the emotional content of the message or tells listeners the speaker is asking a question.

INFORMATION OVERLOAD is including too much information in a speech and is a common problem for informative speakers.

INFORMATIVE PRESENTATIONS transmit knowledge from one organization member or unit to another or to others.

INFORMATIVE SPEECH has the purpose of communicating something new or a new perspective to an audience, and moving listeners to greater understanding or insight.

INFORMATIVE SPEECH CONTENT is based on what the speech is primarily about—objects, processes, events, people, issues, or concepts.

INFORMATIVE SPEECH OBJECTIVES include speaking to describe, explain, or instruct—with emphasis on audience knowledge or ability, and what the audience should know or be able to do by the end of the speech.

INFORMATIVE SPEECH ORGANIZATIONAL PATTERNS include by category, time, space, comparison and contrast, and cause and effect.

INSTRUCTIONS are useful when the objective is to teach the audience something or tell them how to use it. Instructions are also educational presentations, provided by supervisors to one or several workers, outlining what must be done and how to do it, use it, or operate something.

INTERACTION BARRIERS to listening result from characteristics or elements of the particular communication situation and the people involved.

INTERCULTURAL SENSITIVITY involves the various stages of sensitivity to cultural differences people go through in order to arrive at a point where they relate most productively and nonjudgmentally to others.

INTRODUCTION orients the listeners to your speech and engages them in what will be said.

INVENTION calls for discovering or inventing what you will say creatively—the content of your speech.

ISSUE SPEECH examines a debatable topic from various points of view.

LEVELS OF COMMUNICATION refer to the number of people involved in the communication event and the distance between or among the communicators.

LISTENING is the process of receiving, constructing meaning from, and responding to spoken and/or nonverbal messages.

LISTS are all-text visual aids that can communicate a lot of information in a simple way.

LOGICAL APPEAL is based on knowledge and reasoning, which involves how people think.

LOGICAL FALLACIES are errors in reasoning and logic that lead the listeners to false conclusions.

MAIN POINTS are the key ideas that, taken together, support the thesis statement and prove the central claim of the speech.

MANIPULATION is a negative and unethical form of influence that is used to control people's actions or reactions in a devious or deceitful way.

MANUSCRIPT SPEECH is written out ahead of time and read word for word to the audience.

MAPS are a useful visual aid when you want to pinpoint a location or highlight a geographical area.

MASS APPEAL subject areas are those most people probably will find of some interest, such as historical subjects, critical issues and controversial subjects, and widely accepted principles.

MEANING is the interpretation and understanding of a message that is sent or received using various media.

MEDIA are any means or channels people use to transmit and exchange messages with one another.

MEMORIZED SPEECH requires the most time to prepare because it is fully written out and memorized ahead of time, then spoken to the audience word for word.

MESSAGE OVERLOAD refers to the quantity of messages you process and **MESSAGE COMPLEXITY** is about how detailed and complicated those messages are.

MESSAGES are the words, sounds, actions, and gestures that people use to communicate with one another.

METAPHOR implies a comparison between two dissimilar things, but it does so without using the words like or as.

MOTIVATED SEQUENCE organizational pattern is a persuasive structure that moves through a sequence of five steps, designed to psychologically motivate and persuade listeners.

MULTICODALITY calls for retaining your unique way of using words and nonverbal cues, while incorporating some of the unique communication patterns of the listeners into what you say and do.

NARRATIVE THEORY says people are essentially storytellers, and storytelling is one of the oldest and most universal forms of human communication.

NON SEQUITOR is a fallacy that occurs when a claim does not directly follow from the support material that the speaker presents.

NOTE DEPENDENT means you refer to your notes too often and lose contact with the audience when giving the speech.

OBJECT SPEECH is usually about something tangible that can be seen, touched, or otherwise experienced through the physical senses.

OBJECTIVE INFORMATION is from sources such as research studies, reference books, and resources housed in libraries or obtained from the Internet.

OBJECTS including models, are visual aids you can use to show your listeners what something looks like or how it works.

OCCASION refers to any unique aspects of the speaking situation that will impact the presentation, for example, if you are the keynote speaker at a luncheon or dinner.

OMISSIONS are saying sounds incorrectly because of leaving out and not saying part of a word.

ORGANIZATIONAL PATTERN is the structure of the speech that introduces and clearly supports the thesis and logically leads the audience through the main points to the conclusion.

ORGANIZING is the process by which you arrange your main points and support materials into a logical and effective pattern.

PEOPLE SPEECH describes a person in much the same way an object speech describes an object.

PERSONAL OR DEMOGRAPHIC CHARACTERISTICS include the listeners' ages, the types of households they live in, their occupations, income, and education levels.

PERSUASIVE PRESENTATIONS attempt to influence problem solving or decision making in the organization.

PERSUASIVE SPEECH has the purpose of influencing an audience's attitudes, beliefs, values, or behaviors.

PHYSICAL APPEARANCE shapes first impressions and includes your clothing, shoes, jewelry, hairstyle, and even hair adornments.

PHYSICAL BARRIERS include interferences from the physical environment and distracting characteristics or behaviors of the speaker or other listeners.

PICTURE OR PHOTOGRAPH is a visual aid used when a more realistic depiction of a person, a place, or an object is needed in your speech.

PITCH is the highness or lowness of the speaking voice.

PLACE considers where the speech is presented, the physical environment and surroundings.

PLAGIARISM is the unauthorized use or close imitation of other people's ideas, thoughts, language, or words without acknowledging and citing their source.

POSTURE is defined as a position of your bodily parts that communicates your attitude and sense of self to the audience.

PRECISION LISTENING is a type of listening that is a basic tool for gathering and assessing information needed for timely and effective decision making.

PRESENTATION AID is anything other than your spoken words that assists in illustrating or supporting the content of the speech.

PROBLEM-SOLUTION organization first identifies a problem and then proposes a workable solution for the problem.

PROCESS SPEECH is about a system or sequence of steps that lead to a result or change taking place.

PRONUNCIATION means stressing and accenting the right syllables in a word.

PSYCHOLOGICAL BARRIERS include mental and emotional distractions to listening, for instance, daydreaming, being emotionally preoccupied with something else, thinking listening takes too much time, or strong personal reactions to the speaker or the topic.

PSYCHOLOGICAL CHARACTERISTICS include the listeners' *needs* and *motivations* and their *beliefs*, *attitudes*, and *values*.

PUBLIC SPEAKING involves one person or a small group of people speaking to a larger number of people, an audience that typically has little or no "speaking" role except for questions and answers at the end of the presentation.

PUBLIC SPEAKING ANXIETY refers to a person's level of fear or anxiety associated with a real or anticipated public speaking event.

PUBLIC SPEAKING OCCASION includes any factors that will affect how you narrow and focus the topic such as time constraints, the actual physical situation, and the speaking event itself.

PUBLIC VOICE makes use of increased variety in rate and pitch and increased volume, so your words are easily heard and understood by the entire audience.

QUOTATION is another person's exact words.

RATE is the speed at which a speaker delivers a speech.

RECEIVER is the recipient of the message.

RECEIVING means tuning in to a speaker's entire message, including both its verbal and nonverbal aspects, and consciously paying attention to it.

RECOMMENDATIONS are persuasive presentations, ranging from minor issues such as changing a company procedure to major recommendations such as a company wide reorganization, a merger, or the introduction of a new product line.

RED HERRING is a fallacy that diverts the audience's attention from the real issue by presenting arguments or issues that are not relevant to the topic.

REFUTING THE OPPONENT organization dismantles your opponent's argument in order to persuade the audience that your argument is superior.

REPETITION is when the speaker repeats the same word or phrase several times in the same or various section of a speech.

RESPONDING completes the listening process and is the step in which the listener lets the speaker know the message, its verbal and nonverbal content, has been received and understood.

RHETORIC is the art of discovering the available means of persuasion in the situation and influencing an audience through words.

RHETORICAL QUESTION is one that is asked for effect rather than to elicit an answer.

SEVEN BY SEVEN RULE limits each slide to seven lines down and seven words across.

SIMILE is an explicit comparison that compares two unlike things by using the words like or as.

SITUATION ANALYSIS includes careful consideration of the time, place, and occasion for the speech.

SLIPPERY SLOPE reasoning occurs when a speaker suggests that because one event occurs, it automatically leads to a series of other undesirable events.

SLURRING is when a speaker runs sounds and words together.

SOCIAL JUDGMENT THEORY says listeners' attitudes on any topic can be plotted on a continuum ranging from acceptance to rejection, with a noncommitted attitude in the middle between those two positions.

SOCIAL MEDIA involves any sort of communication created by people using highly accessible publishing technologies.

SOPHISTS were a group of Greek philosophers and teachers who began teaching Corax's methods of thinking and speaking persuasively throughout Greece in about 481 BCE.

SOURCE is the sender of a message.

SPACE ORGANIZATIONAL PATTERN includes by category, time, space, comparison and contrast, and cause and effect.

SPEAKING OR PRESENTATIONAL OUTLINE contains only enough information to remind you of what to say at a glance.

SPECIFIC PURPOSE is a statement of the desired end result or response the speaker would like from the audience.

SPEECH TO CHANGE is intended to convince the audience to change what they like or dislike, what they hold to be true or untrue, or what they consider important or unimportant.

SPEECH TO MOVE TO ACTION is intended to influence listeners to either engage in a new and desirable behavior or discontinue an undesirable behavior.

SPEECH TO REINFORCE is intended to influence listeners by strengthening their convictions and taking advantage of their tendency to seek out and attend to messages with which they already agree.

STATISTICS are numerical summaries of facts, figures, and research findings that provide pictures of data about people, ideas, or patterns of behavior.

STORY is just a long example, it serves the same purpose—to illustrate an idea, clarify a concept, or make a point more interesting or real.

STRAW MAN ARGUMENT occurs when the speaker attacks an entire argument by selecting a weak example or aspect of it, discrediting that example, and thus defaming the entire argument.

SUBJECT AREA is a general area of knowledge such as college life, communication, sports, or organic chemistry.

SUBJECTIVE INFORMATION is information speakers recall from their own experiences or obtain from observing or interviewing someone else.

SUBSTITUTIONS are when the speaker replaces part of a word with an incorrect sound.

SWEEPING OR HASTY GENERALIZATIONS cluster ideas, people, or objects into one group and imply that all of the items in the group are the same, thus obscuring vital and relevant differences.

SYMBOLS represent or stand for something else, but it is not that something else.

SYSTEMATIC DESENSITIZATION is a process that changes how you feel about public speaking by using relaxation and positive visualization when you think about a public speaking event.

TABLES are all-text visual aids in which numbers or words are arranged in a grid of columns and rows.

TEAM-BASED ORGANIZATION is composed of a variety of teams with defined responsibilities about which managers provide mostly indirect supervision.

TECHNOLOGY-AIDED SPEECH is developed using a computer software program such as PowerPoint, and it is presented using some form of projection equipment.

TECHNOLOGY BARRIERS ARE listening barriers resulting from the use of cell phones, landlines, the Internet, e-mail, text messages, blogs and social media websites, and television, radio, and music on iPods.

TELECONFERENCING includes meetings held through audio conferencing and videoconferencing systems.

TESTIMONY utilizes the opinion of an expert or the account of an event by a witness to it.

THEME REINFORCERS are the points a speaker presents throughout the speech to support and reinforce the central idea they are trying to get across.

THESIS STATEMENT is the central idea or claim of your speech, which you will say out loud to the audience when you actually deliver the speech.

TIME ORGANIZATIONAL PATTERN is used to describe changes or developments in any situation or circumstance, either historical and linked to actual dates—or sequential and related to a sequence of steps that occur or are performed over time.

TIMING involves when the speech is presented, the time of day, and how much time you are given to speak.

TOPIC is a specific facet or aspect of a subject area.

TRAININGS are formal events in which a professional consultant or presenter, an expert in an area, works with a group of people to teach them a new skill, job, or process.

TRANSITIONS are words, phrases, or sentences that are used within the body of the speech to indicate how the main points are related to each other and they are used to connect the introduction to the body of the speech and the body to the conclusion.

TRANSPARENT DELIVERY means presenting a speech in such a way that the audience doesn't focus on elements of the delivery but instead pays full attention to the message.

UNPROJECTED AIDS are easy to use and include the chalkboard or whiteboard, flip charts and poster boards, and handouts.

UNDERSTANDING occurs when we use messages and media in such a way that we fully grasp the meaning of the other person or persons' message.

VALUES are an extension of your listeners' attitudes and beliefs and reflect what they consider to be important and unimportant.

VIRTUAL TEAM is a group of individuals, managers and other employees, organized and linked together by technology to work on short or long term projects.

VIVID LANGUAGE promotes enthusiasm for a speech by bringing the speaker's message to life and moving the audience emotionally.

VOCAL VARIETY is used to heighten and maintain audience attention and interest in your message.

VOCALIZED PAUSES are the meaningless sounds a speaker utters during moments of silence.

VOLUME is the intensity, the loudness or softness, of the speaker's voice.

WEB CAST PRESENTATIONS involve information and data transmission over the web that is one way and does not allow interaction between the presenter and the audience.

WEB CONFERENCING involves information and data transmission over the web that is two way and allows interaction between the presenter and the audience.

WEBINARS are web-based seminars, workshops, or trainings, transmitted over the web.

WORKING OUTLINE contains most of the detailed information from your research efforts and is, in essence, a work-in-progress.

AUTHOR INDEX